Join us at
www.eatingwell.com
for more delicious recipes and the inspiration and information
you need to make healthy eating a way of life.

EATINGWELL.

COMFORT FOODS MADE HEALTHY

The Classic Makeover Cookbook

Library of Congress Cataloging-in-Publication Data has been applied for.

ISBN 978-0-88150-887-1

Authors: Jessie Price & the Editors of EATINGWELL
Test Kitchen Manager & Makeover Tips: Stacy Fraser | Contributing Writer: Jim Romanoff
Associate Editor & Makeover Profiles: Carolyn Malcoun
Dietitian & Nutrition Advisor: Sylvia Geiger, M.S., R.D.

Managing Editor: Wendy S. Ruopp | Assistant Managing Editor: Alesia Depot
Production Manager: Jennifer B. Brown | Research Editor: Anne C. Treadwell
Test Kitchen: Hilary Meyer (Assistant Editor), Katie Webster (recipe developer, food stylist),
Carolyn Casner (recipe tester), Patsy Jamieson (food stylist), Susan Herr (food stylist)
Indexer: Amy Novick, BackSpace Indexing

Art Director: Michael J. Balzano | Production Designer: Elise Whittemore-Hill
Photographer: Ken Burris

EATINGWELL MEDIA GROUP   CEO: Tom Witschi | Editorial Director: Lisa Gosselin

Front cover photograph: Loaded Twice-Baked Potatoes (*page 106*)

Published by
The Countryman Press, P.O. Box 748, Woodstock, Vermont 05091

Distributed by
W.W. Norton & Company, Inc., 500 Fifth Avenue, New York, New York 10110

Printed in China by R.R. Donnelley

First paperback edition, 2009
10 9 8 7 6 5 4 3 2

EATINGWELL®
COMFORT FOODS
MADE HEALTHY

The Classic Makeover Cookbook

10 Principles of
Healthy Cooking

65 Tips & Tricks for
Successful Makeovers

175 Favorite Recipes
Made Healthier

by Jessie Price
& the Editors of EatingWell

EATINGWELL®
WHERE GOOD TASTE MEETS GOOD HEALTH

The Countryman Press
Woodstock, Vermont

Chicken Potpie (page 134)

CONTENTS

ACKNOWLEDGMENTS

This book is the result of tons of cooking, tasting, testing, writing, thinking and rethinking, photographing and designing by an awesome team. Thank you to the EATINGWELL Test Kitchen: Stacy Fraser, for keeping us cooking, being the "tip Czar" and sharing in this project every step of the way; Carolyn Malcoun, for an unbelievable attention to detail; Hilary Meyer and Carolyn Casner for tireless recipe testing and development with a smile; and Katie Webster for food styling with flair and developing new recipes for this book, even with Lila Jane underfoot. Thank you to the people who make our food look so darned delicious: Ken Burris with his camera and Patsy Jamieson and Susan Herr for food styling. Mike Balzano, thank you for making this book a beautiful package, even with way more tips than any art director would ever want to see. Thank you to Lisa Gosselin, who turned the success of "comfort food recipes" in a newsletter into the vision for this book. Thanks to Jim Romanoff for hiring me in the first place and for his tender buffing of headnotes. Sylvia Geiger and Nicci Micco, thank you for setting a high standard with your nutritional guidance. The team that makes it all come together: Alesia Depot, Jennifer Brown and Wendy Ruopp, it is a pleasure to work on a project like this with you. And finally, thank you to my family and especially my husband, John. —J.P.

ABOUT THE AUTHORS

JESSIE PRICE grew up in a family of great cooks and food fanatics. After graduating from Williams College, she cooked in restaurants in California and Colorado, including The Home Ranch, a Relais & Chateaux property near Steamboat Springs. She started out testing and developing recipes for EATINGWELL and joined the editorial team full-time in 2004 when she moved from San Francisco. Jessie directs the food content for EATINGWELL Magazine; she has written extensively on food and has represented the magazine in media appearances. She has worked on four other EATINGWELL books: *Healthy in a Hurry, EatingWell Serves Two, The EatingWell Diet* and *EatingWell for a Healthy Heart.* She lives in Charlotte, Vermont, where she stays busy growing her own vegetables and tracking down great Vermont food.

The **EATINGWELL MEDIA GROUP**'s mission is to deliver the information and inspiration people need to make healthy eating a way of life. EATINGWELL is a leading publisher of the award-winning EATINGWELL Magazine, whose motto is "Where Good Taste Meets Good Health," as well as a series of cookbooks (most recently, *EatingWell for a Healthy Heart* and *The EatingWell Diet*) and a vibrant website, *www.eatingwell.com.*

RECIPE GUIDELINES & NUTRIENT ANALYSES

NUTRITION ICONS:

Our nutritionists have highlighted recipes likely to be of interest to those following various dietary plans. Recipes that meet specific guidelines are marked with these icons:

H ✳ W

To qualify for the **HEALTHY WEIGHT** icon, an entree has reduced calories, fats and saturated fats, as follows:

CALORIES ≤ **350**   TOTAL FAT ≤ **20g**   SAT FAT ≤ **5g**

For soups, salads and side dishes, the limits are:

CALORIES ≤ **250**   TOTAL FAT ≤ **10g**   SAT FAT ≤ **5g**

For muffins, breads and desserts, the limits are:

CALORIES ≤ **230**   TOTAL FAT ≤ **10g**   SAT FAT ≤ **5g**

L ↓ C

The **LOWER CARBS** icon means a recipe has **22 grams** or less of carbohydrate per serving.

H ↑ F

The **HIGH FIBER** icon means a recipe provides **5 grams** or more of fiber per serving.

H ♥ H

For the **HEALTHY HEART** icon, entrees have 3 grams or less of saturated fat, except for fish entrees, which have 5 grams or less of saturated fat. All other recipes have 2 grams or less of saturated fat.

NUTRITION BONUSES.

Nutrition bonuses are indicated for recipes that provide 15% or more of the Daily Value (dv) of specific nutrients. The daily values are the average daily recommended nutrient intakes for most adults. In addition to the nutrients listed on food labels (vitamins A and C, calcium, iron and fiber), we have included bonus information for other nutrients, such as folate, magnesium, potassium, selenium and zinc, when a recipe is particularly high in one or more of these. We have chosen to highlight these nutrients because of their importance to good health and the fact that many Americans may have inadequate intakes of them.

ANALYSIS NOTES:

Each recipe is analyzed for calories, total fat, saturated (sat) and monounsaturated (mono) fat, cholesterol, carbohydrate, protein, fiber, sodium and potassium. (Numbers less than 0.5 are rounded down to 0; 0.5 to 0.9 are rounded up to 1.) We use Food Processor SQL software (ESHA Research) for analyses.

When a recipe states a measure of salt "or to taste," we analyze the measured quantity. (Readers on sodium-restricted diets can reduce or eliminate the salt.) Recipes are tested with iodized table salt unless otherwise indicated. Kosher or sea salt is called for when the recipe will benefit from the unique texture or flavor. We assume that rinsing with water reduces the sodium in canned foods by 35%.

When alternative ingredients are listed, we analyze the first one suggested. Optional ingredients and garnishes are not analyzed. We do not include trimmings or marinade that is not absorbed in analyses. Portion sizes are consistent with healthy-eating guidelines.

OTHER DEFINITIONS:

Testers in the EATINGWELL Test Kitchen keep track of the time needed for each recipe.

ACTIVE TIME includes prep time (the time it takes to chop, dice, puree, mix, combine, etc. before cooking begins), but it also includes the time spent tending something on the stovetop, in the oven or on the grill—and getting it to the table. If you can't walk away from it for more than 10 minutes, we consider it active time.

TOTAL includes both active and inactive time and indicates the entire amount of time required for each recipe, start to finish.

Recipes ready to eat in **45 MINUTES OR LESS** are marked with this icon.

TO MAKE AHEAD gives storage instructions for dishes that taste good made in advance.

If special **EQUIPMENT** is needed to prepare a recipe, we tell you that too.

INTRODUCTION

Ask a hundred people what their ultimate comfort food is and you're going to get a wide range of answers. There are some all-time favorites—fried chicken, mac and cheese, meatloaf with mashed potatoes and gravy, rich chocolate cake—and you'll find those in this book. But there are plenty of others too, like Turkey Albondigas Soup (*page 65*), which happens to be one of my favorites. What counts as comfort food depends on the type of foods you love, grew up with and have strong feelings about.

It may seem that comfort food, which tends toward oozing cheese, creamy sauces, fatty cuts of meat and decadent sweets, is not a natural fit for EATINGWELL. After all what distinguishes EATINGWELL is that we're all about healthy food. Why not stick with inherently healthy foods like juicy roast chicken or steamed asparagus that are delights in their own right? We embrace those foods too, but who doesn't enjoy their chicken deep-fried or a little hollandaise sauce on their asparagus? We're not willing to give up our favorite comfort foods—we suspect you're not either. With America's appetite for these rich foods and its growing average girth, the moment is ripe for this collection of EATINGWELL comfort food recipes that are trimmed down to meet our healthy nutrition guidelines but still taste great.

And that's where my job comes in. As the Food Editor here at EATINGWELL, I make sure our recipes are delicious. (And the fact that they happen to be healthy… well that's nice too.) At our headquarters in Vermont, my office is just four steps outside of our Test Kitchen. All day long I hop up and rush into the Test Kitchen to taste recipes we're working on for our magazine, website and books. I never get tired of it, even when we're digging into our tenth recipe of the day and the rest of the food team is too full to eat another bite. I still love it! I'll admit this is partly because I truly enjoy food, but the

real reason is that we make irresistible, mouthwatering food here at EATINGWELL.

So how do we make comfort food healthier? To start with, we cook an "original," typical version of a classic recipe. The more fattening and delicious the better. (We love a good challenge!) Using the classic version as a baseline for flavor, taste and appeal, we begin the makeover process. Our goal is to cut calories, sodium, fat and saturated fat. And we try to boost healthy nutrients like fiber, vitamins and minerals. Our recipe developers use a wide range of techniques to achieve these goals. We like to swap whole-wheat pasta for regular pasta to increase fiber, or we bulk up meatballs with bulgur to trim some of the saturated fat while keeping them hearty and flavorful. Plus we make sure that you can actually cook these recipes at home and get dinner on the table quickly. You'll find that many of our makeovers are quicker versions of the classics, like Turkey Tetrazzini on page 135, which we have transformed from a casserole to a quick pan sauté. And there are over 90 recipes in this book that can be on the table in 45 minutes or less.

Through years of testing and experimentation here in our Test Kitchen, EATINGWELL recipe developers and testers have determined the best techniques for improving recipes nutritionally while keeping them tasty. All of our recipes are approved by our team of nutritionists and our staff dietitian. Many of the recipes in this book were adapted from ones that first appeared in our *Rx for Recipes* column, which was developed to respond to reader requests to help them make a favorite recipe healthier. Patsy Jamieson, who was the original author of that column, says, "I loved the problem-solving and extensive testing of the Rx recipes. We really went the extra mile to make them taste good, not just to make them healthier." And today we carry on that tradition in the EATINGWELL Test Kitchen, stringently testing each recipe on average seven times, on different equipment and with several testers.

We've truly enjoyed testing and tasting this delicious collection of recipes and we're sure that whatever your comfort food cravings, you'll find something you love in this book. (We certainly have.) And when you see how satisfying it is to make healthy comfort food that tastes amazing, you'll find that it's easy to make healthy eating a way of life. —*Jessie Price*

....

The EatingWell Test Kitchen team, photographed at Libby's Diner, Colchester, Vermont.

OUR COMFORT FOOD FAVORITES

Above, from left to right: Food stylist **Katie Webster** and her sister, Food Editor **Jessie Price**, both fondly associate the Monte Cristo sandwich with their Grandma Rutter. Katie says, "It's all about the salty and sweet combination. It's the kind of thing I could eat any time of day." Growing up in a Lebanese family, Associate Editor **Carolyn Malcoun** longs for "Brigitte's Delight from my cousin's restaurant: kibbe, hummus, tabbouleh, cabbage rolls and grape leaves." True to the classics, Test Kitchen Manager **Stacy Fraser** adores chicken potpie: "I love flaky crust wrapped around a creamy chicken- and vegetable-studded filling." Assistant Editor **Hilary Meyer** flips for shepherd's pie: "Anything with potatoes is comfort food for me. Yum!" Hilary says. And recipe tester **Carolyn Casner**, who hails from El Paso, Texas, loves "all things Tex-Mex." You'll find a makeover of crispy shelled tacos we did for Carolyn's family on page 94 as well as her recipe for Chilaquiles Casserole on page 183.

10 PRINCIPLES OF HEALTHY COOKING

If your eating habits are anything like those of most Americans and you are looking for the simplest advice possible we would tell you to eat more vegetables, fruits and whole grains and less of just about everything else. But if you're ready for just a bit more guidance, our 10 principles of healthy cooking will get you started:

USE SMART FATS – Not all fat is bad. Opt for unsaturated (e.g., olive oil) over saturated fats such as butter. But still use them in moderation because all fats are loaded with calories.

GO UNREFINED – Pick whole grains over refined grains. Whole grains like brown rice and bulgur have their bran intact and thus have more fiber, B vitamins, magnesium, zinc and other nutrients.

EAT MORE FRUITS AND VEGETABLES – Most people don't get enough! Aim for 5 to 13 servings of fruits and vegetables a day. Pick produce in a variety of colors to get a range of antioxidants and vitamins. A serving size is ½ to 1 cup depending on the fruit or vegetable.

IT'S NOT ALL ABOUT THE MEAT – Meat is a great source of protein but it's also a big source of saturated fat in many people's diets. So eat small amounts of lean meat, fish and poultry. Fill up the rest of your plate with healthy vegetables and whole grains.

CHOOSE LOW-FAT DAIRY – Dairy products like milk, sour cream and yogurt are a good source of calcium. Replacing whole-milk dairy products with low-fat or non-fat is an easy way to cut saturated fat in your diet.

KEEP PORTIONS REASONABLE – Even though we would all like a magic bullet for weight control, it really boils down to calories. One of the easiest ways to manage calorie intake is by eating healthy portions. For handy tips, see page 18.

USE SWEETENERS JUDICIOUSLY – Sugars of any kind, whether corn syrup, white sugar, brown sugar, honey or maple syrup, add significant calories without any nutritive value.

KEEP AN EYE ON SODIUM – Whether you have high blood pressure or not, it's wise to watch your sodium intake. The USDA's dietary guidelines for Americans recommend consuming less than 2,300 mg (about 1 teaspoon salt) daily.

GO FOR THE FLAVOR – Enhance food with bold flavors from healthy ingredients like fresh herbs, spices and citrus. When your food has great flavor, there's no reason to feel deprived.

BE MINDFUL AND ENJOY – Make conscious food decisions rather than grabbing for what is most convenient. Make sure it is something delicious and savor it. When you enjoy what you eat, you feel satisfied. For more on mindful eating, see page 17.

MAKEOVER SECRETS

The success of many of the recipe makeovers in this book is the result of simple techniques that are easy to incorporate into your cooking repertoire. (Look for Makeover Tips highlighted throughout this book.) We start by evaluating the makeover candidate recipe. These are some of the questions we ask and things we consider that you should think about whenever you take a look at a less-healthy recipe.

ASK THESE QUESTIONS ABOUT THE RECIPE:

Is the serving size too large? Consider whether the servings are appropriate. See page 18 for some easy ways to judge appropriate servings.

Is this a whole meal or should I add a vegetable side dish or salad to boost nutrition? Remember that it's important to make salads and vegetables a part of meals, so you may need to eat a smaller amount of meat or pasta to make room for them.

Can I add more vegetables? Sautéed onions, shredded zucchini or baby spinach are easy to integrate into many dishes. Sometimes you can simply increase the amount of vegetables already in a recipe.

Are the meat portions appropriate? Will it work with less meat? 3 ounces of cooked meat (about 4 ounces uncooked) is recommended for one serving.

Will it work with a leaner cut of meat?

Can I replace butter (high in saturated fat) with an oil like canola or olive oil (low in saturated fat)?

Can I substitute some egg whites for whole eggs? An egg white has only 17 calories and 0 grams of fat compared with 70 calories and 4 grams of fat for a whole egg. In many recipes it's as simple as swapping out a few of the eggs for egg whites. Two egg whites are about the equivalent of 1 whole egg.

How much cheese do I really need to make this taste great? Could I use a cheese with a bigger flavor? Reducing the amount of cheese in a recipe is an easy way to cut calories and fat. Choosing a cheese with bolder flavor like sharp Cheddar over regular Cheddar or imported Italian Parmesan over domestic Parmesan helps a smaller amount have more impact in the recipe.

Do I need all the mayonnaise? Low-fat mayonnaise, reduced-fat sour cream and nonfat yogurt are all great substitutes for regular mayonnaise. Sometimes a blend is best.

Can I replace full-fat dairy products like milk, yogurt or sour cream with their reduced-fat counterparts? Often this can be done with no compromise in flavor.

Will whole-grain flour work in place of all-purpose flour?

Can I replace white bread, pasta or rice with their whole-grain counterparts?

CONSIDER A HEALTHIER COOKING TECHNIQUE:

Does this dish need to be deep fried? Deep frying adds a lot of calories and fat. Most of the time the taste and texture can be replicated with healthier techniques like oven-frying or pan-frying with just a bit of oil.

Could I use cooking spray to decrease the amount of oil in a recipe? Either store-bought cooking spray or an oil spray bottle with canola or olive oil are great tools to have in the kitchen. Cooking spray works for "oven-frying" foods or for sautéing with less oil or butter in a pan.

Is cream the only way to thicken? Reduced-fat sour cream or low-fat milk thickened with flour work well in sauces. Pureed cooked rice will thicken a soup.

How much oil do I really need in my pan to sauté? Often recipes call for more oil than you really need. A nonstick pan can help reduce the amount of oil you need from tablespoons to teaspoons.

Can I skip tossing my vegetables with butter? Try roasting them instead to bring out their flavor.

AT THE MARKET

Healthy cooking starts at the supermarket, the farmers' market, the local co-op or wherever you shop for groceries. To make it as easy as possible, it's best to get organized. Here are some helpful tips for healthy and easy shopping:

MAKE A DETAILED SHOPPING LIST grouped by the layout of your favorite supermarket. It makes your trip much less stressful if you don't have to backtrack through the store because you realize you forgot the carrots when you're already at the register. You can download a handy shopping list format divided into sections of the grocery store from our website at *eatingwell.com.*

EAT SEASONALLY. Fruits and vegetables are fresher and more flavorful when they are in season and picked recently. (Just think of juicy fresh-picked ripe strawberries as compared with the ones you get in December.) When you start with the best and freshest ingredients you don't need to embellish much to make them delicious.

BUY PERISHABLE PRODUCTS LAST and get them into your refrigerator and freezer first when you get home.

SHOP THE PERIMETER. The outer sections of most supermarkets—produce, seafood, meat and dairy departments—are where the healthiest and least processed ingredients tend to be. In the freezer section, head for frozen vegetables and fruits.

LET THE STORE DO THE WORK FOR YOU. To keep your time in the kitchen down, ask the butcher to trim the fat off your meat. Prewashed lettuce or prepared vegetables also cut down on prep time.

SMART CHOICES TO REDUCE SODIUM:

CANNED BEANS AND TOMATOES – We love the convenience of canned beans and tomatoes but they often come with added sodium. Look for ones labeled "no-sodium" or "low-sodium" and rinse the beans before you use them to remove some of the excess sodium.

VEGETABLES – We prefer to use fresh produce whenever possible, but for convenience, frozen vegetables are a good option with little added salt. Canned vegetables like corn, green beans or peas have a lot of added sodium, less nutrients and a mushy texture.

SOY SAUCE – This condiment is essential in the EATINGWELL pantry, but we opt for the reduced-sodium variety as an easy way to maintain flavor while keeping the sodium down.

BROTH – If you have time, making homemade broth is often tastier and healthier. Store-bought broths tend to have a lot of sodium so if you are buying it choose low- or reduced-sodium varieties.

BREAD – Most store-bought bread including rolls, pita bread, regular sandwich bread and pizza dough has a significant amount of salt added to it. Check and compare nutrition information when choosing.

MEAT – Check the label to avoid meat, especially turkey and pork, "enhanced" with a sodium solution.

CHEESE – Many cheeses, especially ones like feta, Cheddar and Parmesan (some of our favorites) are high in sodium, so use them judiciously.

ROASTED RED PEPPERS – Jarred roasted red peppers are a convenient pantry staple. They add tons of flavor to recipes, but they also tend to be high in sodium, so use them sparingly. Roast your own peppers and then freeze them if you have the time. (Find out how to do it at *eatingwell.com.*)

OLIVES, CAPERS AND ANCHOVIES – Some of our favorite savory treats also happen to be the saltiest! Use them in moderation.

THE HEALTHY PANTRY

While a good shopping list is the key to a quick and painless trip to the supermarket, a well-stocked pantry is the best way to ensure you'll have everything you need to cook once you get home. Our Healthy Pantry includes all the items you need to prepare the recipes in this book plus a few other ingredients that will make impromptu meals easier.

OILS, VINEGARS & CONDIMENTS
Extra-virgin olive oil

Canola oil

VINEGARS: balsamic, red-wine, white-wine, rice, cider

ASIAN CONDIMENTS: reduced-sodium soy sauce, fish sauce, hoisin sauce, oyster sauce, chile-garlic sauce, toasted sesame oil

Dijon mustard

Ketchup

Barbecue sauce

Worcestershire sauce

Mayonnaise, low-fat

FLAVORINGS
Kosher salt, iodized table salt

Black peppercorns

Assorted dried herb and spices

Onions

Fresh garlic

Fresh ginger

Kalamata olives, green olives

Capers

Anchovies or anchovy paste

Lemons, limes, oranges (the zest is as valuable as the juice)

DRY GOODS
Assorted whole-wheat pastas

Brown rice, instant brown rice

Wild rice

Pearl barley, quick-cooking barley

Whole-wheat couscous

Bulgur

Dried lentils

Whole-wheat flour and whole-wheat pastry flour (store opened packages in the refrigerator or freezer)

All-purpose flour

Rolled oats

Cornmeal

Plain dry breadcrumbs

Buttermilk powder

Dried egg whites

Unsweetened cocoa powder, natural and/or Dutch-processed

Bittersweet chocolate

SWEETENERS: granulated sugar, brown sugar, honey, maple syrup

CANNED & BOTTLED GOODS
Reduced-sodium chicken broth, beef broth and/or vegetable broth (or go to *eatingwell.com* for homemade broth recipes)

Clam juice

"Lite" coconut milk

Tomatoes, tomato paste

BEANS: cannellini beans, great northern beans, chickpeas, black beans, red kidney beans, pinto beans

Lentils

Chunk light tuna, wild salmon

Red wine

NUTS, SEEDS & FRUITS
(Store opened packages of nuts and seeds in the refrigerator or freezer.)

NUTS: walnuts, pecans, almonds, hazelnuts, peanuts, pine nuts

Sesame seeds

Natural peanut butter

Tahini (sesame paste)

DRIED FRUITS: apricots, prunes, cherries, cranberries, dates, figs, raisins

REFRIGERATOR ITEMS
Low-fat or nonfat milk

Low-fat or nonfat plain yogurt and/or vanilla yogurt

Reduced-fat or nonfat sour cream

Good-quality Parmesan cheese

Sharp Cheddar cheese

Eggs (large) or egg substitute, such as Egg Beaters

Orange juice

Dry white wine (or nonalcoholic wine)

Water-packed tofu

FREEZER BASICS
Fruit-juice concentrates (orange, apple, pineapple)

FROZEN VEGETABLES: peas, spinach, broccoli, bell pepper and onion mix, corn, uncooked hash browns

Frozen berries and other fruit

Low-fat vanilla ice cream or frozen yogurt

WHAT TO LOOK FOR ON NUTRITION LABELS

By law, packaged foods sold in the U.S. have a standardized Nutrition Facts Panel, which gives a lot of helpful information—if you focus on these key areas.

SERVING SIZE: To make comparing foods easier, similar foods must have similar serving sizes—but "one serving" might not be what you consume in one sitting. Always check serving size and adjust accordingly.

Nutrition Facts

Serving Size	4 Crackers (14g)
Servings Per Container	About 32

Amount per serving

Calories 70	Calories from Fat 25

	% Daily Value *
Total Fat 3g	**5**%
Saturated Fat 1g	**5**%
Trans Fat 0g	
Polyunsaturated Fat 1g	
Monounsaturated Fat 1g	
Cholesterol 0mg	**0**%
Sodium 150mg	**6**%
Total Carbohydrate 9g	**3**%
Dietary Fiber less than 1g	**1**%
Sugars 1g	
Protein 1g	

Vitamin A	0%	•	Vitamin C	0%
Calcium	0%	•	Iron	2%

* Percent Daily Values are based on a 2,000 calorie diet. Your daily values may be higher or lower depending on your calorie needs:

	Calories	2,000	2,500
Total Fat	Less than	65g	80g
Sat. Fat	Less than	20g	25g
Cholesterol	Less than	300mg	300mg
Sodium	Less than	2,400mg	2,400mg
Total Carbohydrate		300g	375g
Dietary Fiber		25g	30g

Ingredients: Enriched flour (wheat flour, niacin, reduced iron, thiamin mononitrate...

CALORIES: Again, these just reflect a count for a single serving, and you'll need to adjust if you eat more or less.

TOTAL FAT: Reflects the total grams of fat per serving and the calories coming from fat. This information is less useful than the breakdown of the type of fat in the foods.

SATURATED FAT: Look for as low as possible. Current dietary recommendations say that people should eat 7 percent or less calories from saturated fat. For 2,000-calorie intake, this translates into a total of 16 grams per day.

TRANS FAT: Look for "0." But keep in mind that food with less than 0.5 gram of trans fat per serving can be labeled as "0." Instead look on the ingredient list for any "partially hydrogenated" or "hydrogenated" ingredients, which are a source of trans fats.

CHOLESTEROL: As low as possible (aim for 300 mg or less).

SODIUM: As low as possible (USDA Dietary Guidelines recommend 2,300 mg/day or less).

DIETARY FIBER: As high as possible (aim for 25 grams or more).

SUGARS: Interesting but not always useful, since labels don't discriminate between naturally occurring sugars (such as in milk or fruit) and added sugars.

VITAMINS AND MINERALS: Vitamins A and C, calcium and iron are required to be listed on labels since consuming enough of these nutrients can improve your health and reduce your risk of some diseases. They're shown in the form of Daily Values.

PERCENT DAILY VALUES (DV): These are reference amounts set by the Food and Drug Administration (FDA). You can use Daily Values to help you track how much of your nutrient needs a food fills. But take note: the DVs are set according to how many calories you eat—and labels usually use 2,000 calories as a reference for the vitamin and mineral recommendations and 2,500 calories as the reference for other nutrients. If you're only eating 1,500 calories daily, for example, your DV goals will be approximately one-fourth to one-third lower than what's on the label.

ESSENTIAL TOOLS FOR THE HEALTHY KITCHEN

To make your kitchen an enjoyable, easy place to work, make sure your tools and ingredients are handy, your sink is cleared out and your work surfaces are clean. Like any good workspace, your kitchen needs good tools. The following recommendations include what you'll need to cook the recipes in this book, as well as a few other useful items.

MEASURING SPOONS & CUPS: One full set of measuring spoons and two sets of measuring cups. One set should be for measuring liquids—those measuring cups usually have handles and pour spouts—and one set for measuring dry ingredients that can be leveled off.

KNIVES: Those butcher blocks full of knives look nice on your counter, but you really only need three: a serrated knife, a 9- to 10-inch-long chef's knife and a paring knife. Make sure you hold a knife before you buy it; it should feel natural in your hand. Buy the best knives you can afford—they will last for many years.

CUTTING BOARDS: Two cutting boards are ideal—one for raw proteins and one for cooked foods and produce—to avoid cross-contamination when cooking. Cutting boards made of polyethylene plastic are inexpensive, durable and easy to clean. Look for ones that are dishwasher-safe.

COOKWARE: Nonstick skillets are great tools for beginner cooks but remember never to use them over high heat or use metal utensils on nonstick pans—scratched surfaces negatively affect their nonstick surfaces. You'll want both small and large nonstick skillets. You'll also want small and large stainless-steel skillets, as well as small and large saucepans and a stockpot.

BOWLS: A set of 3 stainless-steel mixing bowls that fit inside one another is a space saver. They are inexpensive, versatile and will last a lifetime.

BLENDER: Handy for blending up a smoothie or salad dressing.

ELECTRIC HAND MIXER: Baked goods are so much easier with a hand mixer. You can get one for as little as $15.

BAKEWARE: At least one 9-by-13-inch baking pan, roasting pan and rack, pizza pan, baking sheets, 3-quart rectangular and 8-inch-square glass baking dishes.

COLANDER: One that has feet and is the right size for your family (think about how much pasta you need to drain at once). Also make sure it will fit in your sink.

UTENSILS: Heat-resistant nonstick spatulas, vegetable peeler, rolling pin, meat mallet, a slotted spoon for draining, a wire whisk, tongs, a few wooden spoons, ladle.

SLOW COOKER: Buy one that's the right size for your family. A great tool for someone on the go: a lot of recipes can be thrown together in minutes before work and are ready to eat when you get home.

STORAGE CONTAINERS: Storage containers aren't just for storing leftovers, but can also hold any unused ingredients that come from making dinner.

INSTANT-READ THERMOMETER: Found in nearly every supermarket meat section or with other kitchen gadgets, an instant-read thermometer is essential for making sure meat and poultry are safely cooked and done to your preference.

PATTERN FOR HEALTHY EATING

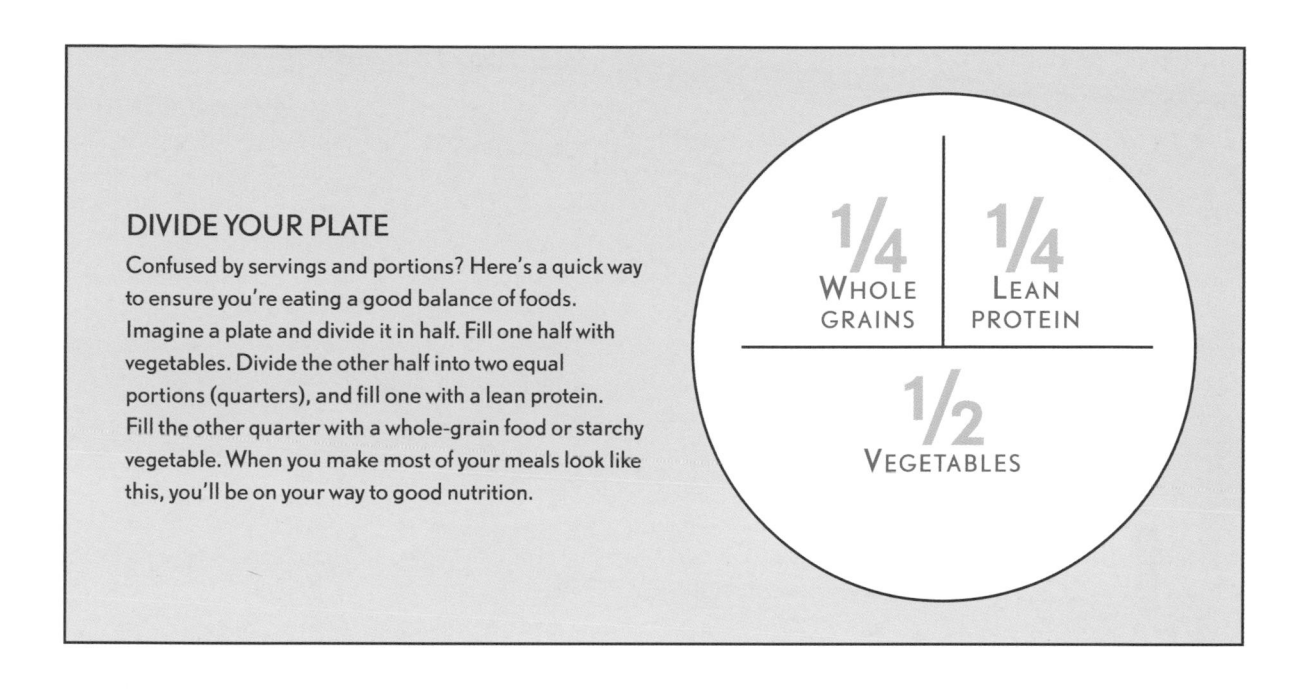

DIVIDE YOUR PLATE

Confused by servings and portions? Here's a quick way to ensure you're eating a good balance of foods. Imagine a plate and divide it in half. Fill one half with vegetables. Divide the other half into two equal portions (quarters), and fill one with a lean protein. Fill the other quarter with a whole-grain food or starchy vegetable. When you make most of your meals look like this, you'll be on your way to good nutrition.

HOW TO EAT MINDFULLY

Your eating patterns—such as the timing between mouthfuls and the order in which you eat the food on your plate—can have a real impact on how many calories you consume in a day. To make sure that you don't eat too much, be mindful of what you're eating and enjoy your meals. Here are a couple of easy ways to do that:

SLOW DOWN AND SAVOR YOUR MEAL. It takes about 20 minutes for "I'm full" signals to reach your brain. If you've inhaled an entire meal in 13 minutes, those satiety messages haven't had enough time to signal that you've eaten four portions. So put down your fork or spoon between each bite. (Some people find that eating with smaller utensils—like a teaspoon instead of a soup spoon, or chopsticks—helps them stay on a slower pace.) Chat with your dining companions—or if you're alone, take some relaxing breaths.

DON'T TAKE SERVING BOWLS TO THE TABLE. Keep the food on the kitchen counter and just carry your plate to the table. Leaving the serving bowls on the table makes it way too easy to take seconds.

LISTEN TO YOUR BODY. Think of your hunger on a scale of 1 to 5, with 1 being "ravenous" and 5 being "stuffed." Stop eating when you've reached about 3 or 4 on the scale—that point where you're comfortably satisfied, but you could still eat a bit more.

KEEP AN EYE ON PORTION SIZE

A key first step in learning how to make over recipes is to understand what reasonable portions of foods look like. For most of us, that requires a bit of downscaling.

Many nutrition authorities believe our ability to estimate correct portions is deteriorating—largely because we are becoming used to the ever-bigger food helpings served up to us in restaurants and other venues. Unfortunately these overblown portions almost always encourage us to eat more. Several studies have shown that when adults and children are repeatedly served bigger-than-normal portions of food, they tend to eat more—regardless of how hungry they were when they sat down.

The best way to reclaim normal portion sizes, say experts, is by measuring them out repeatedly until it becomes instinctive. Use measuring cups and spoons and, if needed, a kitchen scale to portion out your foods. Take note of how the food looks on a plate—and try to use the same plate each time you eat that item, so you'll have a second visual reference. Continue practicing and measuring until the portions become second nature to you. This can take a few days or a few weeks; some people might opt for always measuring rather than eyeballing.

PORTION-SIZE GUIDE

Measuring your food is the most accurate way to keep track of reasonable serving sizes. But you can also just use some real-life objects as a rough guideline for appropriate servings. Here are a few foods and what the serving looks like:

1 teaspoon oil	The tip of your thumb
1 tablespoon salad dressing	Your whole thumb
2 tablespoons peanut butter	A Ping-Pong ball
1 to 2 ounces nuts	Your cupped hand
1 ½ ounces cheese	A 9-volt battery
½ cup cottage cheese	A tennis ball
1 cup cereal	A baseball
1 small baked potato	A computer mouse
3-ounce serving of meat, fish or poultry	A cassette tape
1 standard pancake or waffle	A 4-inch DVD

MENUS FOR EVERY OCCASION

A HEALTHY THANKSGIVING
Herb-Roasted Turkey & Pan Gravy (*page 129*)
Cornbread & Sausage Stuffing (*page 198*)
Vermont Cheddar Mashed Potatoes (*page 194*)
Roasted Carrots with Cardamom Butter (*page 203*)
Green Bean Casserole (*page 206*)
Pumpkin Pie with Rum (*page 225*)

EASY HOLIDAY ENTERTAINING
Smoked Salmon Spread (*page 43*) on crostini
Mint-Pesto Rubbed Leg of Lamb (*page 115*)
Creamed Spinach (*page 202*)
Au Gratin Potatoes (*page 195*)
Deep-Dish Apple Pie (*page 221*) with Vanilla
  Cream (*page 244*)

GAME-DAY DINNER
Jojo's Party Mix (*page 42*)
The Wedge (*page 83*)
Creamy Hamburger Noodle Casserole (*page 109*)
Old-Fashioned Fruit Crumble (*page 219*) with
  Vanilla Bean Ice Cream (*page 230*)

FOURTH OF JULY BBQ
Ranch Dip & Crunchy Vegetables (*page 39*)
Smoky Buffalo Burger (*page 92*)
Summer Potato Salad (*page 86*)
Corn Pudding (*page 208*)
Strawberry Shortcake (*page 218*)

VEGETARIAN DINNER PARTY
Indonesian Tofu Satés (*page 186*)
Nasi Goreng (*page 184*)
Banana Cream Layer Cake (*page 239*)

MEXICAN FIESTA
Crispy Beef Tacos (*page 94*)
Easy Fiesta Beans (*page 200*)
Key Lime Pie (*page 226*)

KIDS RULE!
Mixed greens with Buttermilk Ranch Dressing
  (*page 89*)
Golden Baked Pork Cutlets (*page 102*)
Steamed broccoli with Light Cheese Sauce (*page 211*)
Oatmeal Chocolate Chip Cookies (*page 243*)

ELEGANT OUTDOOR ENTERTAINING
Cauliflower with New Mornay Sauce (*page 210*)
Grilled Filet Mignon with Herb Butter & Texas Toasts
  (*page 111*)
Peach-Raspberry Pie (*page 222*)

FISH FRIDAY
Oven-Fried Fish & Chips (*page 163*)
Asparagus topped with Creamy Tarragon Sauce
  (*page 210*)
Double Chocolate Brownies (*page 241*)

SOUP & SANDWICH NIGHT
Fresh Corn Chowder (*page 62*)
Southwestern Cheese Panini (*page 181*)
Carrot Cake (*page 236*)

SUMMER PICNIC
Classic Coleslaw (*page 83*)
Oven-Fried Chicken (*page 121*)
Three-Bean Salad (*page 88*)
Lemon Squares (*page 240*)

Baked Apple-Cinnamon French Toast (page 26)

BREAKFAST

DELICIOUS FEEDBACK

Blueberry-Maple Muffins

"These were delicious. Very light, great texture. The trouble
is not eating two of these at a time! Much better than your usual
healthy versions of muffins."

—Kathleen, Thousand Oaks, CA

Strawberry-Topped Multi-Grain Waffles

"These waffles are *so delicious* that I always make a double batch and
freeze them. I can pop one in the toaster any day of the week for a
special treat for the kids—and it's healthy!"

—Rachael, Dallas, TX

SCRAMBLED EGGS WITH SMOKED SALMON

H)(W   L↓C   H♥H

ACTIVE TIME: 10 MINUTES | **TOTAL:** 10 MINUTES

Smoked salmon has such a rich and salty flavor that a little bit goes a long way in this sophisticated take on scrambled eggs. Consider a slice of hearty German rye bread with a schmear of Neufchâtel cheese to accompany this savory dish.

4   large eggs
4   large egg whites
    Freshly ground pepper to taste

1   teaspoon canola oil
2   scallions, green tops only, thinly sliced
1   ounce smoked salmon, thinly sliced

1. Whisk eggs, egg whites and pepper in a small bowl until well blended.

2. Heat oil in a nonstick skillet over medium-low heat. Add scallion greens and cook, stirring, until softened, about 30 seconds. Pour the eggs into the pan and cook until they just begin to set, about 10 seconds; stir in salmon. Cook, stirring gently from time to time, until the eggs have thickened into soft, creamy curds, 3 to 5 minutes. Serve immediately.

MAKES 4 SERVINGS.

PER SERVING: 108 calories; 6 g fat (2 g sat, 2 g mono); 213 mg cholesterol; 1 g carbohydrate; 11 g protein; 0 g fiber; 182 mg sodium; 155 mg potassium.

NUTRITION BONUS: Selenium (36% daily value), good source of omega-3s.

QUICHE LORRAINE LIGHT

H⚡W L↓C H♥H

ACTIVE TIME: 30 MINUTES | **TOTAL:** 1 ¼ HOURS
TO MAKE AHEAD: Prepare through Step 3; cover and refrigerate for up to 2 days or freeze for up to 1 month.

Quiche has a reputation as a light dish even though its custardlike texture comes from whole eggs and heavy cream. You can lose a few egg yolks and use a blend of nonfat milk and nonfat evaporated milk to achieve truly light results without sacrificing texture.

CRUST
- ¾ cup whole-wheat pastry flour
- ½ cup all-purpose flour
- ¼ teaspoon salt
- 1 tablespoon butter
- 3 tablespoons canola oil
- 1-2 tablespoons ice water

FILLING
- 2 large eggs
- 4 large egg whites
- ¾ cup nonfat milk
- ¾ cup nonfat evaporated milk
- ¼ teaspoon freshly ground nutmeg
- ¼ teaspoon salt
- ¼ teaspoon freshly ground pepper
- Pinch of cayenne pepper
- ½ cup shredded Gruyère cheese
- ¼ cup diced smoked ham
- ¼ cup chopped scallions
- 1 tablespoon freshly grated Parmesan cheese

1. TO PREPARE CRUST: Position rack in lower third of oven; preheat to 425°F.

2. Stir whole-wheat flour, all-purpose flour and ¼ teaspoon salt in a medium bowl. Melt butter in a small saucepan over low heat. Cook, swirling the pan, until the butter is a light, nutty brown, 30 seconds to 4 minutes (depending on your stove). Pour into a small bowl and let cool. Stir in oil. Using a fork, slowly stir the butter-oil mixture into the flour mixture until it is crumbly. Gradually stir in enough ice water so that the dough will hold together. Knead the dough in the bowl a few times to help it come together. Press the dough into a disk.

3. Place the dough between sheets of parchment or wax paper and roll into a 12-inch circle. Remove the top sheet and invert the dough into a 9-inch pie pan. Remove the remaining paper and patch any tears in the dough. Fold the edges under at the rim and crimp with a fork.

4. Line the dough with a piece of foil or parchment paper large enough to lift out easily; fill evenly with pie weights or dried beans. Bake for 7 minutes. Remove the foil or paper and weights and continue baking just until lightly browned, 3 to 5 minutes more. (The crust will not be fully baked.) Let cool to room temperature on a wire rack. Reduce oven temperature to 350°.

5. TO PREPARE FILLING: Whisk eggs and egg whites well in a large bowl. Add milk, evaporated milk, nutmeg, ¼ teaspoon salt, pepper and cayenne, stirring gently to avoid creating many bubbles.

6. TO ASSEMBLE & BAKE QUICHE: Sprinkle Gruyère, ham and scallions over the bottom of the prebaked crust. Carefully pour in the filling. Sprinkle with Parmesan. Bake the quiche until a knife inserted in the center comes out clean, 35 to 40 minutes. Let cool on a wire rack for 10 to 15 minutes before serving hot or warm.

MAKES 8 SERVINGS.

PER SERVING: 208 calories; 11 g fat (3 g sat, 5 g mono); 68 mg cholesterol; 17 g carbohydrate; 11 g protein; 1 g fiber; 297 mg sodium; 221 mg potassium.

NUTRITION BONUS: Selenium (18% daily value).

HAM & CHEESE BREAKFAST CASSEROLE

H�W

ACTIVE TIME: 30 MINUTES | **TOTAL:** 1 ¾ HOURS

TO MAKE AHEAD: Prepare casserole through Step 2; refrigerate overnight. Let stand at room temperature while the oven preheats. Bake as directed in Step 3.

This healthy update of a traditionally rich and cheesy breakfast strata is made lighter primarily by losing a few egg yolks and using nonfat milk. Gruyère cheese has a delicious, nutty aroma and flavor, which means that with the relatively small amount in this recipe you still get a big impact. To finish the makeover use nutritious, fiber-rich, whole-grain bread instead of white. The results: plenty of flavor, half the calories and one-third the fat of the original.

4	large eggs	4	cups whole-grain bread, crusts removed if desired, cut into 1-inch cubes (about ½ pound, 4-6 slices)
4	large egg whites		
1	cup nonfat milk		
2	tablespoons Dijon mustard	1	cup diced ham steak (5 ounces)
1	teaspoon minced fresh rosemary	½	cup chopped jarred roasted red peppers
¼	teaspoon freshly ground pepper	¾	cup shredded Gruyère *or* Swiss cheese
5	cups chopped spinach, wilted (*see Tip*)		

TIP:

To wilt spinach, rinse thoroughly with cool water. Transfer to a large microwave-safe bowl. Cover with plastic wrap and punch several holes in it. Microwave on High until wilted, 2 to 3 minutes. Squeeze out excess moisture before adding the spinach to the recipe.

MAKEOVER TIP

WHEN YOU REDUCE THE CHEESE IN BAKED DISHES, USE IT JUST AS A TOPPING, RATHER THAN BAKING THE CHEESE INTO THE FILLING, FOR THE BIGGEST FLAVOR IMPACT.

1. Preheat oven to 375°F. Coat a 7-by-11-inch glass baking dish or a 2-quart casserole with cooking spray.

2. Whisk eggs, egg whites and milk in a medium bowl. Add mustard, rosemary and pepper; whisk to combine. Toss spinach, bread, ham and roasted red peppers in a large bowl. Add the egg mixture and toss well to coat. Transfer to the prepared baking dish and push down to compact. Cover with foil.

3. Bake until the custard has set, 40 to 45 minutes. Uncover, sprinkle with cheese and continue baking until the pudding is puffed and golden on top, 15 to 20 minutes more. Transfer to a wire rack and cool for 15 to 20 minutes before serving.

MAKES 6 SERVINGS.

PER SERVING: 286 calories; 10 g fat (4 g sat, 3 g mono); 167 mg cholesterol; 23 g carbohydrate; 23 g protein; 4 g fiber; 813 mg sodium; 509 mg potassium.

NUTRITION BONUS: Vitamin A (70% daily value), Folate (37% dv), Calcium (30% dv), Vitamin C (20% dv).

BAKED APPLE-CINNAMON FRENCH TOAST

H)(W H♥H

ACTIVE TIME: 25 MINUTES | **TOTAL:** 9½ HOURS (INCLUDING 8 HOURS REFRIGERATION TIME)
TO MAKE AHEAD: Prepare through Step 3 and refrigerate for up to 1 day.

French toast is like having an indulgent dessert for breakfast, but with this recipe you can enjoy it guilt-free. By using nonfat instead of whole milk and eliminating the egg yolks, the calories are cut by half and the fat is reduced by nearly 80 percent in our baked (not griddled) version. Best of all, the whole thing can be prepared up to a day in advance and then simply popped in the oven for a leisurely and luxurious weekend morning. (*Photograph: page 20.*)

3 cups nonfat milk	1 1-pound loaf sliced whole-wheat bread
2 cups pasteurized liquid egg whites, such as Egg Beaters	1 cup chopped dried apples (3 ounces)
3 tablespoons honey	½ cup raisins
1½ teaspoons vanilla extract	1½ teaspoons ground cinnamon
¼ teaspoon salt	½ teaspoon ground nutmeg
	1 tablespoon confectioners' sugar

MAKEOVER TIP

TRY USING EGG WHITES IN PLACE OF WHOLE EGGS IN RECIPES LIKE FRENCH TOAST. FOR EACH WHOLE EGG, SUBSTITUTE 2 EGG WHITES OR ¼ CUP OF LIQUID EGG WHITES, SUCH AS EGG BEATERS. JUST ELIMINATING 1 YOLK FROM A RECIPE SAVES 4 GRAMS OF FAT AND 53 CALORIES.

1. Whisk milk, egg whites, honey, vanilla and salt in a large bowl.

2. Trim crusts off 8 bread slices and set aside. Cut the crusts and the remaining bread into 1-inch pieces. Toss with dried apples, raisins, cinnamon and nutmeg in another large bowl.

3. Coat a 9-by-13-inch baking pan with cooking spray. Transfer the bread mixture to the pan. Lay the reserved crustless slices evenly on top, trimming to fit. Whisk the milk mixture one more time, then pour evenly over the bread. Press the bread down with the back of a wooden spoon, making sure it's evenly moist. Cover with parchment paper, then foil, and refrigerate for at least 8 hours or up to 24 hours.

4. Preheat oven to 350°F.

5. Bake the casserole, covered, for 40 minutes. Uncover and continue baking until puffed, set and lightly browned, about 20 minutes more. Let stand for 10 minutes; dust with confectioners' sugar and serve.

MAKES 12 SERVINGS.

PER SERVING: 183 calories; 1 g fat (0 g sat, 1 g mono); 1 mg cholesterol; 33 g carbohydrate; 10 g protein; 4 g fiber; 344 mg sodium; 312 mg potassium.

NUTRITION BONUS: Selenium (21% daily value).

MAKING GRANOLA TRULY WHOLESOME

"My mom found the enclosed granola recipe years ago on a box of oats," wrote Susan Kirby of Buffalo, New York. "It's delicious and has become a tradition; we make large batches and give it as a Christmas gift. I've tried 'lightening' it up myself, with poor results. Please try doctoring it. I rarely make this during the year because of the high fat content."

Granola's image as a health food has led many people to believe that it is a healthier alternative to high-fat snacks and cereals. However, most homemade and commercial granolas derive 40 to 50 percent of their calories from fat, compared to the 1 percent fat-calories from most fruit- and grain-based cereals. Even though granola recipes often contain nutritious oats and wheat germ,

lots of fatty ingredients, such as coconut, almonds, sweetened condensed milk and canola oil, are not only calorie-dense, but they add up to 13 grams of fat per serving.

To transform granola into a truly wholesome food, we shifted the ingredient balance to more fruits and whole grains. Not wanting to sacrifice the flavor and texture of the almonds and coconut, we used a judicious amount and included prunes and dried apricots for more flavor, fiber, vitamins and minerals. A mixture of nonfat dry milk, sugar, water and canola oil moistens the dry ingredients, negating the need for full-fat condensed milk.

The result is satisfying—a crunchy, not-too-sweet granola with about a third the fat of the original and, cup for cup, 138 fewer calories.

COCONUT-ALMOND GRANOLA

H ⬆ F H ❤ H

ACTIVE TIME: 30 MINUTES | **TOTAL:** 2½ HOURS (INCLUDING 1 HOUR CHILLING TIME)
TO MAKE AHEAD: Prepare through Step 1; refrigerate overnight. Store the granola in an airtight container for up to 2 weeks.

The secret to keeping granola nutritious, yet tasty, is in the balance of ingredients. We go heavy on the whole grains and add just the right amount of nuts and dried fruit. **SHOPPING TIP:** Wheat flakes are simply wheat kernels that have been steamed and rolled, oatmeal-style. Look for them in natural-foods stores.

⅔ cup sugar	¼ cup chopped almonds
⅓ cup boiling water	¼ cup unsweetened shredded coconut
1 cup nonfat dry milk	1 teaspoon salt
2 tablespoons corn syrup	2 tablespoons canola oil
2½ cups rolled oats	1 cup raisins
1 cup wheat flakes (*see Shopping Tip*)	½ cup pitted prunes, chopped
½ cup toasted wheat germ	½ cup dried apricots, chopped

1. Dissolve sugar in boiling water in a medium bowl. Stir in dry milk and corn syrup and beat with an electric mixer until smooth and creamy, about 2 minutes. Cover and refrigerate for 1 hour or overnight.
2. Preheat oven to 300°F. Combine oats, wheat flakes, wheat germ, almonds, coconut and salt in a large bowl. Add oil and the reserved milk mixture and mix thoroughly. Spread on a baking sheet. Bake the granola, stirring occasionally, until golden brown, 40 to 50 minutes. Stir in raisins, prunes and apricots. Bake for 5 minutes more. Let cool.

MAKES 8 CUPS.

PER ½-CUP SERVING: 246 calories; 5 g fat (1 g sat, 2 g mono); 0 mg cholesterol; 46 g carbohydrate; 7 g protein; 5 g fiber; 179 mg sodium; 372 mg potassium.

STRAWBERRY-TOPPED MULTI-GRAIN WAFFLES

H⋈W H♥H

ACTIVE TIME: 35 MINUTES | **TOTAL:** 50 MINUTES

TO MAKE AHEAD: Wrap any leftover waffles individually in plastic wrap and refrigerate for up to 2 days or freeze for up to 1 month. Reheat in a toaster or toaster oven.

The batter, which makes great pancakes as well, is chock-full of nutty-tasting whole grains. Add Vanilla Cream (*page 244*) along with the strawberries for a truly decadent topping.

4 cups strawberries, hulled and sliced	1 teaspoon ground cinnamon
3 tablespoons granulated sugar	1/2 teaspoon baking soda
2 cups nonfat buttermilk (*see Tip, page 246*)	1/4 teaspoon salt
1/2 cup rolled oats	2 large eggs, lightly beaten
2/3 cup whole-wheat flour	1/4 cup packed brown sugar
2/3 cup all-purpose flour	1 tablespoon canola oil
1/4 cup toasted wheat germ *or* cornmeal	2 teaspoons vanilla extract
1 1/2 teaspoons baking powder	

PANCAKE VARIATION

Coat a large nonstick skillet with cooking spray; heat over medium heat. Using about 1/4 cup batter for each pancake, cook until the bottoms are golden and small bubbles start to form on the tops, about 3 minutes. Flip and cook until browned and cooked through, 1 to 2 minutes longer. MAKES 16 PANCAKES.

MAKEOVER TIP

ADDING OATS AND WHEAT GERM TO WAFFLE OR PANCAKE BATTER PROVIDES CHOLESTEROL-LOWERING SOLUBLE FIBER AND GREAT TEXTURE.

1. Combine strawberries and granulated sugar in a medium bowl; toss to coat. Let stand at room temperature until the strawberries start to give off juice, 20 to 30 minutes.

2. Meanwhile, mix buttermilk and oats in a medium bowl; let stand for 15 minutes.

3. Whisk whole-wheat flour, all-purpose flour, wheat germ (or cornmeal), baking powder, cinnamon, baking soda and salt in a large bowl.

4. Stir eggs, brown sugar, oil and vanilla into the oat mixture. Add the wet ingredients to the dry ingredients; mix with a rubber spatula just until moistened.

5. Coat a waffle iron with cooking spray and preheat. Spoon in enough batter to cover three-fourths of the surface (about 2/3 cup for an 8-by-8-inch waffle iron). Cook until the waffles are crisp and golden brown, 4 to 5 minutes. Repeat with the remaining batter. Serve topped with the strawberries.

MAKES 8 SERVINGS (2 waffles & 1/2 cup strawberries each).

PER SERVING: 237 calories; 4 g fat (1 g sat, 2 g mono); 54 mg cholesterol; 43 g carbohydrate; 9 g protein; 4 g fiber; 319 mg sodium; 258 mg potassium.

NUTRITION BONUS: Vitamin C (82% daily value).

GERMAN APPLE PANCAKE

H)(W   H ♥ H

ACTIVE TIME: 30 MINUTES | **TOTAL:** 1 HOUR 10 MINUTES
TO MAKE AHEAD: The topping (STEPS 1-2) will keep, covered, in the refrigerator for up to 2 days. Reheat before serving.

A judicious use of butter and sugar give this classic breakfast—also known as a Dutch baby—less than a third of the fat and considerably fewer calories than the original. The topping—sautéed apples glazed with apple-cider syrup—is wonderful on oatmeal, waffles and frozen yogurt too.

APPLE TOPPING

- 1½ teaspoons butter
- 1½ teaspoons canola oil
- 4 Granny Smith apples, peeled and sliced
- 3 tablespoons sugar
- ½ teaspoon vanilla extract
- ¼ teaspoon ground cinnamon
- 1 cup apple cider

PANCAKE

- 3 large eggs
- ¼ cup all-purpose flour
- 2 teaspoons sugar
- ¼ teaspoon salt
- 1 cup low-fat milk
- Confectioners' sugar for dusting

1. TO PREPARE TOPPING: Heat butter and oil in a large nonstick skillet over medium heat until melted. Add apples and 3 tablespoons sugar; cook, stirring, until the apples are tender and golden, about 20 minutes. Stir in vanilla and cinnamon.

2. Meanwhile, bring cider to a boil in a medium saucepan over medium-high heat. Cook until reduced to ⅓ cup, 10 to 15 minutes. Stir into the sautéed apples. Set aside.

3. TO PREPARE PANCAKE: Preheat oven to 400°F. Coat a 12-inch cast-iron or other ovenproof skillet with cooking spray.

4. Whisk eggs, flour, 2 teaspoons sugar and salt in a mixing bowl until smooth. Gradually add milk, whisking until smooth. Pour the batter into the prepared skillet.

5. Bake the pancake for 15 minutes. Reduce oven temperature to 350°; bake until the pancake is golden and puffed, 15 minutes more. (The pancake will deflate when removed from the oven.)

6. Meanwhile, gently reheat the apple topping, if necessary. Dust the pancake with confectioners' sugar and cut into wedges. Serve immediately, with the warm apple topping.

MAKES 4 SERVINGS.

PER SERVING: 282 calories; 8 g fat (3 g sat, 3 g mono); 166 mg cholesterol; 47 g carbohydrate; 9 g protein; 2 g fiber; 230 mg sodium; 175 mg potassium.

NUTRITION BONUS: Selenium (17% daily value).

PINEAPPLE COFFEE CAKE

H ♥ H

ACTIVE TIME: 15 MINUTES | **TOTAL:** 1 ½ HOURS

Nonfat plain yogurt stands in for sour cream to add moisture and tenderness to this lightened-up classic coffee cake. Best of all, you can mix the batter and have this wholesome breakfast treat in the oven in under 15 minutes—that's healthy in a hurry.

1 cup whole-wheat pastry flour	1 cup nonfat plain yogurt
1 cup all-purpose flour	¼ cup canola oil
½ cup plus 2 tablespoons sugar, divided	1 teaspoon vanilla extract
1 tablespoon baking powder	1 ½ cups diced fresh *or* canned pineapple chunks, blotted dry and coarsely chopped
1 teaspoon baking soda	¼ cup chopped pecans
½ teaspoon salt	
1 large egg	

1. Preheat oven to 350°F. Coat an 8-inch-square baking pan with cooking spray.

2. Whisk whole-wheat flour, all-purpose flour, ½ cup sugar, baking powder, baking soda and salt in a medium bowl.

3. Whisk egg, yogurt, oil and vanilla in a large bowl until smooth. Add the dry ingredients and stir with a rubber spatula until just blended. (Do not overmix.) Fold in pineapple. Scrape the batter into the prepared pan.

4. Combine pecans and the remaining 2 tablespoons sugar in a small bowl. Sprinkle over the batter.

5. Bake the cake until the top is golden and a skewer inserted in the center comes out clean, 50 to 55 minutes. Let cool in the pan on a wire rack for about 20 minutes. Cut into squares and serve warm.

MAKES 9 SERVINGS.

PER SERVING: 253 calories; 9 g fat (1 g sat, 6 g mono); 24 mg cholesterol; 38 g carbohydrate; 5 g protein; 2 g fiber; 476 mg sodium; 94 mg potassium.

NUTRITION BONUS: Vitamin C (23% daily value).

VARIATIONS

This quick coffee cake can be made with a variety of fruit. Try rhubarb, blueberries or peaches. If using frozen fruit, increase the baking time by 10 to 15 minutes.

MAKEOVER TIP

USING WHOLE-WHEAT PASTRY FLOUR IN PLACE OF SOME (OR ALL) OF THE ALL-PURPOSE FLOUR IN BAKED GOODS INCREASES FIBER. ONE CUP OF WHOLE-WHEAT PASTRY FLOUR HAS 12 GRAMS OF FIBER WHILE 1 CUP OF ALL-PURPOSE FLOUR HAS JUST 3 GRAMS.

BANANA-NUT-CHOCOLATE CHIP QUICK BREAD

ACTIVE TIME: 25 MINUTES | **TOTAL:** 1 ¼ HOURS (MUFFINS, MINI BUNDTS), 1 ½ HOURS (MINI LOAVES), 2 ¼ HOURS (LARGE LOAF), including cooling times

TO MAKE AHEAD: Store, individually wrapped, at room temperature for up to 2 days or in the freezer for up to 1 month.

Banana quick breads are always a crowd-pleaser but they're usually loaded with oil and butter. This version reduces the fat substantially and uses nonfat buttermilk to make the results extremely moist and tender. Plenty of chocolate chips and toasted heart-healthy walnuts guarantee that you get a taste of nuts and chocolate in each bite.

1 ½ cups whole-wheat pastry flour (*see Ingredient Note, page 248*) *or* whole-wheat flour	1 cup nonfat buttermilk (*see Tip, page 246*)
1 cup all-purpose flour	⅔ cup brown sugar
1 ½ teaspoons baking powder	2 tablespoons butter, melted
1 teaspoon ground cinnamon	2 tablespoons canola oil
½ teaspoon baking soda	1 teaspoon vanilla extract
¼ teaspoon ground nutmeg	2 cups diced bananas
¼ teaspoon salt	½ cup chopped toasted walnuts (*see Tip, page 247*), plus more for topping if desired
2 large eggs	½ cup mini chocolate chips

PAN OPTIONS:

1 large loaf (9-by-5-inch pan)

3 mini loaves (6-by-3-inch pan, 2-cup capacity)

6 mini Bundt cakes (6-cup mini Bundt pan, scant 1-cup capacity per cake)

12 muffins (standard 12-cup, 2½-inch muffin pan)

1. Preheat oven to 400°F for muffins, mini loaves and mini Bundts or 375°F for a large loaf. (*See pan options, left.*) Coat pan(s) with cooking spray.

2. Whisk whole-wheat flour, all-purpose flour, baking powder, cinnamon, baking soda, nutmeg and salt in a large bowl. Whisk eggs, buttermilk, brown sugar, butter, oil and vanilla in another large bowl until well combined.

3. Make a well in the dry ingredients and stir in the wet ingredients until just combined. Add bananas, walnuts and chocolate chips. Stir just to combine; do not overmix. Transfer the batter to the prepared pan(s). Top with additional walnuts, if desired.

4. Bake until golden brown and a skewer inserted in the center comes out clean, 22 to 25 minutes for muffins or mini Bundts, 35 minutes for mini loaves, 1 hour 10 minutes for a large loaf. Let cool in the pan(s) for 10 minutes, then turn out onto a wire rack. Let muffins and mini Bundts cool for 5 minutes more, mini loaves for 30 minutes, large loaves for 40 minutes.

MAKES 12 SERVINGS.

PER SERVING: 273 calories; 11 g fat (3 g sat, 3 g mono); 41 mg cholesterol; 40 g carbohydrate; 7 g protein; 3 g fiber; 184 mg sodium; 178 mg potassium.

MORNING GLORY MUFFINS

H✕W   H♥H

ACTIVE TIME: 40 MINUTES | **TOTAL:** 1 HOUR

TO MAKE AHEAD: Get a head start on your morning muffins the night before by mixing up the dry and liquid ingredients separately (refrigerate liquids). In the morning, combine the two, scoop and bake.

Grated carrots make this bakery standard a great source of vitamin A, but most versions are high in fat as well. As a substitute for much of the fat, we use apple butter, which makes each bite superbly moist and tender. If raisins aren't your favorite, substitute an equal amount of the dried fruit of your choice.

1 cup whole-wheat flour	2 large egg whites *or* 4 teaspoons dried egg whites (*see Ingredient Note, page 247*), reconstituted according to package directions
1 cup all-purpose flour	
¾ cup sugar	
1 tablespoon ground cinnamon	
1 teaspoon baking powder	½ cup apple butter
1 teaspoon baking soda	¼ cup canola oil
¼ teaspoon salt	1 tablespoon vanilla extract
2 cups grated carrots (4 medium)	2 tablespoons finely chopped walnuts *or* pecans
1 apple, peeled and finely chopped	
½ cup raisins	2 tablespoons toasted wheat germ
1 large egg	

1. Preheat oven to 375°F. Coat 18 muffin cups with cooking spray.

2. Whisk whole-wheat flour, all-purpose flour, sugar, cinnamon, baking powder, baking soda and salt in a large bowl. Stir in carrots, apple and raisins. Whisk egg, egg whites, apple butter, oil and vanilla in a medium bowl.

3. Make a well in the dry ingredients and stir in the wet ingredients with a rubber spatula until just combined. Spoon the batter into the prepared muffin cups, filling them about three-fourths full. Combine walnuts and wheat germ in a small bowl; sprinkle over the muffin tops.

4. Bake the muffins until the tops are golden brown and spring back when touched lightly, 15 to 25 minutes. Let cool in the pans for 5 minutes. Loosen edges and turn muffins out onto a wire rack to cool.

MAKES 18 MUFFINS.

PER MUFFIN: 163 calories; 4 g fat (0 g sat, 2 g mono); 12 mg cholesterol; 29 g carbohydrate; 3 g protein; 2 g fiber; 154 mg sodium; 149 mg potassium.

MAKEOVER TIP

APPLE BUTTER CAN BE USED AS A FAT REPLACER IN BAKED GOODS. IN THESE MUFFINS, WE USE IT TO REPLACE HALF THE OIL.

BLUEBERRY-MAPLE MUFFINS

H)(W   H♥H

ACTIVE TIME: 30 MINUTES | **TOTAL:** 1 HOUR

Whole-wheat flour and flaxseeds give these maple syrup-sweetened muffins a delicious, nutty flavor. Compared to a traditional version of the recipe, they have four times the dietary fiber and substitute healthful monounsaturated fat (canola oil) for saturated fat (butter).

⅓ cup whole flaxseeds	½ cup pure maple syrup
1 cup whole-wheat flour	1 cup nonfat buttermilk (*see Tip, page 246*)
¾ cup plus 2 tablespoons all-purpose flour	¼ cup canola oil
1½ teaspoons baking powder	2 teaspoons freshly grated orange zest
1 teaspoon ground cinnamon	1 tablespoon orange juice
½ teaspoon baking soda	1 teaspoon vanilla extract
¼ teaspoon salt	1½ cups fresh blueberries
2 large eggs	1 tablespoon sugar

1. Preheat oven to 400°F. Coat 12 muffin cups with cooking spray.

2. Grind flaxseeds in a spice mill (such as a clean coffee grinder) or dry blender. Transfer to a large bowl. Add whole-wheat flour, all-purpose flour, baking powder, cinnamon, baking soda and salt; whisk to blend. Whisk eggs and maple syrup in a medium bowl until smooth. Add buttermilk, oil, orange zest, orange juice and vanilla; whisk until blended.

3. Make a well in the dry ingredients and stir in the wet ingredients with a rubber spatula just until moistened. Fold in blueberries. Scoop the batter into the prepared muffin cups. Sprinkle the tops with sugar.

4. Bake the muffins until the tops are golden brown and spring back when touched lightly, 15 to 25 minutes. Let cool in the pan for 5 minutes. Loosen edges and turn muffins out onto a wire rack to cool slightly.

MAKES 12 MUFFINS.

PER MUFFIN: 208 calories; 8 g fat (1 g sat, 4 g mono); 36 mg cholesterol; 31 g carbohydrate; 6 g protein; 3 g fiber; 184 mg sodium; 149 mg potassium.

MAKEOVER TIP

ADD FLAXSEEDS TO BAKED GOODS TO PROVIDE OMEGA-3 FATTY ACIDS AND EXTRA FIBER. THE SEEDS NEED TO BE GROUND FOR YOUR BODY TO ABSORB THE BENEFITS. FIND THEM IN THE NATURAL-FOODS SECTION OF LARGE SUPERMARKETS AND IN NATURAL-FOODS STORES.

Southwestern Layered Bean Dip (page 38)

APPETIZERS

DELICIOUS FEEDBACK

Steak-&-Boursin-Wrapped Bells

"These are surprisingly good for such a simple ingredient list.
All of my guests loved them, as did I, even though I'm not
a big meat fan."

—Anonymous, Duxbury, VT

Southwestern Layered Bean Dip

"This is probably my current favorite EATINGWELL recipe.
My husband requests it every weekend. It is so much healthier than
the 7-layer dip sold at grocery stores. I eat mine nacho-style with
homemade whole-wheat baked pita chips. Wonderful."

—Anonymous, Charlotte, NC

SOUTHWESTERN LAYERED BEAN DIP

H⇥W L⬇C H⬆F

ACTIVE TIME: 20 MINUTES | **TOTAL:** 20 MINUTES
TO MAKE AHEAD: Prepare through Step 1, cover and refrigerate for up to 1 day. To serve, continue with Steps 2 & 3.

You'll want to have lots of baked tortilla chips on hand when you serve this delicious dip. Plenty of black beans, salsa and chopped fresh vegetables mean a healthy amount of dietary fiber. We use reduced-fat sour cream along with full-fat (and full-flavored) cheese to make the dip lighter without compromising great taste. (*Photograph: page 36.*)

1 16-ounce can nonfat refried beans, preferably "spicy"	1 cup shredded Monterey Jack *or* Cheddar cheese
1 15-ounce can black beans, rinsed	½ cup reduced-fat sour cream
4 scallions, sliced	1½ cups chopped romaine lettuce
½ cup prepared salsa	1 medium tomato, chopped
½ teaspoon ground cumin	1 medium avocado, chopped
½ teaspoon chili powder	¼ cup canned sliced black olives (optional)
¼ cup pickled jalapeño slices, chopped	

1. Combine refried beans, black beans, scallions, salsa, cumin, chili powder and jalapeños in a medium bowl. Transfer to a shallow 2-quart microwave-safe dish; sprinkle with cheese.

2. Microwave on High until the cheese is melted and the beans are hot, 3 to 5 minutes.

3. Spread sour cream evenly over the hot bean mixture, then scatter with lettuce, tomato, avocado and olives (if using).

MAKES 12 SERVINGS, ABOUT ½ CUP EACH.

PER SERVING: 146 calories; 7 g fat (3 g sat, 3 g mono); 12 mg cholesterol; 15 g carbohydrate; 7 g protein; 5 g fiber; 288 mg sodium; 164 mg potassium.

NUTRITION BONUS: Fiber (20% daily value), Vitamin A & Vitamin C (15% dv).

RANCH DIP & CRUNCHY VEGETABLES

H)(W   L↓C   H♥H

ACTIVE TIME: 15 MINUTES | **TOTAL:** 15 MINUTES
TO MAKE AHEAD: Cover and refrigerate the dip for up to 3 days.

Adults and kids alike love the tanginess of this ranch-style dip. By using nonfat buttermilk and low-fat mayonnaise for the creamy base we've cut the fat substantially and eliminated the saturated fat. It only takes 15 minutes to make and keeps for 3 days so it's perfect for a healthy snack in a pinch.

½   cup nonfat buttermilk (*see Tip, page 246*)
⅓   cup low-fat mayonnaise
2   tablespoons minced fresh dill *or* 2 teaspoons dried
1   tablespoon lemon juice
1   teaspoon Dijon mustard
1   teaspoon honey

½   teaspoon garlic powder
⅛   teaspoon salt
6   cups vegetables, such as baby carrots, sliced red bell peppers, snap peas, broccoli and cauliflower florets, cucumber spears, grape tomatoes

Whisk buttermilk, mayonnaise, dill, lemon juice, mustard, honey, garlic powder and salt in a medium bowl until combined. Serve the dip with vegetables of your choice.

MAKES 6 SERVINGS, 2½ TABLESPOONS DIP & 1 CUP VEGETABLES EACH.

PER SERVING: 61 calories; 1 g fat (0 g sat, 0 g mono); 0 mg cholesterol; 11 g carbohydrate; 3 g protein; 2 g fiber; 224 mg sodium; 196 mg potassium.

NUTRITION BONUS: Vitamin C (100% daily value), Vitamin A (80% dv).

MAKEOVER TIP

TANGY NONFAT BUTTERMILK MIXED WITH LOW-FAT MAYONNAISE CAN BE USED IN PLACE OF SOUR CREAM OR FULL-FAT MAYONNAISE IN CREAMY VEGETABLE DIPS.

RICH CRAB DIP

ACTIVE TIME: 20 MINUTES | **TOTAL:** 50 MINUTES

In our healthier version of this ultra-rich dip, the crabmeat plays a starring role while a blend of pureed nonfat cottage cheese and reduced-fat cream cheese provides all the creaminess you would expect. Serve with slices of whole-grain baguette.

½ cup nonfat cottage cheese
4 ounces reduced-fat cream cheese (Neufchâtel)
2 small cloves garlic, minced
½ teaspoon freshly ground pepper
¼ teaspoon Worcestershire sauce
¼ teaspoon Old Bay seasoning
¼ teaspoon cayenne pepper
8 ounces crabmeat, any shells or cartilage removed, drained and patted dry
1 tablespoon lemon juice

MAKEOVER TIP

TO REDUCE CALORIES AND FAT IN DIPS, TRY A COMBINATION OF PUREED NONFAT COTTAGE CHEESE AND REDUCED-FAT CREAM CHEESE INSTEAD OF SOUR CREAM.

Place cottage cheese in a fine-mesh sieve and press on it to remove excess moisture. Transfer the cottage cheese to a food processor or blender; add cream cheese and blend until smooth. Transfer to a medium saucepan and add garlic, pepper, Worcestershire, Old Bay and cayenne. Heat over low heat, stirring frequently, until warm, 2 to 3 minutes. Add crab and lemon juice; stir well. Heat until warm, 30 to 40 seconds. Remove from heat and serve immediately.

MAKES ABOUT 1½ CUPS.

PER 2-TABLESPOON SERVING: 48 calories; 2 g fat (1 g sat, 1 g mono); 21 mg cholesterol; 1 g carbohydrate; 6 g protein; 0 g fiber; 99 mg sodium; 86 mg potassium.

HOT ARTICHOKE DIP

ACTIVE TIME: 10 MINUTES | **TOTAL:** 20-30 MINUTES
TO MAKE AHEAD: Prepare through Step 1. Cover and refrigerate for up to 2 days.

When you cut fat and salt you run the risk of diminishing flavor. That's not a problem with this recipe which has more artichokes and plenty of Parmesan cheese, garlic and lemon zest for flavor. Who says healthier can't taste better?

2 14-ounce cans artichoke hearts, rinsed	2 teaspoons freshly grated lemon zest
2 cups plus 2 tablespoons freshly grated Parmesan cheese, divided	Cayenne pepper to taste
½ cup low-fat mayonnaise	¼ teaspoon salt
2 cloves garlic, minced	Freshly ground pepper to taste

1. Preheat oven to 400°F. Chop artichoke hearts in a food processor. Add 2 cups Parmesan, mayonnaise, garlic, lemon zest, cayenne, salt and pepper; puree until smooth. Divide between two 2-cup gratin or other shallow baking dishes. Sprinkle each with 1 tablespoon Parmesan.
2. Bake the dip until golden on top and heated through, 10 to 20 minutes.

MAKES ABOUT 2⅔ CUPS.

PER 2-TABLESPOON SERVING: 61 calories; 3 g fat (1 g sat, 1 g mono); 7 mg cholesterol; 6 g carbohydrate; 4 g protein; 3 g fiber; 327 mg sodium; 120 mg potassium.

MAKEOVER TIP

SUBSTITUTE LOW-FAT MAYONNAISE FOR THE FULL-FAT VERSION TO SAVE CALORIES AND FAT. ONE TABLESPOON OF REGULAR MAYONNAISE HAS 90 CALORIES AND 10 GRAMS FAT COMPARED WITH 15 CALORIES AND 1 GRAM FAT FOR LOW-FAT.

JOJO'S PARTY MIX

ACTIVE TIME: 5 MINUTES | **TOTAL:** 45 MINUTES

Our more sophisticated version of crunchy party mix gets its irresistible, rich taste from olive oil and a bit of Parmesan cheese rather than the better part of a stick of butter, or worse, margarine. With two-thirds less fat (none of it saturated) you can forget about that other stuff.

4   cups mixed Rice and Wheat Chex cereals
2   cups mini pretzels
2   tablespoons freshly grated Parmesan cheese
½   teaspoon garlic salt
¼   teaspoon onion powder

¼   teaspoon pepper
⅛   teaspoon cayenne pepper
1   tablespoon extra-virgin olive oil
1   teaspoon Worcestershire sauce

Preheat oven to 350°F. Mix cereals, pretzels, Parmesan, garlic salt, onion powder, pepper and cayenne in a large bowl. Toss with oil and Worcestershire. Spread on a lightly oiled baking sheet. Bake, stirring often, until toasted, 40 minutes.

MAKES ABOUT 6 CUPS.

PER ½-CUP SERVING: 61 calories; 2 g fat (0 g sat, 1 g mono); 1 mg cholesterol; 11 g carbohydrate; 1 g protein; 1 g fiber; 189 mg sodium; 35 mg potassium.

NUTRITION BONUS: Folate (29% daily value), Iron (15% dv).

SMOKED SALMON SPREAD

ACTIVE TIME: 15 MINUTES | **TOTAL:** 45 MINUTES
TO MAKE AHEAD: Cover and refrigerate for up to 2 days.

A splash of pepper-flavored vodka gives this salmon spread a sophisticated flair. If you like, use plain vodka instead but be sure to season generously with freshly cracked pepper before serving. Smoothly pureed nonfat cottage cheese replaces cream cheese and sour cream to cut the fat by about 80 percent.

8 ounces smoked salmon	2 tablespoons lemon juice
1 ½ cups nonfat cottage cheese	2 teaspoons Dijon mustard
3 tablespoons pepper-flavored vodka, such as Absolut Peppar	1 teaspoon prepared horseradish

Cut half the salmon into chunks. Dice the remaining salmon. Place cottage cheese in a fine-mesh sieve and press on it to remove excess moisture. Transfer the cottage cheese to a food processor. Add the salmon chunks, vodka, lemon juice, mustard and horseradish. Process until smooth. Transfer the mixture to a bowl and fold in the diced salmon. Refrigerate until chilled.

MAKES ABOUT 2 CUPS.

PER 2-TABLESPOON SERVING: 41 calories; 1 g fat (0 g sat, 0 g mono); 4 mg cholesterol; 1 g carbohydrate; 5 g protein; 0 g fiber; 213 mg sodium; 29 mg potassium.

BONELESS BUFFALO WINGS

H)(W   L↓C

ACTIVE TIME: 30 MINUTES | **TOTAL:** 40 MINUTES
TO MAKE AHEAD: The chicken can marinate (STEP 1) for up to 1 hour.

Even though boneless Buffalo wings are made with healthy white-meat chicken, they're usually deep-fried and drenched in hot sauce laced with butter. The solution: chicken tenders are dredged in seasoned whole-wheat flour and cornmeal, pan-fried in only a small amount of oil and then drizzled with a tangy hot pepper sauce. With a fraction of the fat, calories and sodium, these boneless wings are reason enough to throw a party.

- 3 tablespoons nonfat buttermilk (*see Tip, page 246*)
- 3 tablespoons hot sauce, such as Frank's RedHot, divided
- 3 tablespoons distilled white vinegar, divided
- 2 pounds chicken tenders (*see Ingredient Note, page 247*)

- 6 tablespoons whole-wheat flour
- 6 tablespoons cornmeal
- ½ teaspoon cayenne pepper
- 2 tablespoons canola oil, divided
- 2 cups carrot sticks
- 2 cups celery sticks
  Spicy Blue Cheese Dip (*page 215*)

1. Whisk buttermilk, 2 tablespoons hot sauce and 2 tablespoons vinegar in a large bowl until combined. Add chicken; toss to coat. Transfer to the refrigerator and let marinate for at least 10 minutes or up to 1 hour, stirring occasionally.
2. Meanwhile, whisk flour and cornmeal in a shallow dish. Whisk the remaining 1 tablespoon hot sauce and 1 table-spoon vinegar in a small bowl; set aside.
3. Remove the chicken from the marinade and roll in the flour mixture until evenly coated. (Discard remaining marinade and flour mixture.) Sprinkle both sides of the chicken with cayenne.
4. Heat 1 tablespoon oil in a large nonstick skillet over medium-high heat. Add half the chicken, placing each piece in a little oil. Cook until golden brown and cooked through, 3 to 4 minutes per side. Transfer to a serving platter. Repeat with the remaining 1 tablespoon oil and chicken, reducing the heat if necessary to prevent burning. Transfer to the platter. Drizzle the chicken with the reserved hot sauce mixture. Serve with carrots, celery and Spicy Blue Cheese Dip.

MAKES 8 SERVINGS (2 "wings," ½ cup vegetables & 2 tablespoons dip each).

PER SERVING: 256 calories; 10 g fat (4 g sat, 4 g mono); 83 mg cholesterol; 12 g carbohydrate; 31 g protein; 2 g fiber; 353 mg sodium; 248 mg potassium.

NUTRITION BONUS: Vitamin A (120% daily value).

TACKLING A WEIGHT PROBLEM WITH GAME-DAY FAVORITES

Nacho chips smothered in cheese sauce. Spicy chicken wings begging to be dunked in creamy blue cheese dressing—those were Anthony Davis' favorite. "Mmm… they were so good that I could never resist them," says Davis, former NFL player and legendary University of Southern California running back. But too many football Sundays spent in the VIP box noshing on fattening appetizers didn't do much for his health.

In 2006, he got a wake-up call. The same year he was "enshrined" into the College Football Hall of Fame, he was diagnosed with type 2 diabetes. He suffered from painful flare-ups of gout (an inflammatory disease linked with obesity). Davis also struggled with sleep apnea, an obesity-related condition in which one stops breathing several times a night. When months of dieting proved unsuccessful, he and his doctors concluded that changing his life would require drastic measures. He scheduled gastric bypass surgery for March 11, 2006.

Now, Davis is 90 pounds lighter and he feels better than ever. "I have so much energy," he says. "My diabetes, gout and sleep apnea are gone." While the surgery jump-started his weight loss, only regular exercise and a healthy diet will keep the pounds from creeping back. Physical exercise is again part of his daily routine. "I walk everywhere now," says Davis. "And I've started working out at the gym again too."

Come this football season, Davis will opt for leaner snacks, like Boneless Buffalo Wings—with less than half the calories and 80 percent less sodium than traditional versions—and Southwestern Layered Bean Dip (*page 38*). With plenty of the good stuff—tomato, lettuce and protein-rich beans—and few ingredients high in calories or fat, our dip comes in with less than half the calories and one-quarter the saturated fat of the original. So go ahead and chow down with these healthy appetizers.

GAME-DAY MAKEOVER RECIPES

Boneless Buffalo Wings (*page 44*)

Spicy Blue Cheese Dip (*page 215*)

Southwestern Layered Bean Dip (*page 38*)

CLAMS CASINO

H⧓W L↓C H♥H

ACTIVE TIME: 40 MINUTES | **TOTAL:** 1 HOUR
TO MAKE AHEAD: Prepare the stuffed clams through Step 4; wrap and freeze for up to 1 month. Remove from the freezer and bake at 450°F until well browned, 20 to 25 minutes.

Lean Canadian bacon, Parmesan cheese and an aromatic blend of chopped vegetables and herbs give our baked, stuffed clams so much flavor and crunch that you won't even miss the 6 tablespoons of butter that typically goes into this classic appetizer. They make a fabulous starter for a dinner party or a light summer entree with a fresh salad.

18 littleneck clams, scrubbed	¾ cup fresh breadcrumbs, preferably whole-wheat (*see Tip, page 246*)
2 bay leaves	½ cup grated Parmesan cheese
½ cup water	2 tablespoons chopped fresh chives
1 tablespoon extra-virgin olive oil	2 teaspoons minced fresh oregano *or* 1 teaspoon dried
2 medium shallots, minced	
1 small green bell pepper, minced	½ teaspoon smoked *or* regular paprika (*see Ingredient Note, page 248*)
2 ounces Canadian bacon, finely chopped (about ½ cup)	
2 teaspoons white-wine vinegar	½ teaspoon freshly ground pepper

MAKEOVER TIP

SUBSTITUTE EXTRA-VIRGIN OLIVE OIL FOR BUTTER TO REDUCE SATURATED FAT AND ADD HEART-HEALTHY MONO-UNSATURATED FAT.

1. Preheat oven to 450°F.

2. Place clams, bay leaves and water in a large pot; cover and bring to a boil. Reduce heat to medium and cook the clams until they open, 6 to 8 minutes. Drain in a colander. (Discard any clams that do not open.) Discard the bay leaves.

3. Meanwhile, heat oil in a large skillet over medium heat. Add shallots and bell pepper; cook, stirring often, until soft, 2 to 3 minutes. Add Canadian bacon; cook, stirring frequently, until heated and fragrant, about 1 minute. Stir in vinegar; transfer the mixture to a large bowl. Stir in breadcrumbs, Parmesan, chives, oregano, paprika and pepper.

4. Remove clam meat from shells (reserving the shells), chop and stir into the breadcrumb mixture. Pull clamshells apart and spoon the breadcrumb mixture into the half shells, packing lightly and mounding slightly (you may have a few shells left over).

5. Place the stuffed clamshells on a large baking sheet. Bake until well browned, about 20 minutes.

MAKES 4 SERVINGS, ABOUT 8 HALF SHELLS EACH.

PER SERVING: 176 calories; 8 g fat (3 g sat, 4 g mono); 36 mg cholesterol; 9 g carbohydrate; 16 g protein; 1 g fiber; 370 mg sodium; 342 mg potassium.

NUTRITION BONUS: Iron (60% daily value), Vitamin C (40% dv), Selenium (34% dv), Calcium (15% dv).

PROSCIUTTO-WRAPPED SCALLOPS

ACTIVE TIME: 15 MINUTES | **TOTAL:** 15 MINUTES
EQUIPMENT: 12 wooden toothpicks or four 10-inch skewers

Plump and juicy scallops don't really need butter and bacon to make them shine. Here we use mellow prosciutto as a foil for the sweetness of the shellfish. Use a better-quality prosciutto for superior flavor—it may cost a bit more but you only need a small amount for this dish.

12	large dry sea scallops (about 1 pound; *see Ingredient Note*), tough muscle removed	2	tablespoons extra-virgin olive oil
¼	teaspoon lemon pepper	½	teaspoon freshly grated lemon zest
1¼	ounces very thinly sliced prosciutto (about 3 slices), cut into 12 long strips	1	teaspoon lemon juice
		⅛	teaspoon salt
			Freshly ground pepper to taste

INGREDIENT NOTE:

Be sure to buy "dry" sea scallops (scallops that have not been treated with sodium tripolyphosphate, or STP). Scallops that have been treated with STP ("wet" scallops) have been subjected to a chemical bath and are not only mushy and less flavorful, but will not brown properly.

1. Place rack in upper third of oven; preheat broiler. Coat a large baking sheet with cooking spray.

2. Pat scallops dry and sprinkle both sides with lemon pepper. Wrap 1 strip of prosciutto around each scallop. Thread the scallops onto toothpicks (or skewers), securing the prosciutto to the scallop, and place on the prepared baking sheet. Broil until just cooked through, about 6 minutes.

3. Meanwhile, whisk oil, lemon zest, lemon juice, salt and pepper in a small bowl. Serve the scallops drizzled with the vinaigrette.

MAKES 1 DOZEN SCALLOPS.

PER SCALLOP: 63 calories; 3 g fat (1 g sat, 2 g mono); 16 mg cholesterol; 1 g carbohydrate; 7 g protein; 0 g fiber; 153 mg sodium; 123 mg potassium.

SEE IT : MAKE IT

SMOKED SALMON TARTARE

Combine chopped dill with reduced-fat sour cream. Top radish slices with chopped smoked salmon, a dollop of the dill sour cream and a sprig of fresh dill.

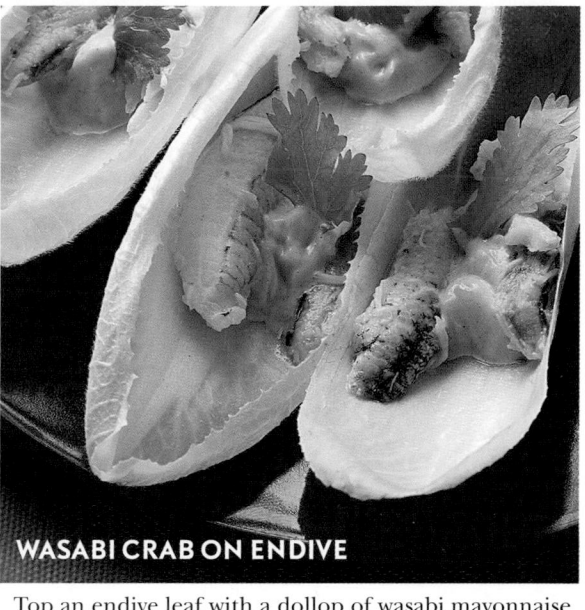

WASABI CRAB ON ENDIVE

Top an endive leaf with a dollop of wasabi mayonnaise and cooked lump crabmeat. Garnish with a sprig of cilantro and a squeeze of lemon or lime juice.

STEAK-&-BOURSIN-WRAPPED BELLS

Roll thinly sliced grilled steak, such as filet mignon, around a small dollop of light Boursin cheese and thin slices of bell pepper.

CAVIAR-STUFFED NEW POTATOES

Boil red potatoes; chill. Slice off one end for a base. Hollow out a small "bowl" in the other end and fill with caviar. Garnish with crème fraîche and chives.

Quick French Onion Soup (page 52)

SOUPS

DELICIOUS FEEDBACK

Broccoli-Cheese Chowder

"That's it! No more looking for better broccoli soup recipes!
This is the best—*and* it's healthy!"

—Anonymous, Chula Vista, CA

Turkey Albondigas Soup

"This soup is a staple in my house. It is absolutely
the most flavorful soup I have ever made.
So many complex flavors...yum!"

—Emily, Boston, MA

QUICK FRENCH ONION SOUP

H ↑ F

ACTIVE TIME: 45 MINUTES | **TOTAL:** 45 MINUTES

French onion soup is a favorite but it usually isn't substantial enough to make a complete meal. We've solved this problem by adding fiber-rich chickpeas to a broth flavored with sherry and three kinds of onions. Of course, we didn't forget the gooey topping, we've just made it a little lighter and a lot easier to prepare at home—simply top toasted whole-wheat bread with cheese and pour the soup on to melt it. (*Photograph: page 50.*)

1 tablespoon extra-virgin olive oil
2 large sweet onions, sliced
2 cups chopped spring onions *or* leeks, whites and light green parts only
2 tablespoons chopped garlic
1 teaspoon chopped fresh thyme *or* ¼ teaspoon dried
¼ cup dry sherry (*see Ingredient Note, page 248*)

½ teaspoon freshly ground pepper
3 14-ounce cans reduced-sodium beef broth
1 15-ounce can chickpeas, rinsed
¼ cup minced fresh chives or scallions
6 slices whole-wheat country bread
1 cup shredded Gruyère *or* fontina cheese

1. Heat oil in a large saucepan over medium-high heat. Add sweet onions and stir to coat. Cover, reduce heat to medium and cook, stirring often, until softened and starting to brown, 6 to 8 minutes. Add spring onions (or leeks), garlic and thyme and cook, uncovered, stirring often, until starting to soften, 3 to 4 minutes.
2. Stir in sherry and pepper; increase heat to medium-high and bring to a simmer. Cook, stirring often, until most of the liquid has evaporated, 1 to 2 minutes. Stir in broth and chickpeas and bring to a boil. Reduce heat to a simmer and cook until the vegetables are tender, about 3 minutes. Remove from the heat and stir in chives (or scallions).
3. Meanwhile, toast bread and divide it among 6 bowls; top with cheese. Ladle the soup over the bread and cheese and serve immediately.

MAKES 6 SERVINGS, 1 ½ CUPS EACH.

PER SERVING: 374 calories; 10 g fat (4 g sat, 4 g mono); 20 mg cholesterol; 48 g carbohydrate; 18 g protein; 6 g fiber; 591 mg sodium; 555 mg potassium.

NUTRITION BONUS: Calcium, Folate & Vitamin C (25% daily value).

CURRIED BUTTERNUT SQUASH BISQUE

H✳W H♥H

ACTIVE TIME: 30 MINUTES | **TOTAL:** 1 HOUR
TO MAKE AHEAD: Prepare through Step 2, cover and refrigerate for up to 2 days.

This exotic, spicy soup takes advantage of the affinity between butternut squash and curry. Pureed squash has a velvety texture, which means you can forgo using cream. We serve the soup with some nonfat yogurt for a tangy note. And if you're looking for more vitamin A in your diet, look no further: this soup gives you 200 percent of the daily recommendation.

2	teaspoons canola oil	½	cup white rice
2	onions, chopped	2	pounds butternut squash, peeled, seeded and cubed (about 6 cups)
3	cloves garlic, minced		
1	tablespoon curry powder	½	teaspoon salt
½	teaspoon ground cumin		Freshly ground pepper to taste
6	cups reduced-sodium chicken broth	½	cup nonfat plain yogurt
1	cup apple cider	2	tablespoons nonfat milk

1. Heat oil in a Dutch oven or heavy soup pot over medium heat. Add onions and garlic; cook, stirring, until slightly softened, 2 to 3 minutes. Stir in curry and cumin and cook for 1 minute. Add broth, cider, rice and squash; bring to a boil. Reduce heat to low, cover and simmer until the squash is tender, 30 to 40 minutes.

2. Pour the mixture through a strainer set over a large bowl. Puree the solids in a food processor or blender until very smooth. (Use caution when pureeing hot liquids.) Return the puree and liquid to the pot. Heat the soup gently and season with salt and pepper.

3. To serve, stir yogurt and milk in a small bowl. Ladle the soup into bowls and add a dollop of the yogurt mixture. Draw the tip of a knife or a toothpick through the yogurt to make decorative swirls.

MAKES 8 SERVINGS, ABOUT 1 CUP EACH.

PER SERVING: 153 calories; 2 g fat (1 g sat, 1 g mono); 4 mg cholesterol; 30 g carbohydrate; 6 g protein; 4 g fiber; 267 mg sodium; 356 mg potassium.

NUTRITION BONUS: Vitamin A (204% daily value), Vitamin C (40% dv), Folate (16% dv).

CREAM OF MUSHROOM & BARLEY SOUP

H✕W   H✚F

ACTIVE TIME: 50 MINUTES | **TOTAL:** 1 ¼ HOURS

This sophisticated take on creamy mushroom soup is rich with earthy porcini mushrooms and has the added good-ness of whole-grain barley. **SHOPPING TIP:** Look for mushroom broth in aseptic containers in well-stocked super-markets or natural-foods stores.

½ cup pearl barley
4½ cups reduced-sodium chicken broth *or* mushroom broth (*see Shopping Tip*), divided
1 ounce dried porcini mushrooms
2 cups boiling water
2 teaspoons butter
1 tablespoon extra-virgin olive oil
1 cup minced shallots (about 4 medium)
8 cups sliced white mushrooms (about 20 ounces)

2 stalks celery, finely chopped
1 tablespoon minced fresh sage *or* 1 teaspoon dried
½ teaspoon salt
½ teaspoon freshly ground pepper
2 tablespoons all-purpose flour
1 cup dry sherry (*see Ingredient Note, page 248*)
½ cup reduced-fat sour cream
¼ cup minced fresh chives

MAKEOVER TIP

TRY ADDING REDUCED-FAT SOUR CREAM TO A SOUP THAT'S TRADITIONALLY MADE WITH HEAVY CREAM—YOU'LL GET A GREAT CREAMY TEXTURE WITH A FRACTION OF THE FAT.

1. Bring barley and 1½ cups broth to a boil in a small saucepan over high heat. Cover, reduce heat to low and simmer until tender, 30 to 35 minutes.

2. Meanwhile, combine porcinis and boiling water in a medium bowl and soak until softened, about 20 minutes. Line a sieve with paper towels, set it over a bowl and pour in mushrooms and soaking liquid. Reserve the soak-ing liquid. Transfer the mushrooms to a cutting board and finely chop.

3. Heat butter and oil in a Dutch oven over medium-high heat. Add shallots and cook, stirring often, until softened, about 2 minutes. Add white mush-rooms and cook, stirring often, until they start to brown, 8 to 10 minutes. Add the porcinis, celery, sage, salt and pepper and cook, stirring often, until beginning to soften, about 3 minutes. Sprinkle flour over the vegetables and cook, stirring, until the flour is incorporated, about 1 minute. Add sherry and cook, stirring, until most of the sherry has evaporated, about 1 minute.

4. Add the soaking liquid and the remaining 3 cups broth; increase heat to high and bring to a boil. Reduce heat and simmer, stirring occasionally, until the soup has thickened, 18 to 22 minutes. Add the cooked barley and continue cooking, stirring occasionally, until heated through, about 5 min-utes more. Stir in sour cream until incorporated. Garnish with chives.

MAKES 4 SERVINGS, ABOUT 1¾ CUPS EACH.

PER SERVING: 343 calories; 10 g fat (5 g sat, 4 g mono); 22 mg cholesterol; 38 g carbohydrate; 14 g protein; 7 g fiber; 501 mg sodium; 975 mg potassium.

NUTRITION BONUS: Potassium (28% daily value), Selenium (20% dv), Iron (19% dv), Vitamin A (18% dv).

NEW ENGLAND CLAM CHOWDER

L↓C

ACTIVE TIME: 45 MINUTES | **TOTAL:** 45 MINUTES

A blend of chopped clams, aromatic vegetables and creamy potatoes with low-fat milk and just a half cup of cream gives this chunky soup plenty of rich body. Serve with oyster crackers and a tossed salad to make it a meal.
SHOPPING TIP: Look for fresh clam strips at the seafood counter.

- 2 teaspoons canola oil
- 4 slices bacon, chopped
- 1 medium onion, chopped
- 2 stalks celery, chopped
- 2 teaspoons chopped fresh thyme *or* 1 teaspoon dried
- 1 medium red potato, diced
- 1 8-ounce bottle clam juice
- 1 bay leaf

- 3 cups low-fat milk
- ½ cup heavy cream
- ⅓ cup all-purpose flour
- ¾ teaspoon salt
- 12 ounces fresh clam strips (*see Shopping Tip*), chopped, *or* 3 6-ounce cans chopped baby clams, rinsed
- 2 scallions, thinly sliced

MAKEOVER TIP

CHECK SODIUM CAREFULLY WHEN USING CLAM JUICE BECAUSE THE AMOUNT OF SODIUM CAN VARY DRAMATICALLY BETWEEN BRANDS. WE USE BAR HARBOR CLAM JUICE WITH ONLY 120 MG SODIUM PER 2-OUNCE SERVING.

1. Heat oil in a large saucepan over medium heat. Add bacon and cook until crispy, 4 to 6 minutes. Transfer half of the cooked bacon to a paper towel-lined plate with a slotted spoon. Add onion, celery and thyme to the pan; cook, stirring, until beginning to soften, about 2 minutes. Add potato, clam juice and bay leaf. Bring to a simmer, cover and cook until the vegetables are just tender, 8 to 10 minutes.

2. Whisk milk, cream, flour and salt together in a medium bowl. Add to the pan and return to a simmer, stirring, over medium-high heat. Cook, stirring, until thickened, about 2 minutes. Add clams and cook, stirring occasionally, until the clams are just cooked through, about 3 minutes more.

3. To serve, discard bay leaf. Ladle into bowls and top each serving with some of the reserved bacon and scallions.

MAKES 6 SERVINGS, GENEROUS 1 CUP EACH.

PER SERVING: 253 calories; 13 g fat (6 g sat, 4 g mono); 59 mg cholesterol; 20 g carbohydrate; 16 g protein; 1 g fiber; 585 mg sodium; 392 mg potassium.

NUTRITION BONUS: Iron (50% daily value), Vitamin C (23% dv), Calcium (21% dv), Vitamin A (17% dv).

OYSTER BISQUE

H✳W   L↓C   H♥H

ACTIVE TIME: 25 MINUTES | **TOTAL:** 1 HOUR
TO MAKE AHEAD: Prepare through Step 2. Refrigerate the vegetable garnish (STEP 1) and puree (STEP 2) in separate covered containers for up to 8 hours.

This oyster soup bursts with the heady flavors of the sea. Rather than heavy cream, this recipe uses pureed rice to add body and the mellow sweetness needed to balance the oysters. It makes an elegant starter for a dinner party.

2 carrots, cut into 2-inch-long matchsticks
2 leeks, trimmed, washed (*see Tip, page 246*) and cut into 2-inch-long matchsticks
1 tablespoon canola oil
2 onions, finely chopped
½ cup long-grain white rice
3 cups water, divided

3 cups clam juice (*see Makeover Tip, page 56*), divided
1 cup low-fat milk
1 pint shucked oysters with their liquor
⅛ teaspoon salt
  Freshly ground pepper to taste

1. Bring a large pot of water to a boil over high heat. Add carrots and leeks and cook until tender, 1 to 2 minutes. Drain and rinse with cold running water. Spread the vegetables on paper towels and pat dry; set aside.

2. Heat oil in a large saucepan over medium-high heat. Add onions and cook, stirring often, until softened, about 2 minutes. Stir in rice and cook for about 2 minutes. Pour in 1½ cups water and 1½ cups clam juice; increase heat to high. Bring to a boil, stirring often, then reduce heat to medium-low. Cover and cook until the rice is very soft, 25 minutes. Puree the mixture in a blender or food processor until very smooth. (Use caution when pureeing hot liquids.)

3. Return the puree to the pan; pour in milk and the remaining 1½ cups water and 1½ cups clam juice. Bring to a simmer over medium-high heat. Stir in oysters and their liquor and cook gently until the oysters are curled at the edges, 3 minutes. Season with salt and pepper. Ladle the bisque into bowls and garnish with the reserved carrots and leeks.

MAKES 10 SERVINGS, ABOUT ¾ CUP EACH.

PER SERVING: 110 calories; 3 g fat (1 g sat, 1 g mono); 28 mg cholesterol, 15 g carbohydrate; 6 g protein; 1 g fiber; 497 mg sodium; 182 mg potassium.

NUTRITION BONUS: Zinc (300% daily value), Vitamin A (35% dv), Iron (20% dv).

BROCCOLI-CHEESE CHOWDER

H✱W

ACTIVE TIME: 45 MINUTES | **TOTAL:** 1 HOUR 5 MINUTES
TO MAKE AHEAD: Prepare through Step 2. Cover and refrigerate for up to 2 days or freeze for up to 2 months.

Many broccoli chowders have as much as a cup each of cream and cheese to give them their richness. This satisfying remake of the hearty soup benefits from the creamy texture of cooked potatoes and smooth, tangy reduced-fat sour cream. Not only is the flavor vibrant, but a single serving gives you over half of the daily recommendation for vitamin C.

1	tablespoon extra-virgin olive oil
1	large onion, chopped
1	large carrot, diced
2	stalks celery, diced
1	large potato, peeled and diced
2	cloves garlic, minced
1	tablespoon all-purpose flour
½	teaspoon dry mustard
⅛	teaspoon cayenne pepper

2	14-ounce cans vegetable broth *or* reduced-sodium chicken broth
8	ounces broccoli crowns (*see Ingredient Note, page 247*), cut into 1-inch pieces, stems and florets separated
1	cup shredded reduced-fat Cheddar cheese
½	cup reduced-fat sour cream
⅛	teaspoon salt

MAKEOVER TIP

USE REDUCED-FAT CHEESE INSTEAD OF REGULAR CHEESE TO DECREASE CALORIES AND FAT. COMPARED WITH 1 CUP OF SHREDDED CHEDDAR, THE SAME AMOUNT OF REDUCED-FAT CHEDDAR SAVES ABOUT 90 CALORIES, 14 GRAMS OF FAT AND 8 GRAMS OF SATURATED FAT.

1. Heat oil in a Dutch oven or large saucepan over medium-high heat. Add onion, carrot and celery; cook, stirring often, until the onion and celery soften, 5 to 6 minutes. Add potato and garlic; cook, stirring, for 2 minutes. Stir in flour, dry mustard and cayenne; cook, stirring often, for 2 minutes.

2. Add broth and broccoli stems; bring to a boil. Cover and reduce heat to medium. Simmer, stirring occasionally, for 10 minutes. Stir in florets; simmer, covered, until the broccoli is tender, about 10 minutes more. Transfer 2 cups of the chowder to a bowl and mash; return to the pan.

3. Stir in Cheddar and sour cream; cook over medium heat, stirring, until the cheese is melted and the chowder is heated through, about 2 minutes. Season with salt.

MAKES 6 SERVINGS, 1 CUP EACH.

PER SERVING: 205 calories; 9 g fat (4 g sat, 3 g mono); 21 mg cholesterol; 23 g carbohydrate; 9 g protein; 4 g fiber; 508 mg sodium; 436 mg potassium.

NUTRITION BONUS: Vitamin C (61% daily value), Vitamin A (64% dv), Calcium (34% dv).

CHEDDAR-ALE SOUP

H ↑ F

ACTIVE TIME: 35 MINUTES | **TOTAL:** 35 MINUTES

Our cheese- and beer-lover's soup has only a fraction of the fat and sodium of a traditional recipe. We use low-fat milk and only a little oil and keep the flavor strong with zesty, sharp Cheddar cheese. Precooked diced potatoes, which you can get at many supermarkets, keep this recipe super speedy. Regular diced red potatoes also work—you'll just need to increase the cooking time.

1	tablespoon canola oil
1	large onion, chopped
1	12-ounce bottle beer, preferably ale
2	18-ounce bags precooked diced peeled potatoes (*see Ingredient Note, page 248*)
1	14-ounce can vegetable broth *or* reduced-sodium chicken broth

1	cup water
2½	cups nonfat *or* low-fat milk
¼	cup all-purpose flour
1½	cups shredded sharp Cheddar cheese, divided
1	small red bell pepper, thinly sliced or finely chopped

MAKEOVER TIP

MAKE THICK AND CREAMY SOUP BY ADDING FLOUR WHISKED INTO NONFAT MILK INSTEAD OF THICKENING IT WITH HEAVY CREAM AND/OR BUTTER.

1. Heat oil in a Dutch oven over medium heat. Add onion and cook, stirring, until softened, about 3 minutes. Add beer; bring to a boil and boil for 5 minutes. Add potatoes, broth and water; cover and return to a boil. Reduce the heat to maintain a simmer, and cook until the potatoes are tender, about 4 minutes. Remove from the heat and mash the potatoes with a potato masher to the desired consistency.

2. Whisk milk and flour and add to the soup. Bring to a simmer over medium-high heat and cook, whisking occasionally, until thickened, about 3 minutes. Remove from the heat; stir in 1¼ cups Cheddar and stir until melted. Ladle the soup into bowls and garnish with the remaining ¼ cup cheese and bell pepper.

MAKES 6 SERVINGS, 1 3/4 CUPS EACH.

PER SERVING: 389 calories; 12 g fat (5 g sat, 2 g mono); 32 mg cholesterol; 50 g carbohydrate; 16 g protein; 5 g fiber; 408 mg sodium; 238 mg potassium.

NUTRITION BONUS: Calcium (34% daily value), Vitamin C (32% dv), Vitamin A (19% dv).

FRESH CORN CHOWDER

H✥W   H♥H

ACTIVE TIME: 1 HOUR | **TOTAL:** 1 ¼ HOURS

Turkey bacon gives this soup a fabulous flavor without adding a lot of saturated fat. The chowder has less than 190 calories per serving so it's an excellent choice if you are watching your weight. If you don't have fresh corn, frozen will work just as well.

1 ½	teaspoons canola oil		3	medium ears corn, kernels cut from cob (*see Tip, page 246*)
2	slices turkey bacon, diced		2	medium potatoes, peeled and diced
1	medium onion, diced		1 ½	cups low-fat milk
1	red bell pepper, diced		1	teaspoon salt
1	stalk celery, diced			Freshly ground pepper to taste
¼	cup all-purpose flour		2	tablespoons chopped fresh parsley
2	14-ounce cans reduced-sodium chicken broth			

1. Heat oil in a large saucepan over medium heat. Add bacon, onion, bell pepper and celery. Cook, stirring frequently, until softened and beginning to brown, 7 to 8 minutes. Sprinkle flour over the vegetables and cook, stirring, for 1 minute more. Add broth and bring to a boil, whisking constantly. Reduce heat to low and simmer, uncovered, stirring occasionally, until slightly thickened, about 15 minutes.

2. Add corn kernels, potatoes, milk and salt to the pan. Return to a simmer and cook, uncovered, until the vegetables are tender, 20 to 30 minutes. Season with pepper. Serve garnished with parsley.

MAKES 6 SERVINGS, GENEROUS 1 CUP EACH.

PER SERVING: 188 calories; 5 g fat (1 g sat, 2 g mono); 14 mg cholesterol; 29 g carbohydrate; 9 g protein; 3 g fiber; 605 mg sodium; 455 mg potassium.

NUTRITION BONUS: Vitamin C (69% daily value), Vitamin A (19% dv).

CREAMY TOMATO BISQUE WITH MOZZARELLA CROSTINI

H)((W   H ♥ H

ACTIVE TIME: 20 MINUTES | **TOTAL:** 35 MINUTES

TO MAKE AHEAD: Prepare the soup (STEPS 1 & 3), cover and refrigerate for up to 2 days. When ready to serve, make crostini and reheat the soup (STEPS 2 & 4).

We use high-in-protein and low-in-fat silken tofu and a bit of rice instead of heavy cream to thicken this French-inspired soup. Topped with a melted-cheese crostini it's almost like getting your grilled cheese and tomato soup all in one.

2 tablespoons extra-virgin olive oil	½ cup silken tofu
1 large onion, chopped	1 tablespoon rice vinegar
4 cloves garlic, crushed and peeled	6 ¾-inch-thick slices baguette, preferably whole-grain
1 14-ounce can reduced-sodium chicken broth	3 tablespoons shredded part-skim mozzarella cheese
2 cups water	
¼ cup white rice	
1 28-ounce can crushed tomatoes	

1. Heat oil in a Dutch oven over medium heat. Add onion and garlic and cook, stirring occasionally, until beginning to soften, about 3 minutes. Stir in broth, water and rice; bring to a boil. Reduce heat to a simmer and cook, stirring occasionally, until the rice is very tender, about 15 minutes.

2. Preheat oven to 450°F.

3. Stir tomatoes, tofu and vinegar into the soup. Remove from the heat and puree, in batches, in a blender. (Use caution when pureeing hot liquids.) Return the soup to the pot and reheat over medium-high heat, stirring often.

4. Meanwhile, top slices of baguette with mozzarella and place on a baking sheet. Bake until the cheese is melted and bubbly, about 5 minutes. Ladle soup into bowls and top each serving with a cheesy crostini.

MAKES 6 SERVINGS, ABOUT 1 ½ CUPS EACH.

PER SERVING: 218 calories; 8 g fat (1 g sat, 4 g mono); 3 mg cholesterol; 31 g carbohydrate; 8 g protein; 4 g fiber; 355 mg sodium; 478 mg potassium.

NUTRITION BONUS: Vitamin C (25% daily value), Vitamin A (20% dv), Iron (15% dv).

TURKEY ALBONDIGAS SOUP

H✕W   H↑F   H♥H

ACTIVE TIME: 45 MINUTES | **TOTAL:** 1 HOUR
TO MAKE AHEAD: Prepare through Step 2. Cover and refrigerate the soup and meatballs separately for up to 1 day. To serve, reheat soup in a Dutch oven and proceed with Step 3.

Albondigas, Spanish for "meatballs," star in the traditional broth-based Mexican *Sopa de Albondigas.* Our version uses turkey rather than beef or pork for the meatballs, and we've pumped up the volume of fresh vegetables in the mix.
SHOPPING TIP: Poblano peppers can be fiery or relatively mild; there's no way to tell until you taste them. Find them at most large supermarkets. Or substitute 2 green bell peppers plus one minced jalapeño pepper (or more to taste).

1	pound 93%-lean ground turkey		2	carrots, diced
1	cup fresh whole-wheat breadcrumbs (*see Tip, page 246*)		3	poblano peppers (*see Shopping Tip*), diced
1	large egg		3	plum tomatoes, diced
2	teaspoons ground cumin, divided		6	cups reduced-sodium chicken broth
2	teaspoons dried oregano, divided		½	cup instant brown rice *or* ½ cup cooked brown rice
¾	teaspoon freshly ground pepper, divided		2	tablespoons lime juice
½	teaspoon salt, divided		1	jalapeño, minced
1	tablespoon canola oil		2	tablespoons minced fresh cilantro
1	large white onion, diced			

1. Line a large baking sheet with wax paper. Place turkey, breadcrumbs, egg, 1½ teaspoons cumin, 1½ teaspoons oregano, ½ teaspoon pepper and ¼ teaspoon salt in a medium bowl. Mix gently until combined. Shape the mixture into 1½-inch balls and transfer to the baking sheet. (You should have about 20 meatballs.) Place in the refrigerator and chill for at least 20 minutes or until ready to use.
2. Heat oil in a Dutch oven over medium-high heat. Add onion and carrots and cook, stirring often, until beginning to soften, about 4 minutes. Add peppers, tomatoes, the remaining ½ teaspoon cumin, ½ teaspoon oregano, ¼ teaspoon pepper and ¼ teaspoon salt; cook, stirring, until fragrant, about 1 minute. Add broth, increase heat to high and bring to a boil; reduce heat and simmer for 5 minutes.
3. Carefully submerge the meatballs in the simmering soup; return to a simmer and cook for 8 minutes. Add rice and cook, stirring occasionally, until tender, about 5 minutes. Remove from the heat and stir in lime juice. Garnish with jalapeño and cilantro.

MAKES 6 SERVINGS, ABOUT 1⅔ CUPS EACH.

PER SERVING: 288 calories; 10 g fat (2 g sat, 2 g mono); 84 mg cholesterol; 27 g carbohydrate; 24 g protein; 6 g fiber; 438 mg sodium; 421 mg potassium.

NUTRITION BONUS: Vitamin A (110% daily value), Iron & Vitamin C (17% dv).

CHICKEN NOODLE SOUP WITH DILL

H✕W L↓C H♥H

ACTIVE TIME: 20 MINUTES | **TOTAL:** 50 MINUTES
TO MAKE AHEAD: Cover and refrigerate for up to 2 days.

Most versions of chicken noodle soup aren't in dire need of a makeover, though we did come across one with heavy cream and a cup of Parmesan when we were researching this book. It is however undeniably comfort food for many (especially sick) people and so we had to include it. And we were able to give it a little makeover—whole-wheat egg noodles as opposed to regular add fiber and nutrients and the reduced-sodium chicken broth cuts the sodium. By all means use homemade chicken broth if you have it.

10 cups reduced-sodium chicken broth
3 medium carrots, diced
1 large stalk celery, diced
3 tablespoons minced fresh ginger
6 cloves garlic, minced

4 ounces whole-wheat egg noodles (3 cups)
4 cups shredded cooked skinless chicken breast (about 1 pound; *see Tip, page 246*)
3 tablespoons chopped fresh dill
1 tablespoon lemon juice, or to taste

1. Bring broth to a boil in a Dutch oven. Add carrots, celery, ginger and garlic; cook, uncovered, over medium heat until vegetables are just tender, about 20 minutes.

2. Add noodles and chicken; simmer until the noodles are just tender, 8 to 10 minutes. Stir in dill and lemon juice.

MAKES 6 SERVINGS, ABOUT 1½ CUPS EACH.

PER SERVING: 267 calories; 4 g fat (2 g sat, 1 g mono); 90 mg cholesterol; 18 g carbohydrate; 38 g protein; 2 g fiber; 329 mg sodium; 330 mg potassium.

NUTRITION BONUS: Vitamin A (104% daily value).

MATZO BALL SOUP

H✡W L↓C H♥H

ACTIVE TIME: 45 MINUTES | **TOTAL:** 1 ¾ HOURS
TO MAKE AHEAD: Prepare through Step 1; cover and refrigerate overnight.

Matzo balls are traditionally made with chicken fat—lots of flavor and lots of saturated fat. Floating in a flavorful broth, our matzo balls are light and fluffy but bound together with whisked eggs and only a small amount of canola oil rather than chicken fat. Plus, this version of Jewish penicillin has plenty of added vegetables, making it a good source for vitamins A and C. Now that's what Doctor Mom ordered! **SHOPPING TIP:** Look for matzo meal in the kosher section of the supermarket.

2 large eggs	2 parsnips, peeled and chopped
1 large egg white	1 large carrot, peeled and chopped
½ teaspoon salt	1 onion, chopped
¾ cup matzo meal (*see Shopping Tip*)	1 cup broccoli florets
1 tablespoon canola oil	1 cup sliced mushrooms
3 tablespoons cold water	2 tablespoons chopped fresh dill *or* parsley
8 cups reduced-sodium chicken broth	

1. Whisk eggs, egg white and salt in a medium bowl. Whisk in matzo meal, oil and water. Cover and chill for at least 1 hour or overnight.

2. Bring broth to a boil in a large pot. Add parsnips, carrot and onion; reduce the heat to a simmer and cook for 5 minutes.

3. Gently roll level teaspoonfuls of the chilled matzo dough into balls, dropping them into the simmering broth as you work. Cover and cook for 15 minutes. Do not lift the lid: the broth must simmer rapidly to allow the matzo balls to expand properly.

4. Add broccoli and mushrooms and simmer, uncovered, until the broccoli is just tender, 2 to 3 minutes. Ladle into bowls, sprinkle with dill (or parsley) and serve.

MAKES 8 SERVINGS, 1 ¼ CUPS EACH.

PER SERVING: 142 calories; 4 g fat (1 g sat, 2 g mono); 58 mg cholesterol; 20 g carbohydrate; 8 g protein; 3 g fiber; 324 mg sodium; 262 mg potassium.

NUTRITION BONUS: Vitamin A (35% daily value), Vitamin C (25% dv).

JUMPIN' JIMMY'S GUMBO

H)(W H⬆F H♥H

ACTIVE TIME: 40 MINUTES | **TOTAL:** 1 ¼ HOURS

Lean chicken breast and a small amount of spicy andouille sausage are at the heart of this version of the Cajun stew, traditionally served on Good Friday. With significantly less fat and sodium plus loads of vegetables, you can feel good about eating this gumbo any day of the year.

⅓ cup all-purpose flour	1 15-ounce can diced tomatoes
3 teaspoons canola oil, divided	1 10-ounce package frozen okra, slightly thawed, sliced
8 ounces boneless, skinless chicken breasts, cut into thin strips	2 habanero chiles *or* 4 jalapeños, pierced all over with a fork
3 ounces andouille (*see Ingredient Note, page 247*) *or* kielbasa sausage, thinly sliced	1 bay leaf
1 onion, chopped	½ teaspoon dried thyme
1 large green bell pepper, diced	¼ teaspoon hot sauce, or to taste
1 stalk celery, finely chopped	⅛ teaspoon salt
4 cloves garlic, minced	Freshly ground pepper to taste
3 cups reduced-sodium chicken broth	3 cups cooked brown rice

MAKEOVER TIP

TOASTING FLOUR IN A HEAVY DRY SKILLET, AS WE DO IN THIS GUMBO RECIPE, COMES VERY CLOSE TO THE DEEP FLAVOR OF A TRADITIONAL ROUX (A FLOUR-AND-FAT MIXTURE USED AS A THICKENER), WITHOUT ANY OF THE FAT.

1. Heat a heavy cast-iron skillet over medium heat. Add flour and cook, stirring constantly with a wooden spoon, until it turns deep golden, 7 to 10 minutes. There will be a strong aroma like burnt toast. Be careful not to let the flour burn; reduce the heat if it's browning too quickly. (*Alternatively, toast flour in a pie pan in a 400°F oven for 20 minutes.*) Transfer to a plate to cool.

2. Heat 1½ teaspoons oil in a Dutch oven or heavy soup pot over high heat. Add chicken and sausage; cook, stirring, until browned on all sides, about 3 minutes. Transfer to a plate.

3. Reduce heat to medium and add the remaining 1½ teaspoons oil. Add onion, bell pepper, celery and garlic; cook, stirring, until the onion is lightly browned, about 7 minutes. Stir in the toasted flour. Gradually stir in broth and bring to a simmer, stirring.

4. Add tomatoes and their juice, okra, chiles, bay leaf and thyme. Reduce heat to low, cover and simmer for 30 minutes.

5. Add the reserved chicken and sausage and simmer for 5 minutes more. Discard the chiles and bay leaf. Season with hot sauce, salt and pepper. Serve with rice, passing additional hot sauce.

MAKES 6 SERVINGS, GENEROUS 1 CUP EACH.

PER SERVING: 284 calories; 7 g fat (2 g sat, 2 g mono); 49 mg cholesterol; 34 g carbohydrate; 22 g protein; 6 g fiber; 337 mg sodium; 374 mg potassium.

NUTRITION BONUS: Vitamin C (67% daily value), Selenium (30% dv), Folate & Magnesium (21% dv).

HEARTY MINESTRONE

H✂W H⬆F H♥H

ACTIVE TIME: 45 MINUTES | **TOTAL:** 45 MINUTES

This quintessential Italian soup is packed with leeks, potatoes, beans, zucchini, spinach and orzo, making it perfect for a hearty lunch or supper on a cold winter's night. To make a vegetarian version use vegetable rather than chicken broth. Top each bowl with freshly grated Parmigiano-Reggiano for a zesty burst of flavor.

2 teaspoons extra-virgin olive oil	½ teaspoon freshly ground pepper
3 medium leeks, trimmed, washed (*see Tip, page 246*) and thinly sliced	½ cup whole-wheat orzo
	1 15-ounce can white beans, rinsed
4 cups reduced-sodium chicken broth *or* vegetable broth	2 medium zucchini, quartered and thinly sliced
1 cup water	1 pound fresh spinach, stems removed
1 large red potato, diced	2 tablespoons cider vinegar
2 teaspoons dried thyme	2 tablespoons freshly grated Parmesan cheese, preferably Parmigiano-Reggiano
¼ teaspoon salt	

1. Heat oil in a Dutch oven or large soup pot over medium-high heat. Add leeks and cook, stirring occasionally, until soft, about 3 minutes. Add broth, water, potato, thyme, salt and pepper. Bring to a boil, reduce heat to low and simmer, covered, for 5 minutes.

2. Add orzo and cook, partially covered, stirring occasionally to prevent sticking, for 5 minutes. Add beans and zucchini and continue to cook, partially covered, until the vegetables and pasta are tender, about 8 minutes more.

3. Stir in spinach and cook, stirring, until wilted, about 2 minutes. Season the soup with vinegar. Ladle into bowls and garnish with Parmesan.

MAKES 4 SERVINGS, 2 CUPS EACH.

PER SERVING: 307 calories; 5 g fat (1 g sat, 2 g mono); 7 mg cholesterol; 54 g carbohydrate; 19 g protein; 14 g fiber; 656 mg sodium; 1,475 mg potassium.

NUTRITION BONUS: Vitamin A (239% daily value), Vitamin C (100% dv), Folate (75% dv), Potassium (42% dv), Calcium (25% dv).

MAKEOVER TIP

STORE-BOUGHT BROTHS CAN BE VERY HIGH IN SODIUM. CHOOSING REDUCED SODIUM-BROTH SAVES ABOUT 790 MG OF SODIUM PER CUP.

COLLARD GREEN & BLACK-EYED PEA SOUP

H⟩⟨W   H⬆F   H❤H

ACTIVE TIME: 45 MINUTES | **TOTAL:** 45 MINUTES

Antioxidant-rich collard greens and fiber-packed black-eyed peas—it doesn't get much healthier than that. There's no need for loads of ham or salt pork in this soup. Just a small amount of bacon gives it a wonderful smoky flavor. You can skip the bacon and substitute vegetable broth for chicken broth for a great vegetarian dish.

1   tablespoon extra-virgin olive oil
1   large onion, diced
1   large carrot, sliced
1   stalk celery, sliced
5   cloves garlic (4 sliced and 1 whole), divided
1   sprig fresh thyme
¼   teaspoon crushed red pepper, or to taste
4   cups reduced-sodium chicken broth
1   15-ounce can diced tomatoes

5   cups chopped collard greens *or* kale leaves (about 1 bunch), tough stems removed
1   15-ounce can black-eyed peas, rinsed
6   ½-inch-thick slices baguette, preferably whole-grain, cut on the diagonal
6   tablespoons shredded Gruyère *or* Swiss cheese
2   slices cooked bacon, finely chopped

1. Heat oil in a Dutch oven over medium heat. Add onion, carrot and celery and cook, stirring, until just tender, 5 to 7 minutes. Add sliced garlic, thyme and crushed red pepper and cook, stirring, until fragrant, about 15 seconds. Increase heat to high and add broth, tomatoes and their juice. Bring to a boil, scraping up any browned bits. Stir in collard greens (or kale), reduce heat to maintain a simmer and cook, stirring occasionally, until the greens are tender, 5 to 10 minutes. Discard the thyme sprig. Stir in black-eyed peas; remove from the heat and cover.

2. Position rack in upper third of oven; preheat broiler.

3. Place baguette slices on a baking sheet and broil until lightly toasted, 2 to 4 minutes. Rub each bread slice with the remaining garlic clove. (Discard garlic.) Turn the slices over and top with cheese. Broil until the cheese is melted, 1 to 3 minutes. Serve the soup topped with the cheese toasts and bacon.

MAKES 6 SERVINGS, ABOUT 1 ⅓ CUPS EACH.

PER SERVING: 192 calories; 6 g fat (2 g sat, 3 g mono); 13 mg cholesterol; 23 g carbohydrate; 12 g protein; 5 g fiber; 518 mg sodium; 253 mg potassium.

NUTRITION BONUS: Vitamin A (50% daily value), Vitamin C (25% dv), Fiber (16% dv).

The EatingWell Cobb Salad (page 74)

SALADS

DELICIOUS FEEDBACK

Taco Salad

"This has become a staple in our house. It's easy and fast,
it tastes much better than high-sodium taco mixes. I like the
fact that it's a salad, and my kids eat it all."

—Anonymous, Arlington, VA

Maple-Mustard Vinaigrette

"This is my all-time *favorite* dressing. I have varied it with different
vinegars (balsamic, organic cider, white wine) and different
mustards (pub style, Dijon, Dakin's Maple Horseradish). It is
incredible no matter what. It takes 3 minutes to whip up.
I don't even buy bottled vinaigrettes anymore."

—Cheryl, Milton, VT

THE EATINGWELL COBB SALAD

L↓C H↑F

ACTIVE TIME: 40 MINUTES | **TOTAL:** 40 MINUTES

Hollywood restaurateur Bob Cobb would be proud of our interpretation of his creation. We've been true to the original with all the good stuff—chicken, eggs, bacon, avocado and a tangy dressing. But we cut the saturated fat in half and doubled the amount of healthy monounsaturated fat. We've left the blue cheese optional, but the salad is so nutritious you might just want to go ahead and indulge yourself with a little bit anyway. (*Photograph: page 72.*)

3 tablespoons white-wine vinegar	2 large eggs, hard-boiled (*see Tip, page 246*), peeled and chopped
2 tablespoons finely minced shallot	2 medium tomatoes, diced
1 tablespoon Dijon mustard	1 large cucumber, seeded and sliced
1 teaspoon freshly ground pepper	1 avocado, diced
¼ teaspoon salt	2 slices cooked bacon, crumbled
3 tablespoons extra-virgin olive oil	½ cup crumbled blue cheese (optional)
10 cups mixed salad greens	
8 ounces shredded cooked chicken breast (about 1 large breast half; *see Tip, page 246*)	

1. Whisk vinegar, shallot, mustard, pepper and salt in a small bowl to combine. Whisk in oil until combined. Place salad greens in a large bowl. Add half of the dressing and toss to coat.

2. Divide the greens among 4 plates. Arrange equal portions of chicken, egg, tomatoes, cucumber, avocado, bacon and blue cheese (if using) on top of the lettuce. Drizzle the salads with the remaining dressing.

MAKES 4 SERVINGS.

PER SERVING: 346 calories; 23 g fat (4 g sat, 15 g mono); 142 mg cholesterol; 18 g carbohydrate; 21 g protein; 8 g fiber; 397 mg sodium; 711 mg potassium.

NUTRITION BONUS: Vitamin A (117% daily value), Vitamin C (27% dv), Potassium (20% dv), Folate (18% dv), Iron (15% dv).

CAESAR SALAD

H✂W H♥H

ACTIVE TIME: 20 MINUTES | **TOTAL:** 1 HOUR
TO MAKE AHEAD: Cover and refrigerate the dressing (STEPS 1-3) for up to 2 days.

A considerable amount of oil and egg yolks combine to give the typical Caesar salad dressing its creamy consistency. Our dressing uses pureed roasted garlic as a flavor-packed, lower-fat and lower-calorie substitute without losing any of the richness you expect in a Caesar. Add some grilled chicken breast to this salad and you've got a complete meal.

ROASTED GARLIC DRESSING

- 2 heads garlic
- ¼ cup reduced-sodium chicken broth *or* water
- 3 tablespoons white-wine vinegar *or* cider vinegar
- 2 tablespoons extra-virgin olive oil
- 2 teaspoons Dijon mustard
- 3 anchovy fillets, rinsed and coarsely chopped
- 2 teaspoons Worcestershire sauce
- ⅛ teaspoon salt
  Freshly ground pepper to taste

CROUTONS & SALAD

- 2 cups cubed French bread, preferably whole-grain (1-inch pieces)
- 1 clove garlic, peeled
- ½ teaspoon salt
- 2 teaspoons extra-virgin olive oil
- 10 cups torn romaine lettuce (2 medium heads)
- ½ ounce Parmesan cheese, shaved (*see Tip*)
  Freshly ground pepper to taste
- 3 anchovy fillets, rinsed and halved lengthwise (optional)

1. TO PREPARE ROASTED GARLIC DRESSING: Preheat oven to 400°F.

2. Remove loose papery skin from garlic, without separating the cloves. Slice the tips off each head, exposing the cloves. Wrap the heads in foil. Roast until the cloves are very soft, about 40 minutes.

3. Unwrap the garlic and let cool slightly. Squeeze the cloves out of their skins into a blender or food processor. Add broth (or water), vinegar, 2 tablespoons oil, mustard, anchovies and Worcestershire sauce; blend until smooth. Season with ⅛ teaspoon salt and pepper.

4. TO PREPARE CROUTONS & SALAD: Spread bread cubes on a baking sheet. Toast in a 400° oven until golden and crisp, 10 to 15 minutes.

5. Coarsely chop garlic clove, sprinkle with ½ teaspoon salt and mash with the side of the knife blade. Heat 2 teaspoons oil in a nonstick skillet. Add the mashed garlic and cook, stirring, until golden brown, about 30 seconds. Remove from the heat, add bread and toss until the garlic is well distributed.

6. Combine lettuce with the dressing in a large bowl and toss well. Add the croutons and Parmesan. Grind pepper over the top, toss once and serve topped with anchovy fillets, if using.

MAKES 6 SERVINGS.

PER SERVING: 192 calories; 8 g fat (2 g sat, 5 g mono); 4 mg cholesterol; 24 g carbohydrate; 7 g protein; 3 g fiber; 613 mg sodium; 298 mg potassium.

NUTRITION BONUS: Vitamin A (109% daily value), Folate (50% dv), Vitamin C (39% dv), Selenium (16% dv).

TIP:
Use a vegetable peeler to shave curls off a block of hard cheese like Parmigiano-Reggiano or Pecorino Romano.

MAKEOVER TIP

PUREED ROASTED GARLIC YIELDS A CREAMY TEXTURE AND IS A FLAVORFUL, LOW-CALORIE SUBSTITUTE FOR SOME OF THE OIL, EGGS OR FULL-FAT MAYONNAISE IN CREAMY DRESSINGS.

CHINESE CHICKEN & NOODLE SALAD

H ♥ H

ACTIVE TIME: 30 MINUTES | **TOTAL:** 30 MINUTES

TO MAKE AHEAD: Refrigerate the vegetables, toasted noodle mixture, chicken and dressing in separate containers for up to 1 day. Toss together just before serving.

This delicious salad is crisp, crunchy and cool with shredded cabbage, carrots and chicken breast tossed with toasted ramen noodles and slivered almonds. The dressing is an addictive orange, sesame, ginger and soy combination—you may want to double the dressing and save some for a salad the next day.

2	3-ounce packages low-fat ramen-noodle soup mix
½	cup slivered almonds
2	tablespoons sesame seeds
1	tablespoon canola oil
2	pounds boneless, skinless chicken breasts, trimmed
6	¼-inch-thick slices fresh ginger
1	teaspoon salt

6	tablespoons orange juice
6	tablespoons cider vinegar
3	tablespoons reduced-sodium soy sauce
3	tablespoons sugar
1½	teaspoons toasted sesame oil
4	cups shredded green cabbage
2	medium carrots, shredded
1	bunch scallions, chopped

MAKEOVER TIP

BE A SMART SHOPPER—READ NUTRITION LABELS CAREFULLY. DOES YOUR FAVORITE CONVENIENCE PRODUCT HAVE A HEALTHIER ALTERNATIVE, SUCH AS LOW-FAT BAKED RAMEN NOODLES INSTEAD OF FRIED RAMEN?

1. Preheat oven to 350°F.

2. Crumble ramen noodles onto a large rimmed baking sheet (discard seasoning packets). Add almonds, sesame seeds and canola oil; toss to coat. Bake for 10 minutes. Stir, then bake until the noodles are golden brown, about 5 minutes more. Let cool on the pan on a wire rack.

3. Place chicken in a medium skillet or saucepan with water to cover. Add ginger and salt; bring to a boil. Cover, reduce heat to low, and simmer gently until cooked through and no longer pink in the middle, 10 to 15 minutes. Transfer the chicken to a cutting board to cool. Shred into bite-size pieces. (Discard the poaching liquid.)

4. Meanwhile, combine orange juice, vinegar, soy sauce, sugar and sesame oil in a small bowl or jar with a tight-fitting lid. Whisk or shake until the sugar has dissolved.

5. Just before serving, combine the shredded chicken, cabbage, carrots and scallions in a large bowl. Add the toasted noodle mixture and the dressing; mix well.

MAKES 8 SERVINGS.

PER SERVING: 390 calories; 12 g fat (2 g sat, 5 g mono); 96 mg cholesterol; 29 g carbohydrate; 41 g protein; 4 g fiber; 621 mg sodium; 587 mg potassium.

NUTRITION BONUS: Vitamin A (56% daily value), Vitamin C (38% dv), Folate (26% dv), Magnesium (21% dv), Potassium (17% dv).

LIGHTENING UP CHINESE CHICKEN SALAD

"This salad is so popular we can't go to a friend's house or a church picnic without running into it," wrote Jolene Eichorn of Little Canada, Minnesota. "What can be done to lighten it up but keep the great taste?" Indeed, with deep-fried ramen noodles and ½ cup of sugar in the dressing, this ubiquitous crunchy cabbage-and-carrot salad was in need of a makeover.

We were able to reduce the fat by almost 75 percent and knock 160 calories out of every serving, yet keep the taste remarkably close to that of the original. Ramen noodles, usually packaged with a seasoning mix to make instant soup, are a convenient—and seemingly healthful—product. But what you may not realize is that most ramen noodles are deep-fried. A serving of the soup contains 8 grams of fat. Fortunately, you can buy baked ramen, with only 1 gram of fat per serving. Be sure to check the label so you know what you're buying. Toasting crisps up the baked ramen noodles, and maximizes the flavor of the almonds and sesame seeds, allowing you to use a lesser amount. Most of the oil is replaced with vitamin-C-rich orange juice—just a touch of toasted sesame oil adds body and flavor. The sweetness from the orange juice let us greatly reduce the amount of sugar in the dressing as well.

Consider sharing the new version with your friends—the next time it appears at a potluck, everyone will be able to enjoy it worry-free.

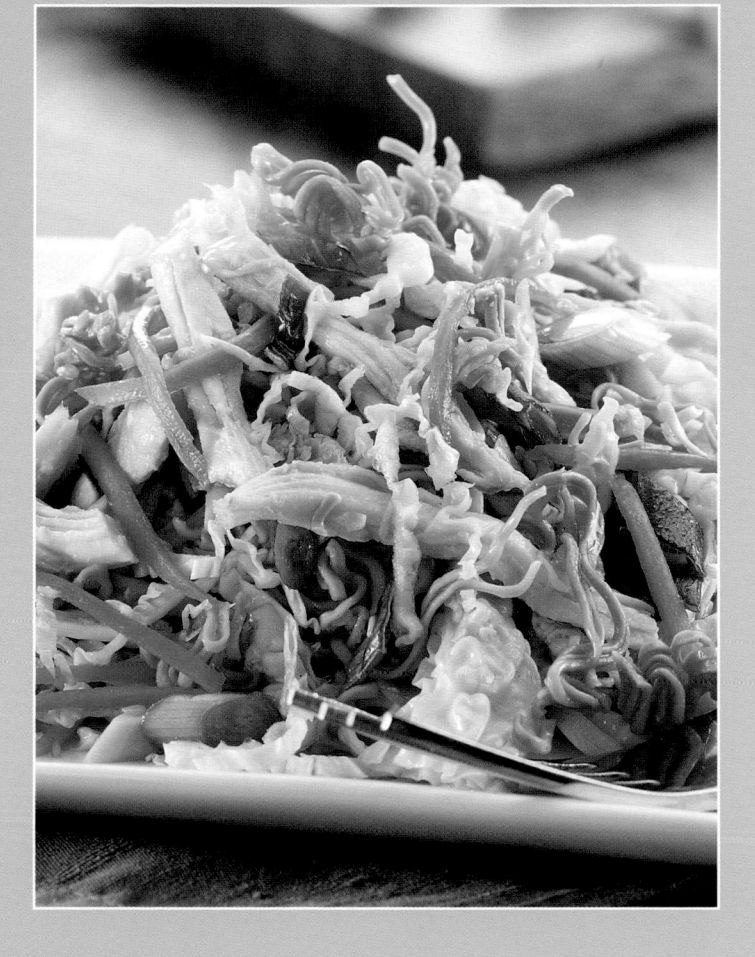

QUICK CHEF'S SALAD

H)(W   L↓C   H↑F   H♥H

ACTIVE TIME: 10 MINUTES | **TOTAL:** 10 MINUTES

Chef's salads are satisfying because they typically contain plenty of protein (but often far more than you need for a healthy meal). Our version keeps the satisfaction level high with lean turkey breast and reduced-fat Swiss cheese, plus adds a blend of colorful carrots, tomatoes and red onions. This salad is also delicious with chicken, ham or roast beef from the deli instead of the turkey. If you want to pack it for lunch, skip tossing the vegetables with the dressing and bring it on the side.

6	cups mixed salad greens	10	cherry tomatoes
1	cup shredded carrots	4	slices roast turkey breast, cut up (3 ounces)
2	tablespoons chopped red onion	2	slices reduced-fat Swiss cheese, cut up (2 ounces)
¼	cup Buttermilk Ranch Dressing (*page 89*) *or* Maple-Mustard Vinaigrette (*page 89*)		

MAKEOVER TIP

TO KEEP SALADS GOOD FOR YOU, DON'T OVERDO IT ON THE DRESSING: 2 TABLESPOONS IS A HEALTHY SERVING SIZE.

Toss greens, carrots and onion with dressing in a large bowl until coated. Divide between 2 plates. Arrange tomatoes, turkey and cheese on top of the salads.

MAKES 2 SERVINGS, ABOUT 4 CUPS EACH.

PER SERVING: 179 calories; 3 g fat (1 g sat, 0 g mono); 27 mg cholesterol; 22 g carbohydrate; 19 g protein; 7 g fiber; 875 mg sodium; 433 mg potassium.

NUTRITION BONUS: Vitamin A (290% daily value), Vitamin C (70% dv), Folate (55% dv), Calcium (40% dv).

SAN FRANCISCO CRAB LOUIS

H)(W L↓C H♥H

ACTIVE TIME: 35 MINUTES | **TOTAL:** 35 MINUTES
TO MAKE AHEAD: Cover and refrigerate the dressing (STEP 2) for up to 1 day.

Crab Louis is a West Coast favorite that has often been called "The King of Salads." But the king has gotten a bit fat over the years so we put him on a diet. To make our dressing, we combine chili sauce and minced shallot with a modest amount of low-fat mayonnaise with regal results. Long live the King!

4 large eggs	¼ cup minced scallions
1 bunch asparagus, trimmed	8 cups shredded romaine lettuce
1 small shallot, minced	12 ounces lump crabmeat, drained, any shells
¼ cup chili sauce, such as Heinz	or cartilage removed
¼ cup low-fat mayonnaise	Freshly ground pepper to taste

1. Place eggs in a large saucepan of cold water; bring to a gentle simmer over medium heat. Simmer for 5 minutes. Add asparagus and continue cooking until the asparagus is bright green, about 3 minutes more. Carefully drain and fill the pan with ice water to cool the eggs and asparagus. Drain again. Peel and slice the eggs; set the asparagus aside.
2. Meanwhile, whisk shallot, chili sauce, mayonnaise and scallions in a large bowl. Reserve ½ cup of the dressing in a medium bowl. Add lettuce to the large bowl; toss to combine. Divide the lettuce among 4 large plates.
3. Add crab to the reserved dressing; stir gently to combine. Mound ½ cup of the crab on each portion of lettuce, arrange some sliced egg and asparagus around it and season with pepper.

MAKES 4 SERVINGS.

PER SERVING: 215 calories; 7 g fat (2 g sat, 2 g mono); 310 mg cholesterol; 13 g carbohydrate; 26 g protein; 3 g fiber; 736 mg sodium; 450 mg potassium.

NUTRITION BONUS: Vitamin A (130% daily value), Folate (60% dv), Vitamin C (50% dv).

GREEN GODDESS SALAD

H✕W   H⬆F   H♥H

ACTIVE TIME: 30 MINUTES | **TOTAL:** 30 MINUTES
TO MAKE AHEAD: Cover and refrigerate the dressing (STEP 1) for up to 1 day.

The beautiful green color of green goddess dressing shouts "healthy," so why spoil things by adding lots of mayonnaise? Our dressing is beautifully green and creamy with avocado (loaded with good-for-you fats) and fresh herbs. Buttermilk and a dash of rice vinegar add tang. Spooned onto a gorgeous salad with fresh shrimp and tasty vegetables—cucumber, artichoke hearts and cherry tomatoes in this case—you've got a satisfying meal.

½ avocado, peeled and pitted
¾ cup nonfat buttermilk
2 tablespoons chopped fresh herbs, such as tarragon, sorrel *and/or* chives
2 teaspoons tarragon vinegar *or* white-wine vinegar
1 teaspoon anchovy paste *or* minced anchovy fillet
8 cups bite-size pieces green leaf lettuce

12 ounces peeled and deveined cooked shrimp (21-25 per pound)
½ cucumber, sliced
1 cup cherry *or* grape tomatoes
1 cup canned chickpeas, rinsed
1 cup rinsed and chopped canned artichoke hearts
½ cup chopped celery

1. Puree avocado, buttermilk, herbs, vinegar and anchovy in a blender until smooth.
2. Divide lettuce among 4 plates. Top with shrimp, cucumber, tomatoes, chickpeas, artichoke hearts and celery. Drizzle the dressing over the salads.

MAKES 4 SERVINGS.

PER SERVING: 292 calories; 7 g fat (1 g sat, 3 g mono); 134 mg cholesterol; 31 g carbohydrate; 28 g protein; 9 g fiber; 790 mg sodium; 843 mg potassium.

NUTRITION BONUS: Vitamin A (90% daily value), Vitamin C (45% dv), Folate (40% dv), Potassium (24% dv), Magnesium (20% dv).

MAKEOVER TIP

INSTEAD OF USING DRIED HERBS IN SALAD DRESSING, TRY USING FRESH— IT HELPS KEEP THE FLAVORS BRIGHT AND SATISFYING.

TACO SALAD

H ⬆ F

ACTIVE TIME: 30 MINUTES | **TOTAL:** 30 MINUTES

A super-quick blend of reduced-fat sour cream and salsa serves double duty as salad dressing and seasoning for the "taco" meat. Depending on the type of salsa you use, the salad will vary in heat. We keep this version light with lean turkey, but lean ground beef (about 95%-lean) would also keep the nutrition marks reasonable. Just hold the deep-fried tortilla bowl and instead serve this salad with tortilla chips and wedges of fresh lime.

½   cup prepared salsa
¼   cup reduced-fat sour cream
1   teaspoon canola oil
1   medium onion, chopped
3   cloves garlic, minced
1   pound 93%-lean ground turkey
2   large plum tomatoes, diced

1   14-ounce can kidney beans, rinsed
2   teaspoons ground cumin
2   teaspoons chili powder
¼   cup chopped fresh cilantro
8   cups shredded romaine lettuce
½   cup shredded sharp Cheddar cheese

MAKEOVER TIP

USE FULL-FLAVORED CHEESES, SUCH AS SHARP OR EXTRA-SHARP CHEDDAR, TO KEEP THE FLAVOR DELICIOUS EVEN WHEN REDUCING THE TOTAL AMOUNT OF CHEESE.

1. Combine salsa and sour cream in a large bowl.

2. Heat oil in a large nonstick skillet over medium heat. Add onion and garlic and cook, stirring often, until softened, about 2 minutes. Add turkey and cook, stirring often and crumbling with a wooden spoon, until cooked through, about 5 minutes. Add tomatoes, beans, cumin and chili powder; cook, stirring, until the tomatoes begin to break down, 2 to 3 minutes. Remove from the heat, stir in cilantro and ¼ cup of the salsa mixture.

3. Add lettuce to the remaining salsa mixture in the bowl; toss to coat. To serve, divide the lettuce among 4 plates, top with the turkey mixture and sprinkle with cheese.

MAKES 4 SERVINGS (1 cup filling & 2 cups salad each).

PER SERVING: 361 calories; 16 g fat (6 g sat, 1 g mono); 86 mg cholesterol; 25 g carbohydrate; 33 g protein; 10 g fiber; 583 mg sodium; 718 mg potassium.

NUTRITION BONUS: Vitamin A (150% daily value), Vitamin C (60% dv), Folate (53% dv), Iron (25% dv), Potassium (22% dv).

THE WEDGE

H✕W L↓C

ACTIVE TIME: 15 MINUTES | **TOTAL:** 15 MINUTES

Found on virtually every steakhouse menu, this salad gets its name from the wedge of iceberg lettuce it's usually made with. Despite its stellar texture, iceberg is a bit of a nutritional wasteland, so we call for more nutrient-rich hearts of romaine. But we stay true to the original with a topping of crumbled bacon and chunks of blue cheese.

2	hearts of romaine, quartered lengthwise and cores removed	2	slices cooked bacon, crumbled
¼	cup chopped fresh chives	2	ounces crumbled blue cheese
		½	cup Buttermilk Ranch Dressing (*page 89*)

Divide romaine among 4 salad plates. Sprinkle with chives, bacon and blue cheese. Drizzle with dressing.

MAKES 4 SERVINGS.

PER SERVING: 95 calories; 6 g fat (3 g sat, 2 g mono); 14 mg cholesterol; 5 g carbohydrate; 6 g protein; 1 g fiber; 499 mg sodium; 72 mg potassium.

NUTRITION BONUS: Vitamin A (25% daily value), Vitamin C (20% dv).

CLASSIC COLESLAW

H✕W L↓C H♥H

ACTIVE TIME: 15 MINUTES | **TOTAL:** 15 MINUTES

There are two schools of coleslaw—vinegary and creamy. For those who prefer the latter, here's one that's rich-tasting with about a third of the calories and 80 percent less fat than a typical version.

1	cup low-fat mayonnaise		Freshly ground pepper to taste
¾	cup reduced-fat sour cream	9	cups shredded green cabbage, preferably Savoy (1 small head)
3	tablespoons cider vinegar		
1	tablespoon Dijon mustard	1	large green bell pepper, quartered and very thinly sliced
1	teaspoon sugar		
⅛	teaspoon salt	2	cups grated carrots

Whisk mayonnaise, sour cream, vinegar, mustard and sugar in a large bowl. Season with salt and pepper. Add cabbage, bell pepper and carrots and toss until well combined.

MAKES 8 SERVINGS.

PER SERVING: 100 calories; 5 g fat (2 g sat, 1 g mono); 9 mg cholesterol; 14 g carbohydrate; 3 g protein; 4 g fiber; 372 mg sodium; 338 mg potassium.

NUTRITION BONUS: Vitamin A (98% daily value), Vitamin C (74% dv).

CURRIED WALDORF SALAD

H)(W   H ♥ H

ACTIVE TIME: 25 MINUTES | **TOTAL:** 25 MINUTES

The famous Waldorf Salad gets a healthful makeover in this delicious curried version. With plenty of fruits and vegetables, it has nearly twice the fiber of typical versions.

- ¼ cup nonfat plain yogurt
- 3 tablespoons low-fat mayonnaise
- ½ teaspoon curry powder
- ⅛ teaspoon salt
  Pinch of cayenne pepper, or to taste
- 1 orange

- 2 tart-sweet red apples, diced
- 1 cup chopped celery
- ⅓ cup golden raisins
- ⅓ cup coarsely chopped walnuts, toasted
  (*see Tip, page 247*)

MAKEOVER TIP

SUBSTITUTE NONFAT PLAIN YOGURT FOR SOME OF THE MAYONNAISE IN CREAMY DRESSINGS. IT PROVIDES GREAT TEXTURE, TANGY FLAVOR AND ONLY 13 CALORIES AND 0 GRAMS OF FAT PER 2 TABLESPOONS, COMPARED WITH 180 CALORIES AND 20 GRAMS OF FAT FOR REGULAR MAYONNAISE.

1. Whisk yogurt, mayonnaise, curry powder, salt and cayenne in a medium bowl. Grate 2 teaspoons zest from the orange and add to the dressing.

2. Using a sharp knife, cut off the peel and white pith from the orange. To make segments, hold the orange over the bowl (to catch the juice) and slice between each segment and its surrounding membranes. Add apples, celery, raisins and walnuts; toss to combine.

MAKES 6 SERVINGS, ¾ CUP EACH.

PER SERVING: 136 calories; 5 g fat (0 g sat, 0 g mono); 0 mg cholesterol; 24 g carbohydrate; 2 g protein; 4 g fiber; 134 mg sodium; 222 mg potassium.

NUTRITION BONUS: Vitamin C (26% daily value).

BROCCOLI-BACON SALAD

H✕W L↓C H♥H

ACTIVE TIME: 20 MINUTES | **TOTAL:** 20 MINUTES
TO MAKE AHEAD: Cover and refrigerate for up to 1 day.

Loaded with vitamins C, K and A, broccoli truly is a healthy, power vegetable. So adding a modest amount of bacon hardly mutes its strengths. Our version of this favorite has plenty of creaminess without all the fat. Make it once and it will become a regular on your backyard barbecue menu.

1 clove garlic, minced
¼ cup low-fat mayonnaise
¼ cup reduced-fat sour cream
2 teaspoons cider vinegar
1 teaspoon sugar
4 cups finely chopped broccoli crowns (*see Tip, page 247*)

1 8-ounce can sliced water chestnuts, rinsed and chopped
3 slices cooked bacon, crumbled
3 tablespoons dried cranberries
  Freshly ground pepper to taste

Whisk garlic, mayonnaise, sour cream, vinegar and sugar in a large bowl. Add broccoli, water chestnuts, bacon, cranberries and pepper; stir to coat with the dressing.

MAKES 6 SERVINGS, 1 SCANT CUP EACH.

PER SERVING: 92 calories; 4 g fat (2 g sat, 1 g mono); 7 mg cholesterol; 12 g carbohydrate; 3 g protein; 3 g fiber; 181 mg sodium; 188 mg potassium.

NUTRITION BONUS· Vitamin C (70% daily value), Vitamin A (30% dv).

MAKEOVER TIP

YOU DON'T HAVE TO GIVE UP BACON, JUST USE IT JUDICIOUSLY. THINK OF IT AS A "FLAVOR ENHANCER," NOT THE STAR INGREDIENT.

SUMMER POTATO SALAD

H)(W   H♥H

ACTIVE TIME: 30 MINUTES | **TOTAL:** 1 HOUR

Our take on this summer staple has a light creamy dressing made with nonfat yogurt and low-fat mayonnaise. It gets a unique hit of richness and flavor with the addition of pureed roasted garlic.

2 large heads garlic
3 pounds medium red potatoes, cut into 1-inch pieces
1 tablespoon white-wine vinegar
1/3 cup low-fat mayonnaise
1/3 cup nonfat plain yogurt
2 tablespoons Dijon mustard
1/2 teaspoon salt, divided
   Freshly ground pepper to taste
4 large hard-boiled eggs (*see Tip, page 246*), peeled, divided

1 cup chopped celery
1 4-ounce jar sliced pimientos, rinsed
1 3-ounce can pitted black olives (1/2 cup), rinsed and chopped
2 tablespoons chopped fresh parsley
2 tablespoons chopped fresh chives *or* scallion greens
   Paprika for garnish
   Chives *or* parsley sprigs for garnish

1. Preheat oven to 400°F. Remove loose papery skin from garlic, without separating the cloves. Slice the tips off each head, exposing the cloves. Wrap the heads in foil. Roast until the cloves are very soft, about 40 minutes. Unwrap the garlic and let cool slightly.

2. Meanwhile, place potatoes in a large saucepan and cover with water. Bring to a boil. Cover and cook over medium heat until tender, 7 to 9 minutes. Drain well and transfer to a large bowl. Toss gently with vinegar; let cool.

3. When the garlic is cool enough to handle, squeeze the cloves out of their skins into a food processor or blender. Add mayonnaise, yogurt and mustard; blend until smooth. Season with 1/4 teaspoon salt and pepper.

4. Add the dressing to the potatoes and toss to coat. Finely chop 3 hard-boiled eggs and add to the potatoes along with celery, pimientos, olives, parsley, chives (or scallion greens), the remaining 1/4 teaspoon salt and pepper. Stir gently to mix. Transfer to a serving dish and sprinkle with paprika. Slice the remaining egg and arrange the slices decoratively on top. Garnish with chives (or parsley sprigs).

MAKES 10 SERVINGS.

PER SERVING: 161 calories; 4 g fat (1 g sat, 2 g mono); 85 mg cholesterol; 27 g carbohydrate; 6 g protein; 3 g fiber; 347 mg sodium; 719 mg potassium.

NUTRITION BONUS: Vitamin C (42% daily value), Potassium (21% dv).

TORTELLINI SALAD

H)(W H↑F H♥H

ACTIVE TIME: 20 MINUTES | **TOTAL:** 40 MINUTES
TO MAKE AHEAD: Cover and refrigerate Tomato Vinaigrette for up to 2 days.

A tomato-rich dressing boosts the flavor and lowers calories and fat in this tortellini salad (the dressing is also great on green salads or grilled fish). Roasted red peppers, artichoke hearts and sun-dried tomatoes add a good dose of vitamins A, C and fiber.

1	pound fresh *or* frozen cheese tortellini, preferably whole-wheat
1	cup sun-dried tomatoes (*not* packed in oil)
1	14-ounce can artichoke hearts, rinsed and quartered
1	7-ounce jar roasted red peppers, rinsed and chopped
1	cup cherry tomatoes, halved, *or* 2 ripe tomatoes, seeded and chopped
4	scallions, coarsely chopped
½	cup finely chopped fresh basil
1	ounce prosciutto, trimmed and julienned (optional)

⅛	teaspoon salt
	Freshly ground pepper to taste
	Arugula for serving (optional)

TOMATO VINAIGRETTE

2	ripe tomatoes, halved and seeded
2	tablespoons red-wine vinegar
1	tablespoon extra-virgin olive oil
1	teaspoon dried oregano
1	clove garlic, minced
⅛	teaspoon salt
	Freshly ground pepper to taste

1. Bring a large pot of water to a boil. Cook tortellini until just tender, 8 to 12 minutes or according to package directions. Drain and rinse under cold water. Transfer to a large bowl.

2. Meanwhile, place sun-dried tomatoes in a small bowl and cover with more boiling water. Let stand for 30 minutes. Drain and coarsely chop.

3. Add the sun-dried tomatoes to the tortellini along with artichoke hearts, roasted red peppers, tomatoes, scallions, basil and prosciutto, if using. Season with salt and pepper.

4. TO PREPARE TOMATO VINAIGRETTE: Working over a bowl, rub tomato halves on the large-holed side of a box grater until only the skins remain. Discard the skins. Add vinegar, oil, oregano, garlic, salt and pepper to the tomato juice and whisk until blended.

5. Add the Tomato Vinaigrette to the tortellini salad and toss. Serve the salad on a bed of arugula, if desired.

MAKES 8 SERVINGS, ABOUT 1¼ CUPS EACH.

PER SERVING: 278 calories; 7 g fat (3 g sat, 3 g mono); 27 mg cholesterol; 42 g carbohydrate; 8 g protein; 5 g fiber; 451 mg sodium; 229 mg potassium.

NUTRITION BONUS: Vitamin A (27% daily value), Vitamin C (24% dv).

> ## MAKEOVER TIP
>
> **RINSING CANNED OR MARINATED VEGETABLES CUTS THE SODIUM BY UP TO 35%.**

THREE-BEAN SALAD

H✱W L↓C H↑F H♥H

ACTIVE TIME: 30 MINUTES | **TOTAL:** 30 MINUTES
TO MAKE AHEAD: Prepare the dressing (STEP 2), cover and refrigerate for up to 8 hours. Finish with Steps 3-4 just before serving.

It's true, beans are good for your heart, and this tangy cold salad makes it a delight to get more of them in your diet. Plenty of added veggies supply crunch along with nutrients and fiber. This salad is great made in advance so it's perfect for a potluck.

3 tablespoons cider vinegar
3 tablespoons rice vinegar
1 tablespoon sugar
1 tablespoon whole-grain mustard
1 tablespoon canola oil
½ teaspoon salt
  Freshly ground pepper to taste
⅓ cup diced red onion

1 15-ounce can black-eyed peas *or* chickpeas, rinsed
1 10-ounce package frozen baby lima beans *or* shelled edamame
1 pound green beans, trimmed and cut into 1-inch pieces
2 tablespoons chopped fresh parsley

MAKEOVER TIP

WHEN CONVENIENT, USE FRESH VEGETABLES IN PLACE OF HIGHER-SODIUM CANNED VEGETABLES AND LET THEM BE THE STAR OF THE RECIPE LIKE THE FRESH GREEN BEANS IN THIS SALAD.

1. Put a large saucepan of water on to boil. Fill a large bowl half full with cold water.
2. Whisk cider vinegar, rice vinegar, sugar, mustard, oil, salt and pepper in a large bowl until blended. Add onion and black-eyed peas (or chickpeas); toss to coat.
3. Cook lima beans (or edamame) in the boiling water until tender, about 5 minutes. Remove with a slotted spoon and refresh in the cold water. Pat dry and add to the bowl.
4. Cook green beans in the boiling water until just tender, 3 to 6 minutes. Drain and refresh in the cold water. Pat dry and add to the salad along with parsley; toss well.

MAKES 8 SERVINGS, ABOUT 1 CUP EACH.

PER SERVING: 110 calories; 2 g fat (0 g sat, 1 g mono); 0 mg cholesterol; 18 g carbohydrate; 5 g protein; 6 g fiber; 315 mg sodium; 384 mg potassium.

NUTRITION BONUS: Fiber (23% daily value), Vitamin C (15% dv).

SEE IT : MAKE IT

CREAMY BLUE CHEESE DRESSING

Whisk ⅓ cup each low-fat mayonnaise, buttermilk and nonfat plain yogurt, 2 tablespoons white-wine vinegar, 1 tablespoon Dijon mustard, ½ teaspoon each salt and pepper. Stir in ¼ cup crumbled blue cheese.

MAKES 1 ¼ CUPS. | PER TABLESPOON: 14 calories; 1 g fat (0 g sat); 132 mg sodium.

MAPLE-MUSTARD VINAIGRETTE

Whisk ½ cup walnut *or* canola oil, ¼ cup each maple syrup and cider vinegar, 2 tablespoons each coarse-grained mustard and reduced-sodium soy sauce, ½ teaspoon each salt and pepper.

MAKES 1 ¼ CUPS. | PER TABLESPOON: 62 calories; 6 g fat (1 g sat); 149 mg sodium.

BUTTERMILK RANCH DRESSING

Whisk ½ cup buttermilk, ¼ cup low-fat mayonnaise, 2 tablespoons white-wine vinegar, ½ teaspoon each granulated garlic, salt and pepper. Stir in ⅓ cup chopped fresh herbs, such as chives and/or dill.

MAKES 1 CUP. | PER TABLESPOON: 8 calories; 1 g fat (0 g sat); 112 mg sodium.

FRENCH DRESSING

Puree ¾ cup low-sodium tomato juice, 2 tablespoons olive oil, 1 tablespoon cider vinegar, 1 teaspoon each Dijon mustard and sugar, 1 garlic clove, 1½ teaspoons fresh thyme, salt and pepper to taste in a blender.

MAKES ABOUT 1 CUP. | PER TABLESPOON: 18 calories; 2 g fat (0 g sat); 83 mg sodium.

Smoky Buffalo Burger (page 92)

MEAT

DELICIOUS FEEDBACK

Beef & Portobello Mushroom Stroganoff

"Very easy and tasty recipe. The portobello mushrooms
have such a meaty texture that the beef could be left out
for a vegetarian option."

—Anonymous, MI

EatingWell Sloppy Joes

"These were really very good—they got rave reviews
at my house, which isn't very common with
my 'makeover' type recipes."

—Sonya, Ocala, FL

SMOKY BUFFALO BURGER

H↑F

ACTIVE TIME: 40 MINUTES | **TOTAL:** 40 MINUTES
TO MAKE AHEAD: Cover and refrigerate the barbecue mayonnaise (STEP 3) for up to 5 days.

Smoky flavors are an ideal match for sweet, beefy buffalo (bison). Instead of melted on top, cheese is used here to season the meat—adding moisture and smoky flavor inside the burger. Wild rice bulks up the serving size (and adds vitamins and minerals), while keeping it lean. Plus the flavor and chewy texture are a wonderful complement to the meat. If you can't find buffalo in your store, substitute 90%-lean ground beef. (*Photograph: page 90.*)

1 pound ground buffalo (bison)
½ cup cooked wild rice (*see Kitchen Tip*)
½ cup shredded smoked cheese, such as Cheddar, gouda *or* mozzarella
2 tablespoons smoky barbecue sauce, divided
1 tablespoon paprika, preferably sweet Hungarian
2 teaspoons Dijon mustard
1 teaspoon minced garlic

¾ teaspoon freshly ground pepper
¼ teaspoon salt
¼ cup low-fat mayonnaise
1 tablespoon sweet pepper relish *or* pickle relish
2 teaspoons prepared horseradish
4 whole-wheat hamburger buns, toasted
4 slices tomato
4 thin slices sweet onion, such as Vidalia

KITCHEN TIP:

Be sure to plan ahead for cooking the wild rice—it takes 40 to 50 minutes. To cut down on cooking time, look for "quick" wild rice—a whole-grain rice that cooks in less than 30 minutes—or "instant" wild rice that's done in 10 minutes or less.

MAKEOVER TIP

ADD WHOLE-GRAINS LIKE WILD RICE TO YOUR BURGERS TO REPLACE SOME OF THE MEAT AND KEEP THEM MOIST.

1. Preheat grill to medium.
2. Place meat, rice, cheese, 1 tablespoon barbecue sauce, paprika, mustard, garlic, pepper and salt in a large bowl. Gently combine, without overmixing, until evenly incorporated. Form into 4 equal patties, ½ to ¾ inch thick.
3. Combine the remaining 1 tablespoon barbecue sauce, mayonnaise, relish and horseradish in a small bowl.
4. Oil the grill rack (*see Tip, page 246*). Grill the burgers until an instant-read thermometer inserted in the center registers 155°F, 5 to 6 minutes per side.
5. Assemble the burgers on buns with the barbecue mayonnaise sauce, tomato and onion.

MAKES 4 SERVINGS.

PER SERVING: 434 calories; 19 g fat (7 g sat, 2 g mono); 65 mg cholesterol; 36 g carbohydrate; 29 g protein; 5 g fiber; 721 mg sodium; 301 mg potassium.

NUTRITION BONUS: Vitamin A (25% daily value), Iron (20% dv), Calcium (15% dv).

MEATLOAF

H❯❮W   H⬆F   H♥H

ACTIVE TIME: 40 MINUTES | **TOTAL:** 1 ¾ HOURS

Here's an American standard made better. The addition of richly flavored dried mushrooms and the whole-grain goodness of bulgur increases the vitamins and minerals and decreases the saturated fat. The loaf is free-form, rather than baked in a loaf pan, which means more delicious, browned crust. This recipe is large enough to feed a big group or, even better, have leftovers for a cold sandwich the next day.

1   cup dried mushrooms, such as shiitake, porcini *or* chanterelle
1   cup bulgur (*see Ingredient Note, page 247*)
1   cup boiling water
2   teaspoons extra-virgin olive oil
1   small onion, chopped
1   stalk celery, chopped
2   cloves garlic, minced
1   tablespoon Worcestershire sauce
1   15-ounce can diced tomatoes, drained

½   cup nonfat evaporated milk
½   cup ketchup
1   large egg
2   large egg whites
1 ½   pounds 90%-lean ground beef
1   cup fine dry breadcrumbs
¼   cup chopped fresh parsley
2   teaspoons dried thyme
½   teaspoon salt

1. Place mushrooms in a small bowl and cover with warm water; let stand for 30 minutes. Combine bulgur with the boiling water in another small bowl and let soak until the bulgur is tender and the water has been absorbed, about 30 minutes. Remove the mushrooms from the liquid; trim stems and coarsely chop caps.

2. Preheat oven to 350°F. Coat a baking sheet with cooking spray.

3. Heat oil in a small skillet over medium-low heat and add onion, celery and garlic. Cook, stirring occasionally, until the vegetables are softened, 5 to 7 minutes. Add Worcestershire and cook for 3 minutes, scraping the pan well as the mixture becomes sticky. Add tomatoes, evaporated milk and ketchup; stir to combine. Continue cooking until the mixture is very thick, about 3 minutes. Remove from the heat and let cool.

4. Whisk egg and egg whites in a large bowl. Add beef, breadcrumbs, the soaked bulgur, the mushrooms and the tomato mixture. Stir in parsley, thyme and salt. Mix gently but thoroughly with your hands.

5. Mound the meatloaf mixture into a free-form loaf on the prepared baking sheet. Bake until the internal temperature reaches 165°F, 50 to 60 minutes. Let cool for 10 minutes before slicing and serving.

MAKES 10 SERVINGS.

PER SERVING: 313 calories; 10 g fat (3 g sat, 4 g mono); 66 mg cholesterol; 32 g carbohydrate; 24 g protein; 6 g fiber; 467 mg sodium; 488 mg potassium.

NUTRITION BONUS: Iron (34% daily value), Zinc (26% dv), Selenium (25% dv).

CRISPY BEEF TACOS

H)(W H↟F H♥H

ACTIVE TIME: 50 MINUTES | **TOTAL:** 50 MINUTES

TO MAKE AHEAD: Store taco shells in an airtight container for up to 2 days. Reheat at 375°F for 1 to 2 minutes before serving. Refrigerate taco meat in an airtight container for up to 1 day. Reheat just before serving.

EQUIPMENT: Baked-taco rack (OR SEE TIP, PAGE 247)

Building the perfect taco is a very personal task. Fill your baked crispy taco shells with our lean and spicy taco meat, then add plenty of fresh toppings. With a side of Easy Fiesta Beans (*page 200*) you'll have a meal that's as healthy as it is fun.

CRISPY TACO SHELLS

- 12 6-inch corn tortillas
     Canola oil cooking spray
- ¾ teaspoon chili powder, divided
- ¼ teaspoon salt, divided

LEAN & SPICY TACO MEAT

- 8 ounces 93%-lean ground beef
- 8 ounces 99%-lean ground turkey breast
- ½ cup chopped onion
- 1 10-ounce can diced tomatoes with green chiles *or* 1 ¼ cups petite-diced tomatoes
- ½ teaspoon ground cumin
- ½ teaspoon ground chipotle chile pepper (*see Ingredient Note, page 247*) *or* 1 teaspoon chili powder
- ½ teaspoon dried oregano

TOPPINGS

- 3 cups shredded romaine lettuce
- ¾ cup shredded reduced-fat Cheddar cheese
- ¾ cup diced tomatoes
- ¾ cup prepared salsa
- ¼ cup diced red onion

1. TO PREPARE TACO SHELLS: Preheat oven to 375°F.

2. Wrap 4 tortillas in a barely damp cloth or paper towel and microwave on High until steamed, about 30 seconds. (*Alternatively, wrap in foil and heat in the preheated oven until steaming, 5 to 7 minutes.*) Coat both sides with cooking spray; sprinkle a little chili powder and salt on one side.

3. Drape each tortilla over a panel on a baked-taco rack and bake until crispy and brown, 7 to 10 minutes. (*Or see Tip, page 247.*)

4. Remove the shells from the rack and repeat Steps 2 and 3 with the remaining 8 tortillas.

5. TO PREPARE TACO MEAT: Place beef, turkey and onion in a large nonstick skillet over medium heat. Cook, breaking up the meat with a wooden spoon, until cooked through, about 10 minutes. Transfer to a colander to drain off fat. Wipe out the pan. Return the meat to the pan and add tomatoes, cumin, ground chipotle (or chili powder) and oregano. Cook over medium heat, stirring occasionally, until most of the liquid has evaporated, 3 to 6 minutes.

6. TO ASSEMBLE: Fill each taco shell with a generous 3 tablespoons taco meat, ¼ cup lettuce, 1 tablespoon cheese, 1 tablespoon tomato, 1 tablespoon salsa and 1 teaspoon onion.

MAKES 6 SERVINGS, 2 FILLED TACOS EACH.

PER SERVING: 261 calories; 5 g fat (1 g sat, 1 g mono); 38 mg cholesterol; 31 g carbohydrate; 24 g protein; 5 g fiber; 582 mg sodium; 272 mg potassium.

NUTRITION BONUS: Vitamin A (40% daily value), Vitamin C (25% dv), Zinc (17% dv), Iron (15% dv).

CRISPY TEX-MEX TACOS GO HEALTHY

Eatingwell recipe tester Carolyn Casner knows Tex-Mex: she grew up on the border in El Paso, Texas. So when it's taco night at her house, she has a clear culinary memory: "The world's best tacos come from Julio's Café Corona, where my family and I always went after church," she recalls. "They're greasy, messy and delicious."

Carolyn and husband Jeb Wallace-Brodeur, a photojournalist, savor Julio's tacos when they're able, along with son Aidan, 9. But with two busy work schedules, their home version of taco night is more humble: store-bought taco shells with an assortment of fillings like ground beef, refried beans, shredded cheese and lettuce, salsa and chopped onions. Once in a while, Carolyn admits, she'll save time by using a boxed taco kit.

But all that meat, cheese and seasoning loads a taco meal with grease and salt, more like fast-food tacos than homemade. For instance, two Taco Bell "Original" beef tacos weigh in at 340 calories and 20 grams of fat (8 saturated) and 700 milligrams of sodium. Carolyn wishes there were more vegetables, too; Aidan won't put any in his tacos. "He doesn't like mixing."

Eatingwell's taco-night plan adds more vegetables to the menu, by seasoning the taco meat with tomatoes and onion. It also cuts out much of the fat and sodium. A key switch: using homemade, oven-baked tortilla shells, which eliminate the saturated and trans fats found in most store-bought brands.

When Aidan dug into a fully loaded taco (with lettuce and tomatoes), he pronounced it "yummy!" and promptly forgot his "no mixing" rule. He especially loved Easy Fiesta Beans, which he scooped into a taco shell.

"It's nice to feel content, and not stuffed," Carolyn pronounced. Jeb's verdict: "When can we do taco night again?"

TACO NIGHT MAKEOVER RECIPES

Crispy Beef Tacos (*page 94*)

Easy Fiesta Beans (*page 200*)

PULLED PORK

H✕W L↓C

ACTIVE TIME: 1 HOUR | **TOTAL:** 5-6 HOURS
TO MAKE AHEAD: Cover and refrigerate for up to 3 days or freeze for up to 2 months.

The trick to making pulled pork healthy is to trim the meat well and then skim any extra fat off the sauce after cooking. Serve on a soft whole-grain bun with crisp, cool coleslaw (*see page 83*). **SHOPPING TIP:** Boston butt (or "Boston-style butt," "fresh pork butt," "pork shoulder") can weigh upwards of 10 pounds, so you may have to ask your butcher to cut one down for this recipe.

1 tablespoon extra-virgin olive oil	¾ cup cider vinegar
2 medium yellow onions, diced	½ cup whole-grain mustard
2 tablespoons chili powder	2 tablespoons tomato paste
1 tablespoon ground cumin	1 canned chipotle pepper in adobo sauce, minced, plus 1 tablespoon adobo sauce (*see Ingredient Note, page 247*)
2 teaspoons paprika	
1 teaspoon cayenne pepper	
12 ounces beer, preferably lager (1 ½ cups)	1 5-pound bone-in Boston butt (*see Shopping Tip*)
¾ cup ketchup	

MAKEOVER TIP

EVEN DECADENT-SOUNDING FOODS LIKE PULLED PORK CAN STAY ON THE MENU AS LONG AS YOU KEEP THE PORTION SIZE IN CHECK. A HEALTHY PORTION SIZE FOR MEAT IS 3 OUNCES (COOKED), OR ABOUT THE SIZE OF A DECK OF CARDS. FOR MORE ABOUT PORTION SIZE, SEE PAGE 18.

1. Preheat oven to 300°F. Heat oil in a large Dutch oven over medium-low heat. Add onions and cook, stirring occasionally, until lightly browned and very soft, about 20 minutes.

2. Increase heat to high; add chili powder, cumin, paprika and cayenne and cook, stirring, until fragrant, 1 minute. Add beer, ketchup, vinegar, mustard, tomato paste, chipotle pepper and adobo sauce; bring to a boil. Reduce heat to medium-low and simmer, uncovered, stirring occasionally, until the sauce is slightly thickened, 10 minutes. Meanwhile, trim all visible fat from the pork.

3. Remove the pan from the heat and add the pork, spooning sauce over it. Cover the pan, transfer to the oven and bake for 1½ hours. Turn the pork over, cover, and bake for 1½ hours more. Uncover and bake until a fork inserted into the meat turns easily, 1 to 2 hours more.

4. Transfer the pork to a large bowl and cover with foil. Pour the sauce into a large measuring cup or glass bowl and refrigerate until the fat and sauce begin to separate, 15 minutes. Skim off the fat. Return the sauce to the pan and heat over medium-high until hot, about 4 minutes.

5. Remove the bone and any remaining pieces of fat from the meat. The bone should easily slip away from the tender meat. Pull the pork apart into long shreds using two forks. Add the hot sauce to the meat; stir to combine. Serve hot.

MAKES 12 SERVINGS, 3 OUNCES EACH.

PER SERVING: 283 calories; 13 g fat (4 g sat, 6 g mono); 97 mg cholesterol; 10 g carbohydrate; 29 g protein; 2 g fiber; 489 mg sodium; 529 mg potassium.

NUTRITION BONUS: Selenium (46% daily value), Zinc (29% dv), Vitamin A (17% dv), Potassium (15% dv).

EATINGWELL SLOPPY JOES

H✕W   H⬆F   H♥H

ACTIVE TIME: 35 MINUTES | **TOTAL:** 45 MINUTES
TO MAKE AHEAD: The filling will keep in the freezer for up to 1 month.

Forget the school-lunch standard you may remember from your childhood. Our updated Sloppy Joe takes lean ground beef and adds chopped cremini mushrooms and diced fresh plum tomatoes, all in a zesty sauce. Served on a whole-wheat bun, it's a hearty dinner sandwich that will please adults and kids alike.

12 ounces 90%-lean ground beef	½ cup water
1 large onion, finely diced	¼ cup cider vinegar
2 cups finely chopped cremini mushrooms (about 4 ounces)	¼ cup chili sauce, such as Heinz
5 plum tomatoes, diced	¼ cup ketchup
2 tablespoons all-purpose flour	8 whole-wheat hamburger buns, toasted if desired

1. Crumble beef into a large nonstick skillet; cook over medium heat until it starts to sizzle, about 1 minute. Add onion and mushrooms and cook, stirring occasionally, breaking up the meat with a wooden spoon, until the vegetables are soft and the moisture has evaporated, 8 to 10 minutes.

2. Add tomatoes and flour; stir to combine. Stir in water, vinegar, chili sauce and ketchup and bring to a simmer, stirring often. Reduce heat to a low simmer and cook, stirring occasionally, until the sauce is thickened and the onion is very tender, 8 to 10 minutes. Serve warm on buns.

MAKES 8 SERVINGS, GENEROUS ½ CUP FILLING EACH.

PER SERVING: 233 calories; 6 g fat (2 g sat, 2 g mono); 28 mg cholesterol; 31 g carbohydrate; 14 g protein; 5 g fiber; 436 mg sodium; 504 mg potassium.

NUTRITION BONUS: Zinc (20% daily value), Vitamin C (15% dv).

MAKEOVER TIP

"WHEAT" BUNS MAY SOUND HEALTHY, BUT THEY ARE OFTEN MADE WITH REFINED FLOUR. LOOK FOR "WHOLE-WHEAT" AND CHECK THE INGREDIENT LIST— THE FIRST INGREDIENT IN WHOLE-WHEAT BUNS SHOULD BE WHOLE-WHEAT FLOUR.

PHILLY CHEESE STEAK SANDWICH

H ↑ F

ACTIVE TIME: 35 MINUTES | **TOTAL:** 35 MINUTES

You may be wondering whether we kept the Cheez Whiz that's often served in this staple from the city of brotherly love…and the answer is no. But the rest of the good stuff, from thin-sliced steak, onions, peppers and mushrooms to slightly-less-gooey but more flavorful provolone cheese, is all there. We adore spicy banana peppers as a topping, but omit them if you can do without the heat.

2 teaspoons extra-virgin olive oil
1 medium onion, sliced
8 ounces mushrooms, sliced
1 red *or* green bell pepper, sliced
2 tablespoons minced fresh oregano *or*
2 teaspoons dried
½ teaspoon freshly ground pepper
1 pound sirloin steak, trimmed and thinly sliced
(*see Kitchen Tip*)

½ teaspoon salt
1 tablespoon all-purpose flour
½ cup sliced hot banana peppers (optional)
¼ cup reduced-sodium chicken broth
3 ounces thinly sliced reduced-fat provolone cheese
4 whole-wheat buns, split and toasted

KITCHEN TIP:

It is easiest to cut meat into thin slices if it is partially frozen. If you have time, freeze it for 20 minutes before slicing.

1. Heat oil in a large nonstick skillet over medium-high heat. Add onion and cook, stirring often, until soft and beginning to brown, 2 to 3 minutes. Add mushrooms, bell pepper, oregano and pepper and cook, stirring often, until the vegetables are wilted and soft, about 7 minutes. Add steak and salt and cook, stirring, until the meat is just cooked through, about 4 minutes.
2. Reduce heat to low. Sprinkle the vegetables and meat with flour; stir to coat. Stir in banana peppers (if using) and broth; bring to a simmer. Remove from the heat; lay cheese slices on top of the vegetables and meat, cover and let stand until melted, 1 to 2 minutes.
3. Divide into 4 portions with a spatula, leaving the melted cheese layer on top. Scoop a portion onto each bun and serve immediately.

MAKES 4 SERVINGS.

PER SERVING: 440 calories; 15 g fat (6 g sat, 6 g mono); 74 mg cholesterol; 31 g carbohydrate; 45 g protein; 5 g fiber; 766 mg sodium; 875 mg potassium.

NUTRITION BONUS: Vitamin C (72% daily value), Calcium & Potassium (25% dv), Iron (22% dv), Vitamin A (21% dv).

MONTE CRISTO

ACTIVE TIME: 30 MINUTES | **TOTAL:** 30 MINUTES

If you're not familiar with the Monte Cristo sandwich, think of it as a cross between a ham-and-cheese sandwich and deep-fried French toast. It's especially tasty with the currant or raspberry jam it's usually served with. We forgo the deep frying for a quick turn in a skillet with a bit of oil until the cheese is melted and the bread is golden.

1 large egg
3 large egg whites
¼ cup low-fat milk
   Pinch of ground nutmeg
8 teaspoons raspberry jam

8 slices whole-wheat sandwich bread
4 thin slices roasted deli turkey (about 4 ounces)
4 thin slices deli ham (about 4 ounces)
1 cup finely shredded Swiss cheese

1. Preheat oven to 275°F. Set a wire rack on a baking sheet and lightly coat with cooking spray. Place the baking sheet in the oven.

2. Whisk egg, egg whites, milk and nutmeg in a shallow dish until combined.

3. Spread 1 teaspoon jam on each slice of bread. Divide turkey, ham and cheese evenly among 4 slices. Top each sandwich with another slice of bread, jam-side down.

4. Coat a large nonstick skillet with cooking spray and heat over medium-low heat. Dip 2 sandwiches into the egg mixture, making sure to coat both sides. Place the battered sandwiches in the pan, cover and cook until browned and the cheese is melted, 3 to 5 minutes per side. Transfer to the oven to keep warm. Repeat with the remaining 2 sandwiches. Serve warm.

MAKES 4 SERVINGS.

PER SERVING: 355 calories; 11 g fat (5 g sat, 3 g mono); 106 mg cholesterol; 35 g carbohydrate; 29 g protein; 4 g fiber; 719 mg sodium; 213 mg potassium.

NUTRITION BONUS: Selenium (50% daily value), Calcium (25% dv).

CHICKEN-FRIED STEAK & GRAVY

H✕W L↓C H♥H

ACTIVE TIME: 35 MINUTES | **TOTAL:** 35 MINUTES

Can you really make a chicken-fried steak that isn't loaded with saturated fat and salt? Absolutely. We skip the deep frying, but with rich country gravy as consolation, you won't miss it. Our pan-fried, crispy cube steak has less than one-third of the fat and about 80 percent less sodium.

¼ cup all-purpose flour
2 large egg whites, lightly beaten
¼ cup cornmeal
¼ cup whole-wheat flour
¼ cup plus 1 tablespoon cornstarch, divided
1 teaspoon paprika
1 pound cube steak, cut into 4 portions

¾ teaspoon kosher salt, divided
½ teaspoon freshly ground pepper
2 tablespoons canola oil, divided
1 14-ounce can reduced-sodium beef broth
1 tablespoon water
¼ cup half-and-half

1. Preheat oven to 350°F. Coat a baking sheet with cooking spray.

2. Place all-purpose flour on a large plate. Place egg whites in a shallow dish. Whisk cornmeal, whole-wheat flour, ¼ cup cornstarch and paprika in another shallow dish. Season both sides of steak with ½ teaspoon each salt and pepper. Dredge the steak in the flour, shaking off excess; dip in the egg whites, then dredge in the cornmeal mixture.

3. Heat 1 tablespoon oil in a large nonstick skillet over medium-high heat. Reduce heat to medium and add 2 pieces of the steak; cook until browned on both sides, turning once, 3 to 5 minutes total. Transfer the steak to the prepared baking sheet and repeat with the remaining 1 tablespoon oil and 2 pieces of steak. Transfer the baking sheet to the oven and bake until cooked through, about 10 minutes.

4. Meanwhile, add broth to the pan and boil over medium-high heat, stirring occasionally, until reduced to about 1 cup, 3 to 5 minutes. Whisk water and the remaining 1 tablespoon cornstarch until smooth. Remove the pan from the heat and stir in the cornstarch mixture. Return to the heat and cook, stirring, until thickened, 1 to 2 minutes. Stir in half-and-half; season with the remaining ¼ teaspoon salt and pepper. Serve the steak topped with the gravy.

MAKES 4 SERVINGS.

PER SERVING: 315 calories; 13 g fat (3 g sat, 7 g mono); 57 mg cholesterol; 14 g carbohydrate; 33 g protein; 1 g fiber; 312 mg sodium; 379 mg potassium.

NUTRITION BONUS: Selenium (50% daily value), Potassium & Zinc (15% dv).

GOLDEN BAKED PORK CUTLETS

H✕W L↓C H♥H

ACTIVE TIME: 15 MINUTES | **TOTAL:** 35 MINUTES

We love the taste of Shake 'N Bake but wanted a more wholesome homemade version. These quick breaded pork cutlets made with just a few ingredients are so delicious everyone will be wishing they helped make them. Cutting the super-low-fat pork tenderloin into long fillets makes it quick-cooking. Serve with a medley of steamed vegetables and a side of mashed potatoes for a taste of nostalgia.

1 pound pork tenderloin, trimmed	1/2 teaspoon onion powder
1/2 cup dry breadcrumbs, preferably whole-wheat (*see Tip, page 246*)	1/2 teaspoon salt
1 teaspoon sugar	4 teaspoons canola oil
1/2 teaspoon paprika	1 large egg white, lightly beaten
	4 teaspoons cornstarch

1. Preheat oven to 400°F. Coat a rimmed baking sheet with cooking spray.

2. Holding a chef's knife at a 45° angle and perpendicular to the tenderloin, slice the pork into 4 long, thin "fillets."

3. Mix breadcrumbs, sugar, paprika, onion powder and salt in a shallow dish. Drizzle with oil and mash with a fork until the oil is thoroughly incorporated. Lightly beat egg white with a fork in another shallow dish. Sprinkle cornstarch over the pork slices and pat to coat evenly on both sides. Dip the pork into the egg, then press into the breading mixture until evenly coated on both sides. (Discard leftover mixture.)

4. Place the pork on the prepared baking sheet. Bake until just barely pink in the center and an instant-read thermometer registers 145°F, 14 to 16 minutes.

MAKES 4 SERVINGS.

PER SERVING: 220 calories; 7 g fat (1 g sat, 4 g mono); 74 mg cholesterol; 11 g carbohydrate; 26 g protein; 1 g fiber; 377 mg sodium; 475 mg potassium.

NUTRITION BONUS: Selenium (50% daily value).

MINI SHEPHERD'S PIES

H✣W   H↑F

ACTIVE TIME: 30 MINUTES | **TOTAL:** 40 MINUTES
EQUIPMENT: Four 10-ounce broiler-safe ramekins

EATINGWELL's take on Shepherd's Pie is baked in individual ramekins to guarantee perfectly sized servings and help you get it on the table fast. Replacing the potato topping with convenient, delicious frozen squash puree increases the vitamin A.

2 teaspoons extra-virgin olive oil	6 ounces baby spinach, chopped
½ cup chopped onion	¾ teaspoon salt, divided
12 ounces 93%-lean ground beef	½ teaspoon garlic powder, divided
2 tablespoons all-purpose flour	2 12-ounce packages frozen winter squash
1 tablespoon tomato paste	puree, thawed
1 cup reduced-sodium beef broth	⅓ cup finely shredded Parmesan cheese

1. Position rack in upper third of oven; preheat broiler.

2. Heat oil in a large skillet over medium-high heat. Add onion and cook, stirring, until beginning to soften, about 2 minutes. Reduce heat to medium, stir in beef, flour and tomato paste, and cook, stirring, until the beef is mostly browned, about 3 minutes. Add broth, scraping up any browned bits with a wooden spoon. Bring to a boil and cook, stirring occasionally, until the broth is the consistency of thick gravy, about 4 minutes. Stir in spinach, ¼ teaspoon salt and ¼ teaspoon garlic powder; cook until the spinach is just wilted, about 1 minute. Remove from the heat.

3. Place squash in a fine-mesh sieve and gently press on it to extract excess liquid. Transfer to a bowl. Stir in the remaining ½ teaspoon salt and ¼ teaspoon garlic powder. Divide the meat mixture among four 10-ounce broiler-safe ramekins. Top each with about ½ cup of the squash. Place the ramekins on a baking sheet.

4. Broil until heated through and bubbling around the edges, about 10 minutes. Sprinkle with cheese and broil until it is just melted, about 3 minutes more.

MAKES 4 SERVINGS.

PER SERVING: 336 calories; 13 g fat (5 g sat, 3 g mono); 70 mg cholesterol; 26 g carbohydrate; 29 g protein; 5 g fiber; 708 mg sodium; 421 mg potassium.

NUTRITION BONUS: Vitamin A (175% daily value), Vitamin C (50% dv), Zinc (33% dv), Calcium (15% dv).

CREAMY HAMBURGER NOODLE CASSEROLE

H ⬆ F

ACTIVE TIME: 30 MINUTES | **TOTAL:** 1 HOUR 25 MINUTES

If you've been missing the gooey goodness that a boxed "helper" lends to hamburger, grab a fork. The EATINGWELL Test Kitchen takes lean ground beef and combines it with whole-grain bulgur, egg noodles and a creamy tomato sauce in a baked casserole topped with Cheddar. With less fat and calories than the original skillet meal, this dish is sure to become a new family favorite.

2	bunches scallions, trimmed	¼	teaspoon salt, divided
8	ounces 90%-lean ground beef		Freshly ground pepper to taste
1½	teaspoons canola oil	6	ounces no-yolk whole-wheat egg noodles
½	cup bulgur (*see Ingredient Note, page 247*)	1	cup low-fat cottage cheese
2	cloves garlic, minced	1	cup reduced-fat sour cream
2	8-ounce cans tomato sauce	¼	cup shredded extra-sharp Cheddar cheese
½	cup water		

1. Preheat oven to 350°F. Coat a 2-quart baking dish with cooking spray. Put a large pot of water on to boil.

2. Separate white and green parts of scallions; thinly slice and reserve separately.

3. Cook beef in a large skillet over medium-high heat, breaking up clumps with a wooden spoon, until no longer pink, 3 to 5 minutes. Transfer to a plate lined with paper towels.

4. Wipe out the pan, add oil and reduce heat to medium-low. Add bulgur, garlic and the reserved scallion whites. Cook, stirring, until the scallions soften, 5 to 7 minutes. Add tomato sauce, water and the beef; bring to a simmer. Cover and simmer gently until the bulgur is tender and the sauce is thickened, 15 to 20 minutes. Season with ⅛ teaspoon salt and pepper.

5. Meanwhile, cook noodles until just tender, 6 to 8 minutes or according to package directions. Drain and rinse under cold water.

6. Puree cottage cheese in a food processor until smooth. Transfer to a medium bowl; fold in sour cream and the reserved scallion greens. Season with the remaining ⅛ teaspoon salt and pepper.

7. Spread half the noodles in the prepared pan. Top with half the cottage cheese mixture and half the meat sauce. Repeat with the remaining noodles, cottage cheese and sauce. Sprinkle Cheddar over the top.

8. Bake the casserole until bubbly, 30 to 40 minutes. Let stand for 10 minutes before serving.

MAKES 6 SERVINGS.

PER SERVING: 377 calories; 14 g fat (7 g sat, 4 g mono); 52 mg cholesterol; 41 g carbohydrate; 22 g protein; 5 g fiber; 757 mg sodium; 631 mg potassium.

NUTRITION BONUS: Calcium, Iron & Vitamin C (20% daily value), Magnesium (17% dv), Vitamin A (15% dv).

RIGATONI & SPICY SAUSAGE CASSEROLE

H ↑ F

ACTIVE TIME: 30 MINUTES | **TOTAL:** 1 HOUR

Mushrooms have the perfect meaty texture to complement a modest amount of spicy Italian sausage in this baked rigatoni that has less than one-quarter the fat of the original. Whole-wheat pasta rather than white pasta makes our version a fiber powerhouse with 7 grams per serving. This delicious and cheesy pasta casserole freezes well so you might want to make an extra to have on hand for a ready-to-heat-and-eat meal.

4 ounces hot Italian sausage (2 links)	½ teaspoon salt, divided
1 teaspoon extra-virgin olive oil	Freshly ground pepper to taste
1 large onion, chopped	12 ounces whole-wheat rigatoni, mostaccioli *or* penne
3 cloves garlic, very finely chopped	½ cup part-skim ricotta cheese
8 ounces mushrooms, sliced	¾ cup fresh breadcrumbs, preferably whole-wheat (*see Tip, page 246*)
1 teaspoon crumbled dried rosemary	¼ cup freshly grated Parmesan cheese
2 14-ounce cans diced tomatoes *or* plum tomatoes (chopped)	
¼ cup dry red *or* white wine	

1. Preheat oven to 400°F. Coat a 3-quart shallow baking dish with cooking spray. Put a large pot of water on to boil.

2. Crumble sausage into a large nonstick skillet (discard casing) and cook over medium heat, stirring, until browned and cooked through, 5 to 7 minutes. Transfer to a plate lined with paper towels to drain.

3. Wipe out the pan and add oil; heat over medium-high heat. Add onion and cook, stirring occasionally, until softened, about 5 minutes. Add garlic and cook, stirring, for 1 minute. Add mushrooms and rosemary; cook, stirring, until the mushrooms begin to give off liquid, about 3 minutes. Stir in tomatoes (and their juices), wine and the cooked sausage. Bring to a simmer and cook, uncovered, for 5 minutes. (The sauce will be quite thin.) Season with ¼ teaspoon salt and pepper.

4. Meanwhile, cook pasta until just tender, 8 to 10 minutes or according to package directions. Drain.

5. Add the pasta to the sauce; toss to coat. Spread half in the prepared baking dish. Dot with spoonfuls of ricotta and top with the remaining pasta. Cover with foil. Bake for 20 minutes.

6. Combine breadcrumbs and Parmesan in a small bowl. Season with the remaining ¼ teaspoon salt and pepper. Sprinkle the breadcrumb mixture over the pasta and continue to bake, uncovered, until the top is golden, about 10 minutes more.

MAKES 6 SERVINGS.

PER SERVING: 392 calories; 12 g fat (4 g sat, 4 g mono); 24 mg cholesterol; 53 g carbohydrate; 19 g protein; 7 g fiber; 446 mg sodium; 266 mg potassium.

GRILLED FILET MIGNON WITH HERB BUTTER & TEXAS TOASTS

H✕W L↓C H↑F

ACTIVE TIME: 45 MINUTES | **TOTAL:** 45 MINUTES
TO MAKE AHEAD: Prepare herb butter (STEP 2), wrap in plastic wrap and freeze for up to 1 month.

This dish is simply luxurious: grilled beef tenderloin smothered in a vibrant herb butter served on top of a garlicky slab of whole-grain toast. And yes, with only about 303 calories and 14 grams of fat total, this steak-house-worthy entree can be part of a healthy diet. If you like, make extra herb butter to top chicken, fish or even a grilled pork chop.

1 tablespoon whipped *or* regular butter, slightly softened
3 teaspoons extra-virgin olive oil, divided
1 tablespoon minced fresh chives *or* shallot
1 tablespoon capers, rinsed and chopped
3 teaspoons minced fresh marjoram *or* oregano, divided
1 teaspoon freshly grated lemon zest, divided
1 teaspoon lemon juice

¾ teaspoon kosher salt, divided
½ teaspoon freshly ground pepper, divided
1 tablespoon minced fresh rosemary
2 cloves garlic (1 minced, 1 peeled and halved)
1 pound filet mignon, about 1 ½ inches thick, trimmed and cut into 4 portions
4 slices whole-grain bread
4 cups watercress, trimmed and chopped

1. Preheat grill to high.
2. Mash butter in a small bowl with the back of a spoon until soft and creamy. Stir in 2 teaspoons oil until combined. Add chives (or shallot), capers, 1 teaspoon marjoram (or oregano), ½ teaspoon lemon zest, lemon juice, ½ teaspoon salt and ¼ teaspoon pepper. Cover and place in the freezer to chill.
3. Combine the remaining 1 teaspoon oil, 2 teaspoons marjoram (or oregano), ½ teaspoon lemon zest, ¼ teaspoon salt and pepper, rosemary and minced garlic in a small bowl. Rub on both sides of steak. Rub both sides of bread with the halved garlic clove; discard the garlic.
4. Grill the steak 3 to 5 minutes per side for medium-rare. Grill the bread until toasted, 30 seconds to 1 minute per side. Divide watercress among 4 plates. Place 1 toast on each serving of watercress and top with steak. Spread the herb butter on top of the steaks and let rest for 5 minutes before serving.

MAKES 4 SERVINGS.

PER SERVING: 303 calories; 14 g fat (5 g sat, 6 g mono); 80 mg cholesterol; 15 g carbohydrate; 29 g protein; 5 g fiber; 438 mg sodium; 462 mg potassium.

NUTRITION BONUS: Zinc (46% daily value), Selenium (44% dv), Vitamin C (28% dv), Iron (17% dv).

MAKEOVER TIP

TRY MAKING COMPOUND BUTTER—A BLEND OF BUTTER AND SEASONING—WITH HALF OLIVE OIL AND HALF BUTTER TO REDUCE THE SATURATED FAT. IT'S GREAT SERVED ON TOP OF STEAK, CHICKEN OR VEGETABLES.

BEEF & PORTOBELLO MUSHROOM STROGANOFF

L ↓ C

ACTIVE TIME: 40 MINUTES | **TOTAL:** 40 MINUTES

Flank steak plus a rich-tasting sauce made with a touch of cognac and reduced-fat sour cream combine in this healthy update that would be sure to please even Count Stroganov. Thin slices of portobello mushrooms add to the meatiness of the dish. Serve over whole-wheat egg noodles.

2   teaspoons plus 1 tablespoon canola oil, divided
1   pound flank steak, trimmed
4   large portobello mushrooms, stemmed, halved and thinly sliced
1   large onion, sliced
¾   teaspoon dried thyme
½   teaspoon salt

½   teaspoon freshly ground pepper
3   tablespoons all-purpose flour
1   14-ounce can reduced-sodium beef broth
2   tablespoons cognac *or* brandy
1   tablespoon red-wine vinegar
½   cup reduced-fat sour cream
4   tablespoons chopped fresh chives *or* parsley

MAKEOVER TIP

SUBSTITUTE MEATY PORTOBELLO MUSHROOMS FOR SOME OF THE BEEF IN DISHES LIKE BEEF STROGANOFF. THE EXTRA VEGETABLES KEEP THE SERVINGS HEARTY AND THE MEAT PORTION SIZE IN CHECK.

1. Heat 2 teaspoons oil in a large skillet over high heat until shimmering but not smoking. Add steak and cook until browned on both sides, 3 to 4 minutes per side. (The meat will be rare, but will continue to cook as it rests.) Transfer to a cutting board and let rest for 5 minutes. Cut lengthwise into 2 long pieces then crosswise, across the grain, into ¼-inch-thick slices.
2. Heat the remaining 1 tablespoon oil in the pan over medium heat. Add mushrooms, onion, thyme, salt and pepper and cook, stirring often, until the vegetables are very tender and lightly browned, 8 to 12 minutes. Sprinkle flour over the vegetables; stir to coat. Stir in broth, cognac (or brandy) and vinegar and bring to a boil, stirring often. Reduce heat to a simmer, and continue cooking, stirring often, until the mixture is thickened, about 3 minutes. Stir in sour cream, chives (or parsley), the sliced steak and any accumulated juices. Bring to a simmer and cook, stirring, until heated through, 1 to 2 minutes more.

MAKES 4 SERVINGS, 1½ CUPS EACH.

PER SERVING: 404 calories; 19 g fat (7 g sat, 8 g mono); 74 mg cholesterol; 14 g carbohydrate; 37 g protein; 2 g fiber; 426 mg sodium; 969 mg potassium.

NUTRITION BONUS: Selenium & Zinc (43% daily value), Potassium (28% dv), Iron (17% dv).

IRISH LAMB STEW

H✖W H♥H

ACTIVE TIME: 30 MINUTES | **TOTAL:** 8½ HOURS
TO MAKE AHEAD: Cover and refrigerate for up to 2 days or freeze for up to 1 month.
EQUIPMENT: 6-quart slow cooker

This is Emerald Isle penicillin: a rich stew that'll cure whatever ails you. In traditional fashion, nothing here is browned first, just all stewed together. To keep it healthy make sure to trim the lamb of any visible fat before you cook it.

2 pounds boneless leg of lamb, trimmed and cut into 1-inch pieces
1¾ pounds white potatoes, peeled and cut into 1-inch pieces
3 large leeks, white part only, halved, washed (*see Tip, page 246*) and thinly sliced
3 large carrots, peeled and cut into 1-inch pieces

3 stalks celery, thinly sliced
1 14-ounce can reduced-sodium chicken broth
2 teaspoons chopped fresh thyme
1 teaspoon salt
1 teaspoon freshly ground pepper
¼ cup packed fresh parsley leaves, chopped

Combine lamb, potatoes, leeks, carrots, celery, broth, thyme, salt and pepper in a 6-quart slow cooker; stir to combine. Put the lid on and cook on low until the lamb is fork-tender, about 8 hours. Stir in parsley before serving.

MAKES 8 SERVINGS, GENEROUS 1 CUP EACH.

PER SERVING: 266 calories; 7 g fat (2 g sat, 3 g mono); 65 mg cholesterol; 27 g carbohydrate; 23 g protein; 4 g fiber; 427 mg sodium; 803 mg potassium.

NUTRITION BONUS: Vitamin A (139% daily value), Vitamin C (26% dv), Potassium (23% dv), Folate & Iron (15% dv).

MINT-PESTO RUBBED LEG OF LAMB

H✴W L⬇C H♥H

ACTIVE TIME: 30 MINUTES | **TOTAL:** 2 HOURS
EQUIPMENT: Kitchen string

If you think lamb is too fatty, think again. In reality leg of lamb is relatively lean—a 3-ounce serving can contain as little as 7 grams of fat, about the same as top sirloin steak. Here, we make a roulade filled and coated with fresh mint pesto, which is a refreshing alternative to the traditional mint jelly that often accompanies lamb. **SHOPPING TIP:** Have your butcher "butterfly" a boneless leg of lamb (that is, open it up to a large, flat cut of meat); ask that any visible fat be trimmed off.

½ cup packed fresh basil leaves
¼ cup packed fresh mint leaves
¼ cup packed fresh parsley leaves
2 tablespoons toasted pine nuts (*see Tip, page 247*)
2 tablespoons grated Parmigiano-Reggiano cheese

2 tablespoons extra-virgin olive oil
1 clove garlic, peeled
1 teaspoon salt, divided
½ teaspoon freshly ground pepper
1 3½-pound boneless leg of lamb, butterflied (*see Shopping Tip*) and trimmed

1. Preheat oven to 350°F.
2. Place basil, mint, parsley, pine nuts, cheese, oil, garlic, ½ teaspoon salt and pepper in a food processor and process until fairly smooth. Sprinkle lamb all over with the remaining ½ teaspoon salt. Reserve 2 tablespoons of the pesto; spread the rest over the top side of the lamb and roll it closed. (It will not be a perfect cylinder.) Tie kitchen string around the roast in five places; do not tie too tightly or the pesto will squeeze out. Rub the reserved pesto over the outside of the lamb and place in a roasting pan.
3. Roast the lamb until a thermometer inserted into the thickest part registers 140°F for medium-rare, about 1 hour 20 minutes. Transfer to a cutting board; let rest for 10 minutes. Carve the lamb, leaving the string in place to help hold the roast together.

MAKES ABOUT 12 SERVINGS.

PER 3-OUNCE SERVING: 192 calories; 10 g fat (3 g sat, 5 g mono); 76 mg cholesterol; 1 g carbohydrate; 25 g protein; 0 g fiber; 228 mg sodium; 313 mg potassium.

NUTRITION BONUS: Selenium (37% daily value), Zinc (29% dv).

TUSCAN PORK LOIN

H)(W L↓C H♥H

ACTIVE TIME: 25 MINUTES | **TOTAL:** 2 HOURS 20 MINUTES (INCLUDING 1 HOUR MARINATING TIME)
EQUIPMENT: Kitchen string

Roasted pork loin is a staple of Italian cooking. In this recipe we coat the lean meat with garlic, rosemary and aromatic lemon zest before it goes in the oven, and then deglaze the pan with vermouth to make a savory gravy. The roast is perfect for entertaining but equally at home for a Sunday family supper.

1	3-pound pork loin, trimmed	2	tablespoons chopped fresh rosemary
1	teaspoon kosher salt	1	tablespoon freshly grated lemon zest
3	cloves garlic, crushed and peeled	¾	cup dry vermouth *or* white wine
2	tablespoons extra-virgin olive oil	2	tablespoons white-wine vinegar

1. Tie kitchen string around pork in three places so it doesn't flatten while roasting. Place salt and garlic in a small bowl and mash with the back of a spoon to form a paste. Stir in oil, rosemary and lemon zest; rub the mixture into the pork. Refrigerate, uncovered, for 1 hour.

2. Preheat oven to 375°F.

3. Place the pork in a roasting pan. Roast, turning once or twice, until a thermometer inserted into the thickest part registers 145°F, 40 to 50 minutes. Transfer to a cutting board; let rest for 10 minutes.

4. Meanwhile, add vermouth (or wine) and vinegar to the roasting pan and place over medium-high heat. Bring to a simmer and cook, scraping up any browned bits, until the sauce is reduced by half, 2 to 4 minutes. Remove the string and slice the roast. Add any accumulated juices to the sauce and serve with the pork.

MAKES ABOUT 10 SERVINGS.

PER 3-OUNCE SERVING: 221 calories; 11 g fat (3 g sat, 6 g mono); 69 mg cholesterol; 1 g carbohydrate; 24 g protein; 0 g fiber; 156 mg sodium; 368 mg potassium.

NUTRITION BONUS: Thiamin (58% daily value), Selenium (50% dv).

Oven-Fried Chicken (page 121)

CHICKEN & TURKEY

DELICIOUS FEEDBACK

Almond-Crusted Chicken Fingers

"I am pregnant and have been craving chicken fingers (something I *never* eat!) but do not want the kind in restaurants with all the trans fats. My husband made these for me and I loved them! I think I'll keep eating them even when the cravings go!"

—Anonymous, Austin, TX

King Ranch Casserole

"This recipe will replace my old one (with soups)—it is fabulous! Wonderful combo of seasonings, too! Kudos to the chef! This one's a keeper!"

—Marilyn, Flower Mound, TX

ALMOND-CRUSTED CHICKEN FINGERS

H✳W L↓C H♥H

ACTIVE TIME: 20 MINUTES | **TOTAL:** 40 MINUTES

How do you avoid the fast-food trap? Simple: make it better yourself, like these family-friendly chicken fingers. Instead of batter-dipped, deep-fried nuggets, we coat chicken tenders in a seasoned almond and whole-wheat flour crust and then oven-fry them to perfection. With half the fat of standard breaded chicken tenders, you can enjoy to your (healthy) heart's content.

Canola oil cooking spray
½ cup sliced almonds
¼ cup whole-wheat flour
1 ½ teaspoons paprika
½ teaspoon garlic powder
½ teaspoon dry mustard
¼ teaspoon salt
⅛ teaspoon freshly ground pepper
1 ½ teaspoons extra-virgin olive oil
4 large egg whites
1 pound chicken tenders (*see Ingredient Note, page 247*)

MAKEOVER TIP

ADDING GROUND ALMONDS TO BREADING, AS WE DO WITH THESE CHICKEN FINGERS, ADDS CRUNCHY TEXTURE AND A BOOST OF HEART-HEALTHY UNSATURATED FAT.

1. Preheat oven to 475°F. Line a baking sheet with foil. Set a wire rack on the baking sheet and coat it with cooking spray.

2. Place almonds, flour, paprika, garlic powder, dry mustard, salt and pepper in a food processor; process until the almonds are finely chopped and the paprika is mixed throughout, about 1 minute. With the motor running, drizzle in oil; process until combined. Transfer the mixture to a shallow dish.

3. Whisk egg whites in a second shallow dish. Add chicken tenders and turn to coat. Transfer each tender to the almond mixture; turn to coat evenly. (Discard any remaining egg white and almond mixture.) Place the tenders on the prepared rack and coat with cooking spray; turn and spray the other side.

4. Bake the chicken fingers until golden brown, crispy and no longer pink in the center, 20 to 25 minutes.

MAKES 4 SERVINGS.

PER SERVING: 174 calories; 4 g fat (1 g sat, 2 g mono); 66 mg cholesterol; 4 g carbohydrate; 27 g protein; 1 g fiber; 254 mg sodium; 76 mg potassium.

NUTRITION BONUS: Selenium (28% daily value).

OVEN-FRIED CHICKEN

H✴W L↓C H♥H

ACTIVE TIME: 20 MINUTES | **TOTAL:** 1 HOUR 35 MINUTES (INCLUDING 30 MINUTES MARINATING TIME)
TO MAKE AHEAD: Marinate the chicken for up to 8 hours.

Great news—crunchy, flavorful fried chicken can be healthy. We marinate skinless chicken in buttermilk to keep it juicy. A light coating of flour, sesame seeds and spices, misted with olive oil, forms an appealing crust during baking. And with only 7 grams of fat per serving rather than the 20 in typical fried chicken—that *is* good news. (*Photograph: page 118.*)

½ cup nonfat buttermilk (*see Tip, page 246*)	2 tablespoons sesame seeds
1 tablespoon Dijon mustard	1½ teaspoons paprika
2 cloves garlic, minced	1 teaspoon dried thyme
1 teaspoon hot sauce	1 teaspoon baking powder
2½-3 pounds whole chicken legs, skin removed, trimmed and cut into thighs and drumsticks	⅛ teaspoon salt
	Freshly ground pepper to taste
½ cup whole-wheat flour	Olive oil cooking spray

1. Whisk buttermilk, mustard, garlic and hot sauce in a shallow glass dish until well blended. Add chicken and turn to coat. Cover and marinate in the refrigerator for at least 30 minutes or for up to 8 hours.

2. Preheat oven to 425°F. Line a baking sheet with foil. Set a wire rack on the baking sheet and coat it with cooking spray.

3. Whisk flour, sesame seeds, paprika, thyme, baking powder, salt and pepper in a small bowl. Place the flour mixture in a paper bag or large sealable plastic bag. Shaking off excess marinade, place one or two pieces of chicken at a time in the bag and shake to coat. Shake off excess flour and place the chicken on the prepared rack. (Discard any leftover flour mixture and marinade.) Spray the chicken pieces with cooking spray.

4. Bake the chicken until golden brown and no longer pink in the center, 40 to 50 minutes.

MAKES 4 SERVINGS.

PER SERVING: 226 calories; 7 g fat (2 g sat, 2 g mono); 130 mg cholesterol; 5 g carbohydrate; 34 g protein; 1 g fiber; 258 mg sodium; 400 mg potassium.

MAKEOVER TIP

REMOVING THE SKIN FROM CHICKEN SAVES 4 GRAMS OF FAT AND 1 GRAM OF SATURATED FAT FOR EACH 3-OUNCE SERVING.

CHICKEN PICCATA WITH PASTA & MUSHROOMS

H↑F H♥H

ACTIVE TIME: 40 MINUTES | **TOTAL:** 40 MINUTES

Lemony Italian piccata sauce is often made with a stick (or more) of butter. Our chicken piccata, served over whole-wheat pasta, has a rich lemon-caper sauce that's made with extra-virgin olive oil and only a touch of butter for flavor. If you like, you can use a mild fish like tilapia or even shrimp instead of chicken breast.

6	ounces whole-wheat angel hair pasta	1	10-ounce package mushrooms, sliced
1/3	cup all-purpose flour, divided	3	large cloves garlic, minced
2	cups reduced-sodium chicken broth	1/2	cup white wine
1/2	teaspoon salt, divided	2	tablespoons lemon juice
1/4	teaspoon freshly ground pepper	1/4	cup chopped fresh parsley
4	chicken cutlets (3/4-1 pound total), trimmed	2	tablespoons capers, rinsed
3	teaspoons extra-virgin olive oil, divided	2	teaspoons butter

1. Bring a large pot of water to a boil. Add pasta and cook until just tender, 4 to 6 minutes or according to package directions. Drain and rinse.

2. Meanwhile, whisk 5 teaspoons flour and broth in a small bowl until smooth. Place the remaining flour in a shallow dish. Season chicken with 1/4 teaspoon salt and pepper and dredge both sides in the flour. Heat 2 teaspoons oil in a large nonstick skillet over medium heat. Add the chicken and cook until browned and no longer pink in the middle, 2 to 3 minutes per side. Transfer to a plate; cover and keep warm.

3. Heat the remaining 1 teaspoon oil in the pan over medium-high heat. Add mushrooms and cook, stirring, until they release their juices and begin to brown, about 5 minutes. Transfer to a plate. Add garlic and wine to the pan and cook until reduced by half, 1 to 2 minutes. Stir in the reserved broth-flour mixture, lemon juice and the remaining 1/4 teaspoon salt. Bring to a simmer and cook, stirring, until the sauce is thickened, about 5 minutes.

4. Stir in parsley, capers, butter and the reserved mushrooms. Measure out 1/2 cup of the mushroom sauce. Toss the pasta in the pan with the remaining sauce. Serve the pasta topped with the chicken and the reserved sauce.

MAKES 4 SERVINGS.

PER SERVING: 397 calories; 9 g fat (3 g sat, 3 g mono); 54 mg cholesterol; 45 g carbohydrate; 28 g protein; 5 g fiber; 544 mg sodium; 609 mg potassium.

NUTRITION BONUS: Selenium (37% daily value), Vitamin C (18% dv), Potassium (17% dv), Iron (16% dv).

MAKEOVER TIP

ADD FIBER TO YOUR DIET BY SUBSTITUTING WHOLE-WHEAT PASTA FOR WHITE PASTA. ONE 2-OUNCE SERVING OF WHOLE-WHEAT PASTA HAS ABOUT 6 GRAMS OF FIBER COMPARED TO ABOUT 2 GRAMS IN A SERVING OF WHITE PASTA.

CREAMY TARRAGON CHICKEN SALAD

H✂W   L⬇C   H♥H

ACTIVE TIME: 30 MINUTES | **TOTAL:** 1¾ HOURS (INCLUDING 1 HOUR CHILLING TIME)
TO MAKE AHEAD: Bake the chicken (STEPS 1-2) and refrigerate for up to 2 days. Cover and refrigerate the salad for up to 1 day; add the nuts just before serving.

Reduced-fat sour cream and mayo make a sumptuous, creamy dressing for a considerably lightened take on chicken salad. Oven-poaching the chicken in broth intensifies its flavor and keeps it moist and succulent. Combined with sweet grapes and aromatic tarragon, this is an elegant version of chicken salad that's wonderful on a bed of mixed greens or a sandwich with nutty whole-grain bread.

2 pounds boneless, skinless chicken breast, trimmed	1 tablespoon dried tarragon
1 cup reduced-sodium chicken broth	½ teaspoon salt
⅓ cup walnuts, chopped	½ teaspoon freshly ground pepper
⅔ cup reduced-fat sour cream	1½ cups diced celery
½ cup low-fat mayonnaise	1½ cups halved red seedless grapes

1. Preheat oven to 450°F.
2. Arrange chicken in a glass baking dish large enough to hold it in a single layer. Pour broth around the chicken. Bake the chicken until no longer pink in the center and an instant-read thermometer inserted in the thickest part of the breast registers 170°F, 30 to 35 minutes. Transfer the chicken to a cutting board until cool enough to handle, then cut into cubes. (Discard broth or save for another use.)
3. Meanwhile, spread walnuts on a baking sheet and toast in the oven until lightly golden and fragrant, about 6 minutes. Let cool.
4. Stir sour cream, mayonnaise, tarragon, salt and pepper in a large bowl. Add celery, grapes, the chicken and walnuts; stir to coat. Refrigerate until chilled, at least 1 hour.

MAKES 8 SERVINGS, 1 CUP EACH.

PER SERVING: 219 calories; 9 g fat (3 g sat, 2 g mono); 71 mg cholesterol; 10 g carbohydrate; 25 g protein; 1 g fiber; 372 mg sodium; 354 mg potassium.

NUTRITION BONUS: Selenium (30% daily value).

EATINGWELL'S PEPPERONI PIZZA

H✴W   H♥H

ACTIVE TIME: 15 MINUTES | **TOTAL:** 35 MINUTES

TO MAKE AHEAD: Use leftover tomato sauce and pumpkin to make a second batch of pizza sauce. Refrigerate for up to 5 days or freeze for 3 months.

Pizza lovers everywhere can rejoice. We've taken a normally high-fat and high-sodium treat and rescued it from the bad-for-you category. Our secret: we use a whole-wheat pizza dough, spread with flavorful sauce that, thanks to the addition of pumpkin puree, provides extra beta carotene and fiber. We've topped the pie with low-fat turkey pepperoni, but if you like, use your favorite sliced vegetables instead. **SHOPPING TIP:** Look for balls of whole-wheat pizza dough at your supermarket, fresh or frozen and without any hydrogenated oils.

1 pound prepared whole-wheat pizza dough (*see Shopping Tip*), thawed if frozen	½ teaspoon garlic powder
1 cup canned unseasoned pumpkin puree	1 cup shredded part-skim mozzarella cheese
½ cup no-salt-added tomato sauce	½ cup grated Parmesan cheese
	2 ounces sliced turkey pepperoni (½ cup)

1. Place oven rack in the lowest position; preheat to 450°F. Coat a large baking sheet with cooking spray.

2. Roll out dough on a lightly floured surface to the size of the baking sheet. Transfer to the baking sheet. Bake until puffed and lightly crisped on the bottom, 8 to 10 minutes.

3. Whisk pumpkin puree, tomato sauce and garlic powder in a small bowl until combined.

4. Spread sauce evenly over the baked crust. Top with mozzarella, Parmesan and pepperoni. Bake until the crust is crispy on the edges and the cheeses have melted, about 12 minutes.

MAKES 6 SERVINGS.

PER SERVING: 280 calories; 6 g fat (3 g sat, 2 g mono); 30 mg cholesterol; 35 g carbohydrate; 16 g protein; 3 g fiber; 602 mg sodium; 153 mg potassium.

NUTRITION BONUS: Vitamin A (120% daily value), Calcium (25% dv).

MAKEOVER TIP

USE LOWER-FAT TURKEY PEPPERONI IN PLACE OF "THE REAL THING" ON PIZZA; YOU WON'T MISS THE FLAVOR AND YOUR HEART WON'T MISS THE SATURATED FAT.

SWEET & SOUR CHICKEN WITH BROWN RICE

H⬆F   H♥H

ACTIVE TIME: 30 MINUTES | **TOTAL:** 35 MINUTES

In about the time it takes to order and pick up Chinese takeout, you can make this much healthier version of sweet & sour chicken. Our version loses all the saturated fat that comes from deep-frying, along with the extra sugar and salt. If you prefer, use tofu instead of chicken, and use your favorite vegetables; just be sure to cut them into similar-size pieces so they all cook at about the same rate.

2 cups instant brown rice
¼ cup seasoned rice vinegar
2 tablespoons reduced-sodium soy sauce
2 tablespoons cornstarch
2 tablespoons apricot preserves
2 tablespoons canola oil, divided
1 pound chicken tenders (*see Ingredient Note, page 247*), cut into bite-size pieces

4 cloves garlic, minced
2 teaspoons finely grated or minced fresh ginger
1 cup reduced-sodium chicken broth
6 cups bite-size pieces of vegetables, such as snow peas, broccoli and bell peppers
1 5-ounce can sliced water chestnuts, drained

MAKEOVER TIP

USING REDUCED-SODIUM SOY SAUCE IN PLACE OF THE FULL-SODIUM VERSION SAVES 530 MG OF SODIUM PER TABLESPOON.

1. Prepare rice according to the package directions.

2. Meanwhile, whisk vinegar, soy sauce, cornstarch and apricot preserves in a small bowl. Set aside.

3. Heat 1 tablespoon oil in a large skillet over medium-high heat. Add chicken and cook, undisturbed, for 2 minutes. Continue cooking, stirring occasionally, until no longer pink on the outside and just starting to brown in spots, about 2 minutes more. Transfer to a plate.

4. Add the remaining 1 tablespoon oil, garlic and ginger to the pan and cook, stirring, until fragrant, 20 to 30 seconds. Add broth and bring to a boil, stirring constantly. Add vegetables, reduce heat to a simmer, cover and cook until the vegetables are tender-crisp, 4 to 6 minutes. Stir in water chestnuts and the chicken. Whisk the reserved sauce and add to the pan. Simmer, stirring constantly, until the sauce is thickened and the chicken is heated through, about 1 minute. Serve with the rice.

MAKES 4 SERVINGS (about 1 ½ cups stir-fry & ½ cup rice each).

PER SERVING: 469 calories; 10 g fat (1 g sat, 4 g mono); 68 mg cholesterol; 62 g carbohydrate; 34 g protein; 7 g fiber; 709 mg sodium; 408 mg potassium.

NUTRITION BONUS: Vitamin C (320% daily value), Vitamin A (70% dv), Fiber (28% dv).

SWEET & SOUR CHICKEN EVEN A DIABETIC CAN LOVE

It's 5:45 p.m. and Chris Howard, 15, is prowling through the fridge looking for something to eat. He looks at the clock, takes a gulp or two of milk, and calls out to his mom, Kathy, who just got home from work, "There's nothing to eat in this house! Can we order Chinese?"

Although Chinese takeout is one of their favorites, Chris and his sisters, Megan, 18, and Molly, 13, only get to eat it when their father, David, is out of town. That's because David has type 1 diabetes. Though he, too, loves Chinese food, experience has taught him to go lightly. "All those sauces are too sweet and the battered and fried meats make it extremely difficult—if not impossible—to regulate my blood sugar," he says.

It's no wonder that people with diabetes or high blood pressure have trouble enjoying what we Americans call "Chinese" food. A lot of it is battered and deep-fried, adding plenty of sodium, calories, carbohydrate and fat, and most of the sauces are loaded with salt, sugar and starch. Round out the meal with a heap of white rice, and you've just gone into a calorie and carbohydrate overload.

Our makeover of Sweet & Sour Chicken with Brown Rice resulted in a healthy dish for everyone. Our version has 235 fewer calories, 18 fewer grams of carbohydrate, 6 grams less saturated fat and half as much sodium.

And the whole family approved. "I like this better than takeout," Megan said. But David was the most pleased. "I'm pretty conscious of the carbohydrates I eat and I have to limit the Chinese takeout or my blood sugar just spikes. This is a good solution."

HERB-ROASTED TURKEY & PAN GRAVY

H✳W   L↓C   H♥H

ACTIVE TIME: 30 MINUTES | **TOTAL:** 3 1/2 HOURS
EQUIPMENT: Large roasting pan, roasting rack, kitchen string, thermometer

This recipe produces a beautiful, moist turkey without coating it with butter, that is as good in sandwiches and soups as it is right out of the oven for Thanksgiving. Make sure you show this beauty off at the table before you carve it. To make it even healthier, discard the skin before serving.

1 10- to 12-pound turkey	1 teaspoon freshly ground pepper
1/4 cup minced fresh herbs, plus 20 whole sprigs, such as thyme, rosemary, sage, oregano *and/or* marjoram, divided	Aromatics: onion, apple, lemon *and/or* orange, cut into 2-inch pieces (1 1/2 cups)
2 tablespoons canola oil	3 cups water, plus more as needed
1 teaspoon salt	Pan Gravy (*page 130*), optional

1. Position rack in lower third of oven; preheat to 475°F.

2. Remove giblets and neck from turkey cavities. Place the turkey, breast-side up, on a rack in a large roasting pan; pat dry with paper towels. Mix minced herbs, oil, salt and pepper in a small bowl. Rub the herb mixture all over the turkey, under the skin and onto the breast meat. Place aromatics and 10 of the herb sprigs in the cavity. Tuck the wing tips under the turkey. Tie the legs together with kitchen string. Add 3 cups water and the remaining 10 herb sprigs to the pan.

3. Roast the turkey until the skin is golden brown, about 45 minutes. Remove the turkey from the oven. If using a remote digital thermometer, insert it into the deepest part of the thigh, close to the joint. Cover the breast with a double layer of foil, cutting as necessary to conform to the breast. Reduce oven temperature to 350° and continue roasting for 1 1/4 to 1 3/4 hours more. If the pan dries out, tilt the turkey to let juices run out of the cavity into the pan and add 1 cup water. The turkey is done when the thermometer (or an instant-read thermometer inserted into the thickest part of the thigh without touching bone) registers 165°F.

4. Transfer the turkey to a serving platter and cover with foil. (If you're making Pan Gravy, start here.) Let the turkey rest for 20 minutes. Remove string and carve.

MAKES 12 SERVINGS (3 ounces each, plus plenty of leftovers)

PER SERVING (WITHOUT SKIN): 155 calories; 5 g fat (1 g sat, 2 g mono); 63 mg cholesterol; 0 g carbohydrate; 25 g protein; 0 g fiber; 175 mg sodium; 258 mg potassium.

NUTRITION BONUS: Selenium (43% daily value), Zinc (16% dv).

BEYOND ORGANIC WITH NELL NEWMAN'S THANKSGIVING

At age 33, Nell Newman decided to make an all-organic Thanksgiving dinner for her father and mother, the actors Paul Newman and Joanne Woodward, and her sisters. Her mission was to get her dad to help her launch Newman's Own Organics. "Dad's idea of the perfect Thanksgiving was always roast turkey, Pepperidge Farm stuffing, canned petit pois, sweet potatoes, cranberry sauce and Mom's pecan pie with maple whipped cream. It's rare for my parents to let me even toy with our favorite family recipes," Nell said.

To convince her father that organic food was not only healthier but delicious, she needed her father to like this "new" food. She brought organic salad greens and vegetables back from California where she lived (at the time, organic produce wasn't widely available in Connecticut). She ordered an organic turkey from Dean & DeLuca and cooked the whole Thanksgiving dinner herself.

"After we ate it I told him it was all organic. His words were, 'You got me, kid!'" Nell said. The meal was a success and Newman's Own Organics was born.

Nell already had the organic thing nailed, so we worked with her on how to make Thanksgiving healthier. Herb-Roasted Turkey & Pan Gravy (*page 129*), as its name implies, is loaded with herbs—you pick the ones you like best—to give it tons of flavor, but we skip rubbing down the bird with butter. Not only are the fat and calories in check, we've also developed a technique for getting the moistest meat (even from the breast) and the most beautiful, dark and delicious gravy. We tested and retested our turkey and gravy to tweak the technique and the timing. We experimented with different roasting pans and different types of turkeys. The result: our best-ever technique for getting a lovely, golden, crisp-skinned bird with delicious, moist meat and a rich, silky gravy.

PAN GRAVY

ACTIVE TIME: 20 MINUTES | **TOTAL:** 20 MINUTES

4½-5½ cups reduced-sodium chicken broth, divided
¼ cup all-purpose flour
¾ cup deglazing liquid, such as white wine, vermouth *or* brandy

1 tablespoon minced fresh herbs (optional)
¼ teaspoon salt (optional)
  Freshly ground pepper to taste

1. After removing the turkey from the roasting pan (*see page 129*), pour any pan juices and fat into a large glass measuring cup and place in the freezer until the fat rises to the top, about 10 minutes. Skim the fat off with a spoon and discard. (*Alternatively, pour the pan juices and fat into a fat separator then pour the defatted juices into a large measuring cup.*) Add any accumulated juices from the resting turkey to the defatted pan juice. Add enough chicken broth so the combined liquids measure 5 cups total.

2. Whisk ½ cup broth and flour in a small bowl until smooth.

3. Set the roasting pan over two burners on medium-high heat. Add deglazing liquid; bring to a boil and cook, scraping up the browned bits from the pan, until the liquid is reduced, about 3 minutes. Add the 5 cups of liquid from Step 1. Increase the heat to high and return to a boil, whisking often and scraping up any remaining browned bits. Boil until reduced to 2¾ cups, 8 to 12 minutes. Whisk the broth-flour mixture into the roasting pan. Boil, whisking constantly, for 2 to 3 minutes. Remove from the heat and pour the gravy through a fine sieve into a large measuring cup. Stir in herbs, if using. Taste and season with salt (if needed) and pepper.

MAKES ABOUT 3 CUPS.

PER 3-TABLESPOON SERVING: 38 calories; 2 g fat (1 g sat, 1 g mono); 3 mg cholesterol; 2 g carbohydrate; 1 g protein; 0 g fiber; 40 mg sodium; 10 mg potassium.

KING RANCH CASSEROLE

H✂W H⬆F H♥H

ACTIVE TIME: 30 MINUTES | **TOTAL:** 1 HOUR

The fat and sodium found in creamy canned soups and several cups of cheese can make this Tex-Mex favorite a nutritional nightmare. Our version has a tangy, creamy sauce made with nonfat milk, nonfat yogurt and reduced-sodium chicken broth, plus we use reduced-fat Cheddar. Add in lots of chopped fresh vegetables and you have a spicy, layered chicken casserole you can feel good about eating.

1½ cups reduced-sodium chicken broth
1 cup nonfat milk
½ cup all-purpose flour
½ cup nonfat plain yogurt
1 14-ounce can diced tomatoes, drained
1 4-ounce can chopped green chiles, drained
¼ cup chopped fresh cilantro *or* parsley
1 tablespoon chili powder
1 teaspoon dried oregano
½ teaspoon ground cumin

⅛ teaspoon salt
  Freshly ground pepper to taste
1½ teaspoons canola oil
1 large onion, chopped
1 red *or* green bell pepper, diced
2 cloves garlic, minced
2 cups diced cooked skinless chicken
10 corn tortillas, cut in quarters
½ cup shredded reduced-fat Cheddar cheese

1. Preheat oven to 375°F.
2. Bring broth to a simmer in a medium saucepan. Whisk milk and flour in a small bowl until smooth. Add to the broth and cook over medium heat, whisking constantly, until thickened and smooth, about 3 minutes. Remove from the heat and stir in yogurt, tomatoes, chiles, cilantro (or parsley), chili powder, oregano and cumin. Season with salt and pepper.
3. Heat oil in a large nonstick skillet over medium-high heat. Add onion, bell pepper and garlic; cook, stirring occasionally, until tender-crisp, about 3 minutes.
4. Line the bottom of a shallow 3-quart baking dish with half the tortillas. Top with half the chicken and half the onion mixture. Spoon half of the sauce evenly over the top. Repeat layers with remaining tortillas, chicken, onion mixture and sauce. Sprinkle with Cheddar. Bake until bubbly, 25 to 30 minutes.

MAKES 6 SERVINGS.

PER SERVING: 301 calories; 5 g fat (1 g sat, 2 g mono); 44 mg cholesterol; 38 g carbohydrate; 25 g protein; 6 g fiber; 458 mg sodium; 400 mg potassium.

NUTRITION BONUS: Vitamin C (90% daily value), Selenium & Vitamin A (30% dv), Calcium (20% dv), Iron (15% dv).

OLD-FASHIONED CHICKEN & DUMPLINGS

H⬆F   H♥H

ACTIVE TIME: 45 MINUTES | **TOTAL:** 1 HOUR

Our revision of this creamy, comfort dish uses whole-wheat flour for the dumplings and adds lots of vegetables to the filling. The delicious, satisfying results are packed with beneficial nutrients and dietary fiber, and because we don't use canned soup for the sauce, sodium levels are drastically reduced. To go even lighter, try the recipe with boneless, skinless chicken breasts.

1 ¾ pounds boneless, skinless chicken thighs, trimmed and cut into 1 ½-inch pieces	2 14-ounce cans reduced-sodium chicken broth
⅔ cup all-purpose flour	1 cup water
2 tablespoons canola oil, divided	1 ½ cups frozen peas, thawed
2 large carrots, diced	**DUMPLINGS**
2 stalks celery, diced	1 cup whole-wheat pastry flour
1 large onion, diced	½ cup all-purpose flour
1 tablespoon poultry seasoning	1 teaspoon poultry seasoning
½ teaspoon salt	½ teaspoon baking soda
½ teaspoon freshly ground pepper	¼ teaspoon salt
	¾ cup nonfat buttermilk (*see Tip, page 246*)

1. Toss chicken with ⅔ cup all-purpose flour in a medium bowl until coated. Heat 1 tablespoon oil in a Dutch oven over medium-high heat. Reserving the remaining flour, add the chicken to the pot and cook, stirring occasionally, until lightly browned, 3 to 5 minutes. Transfer the chicken to a plate.

2. Reduce heat to medium and add the remaining 1 tablespoon oil to the pot. Stir in carrots, celery, onion, 1 tablespoon poultry seasoning, ½ teaspoon salt and pepper. Cover and cook, stirring occasionally, until the vegetables are softened, 5 to 7 minutes. Sprinkle the reserved flour over the vegetables; stir to coat. Stir in broth, water, peas and the reserved chicken. Bring to a simmer, stirring often.

3. TO PREPARE DUMPLINGS: Meanwhile, stir whole-wheat flour, ½ cup all-purpose flour, 1 teaspoon poultry seasoning, baking soda and ¼ teaspoon salt in a medium bowl. Stir in buttermilk.

4. Drop the dough, 1 tablespoon at a time, over the simmering chicken stew, making about 18 dumplings. Adjust heat to maintain a gentle simmer, cover and cook undisturbed until the dumplings are puffed, the vegetables are tender and the chicken is cooked through, about 15 minutes.

MAKES 6 SERVINGS (1 ⅓ cups stew & 3 dumplings each).

PER SERVING: 463 calories; 15 g fat (3 g sat, 7 g mono); 91 mg cholesterol; 45 g carbohydrate; 34 g protein; 6 g fiber; 629 mg sodium; 412 mg potassium.

NUTRITION BONUS: Vitamin A (100% daily value), Selenium (36% dv), Iron (20% dv), Vitamin C (15% dv).

MAKEOVER TIP

ADDING EXTRA VEGETABLES TO DISHES (INSTEAD OF MORE MEAT) KEEPS THE SERVING SIZE GENEROUS AND BUMPS UP THE FIBER AND NUTRIENTS WHILE KEEPING THE CALORIES IN CHECK.

CHICKEN POTPIE

ACTIVE TIME: 15 MINUTES | **TOTAL:** 1 HOUR 5 MINUTES

The savory sauce in this potpie gets a rich taste from reduced-fat sour cream, but with less fat and calories. The whole-wheat biscuit topping stays tender with whole-wheat pastry flour, which is more delicate than regular whole-wheat flour. And it ends up just as delicious and comforting as you expect. (*Photograph: page 4.*)

FILLING

3	teaspoons canola oil, divided
1	cup frozen pearl onions, thawed
1	cup peeled baby carrots
10	ounces cremini mushrooms, halved
2½	cups reduced-sodium chicken broth, divided
¼	cup cornstarch
2½	cups diced cooked chicken *or* turkey
1	cup frozen peas, thawed
¼	cup reduced-fat sour cream
¼	teaspoon salt
	Freshly ground pepper to taste

BISCUIT TOPPING

¾	cup whole-wheat pastry flour
¾	cup all-purpose flour
2	teaspoons sugar
1¼	teaspoons baking powder
½	teaspoon baking soda
½	teaspoon salt
1	teaspoon dried thyme
1½	tablespoons cold butter, cut into small pieces
1	cup nonfat buttermilk *(see Tip, page 246)*
1	tablespoon canola oil

1. TO PREPARE FILLING: Heat 1 teaspoon oil in a large skillet or Dutch oven over medium-high heat. Add onions and carrots; cook, stirring, until golden brown and tender, about 7 minutes. Transfer to a bowl. Heat the remaining 2 teaspoons oil in the pan over medium-high heat. Add mushrooms and cook, stirring often, until browned and their liquid has evaporated, 5 to 7 minutes. Return the onions and carrots to the pan. Add 2 cups broth and bring to a boil; reduce heat to a simmer. Mix cornstarch with the remaining ½ cup broth; add to the pan and cook, stirring, until the sauce thickens. Stir in chicken (or turkey), peas, sour cream, salt and pepper. Transfer the filling to a 2-quart baking dish.

2. TO PREPARE BISCUIT TOPPING & BAKE POTPIE: Preheat oven to 400°F. Whisk whole-wheat flour, all-purpose flour, sugar, baking powder, baking soda, salt and thyme in a large bowl. Using your fingertips or 2 knives, cut butter into the dry ingredients until crumbly. Add buttermilk and oil; stir until just combined. Drop the dough onto the filling in 6 even portions. Set the baking dish on a baking sheet.

3. Bake the potpie until the topping is golden and the filling is bubbling, 30 to 35 minutes. Let cool for 10 minutes before serving.

MAKES 6 SERVINGS.

PER SERVING: 403 calories; 12 g fat (4 g sat, 4 g mono); 64 mg cholesterol; 46 g carbohydrate; 29 g protein; 4 g fiber; 667 mg sodium; 427 mg potassium.

NUTRITION BONUS: Vitamin A (70% daily value), Fiber (16% dv).

TURKEY TETRAZZINI

H✂W L↓C H♥H

ACTIVE TIME: 35 MINUTES | **TOTAL:** 35 MINUTES

For our healthy take on Tetrazzini, we use low-fat milk and skip the five tablespoons of butter that's often in the sherry-Parmesan sauce. As a result, we slash calories and fat in half, and reduce saturated fat by a whopping 80 percent. Even better, we transformed the dish into a fuss-free sauté that's quick enough to prepare even after a busy day.

2 tablespoons extra-virgin olive oil, divided	1 cup low-fat milk
1 pound turkey breast cutlets, ¼ inch thick	⅔ cup frozen peas, thawed
2½ cups sliced mushrooms (about 8 ounces)	½ cup chopped jarred roasted red peppers
3 tablespoons all-purpose flour	¼ cup shredded Parmesan cheese
1 cup reduced-sodium chicken broth	Freshly ground pepper to taste
¼ cup dry sherry	

1. Heat 1 tablespoon oil in a large nonstick skillet over medium-high heat. Add turkey and cook until lightly golden, 2 to 3 minutes per side. Transfer to a plate and cover to keep warm.

2. Heat the remaining 1 tablespoon oil in the pan. Add mushrooms and cook, stirring often, until browned, 4 to 6 minutes. Sprinkle with flour; stir to coat. Stir in broth and sherry; bring to a simmer. Continue simmering, stirring constantly, until the mixture is slightly reduced, 1 to 2 minutes. Add milk, peas and peppers; return to a simmer, stirring often. Cook until thick and slightly reduced, about 2 minutes. Stir in Parmesan and pepper. Return the turkey and any accumulated juices to the pan, turn to coat with sauce and cook until heated through, 1 to 2 minutes.

MAKES 4 SERVINGS.

PER SERVING: 330 calories; 10 g fat (2 g sat, 6 g mono); 54 mg cholesterol; 18 g carbohydrate; 38 g protein; 2 g fiber; 452 mg sodium; 234 mg potassium.

NUTRITION BONUS: Vitamin A (20% daily value), Calcium (17% dv), Iron (15% dv).

> ## MAKEOVER TIP
>
> **DON'T USE THE "COOKING SHERRY" SOLD IN MANY SUPERMARKETS— IT CAN BE SURPRISINGLY HIGH IN SODIUM. INSTEAD, PURCHASE DRY SHERRY THAT'S SOLD WITH OTHER FORTIFIED WINES IN YOUR WINE OR LIQUOR STORE.**

CHICKEN DIVAN

H✳W L↓C

ACTIVE TIME: 30 MINUTES | **TOTAL:** 1 HOUR

Originally made in restaurants with a rich Mornay sauce, the homemade version of this nostalgic comfort classic was usually made with canned cream of mushroom soup, mayonnaise, sour cream and cheese—tasty, yes, but also loaded with fat and salt. Our revised version has all the flavor of the original with only half the calories and a fraction of the sodium. Use leftover cooked chicken breasts, if you have them on hand, for an even faster dinner.

1½ pounds boneless, skinless chicken breast
1 tablespoon extra-virgin olive oil
2 cups diced leek, white and light green parts only (about 1 large; *see Tip, page 246*)
½ teaspoon salt
5 tablespoons all-purpose flour
1 14-ounce can reduced-sodium chicken broth
1 cup low-fat milk
2 tablespoons dry sherry (*see Ingredient Note, page 248*)

½ teaspoon dried thyme
½ teaspoon freshly ground pepper
2 10-ounce boxes frozen chopped broccoli, thawed, *or* 1 pound broccoli crowns (*see Ingredient Note, page 247*), chopped
1 cup grated Parmesan cheese, divided
¼ cup low-fat mayonnaise
2 teaspoons Dijon mustard

MAKEOVER TIP

TO REDUCE SODIUM AND FAT, REPLACE CONDENSED SOUP IN CASSEROLES LIKE CHICKEN DIVAN WITH A COMBINATION OF LOW-FAT MILK AND REDUCED-SODIUM BROTH THICKENED WITH FLOUR.

1. Preheat oven to 375°F. Coat a 7-by-11-inch (2-quart) glass baking dish with cooking spray.

2. Place chicken in a medium skillet or saucepan and add water to cover. Bring to a simmer over high heat. Cover, reduce heat to low and simmer gently until the chicken is cooked through and no longer pink in the center, 10 to 12 minutes. Drain and slice into bite-size pieces.

3. Heat oil in a large nonstick skillet over medium-high heat. Add leek and salt and cook, stirring often, until softened but not browned, 3 to 4 minutes. Add flour; stir to coat. Add broth, milk, sherry, thyme and pepper and bring to a simmer, stirring constantly. Add broccoli; return to a simmer. Remove from heat and stir in ½ cup Parmesan, mayonnaise and mustard.

4. Spread half the broccoli mixture in the prepared baking dish. Top with the chicken, then the remaining broccoli mixture. Sprinkle evenly with the remaining ½ cup Parmesan. Bake until bubbling, 20 to 25 minutes. Let cool for 10 minutes before serving.

MAKES 6 SERVINGS, ABOUT 1⅓ CUPS EACH.

PER SERVING: 308 calories; 10 g fat (4 g sat, 4 g mono); 76 mg cholesterol; 20 g carbohydrate; 35 g protein; 4 g fiber; 712 mg sodium; 401 mg potassium.

NUTRITION BONUS: Vitamin C (70% daily value), Vitamin A (35% dv), Calcium (30% dv), Folate (19% dv).

SAUSAGE, MUSHROOM & SPINACH LASAGNA

H)(W   H↑F

ACTIVE TIME: 30 MINUTES | **TOTAL:** 2 HOURS
TO MAKE AHEAD: Prepare through Step 5 up to 1 day ahead.

Cheesy lasagna with sausage has got to be a nutritional nonstarter, right? Not when you use spicy Italian turkey sausage, whole-wheat noodles and pump up the vegetables. In fact, a serving of this version has about one-third the fat and saturated fat, and only half the calories of the original. Use soy-based sausage for a hearty vegetarian variation.

8	ounces whole-wheat lasagna noodles
1	pound lean spicy Italian turkey sausage, casings removed (*see Variation*)
4	cups sliced mushrooms (10 ounces)
¼	cup water
1	pound frozen spinach, thawed
1	28-ounce can crushed tomatoes, preferably chunky
¼	cup chopped fresh basil
¼	teaspoon salt
	Freshly ground pepper to taste
1	pound part-skim ricotta cheese (2 cups)
8	ounces part-skim mozzarella cheese, shredded (about 2 cups), divided

VEGETARIAN VARIATION:
Use a sausage-style soy product, such as Gimme Lean, or simply omit the sausage altogether.

MAKEOVER TIP

USE ITALIAN TURKEY SAUSAGE IN PLACE OF THE MORE STANDARD PORK VERSION AND SAVE ABOUT 200 CALORIES, 23 GRAMS OF FAT AND 9 GRAMS OF SATURATED FAT PER 3-OUNCE SERVING.

1. Preheat oven to 350°F. Coat a 9-by-13-inch baking dish with cooking spray.
2. Bring a large pot of water to a boil. Add noodles and cook until not quite tender, about 2 minutes less than the package directions. Drain; return the noodles to the pot, cover with cool water and set aside.
3. Coat a large nonstick skillet with cooking spray and heat over medium-high heat. Add sausage; cook, crumbling with a wooden spoon, until browned, about 4 minutes. Add mushrooms and water; cook, stirring occasionally and crumbling the sausage more, until it is cooked through, the water has evaporated and the mushrooms are tender, 8 to 10 minutes. Squeeze spinach to remove excess water, then stir into the pan; remove from heat.
4. Mix tomatoes with basil, salt and pepper in a medium bowl.
5. TO ASSEMBLE LASAGNA: Spread ½ cup of the tomatoes in the prepared baking dish. Arrange a layer of noodles on top, trimming to fit if necessary. Evenly dollop half the ricotta over the noodles. Top with half the sausage mixture, one-third of the remaining tomatoes and one-third of the mozzarella. Continue with another layer of noodles, the remaining ricotta, the remaining sausage, half the remaining tomatoes and half the remaining mozzarella. Top with a third layer of noodles and the remaining tomatoes.
6. Cover the lasagna with foil and bake until bubbling and heated through, 1 hour to 1 hour 10 minutes. Remove the foil; sprinkle the remaining mozzarella on top. Return to the oven and bake until the cheese is just melted but not browned, 8 to 10 minutes. Let rest for 10 minutes before serving.

MAKES 10 SERVINGS.

PER SERVING: 333 calories; 14 g fat (5 g sat, 3 g mono); 41 mg cholesterol; 28 g carbohydrate; 26 g protein; 7 g fiber; 655 mg sodium; 606 mg potassium.

NUTRITION BONUS: Vitamin A (128% daily value), Calcium (23% dv), Iron (21% dv), Folate (19% dv), Potassium (17% dv).

STUFFED PEPPERS

H)(W   H♠F   H♥H

ACTIVE TIME: 30 MINUTES | **TOTAL:** 1 HOUR

Remember stuffed peppers? In this version, lean ground turkey makes a moist, low-fat substitute for the ground beef that's usually in the filling. To add a nutty flavor and boost the nutrition even further, we call for cooked brown rice, but this will also work with white rice.

4 large green bell peppers	1½ cups cooked brown rice
1½ teaspoons canola oil	1 8-ounce can tomato sauce, divided
1 medium onion, chopped	1 tablespoon chopped fresh parsley
1 clove garlic, minced	1 teaspoon salt (optional)
1 pound 93%-lean ground turkey	¼ teaspoon freshly ground pepper

1. Preheat oven to 350°F.

2. Cut out stem ends of bell peppers and discard. Scoop out seeds. Bring 8 cups water to a boil in a large pot and blanch the peppers until tender-crisp, about 1 minute. Drain and cool under cold running water. Set aside.

3. Heat oil in a large nonstick skillet over medium heat. Add onion and garlic and cook, stirring occasionally, until softened, about 3 minutes. Add turkey and cook, crumbling with a wooden spoon, just until it loses its pink color, about 2 minutes. Drain the fat.

4. Transfer the turkey mixture to a medium bowl and mix in rice, ½ cup tomato sauce, parsley, salt (if using) and pepper. Stuff the peppers with the mixture and place them in a 2-quart casserole dish. Spoon the remaining ½ cup tomato sauce over the peppers. Cover and bake until the peppers are tender and the filling is heated through, 30 to 35 minutes.

MAKES 4 SERVINGS.

PER SERVING: 307 calories; 10 g fat (2 g sat, 1 g mono); 65 mg cholesterol; 31 g carbohydrate; 26 g protein; 6 g fiber; 385 mg sodium; 588 mg potassium.

NUTRITION BONUS: Vitamin C (230% daily value), Iron & Vitamin A (20% dv), Potassium (17% dv).

> ## MAKEOVER TIP
>
> **BE SURE TO CHOOSE LEAN GROUND MEAT (TURKEY, BEEF, PORK OR LAMB). ANYTHING LABELED 90%-LEAN OR LEANER IS CONSIDERED A HEALTHY CHOICE.**

TURKEY-STUFFED PORTOBELLO MUSHROOMS

H❂W L↓C

ACTIVE TIME: 20 MINUTES | **TOTAL:** 40 MINUTES

We use portobello caps to make these dinner-sized stuffed mushrooms that are big on flavor without being overly rich. Rather than the traditional sausage filling, this recipe calls for lean ground turkey blended with fresh herbs and spices, topped with golden, melted fontina cheese. Add a tossed salad and a slice of crusty whole-grain bread to complete the meal.

1 tablespoon extra-virgin olive oil	⅛ teaspoon ground nutmeg
1 sweet onion, thinly sliced lengthwise	1 pound 93%-lean ground turkey
2 teaspoons cider vinegar	4 medium-large portobello mushroom caps, gills removed (*see Tip*)
¾ teaspoon ground sage	
½ teaspoon chopped fresh rosemary	1 tablespoon Worcestershire sauce
½ teaspoon salt	½ cup finely shredded fontina cheese
½ teaspoon freshly ground pepper	

1. Position rack in the lowest position; preheat oven to 400°F.

2. Cook oil and onion in a large skillet over medium heat, stirring occasionally and reducing heat as necessary to prevent scorching, until softened and starting to turn golden, about 20 minutes. Stir in vinegar.

3. Meanwhile, combine sage, rosemary, salt, pepper and nutmeg in a small dish. Place turkey in a medium bowl and sprinkle the spice mixture over it. Gently knead to combine. Form into 4 equal balls. Rub mushroom caps on both sides with Worcestershire. Place one turkey ball in each mushroom cap, patting down to fill the cap. Place on a baking sheet.

4. Bake the stuffed mushrooms on the bottom rack until the mushrooms begin to soften, about 20 minutes. Remove from the oven, spread the onion mixture over the filling and top with fontina. Continue baking until the cheese is melted and golden and the turkey is cooked through, about 10 minutes more.

TIP:

The dark gills found on the underside of a portobello are edible, but if you like you can scrape them off with a spoon.

MAKES 4 SERVINGS.

PER SERVING: 283 calories; 15 g fat (5 g sat, 4 g mono); 81 mg cholesterol; 9 g carbohydrate; 28 g protein; 2 g fiber; 530 mg sodium; 570 mg potassium.

NUTRITION BONUS: Selenium (40% daily value), Iron & Potassium (15% dv).

SWEET & SOUR CABBAGE ROLLS

H)(W L↓C H♥H

ACTIVE TIME: 40 MINUTES | **TOTAL:** 2 HOURS
TO MAKE AHEAD: Prepare through Step 6; refrigerate for up to 1 day or freeze for up to 1 month. If frozen, defrost overnight in the refrigerator before baking.

Lean ground turkey and brown rice seasoned with fresh dill and caraway seeds makes a moist filling for these stuffed cabbage rolls. They're baked in a combination of tomato sauce, lemon juice and honey for the familiar sweet-and-sour flavor typical of the dish.

½ cup brown rice	3 tablespoons chopped fresh dill
1 cup water	1 teaspoon caraway seeds
1 large Savoy cabbage (about 3 pounds)	½ teaspoon salt
1 tablespoon canola oil	½ teaspoon freshly ground pepper
1 medium onion, chopped	1½ cups no-salt-added tomato sauce
4 cloves garlic, minced	1 cup reduced-sodium chicken broth
6 tablespoons lemon juice, divided	1 tablespoon honey
1 pound 93%-lean ground turkey	

MAKEOVER TIP

KEEP SODIUM IN CHECK IN RECIPES USING CANNED PRODUCTS, SUCH AS CANNED TOMATO SAUCE, BY CHOOSING AN ALTERNATIVE LIKE "NO-SALT-ADDED" TOMATO SAUCE.

1. Bring rice and water to a boil in a small saucepan. Cover, reduce heat, and simmer until the water is absorbed, 25 to 30 minutes. Set aside to cool.
2. Meanwhile, bring a Dutch oven full of water to a boil over high heat. Boil the 12 largest outer cabbage leaves for 6 minutes. Drain and rinse under cool water until room temperature. Chop enough of the remaining cabbage to equal 2 cups. (Save the rest for another use.)
3. Heat oil in a large saucepan over medium heat. Add onion and the chopped cabbage. Cook, stirring often, until softened, about 3 minutes. Add garlic; cook, stirring, for 30 seconds. Add 4 tablespoons lemon juice; cook, stirring, until the liquid has almost evaporated. Let cool for 10 minutes.
4. Mix turkey, dill, caraway, salt, pepper, the onion mixture and cooled rice in a large bowl.
5. Preheat oven to 375°F. Coat a 9-by-13-inch pan with cooking spray.
6. Lay one cabbage leaf on your work surface; cut out the thick stem. Place about ⅓ cup of the turkey mixture in the leaf's center. Fold the sides over the filling, then roll closed. Place seam-side down in the baking dish. Repeat with the remaining cabbage leaves and filling. Whisk tomato sauce, broth, honey and the remaining 2 tablespoons lemon juice in a medium bowl. Pour evenly over the rolls. Cover the pan tightly with foil.
7. Bake the cabbage rolls for 1 hour. Uncover and continue baking, basting the rolls with sauce several times, for 20 minutes more.

MAKES 6 SERVINGS.

PER SERVING: 272 calories; 8 g fat (2 g sat, 2 g mono); 44 mg cholesterol; 33 g carbohydrate; 20 g protein; 7 g fiber; 318 mg sodium; 640 mg potassium.

NUTRITION BONUS: Vitamin C (98% daily value), Vitamin A (46% dv), Folate (29% dv), Magnesium & Potassium (18% dv), Iron (15% dv).

Shrimp Chili Cornbread Casserole (page 158)

FISH & SEAFOOD

DELICIOUS FEEDBACK

Shrimp Chili Cornbread Casserole

"I've made this twice now, and it has been a hit both times. It is also very good for lunches the following day! It's especially great for using up a bountiful zucchini harvest."

—Anonymous, Saint Peters, PA

Quick Shrimp Enchilada Bake

"It was very good and super easy. It didn't sit heavy in your stomach like some Mexican food can. I have two small children and it was nice to have such a good meal that didn't require a lot of attention in a short amount of time."

—Deena, Bryant Pond, ME

CATFISH AMANDINE

L ↓ C   H ♥ H

ACTIVE TIME: 30 MINUTES | **TOTAL:** 30 MINUTES

A classic "amandine" sauté combines plenty of butter with almonds and garlic in a luxurious sauce. Here, we use healthier extra-virgin olive oil with a bit of butter added for its flavor. The fish fillets are dredged in flour and pan-fried in just a little more oil. The results are delicately flavored and have only a third of the calories, fat and sodium of a classic version.

1 tablespoon plus 1 ½ teaspoons extra-virgin olive oil, divided
1 tablespoon butter
¼ cup sliced almonds
3 cloves garlic, thinly sliced
½ cup low-fat milk
1 large egg, lightly beaten

⅓ cup all-purpose flour
½ teaspoon salt
½ teaspoon cayenne pepper
1 pound catfish, cut into 4 portions
2 tablespoons lemon juice
1 tablespoon chopped fresh parsley

MAKEOVER TIP

REPLACE MOST OF THE BUTTER IN RICH SAUCES WITH HEART-HEALTHY OLIVE OIL—THE EASY CHANGE CUTS SATURATED FAT WITHOUT GIVING UP THE BUTTER FLAVOR.

1. Heat 1 tablespoon oil and butter in a small saucepan over medium heat. Add almonds and garlic and cook until both are just beginning to brown, 1 to 3 minutes. Set aside.

2. Combine milk and egg in a shallow dish. In another shallow dish, combine flour, salt and cayenne. Dip fish in the milk mixture, then in the flour mixture; shake off any excess flour. (Discard any leftover mixtures.)

3. Heat the remaining 1½ teaspoons oil in a large nonstick skillet over medium heat. Add fish and cook until lightly browned and opaque in the center, 4 to 6 minutes per side.

4. Return the almond-garlic sauce to the stove over medium heat. Add lemon juice and heat through, 1 to 2 minutes. Pour the sauce over the fish and sprinkle with parsley.

MAKES 4 SERVINGS.

PER SERVING: 336 calories; 21 g fat (5 g sat, 11 g mono); 117 mg cholesterol; 10 g carbohydrate; 25 g protein; 1 g fiber; 353 mg sodium; 452 mg potassium.

NUTRITION BONUS: Selenium (33% daily value), Vitamin E (20% dv).

SPAGHETTI WITH CLAM SAUCE

H↑F H♥H

ACTIVE TIME: 40 MINUTES | **TOTAL:** 40 MINUTES

A good clam sauce for pasta need not be loaded with butter or cream. We use whole baby clams, chopped plum tomatoes and lots of fresh herbs to create an elegant dish that has only 8 grams of fat per serving. Toasted pine nuts add complexity and rich texture to this classic Italian combination.

1 tablespoon extra-virgin olive oil	⅓ cup chopped fresh parsley
1 onion, chopped	2 tablespoons chopped fresh basil
3 plum tomatoes, seeded and chopped	⅛ teaspoon salt
2 cloves garlic, finely chopped	Freshly ground pepper to taste
½ cup dry white wine	1 tablespoon pine nuts
1 10-ounce can whole baby clams, drained, liquid reserved, *or* 8 ounces minced fresh clams, liquid reserved	12 ounces whole-wheat spaghetti *or* linguine

1. Put a large pot of water on to boil. Heat oil in a large nonstick skillet over medium heat. Add onion and cook, stirring, until softened, about 5 minutes. Add tomatoes and garlic; cook, stirring, until the tomatoes have softened, about 3 minutes. Stir in wine and clam liquid; bring to a simmer. Reduce heat to low and simmer for 5 minutes. Stir in parsley, basil and clams and heat through. Season with salt and pepper.

2. Toast pine nuts in a small dry skillet over medium heat, stirring, until golden, 3 to 4 minutes.

3. Meanwhile, cook pasta in the boiling water until just tender, 8 to 10 minutes or according to package directions. Drain and add to the pan with the sauce. Toss to coat. Sprinkle with the pine nuts and serve immediately.

MAKES 4 SERVINGS.

PER SERVING: 461 calories; 8 g fat (2 g sat, 3 g mono); 57 mg cholesterol; 73 g carbohydrate; 25 g protein; 12 g fiber; 456 mg sodium; 411 mg potassium.

NUTRITION BONUS: Selenium (90% daily value), Iron (22% dv), Calcium & Vitamin A (20% dv).

TUNA MELT

H✂W L⬇C H♥H

ACTIVE TIME: 10 MINUTES | **TOTAL:** 15 MINUTES

In this updated version of a diner favorite we go light on the mayo and add plenty of flavor with minced shallot and a dash of hot sauce. We top that with fresh tomato slices and shredded sharp Cheddar, which allows us to use considerably less cheese while ensuring that there's great cheese flavor in each gooey bite.

12 ounces canned chunk light tuna, drained	Dash of hot sauce
1 medium shallot, minced (2 tablespoons)	Freshly ground pepper to taste
2 tablespoons low-fat mayonnaise	4 slices whole-wheat bread, toasted
1 tablespoon lemon juice	2 tomatoes, sliced
1 tablespoon minced flat-leaf parsley	½ cup shredded sharp Cheddar cheese
⅛ teaspoon salt	

1. Preheat broiler.

2. Combine tuna, shallot, mayonnaise, lemon juice, parsley, salt, hot sauce and pepper in a medium bowl. Spread ¼ cup of the tuna mixture on each slice of toast; top with tomato slices and 2 tablespoons cheese. Place sandwiches on a baking sheet and broil until the cheese is bubbling and golden brown, 3 to 5 minutes.

MAKES 4 SERVINGS.

PER SERVING: 252 calories; 6 g fat (3 g sat, 0 g mono); 66 mg cholesterol; 16 g carbohydrate; 31 g protein; 3 g fiber; 408 mg sodium; 242 mg potassium.

NUTRITION BONUS: Vitamin A & Vitamin C (20% daily value).

MAKEOVER TIP

CHUNK LIGHT TUNA, WHICH COMES FROM THE SMALLER SKIPJACK OR YELLOWFIN, HAS LESS MERCURY THAN CANNED WHITE ALBACORE TUNA. FDA/EPA ADVICE RECOMMENDS NO MORE THAN 6 OUNCES OF ALBACORE A WEEK; UP TO 12 OUNCES CANNED LIGHT IS CONSIDERED SAFE.

BLACKENED SALMON SANDWICH

H↑F H♥H

ACTIVE TIME: 25 MINUTES | **TOTAL:** 25 MINUTES

Blackened salmon is great in a sandwich with a spread of mashed avocado and low-fat mayonnaise plus peppery arugula leaves, cool tomato slices and zesty red onion. We grill our Cajun-style salmon so there is no need for any added cooking oil. Catfish makes an excellent stand-in for the salmon but you'll want to use a grill basket if you have one to keep the fish from breaking apart.

1 pound wild salmon fillet (*see Ingredient Note*), skinned (*see Tip, page 247*) and cut into 4 portions	2 tablespoons low-fat mayonnaise
	4 crusty whole-wheat rolls, split and toasted
	1 cup arugula
2 teaspoons blackening *or* Cajun seasoning	2 plum tomatoes, thinly sliced
1 small avocado, pitted	½ cup thinly sliced red onion

INGREDIENT NOTE:

Wild-caught salmon from the Pacific (Alaska, California, Washington and Oregon) is considered the best choice for the environment. For more information, visit Monterey Bay Aquarium Seafood Watch (*mbayaq.org/cr/seafoodwatch.asp*).

1. Oil grill rack (*see Tip, page 246*); preheat grill to high.

2. Rub salmon on both sides with blackening (or Cajun) seasoning. Grill until cooked through, 3 to 4 minutes per side.

3. Mash avocado and mayonnaise in a small bowl.

4. To assemble sandwiches, spread some of the avocado mixture on each roll and top with salmon, arugula, tomato and onion.

MAKES 4 SERVINGS.

PER SERVING: 414 calories; 14 g fat (2 g sat, 6 g mono); 65 mg cholesterol; 43 g carbohydrate; 33 g protein; 6 g fiber; 775 mg sodium; 756 mg potassium.

NUTRITION BONUS: Fiber (24% daily value), Potassium (22% dv), Vitamin C (18% dv), Folate (15% dv), good source of omega-3s.

SALMON CAKES

H)(W H♥H

ACTIVE TIME: 30 MINUTES | **TOTAL:** 30 MINUTES

Salmon cakes are a delicious, healthy way to use convenient, omega-3-rich canned salmon—but not when you fry them in a half-inch of oil. Here, the fish is combined with frozen hash browns, chopped capers, scallions and just enough egg white and low-fat mayo to hold everything together. We pan-fry them on one side in a small amount of oil, flip them and then finish in a hot oven. The result is light and crispy.

1½ cups frozen hash brown potatoes, thawed	2 teaspoons drained capers, coarsely chopped
1 7-ounce can wild salmon (*see Ingredient Note, page 150*), drained, picked over and flaked	1 scallion, trimmed and thinly sliced
	⅛ teaspoon salt
	Freshly ground pepper to taste
1 large egg white	1 teaspoon extra-virgin olive oil
1 tablespoon low-fat mayonnaise	

1. Preheat oven to 450°F. Partially mash potatoes in a bowl with a fork until they begin to hold together. Add salmon, egg white, mayonnaise, capers, scallion, salt and pepper. Shape the mixture into 4 cakes, each about ½ inch thick.

2. Heat oil in an ovenproof nonstick skillet over medium heat. Add the salmon cakes and cook until browned on the bottom, 4 to 5 minutes. Carefully turn the cakes over with a spatula and transfer the pan to the oven. Bake until heated through and golden brown on the second side, 5 to 7 minutes.

MAKES 2 SERVINGS, 2 CAKES EACH.

PER SERVING: 311 calories; 12 g fat (2 g sat, 2 g mono); 63 mg cholesterol; 30 g carbohydrate; 24 g protein; 3 g fiber; 785 mg sodium; 598 mg potassium.

NUTRITION BONUS: Vitamin C (23% daily value), Calcium (18% dv).

SKILLET TUNA NOODLE CASSEROLE

H↑F H♥H

ACTIVE TIME: 40 MINUTES | **TOTAL:** 40 MINUTES

TO MAKE AHEAD: Prepare through Step 3, spoon into an 8-inch-square glass baking dish, cover with foil and refrigerate for up to 1 day. Sprinkle with breadcrumbs and cheese (STEP 4) and bake, covered, at 350°F for 50 minutes. Uncover and cook until browned and bubbly, about 15 minutes more.

Known as Tuna-Pea Wiggle to some, this family-friendly casserole tends to be made with canned soup and whole milk, which means high fat and sodium. We remedy this by making our own creamy mushroom sauce with nonfat milk thickened with a bit of flour. Look for whole-wheat egg noodles—they have more fiber than regular egg noodles (but this dish will work well and taste great with either).

8 ounces whole-wheat egg noodles
1 tablespoon extra-virgin olive oil
1 medium onion, finely chopped
8 ounces mushrooms, sliced
½ teaspoon salt
½ cup dry white wine
6 tablespoons all-purpose flour
3 cups nonfat milk

½ teaspoon freshly ground pepper
12 ounces canned chunk light tuna (*see Makeover Tip, page 149*), drained
1 cup frozen peas, thawed
1 cup finely grated Parmesan cheese, divided
½ cup coarse dry whole-wheat breadcrumbs (*see Tip, page 246*)

1. Bring a large pot of water to a boil. Cook noodles until just tender, 6 to 8 minutes or according to package directions. Drain and rinse.

2. Position rack in upper third of oven and preheat broiler.

3. Meanwhile, heat oil in a large ovenproof skillet over medium-high heat. Add onion, mushrooms and salt and cook, stirring often, until the onion is softened but not browned, about 5 minutes. Add wine and cook until evaporated, 4 to 5 minutes. Sprinkle flour over the vegetables; stir to coat. Add milk and pepper and bring to a simmer, stirring constantly. Stir in tuna, peas and ½ cup Parmesan until evenly incorporated. Then, stir in the noodles (the pan will be very full). Remove from the heat.

4. Sprinkle the casserole with breadcrumbs and the remaining ½ cup Parmesan. Broil until bubbly and lightly browned on top, 3 to 4 minutes.

MAKES 6 SERVINGS, ABOUT 1⅓ CUPS EACH.

PER SERVING: 406 calories; 8 g fat (3 g sat, 3 g mono); 53 mg cholesterol; 47 g carbohydrate; 32 g protein; 5 g fiber; 684 mg sodium; 593 mg potassium.

NUTRITION BONUS: Calcium (30% daily value), Potassium (17% dv), Iron, Vitamin A & Vitamin C (15% dv), good source of omega-3s.

> ## MAKEOVER TIP
>
> **TRY USING WHOLE-WHEAT BREAD-CRUMBS TO TOP CASSEROLES. LOOK FOR THEM IN THE NATURAL-FOODS SECTION OF THE SUPERMARKET OR MAKE YOUR OWN (*SEE PAGE 246*).**

BAKED COD CASSEROLE

L ↓ C

ACTIVE TIME: 20 MINUTES | **TOTAL:** 40 MINUTES

Dry white wine and Gruyère cheese give this fish casserole a rich flavor that hides its virtue. Before baking, we top the dish with seasoned whole-wheat breadcrumbs, which add a wholesome, nutty flavor and dietary fiber. For variety, you can substitute almost any mild white fish.

2 tablespoons extra-virgin olive oil, divided	½ teaspoon freshly ground pepper
2 medium onions, very thinly sliced	1 ½ cups finely chopped whole-wheat country bread (about 2 slices)
1 cup dry white wine	½ teaspoon paprika
1 ¼ pounds Pacific cod (*see Ingredient Note*), cut into 4 pieces	½ teaspoon garlic powder
2 teaspoons chopped fresh thyme	1 cup finely shredded Gruyère *or* Swiss cheese
½ teaspoon kosher salt	

INGREDIENT NOTE:

Overfishing and trawling have drastically reduced the number of cod in the Atlantic Ocean and destroyed its sea floor. A better choice is Pacific cod (a.k.a. Alaska cod); it is more sustainably fished and has a larger, more stable population, according to Monterey Bay Aquarium Seafood Watch (*mbayaq.org/cr/seafood watch.asp*).

1. Preheat oven to 400°F.

2. Heat 1 tablespoon oil in a large ovenproof skillet over medium-high heat. Add onions and cook, stirring often, until just starting to soften, 5 to 7 minutes. Add wine, increase heat to high and cook, stirring often, until the wine is slightly reduced, 2 to 4 minutes.

3. Place cod on the onions and sprinkle with thyme, salt and pepper. Cover the pan tightly with foil; transfer to the oven and bake for 12 minutes.

4. Toss bread with the remaining 1 tablespoon oil, paprika and garlic powder in a medium bowl. Spread the bread mixture over the fish and top with cheese. Bake, uncovered, until the fish is opaque in the center, about 10 minutes more.

MAKES 4 SERVINGS.

PER SERVING: 381 calories; 17 g fat (6 g sat, 8 g mono); 83 mg cholesterol; 14 g carbohydrate; 32 g protein; 4 g fiber; 352 mg sodium; 395 mg potassium.

NUTRITION BONUS: Selenium (59% daily value), Calcium (25% dv), Magnesium (21% dv), Zinc (20% dv).

CRAB CAKES

H✂W L↓C H♥H

ACTIVE TIME: 30 MINUTES | **TOTAL:** 40 MINUTES

Flecked with scallions and bell pepper, these healthy crab cakes are as flavorful as their higher-fat counterparts. We brown them first on the stovetop and then finish them in a hot oven—no need for frying.

1 pound fresh lump crabmeat (2 cups), picked over and patted dry	⅓ cup finely diced red *or* green bell pepper
1 cup fresh whole-wheat breadcrumbs (*see Tip, page 246*)	1 tablespoon chopped fresh parsley
¼ cup low-fat mayonnaise	1 teaspoon Old Bay seasoning
1 large egg white, lightly beaten	¼ teaspoon freshly ground pepper
2 tablespoons lemon juice	¼-½ teaspoon hot sauce
1 scallion, trimmed and finely chopped	½ cup fine dry breadcrumbs
	1 teaspoon canola oil
	Lemon wedges for garnish

1. Preheat oven to 450°F.

2. Stir crabmeat, fresh breadcrumbs, mayonnaise, egg white, lemon juice, scallion, bell pepper, parsley, Old Bay seasoning, pepper and hot sauce to taste in a large bowl.

3. Place dry breadcrumbs in a shallow dish. Form the crab mixture into six ½-inch-thick patties. (The mixture will be very soft.) Dredge the patties in the dry breadcrumbs, reshaping as necessary.

4. Brush oil evenly over the bottom of a heavy ovenproof skillet. Heat the pan over medium-high heat. Add the crab cakes and cook until the undersides are golden, about 1 minute. Carefully turn the crab cakes over and transfer the pan to the oven. (If you do not have an ovenproof skillet, transfer the patties to a baking sheet.) Bake until heated through, 10 to 12 minutes. Serve with lemon wedges.

MAKES 6 SERVINGS.

PER SERVING: 149 calories; 3 g fat (0 g sat, 1 g mono); 59 mg cholesterol; 13 g carbohydrate; 17 g protein; 1 g fiber; 536 mg sodium; 329 mg potassium.

NUTRITION BONUS: Vitamin C (30% daily value), Folate (20% dv), Selenium (49% dv), Zinc (20% dv).

BANISHING FAT FROM CRAB GRATIN

"Crab gratin is one of my favorite Outer Banks recipes. It may be served over toast, biscuits, noodles, over crackers for hors d'oeuvres or by itself for any meal. Can you make it more healthful?" requested Sybil Basnight of Manteo, North Carolina.

Delicious though it is, almost everything in the original gratin spells trouble. It begins with a roux for thickening, made with equal amounts of butter and flour. Add cream, hard-boiled eggs and mayonnaise to that, and the saturated fat piles up. Even the Ritz crackers that are used for the topping are problematic, since they contain more oil than other plain crackers.

To trim the roux, we cut the butter and simply blended the flour into milk. A combination of nonfat milk and nonfat evaporated milk stands in for the cream.

Nonfat evaporated milk, from which 60 percent of the water has been removed, contains very little fat, and its rich, subtly sweet taste goes particularly well with the crab.

Omitting the mayonnaise made the gratin thin and bland, so we used half the amount of low-fat mayonnaise. Hard-boiled eggs can be replaced by the whites alone. Toasted whole-wheat breadcrumbs were substituted for the Ritz crackers to give a crusty finish. To give the crab more zip, we increased the dry mustard and added a pinch of cayenne and chopped fresh jalapeño pepper.

Our gratin contains only 207 calories and 3 grams of fat per serving, as compared to 336 calories and 29 grams of fat in the original. Try to find fresh or frozen lump crabmeat for this gratin; canned crabmeat or frozen claws will not do this recipe justice.

OUTER BANKS CRAB GRATIN

H)(W   L ⬇ C   H ❤ H

ACTIVE TIME: 30 MINUTES | **TOTAL:** 1 HOUR

When you have delicious lump crabmeat, why cover up the delicate, sweet flavor? Our crab gratin is rich with a whole pound of crabmeat. Serve with brown rice or whole-grain toast points.

- ⅔ cup nonfat milk, divided
- 2 tablespoons all-purpose flour
- ⅔ cup nonfat evaporated milk
- 2 hard-boiled eggs (see Tip, page 246), whites only
- 1 pound lump crabmeat, fresh or frozen and thawed, picked over and patted dry
- 3 tablespoons low-fat mayonnaise

- 1 teaspoon minced jalapeño pepper (optional)
- 1½ teaspoons dry mustard
- ⅛ teaspoon cayenne pepper, or to taste
- ⅛ teaspoon salt
  Freshly ground pepper to taste
- 2 tablespoons coarse dry whole-wheat breadcrumbs (see Tip, page 246)

1. Preheat oven to 350°F.

2. Whisk ⅓ cup milk and flour in a small bowl until smooth. Heat the remaining ⅓ cup milk and evaporated milk in a small saucepan over medium heat until steaming. Whisk in the flour mixture; cook, whisking constantly, until thickened, 30 to 60 seconds. Finely chop egg whites. Combine with crabmeat, mayonnaise, jalapeño (if using), dry mustard, cayenne, salt and pepper in a medium bowl. Stir in the milk mixture. Spoon into a shallow 2-quart baking dish. Sprinkle the toasted breadcrumbs on top. Bake until heated through, about 25 minutes.

MAKES 4 SERVINGS.

PER SERVING: 207 calories; 3 g fat (0 g sat, 0 g mono); 116 mg cholesterol; 13 g carbohydrate; 30 g protein; 1 g fiber; 592 mg sodium; 609 mg potassium.

NUTRITION BONUS: Selenium (74% daily value), Zinc (37% dv), Calcium (31% dv).

SHRIMP CHILI CORNBREAD CASSEROLE

H⚹W H♥H

ACTIVE TIME: 50 MINUTES | **TOTAL:** 1 HOUR 40 MINUTES
TO MAKE AHEAD: Bake, let cool for 1 hour, cover with parchment paper then foil and refrigerate for up to 3 days. Reheat, covered, in a preheated 350°F oven for 1 hour.

This savory cobbler is based on a casserole that is usually made with ground beef. Here we make a low-fat shrimp and vegetable chili (which is quite tasty on its own) and top it with a layer of golden cornbread. The dish serves 12, so it's just right for serving to a crowd gathered to watch a Sunday afternoon game on TV. (*Photograph: page 144.*)

SHRIMP CHILI FILLING
- 2 teaspoons canola oil
- 1 large onion, chopped
- 1 medium green bell pepper, chopped
- 4 cloves garlic, minced
- 3 medium zucchini, diced (about 5 cups)
- 1½ tablespoons chili powder
- 1½ teaspoons ground cumin
- 1 teaspoon ground cinnamon
- 1 teaspoon salt
- 2 14-ounce cans no-salt-added diced tomatoes
- 1½ pounds raw shrimp (41-50 per pound; *see Ingredient Note, page 248*), peeled and deveined

- ½ cup chopped fresh cilantro

CORNBREAD TOPPING
- 1 cup yellow cornmeal
- 1 cup all-purpose flour
- 2 teaspoons baking powder
- ½ teaspoon salt
- ¾ cup nonfat milk
- ¼ cup canola oil
- 1 large egg
- 1 tablespoon honey

1. TO PREPARE FILLING: Heat 2 teaspoons oil in a Dutch oven over medium heat. Add onion and bell pepper; cook, stirring often, until softened, about 3 minutes. Add garlic and cook, stirring, for 30 seconds. Stir in zucchini; cook, stirring often, for 3 minutes. Stir in chili powder, cumin, cinnamon and 1 teaspoon salt; cook for 20 seconds. Pour in tomatoes and their juice; bring to a simmer. Remove from the heat. Stir in shrimp and cilantro. Pour into a 9-by-13-inch baking pan.

2. Preheat oven to 350°F.

3. TO PREPARE CORNBREAD TOPPING: Whisk cornmeal, flour, baking powder and ½ teaspoon salt in a large bowl. Whisk milk, ¼ cup oil, egg and honey in a medium bowl until smooth. Add the wet ingredients to the dry ingredients and stir just until moistened. Drop by heaping tablespoons over the shrimp mixture.

4. Bake the casserole, uncovered, until the top is browned and the filling is bubbling, 40 to 45 minutes. Let stand for 10 minutes before serving.

MAKES 12 SERVINGS.

PER SERVING: 225 calories; 8 g fat (1 g sat, 4 g mono); 104 mg cholesterol; 24 g carbohydrate; 15 g protein; 3 g fiber; 522 mg sodium; 222 mg potassium.

NUTRITION BONUS: Vitamin C (30% daily value), Iron & Vitamin A (15% dv).

QUICK SHRIMP ENCHILADA BAKE

H✕W   H↑F   H♥H

ACTIVE TIME: 20 MINUTES | **TOTAL:** 45 MINUTES | **TO MAKE AHEAD:** Prepare through Step 3, cover and refrigerate for up to 1 day. Allow the cold baking dish to warm slightly before placing in a hot oven.

Shrimp enchiladas offer a taste of coastal Mexican cuisine but some versions contain so much cheese, butter and sour cream that they can pack a whopping 50 grams of fat per serving. Our version has vibrant flavor and only half the calories and 6 grams of fat per serving, plus we use precooked peeled shrimp so you can get the dish on your table fast enough for a weeknight supper. The addition of refried beans helps makes these enchiladas an excellent source of fiber as well.

- 1 pound peeled cooked shrimp (*see Ingredient Note, page 248*), tails removed, diced
- 1 cup frozen corn, thawed
- 2 4-ounce cans chopped green chiles (*not* drained)
- 2 cups canned green enchilada sauce *or* green salsa, divided
- 12 corn tortillas
- 1 15-ounce can nonfat refried beans
- 1 cup reduced-fat shredded cheese, such as Mexican-style cheese blend, Monterey Jack *or* Cheddar
- ½ cup chopped fresh cilantro
- 1 lime, cut into wedges

1. Preheat oven to 425°F. Coat a 9-by-13-inch glass baking dish with cooking spray.

2. Combine shrimp, corn, chiles and ½ cup enchilada sauce (or salsa) in a microwave-safe medium bowl. Cover and microwave on High until heated through, about 2½ minutes.

3. Spread ¼ cup enchilada sauce (or salsa) in the prepared baking dish. Top with a layer of 6 overlapping tortillas. Spread refried beans evenly over the tortillas. Top the beans with the shrimp mixture, followed by the remaining 6 tortillas. Pour the remaining sauce (or salsa) over the tortillas. Cover with foil.

4. Bake the casserole until it begins to bubble on the sides, about 20 minutes. Remove the foil; sprinkle cheese on top. Continue baking until heated through and the cheese is melted, about 5 minutes more. Top with cilantro and serve with lime wedges.

MAKES 6 SERVINGS

PER SERVING: 281 calories; 6 g fat (2 g sat, 0 g mono); 121 mg cholesterol; 37 g carbohydrate; 23 g protein; 6 g fiber, 709 mg sodium; 241 mg potassium.

NUTRITION BONUS: Fiber (24% daily value), Calcium, Iron & Vitamin C (20% dv).

NEW ENGLAND FRIED SHRIMP

H✂W L↓C H♥H

ACTIVE TIME: 20 MINUTES | **TOTAL:** 20 MINUTES

Shrimp are virtually fat-free so it seems a shame (nutritionally) to send them into the deep fryer, which adds hefty amounts of fat and saturated fat. On the other hand, who doesn't love a crunchy fried shrimp! With 9 grams of total fat and 213 calories per serving, you can feel good about enjoying them. Serve with Classic Coleslaw (*page 83*) and Tartar Sauce (*page 212*).

1 cup pale ale *or* other light-colored beer	2 tablespoons canola oil, divided
1 cup whole-wheat pastry flour (*see Ingredient Note, page 248*) *or* all-purpose flour	1 pound raw shrimp (13-15 per pound; *see Ingredient Note, page 248*), peeled and deveined, tails left on
1 teaspoon Dijon mustard	Freshly ground pepper to taste
½ teaspoon salt, divided	

MAKEOVER TIP

PAN-FRY INSTEAD OF DEEP-FRY TO GET FRIED TASTE AND TEXTURE WITH LESS FAT AND CALORIES. USING A NONSTICK PAN ALLOWS YOU TO "FRY" FOOD IN A MINIMAL AMOUNT OF OIL WITHOUT STICKING. HERE WE PAN-FRY SHRIMP IN ONLY 1 TABLESPOON OF EXTRA-VIRGIN OLIVE OIL PER BATCH.

1. Whisk beer, flour, mustard and ¼ teaspoon salt in a medium bowl until smooth.

2. You'll need to cook the shrimp in two batches. Wait to batter the second batch until the first is cooked. For the first batch, heat 1 tablespoon oil in a large nonstick skillet over medium-high heat. Hold shrimp by the tail and dip in the batter one at a time. Let any excess batter drip off, then add the shrimp to the hot oil, making sure they aren't touching. Cook, turning once and adjusting the heat as necessary to prevent burning, until golden brown on the outside and curled, 3 to 4 minutes total. Transfer to a platter.

3. Wipe out the pan. Add the remaining 1 tablespoon oil to the pan and heat over medium-high. Batter and fry the remaining shrimp. Season all the shrimp with the remaining ¼ teaspoon salt and pepper and serve immediately.

MAKES 4 SERVINGS.

PER SERVING: 213 calories; 9 g fat (1 g sat, 5 g mono); 172 mg cholesterol; 7 g carbohydrate; 24 g protein; 1 g fiber; 351 mg sodium; 210 mg potassium.

NUTRITION BONUS: Selenium (61% daily value), Iron (15% dv).

OVEN-FRIED FISH & CHIPS

H)(W   H♥H

ACTIVE TIME: 25 MINUTES | **TOTAL:** 45 MINUTES

Fish and chips are traditionally sold wrapped in paper to soak up all the grease—not a good sign. Here, we coat the delicate fish in a crispy cornflake crust and then bake it along with potato wedges to cut the calories in half and reduce the fat. Cajun spices add a hint of heat to the mix. Serve with malt vinegar or fresh-cut lemon wedges.

Canola *or* olive oil cooking spray
1 ½ pounds russet potatoes, scrubbed and cut into ¼-inch-thick fries
4 teaspoons canola oil
1 ½ teaspoons Cajun *or* Creole seasoning, divided
2 cups cornflakes

¼ cup all-purpose flour
¼ teaspoon salt
2 large egg whites, beaten
1 pound Pacific cod (*see Ingredient Note, page 154*) *or* haddock, cut into 4 portions

1. Position racks in upper and lower third of oven; preheat to 425°F. Coat a large baking sheet with cooking spray. Set a wire rack on another large baking sheet; coat with cooking spray.

2. Place potatoes in a colander. Thoroughly rinse with cold water; then pat dry completely with paper towels. Toss the potatoes, oil and ¾ teaspoon Cajun (or Creole) seasoning in a large bowl. Spread on the baking sheet without the rack. Bake on the lower oven rack, turning every 10 minutes, until tender and golden, 30 to 35 minutes.

3. Meanwhile, place cornflakes in a food processor or blender and pulse until coarsely ground. Transfer to a shallow dish. Place flour and the remaining ¾ teaspoon Cajun (or Creole) seasoning and salt in another shallow dish and egg whites in a third shallow dish. Dredge fish in the flour mixture, dip it in egg white and then coat all sides with the ground cornflakes. Place on the prepared wire rack. Coat both sides of the breaded fish with cooking spray.

4. Bake the fish on the upper oven rack until opaque in the center and the breading is golden brown and crisp, about 20 minutes.

MAKES 4 SERVINGS.

PER SERVING: 325 calories; 5 g fat (0 g sat, 3 g mono); 43 mg cholesterol; 45 g carbohydrate; 24 g protein; 3 g fiber; 331 mg sodium; 955 mg potassium.

NUTRITION BONUS: Vitamin C (58% daily value), Selenium (47% dv), Potassium (27% dv).

> ## MAKEOVER TIP
>
> **STOP PEELING YOUR POTATOES! THE SKIN AND THE LAYER JUST BELOW CONTAIN MANY NUTRIENTS AND EXTRA FIBER.**

STOVETOP CLAMBAKE

H)(W H♥H

ACTIVE TIME: 20 MINUTES | **TOTAL:** 45 MINUTES
EQUIPMENT: Large stockpot, collapsible metal steamer basket

With our stovetop clambake, the flavors of fresh seafood and summery vegetables are the stars. Flavor-packed sauces are served alongside so there's no need for the bowls of melted butter that so often turn otherwise virtuous seafood into a nutritional disaster.

1 pound small red-skinned potatoes	4 ears corn, husked and cut into thirds
2 whole live lobsters (about 1 ½ pounds each)	Cocktail Sauce (*page 213*) *and/or* Tartar Sauce (*page 212*), optional
12 cherrystone, steamer *or* littleneck clams, scrubbed	
½ pound mussels, scrubbed and debearded if necessary (*see Tip, page 246*)	

HOW TO SHELL A LOBSTER:

1. Grasp claw at the knuckle, near the body. With a firm twist, remove the claw from the body. Repeat with the second claw.

2. To remove claw meat, crack through the claw shell using a pair of kitchen shears or a lobster cracker.

3. Holding the body in one hand and firmly grasping the tail in the other, twist and gently pull the tail from the body. (Discard the body.)

4. Cut the tail in half lengthwise with kitchen shears, starting from the underside. Serve halves in the shell or remove the meat.

1. Place a steamer basket in a large stockpot, add 1 inch of water and bring to a boil over high heat. Place potatoes in the basket, cover the pot and steam for 4 minutes. Reduce the heat slightly, if necessary, to prevent boiling over.

2. Place lobsters on top of the potatoes; cover and steam for 4 minutes. Place clams and mussels on top of the lobsters and potatoes; cover and continue steaming for 4 minutes more. Place corn on top of the shellfish; cover and continue steaming until the clams have opened and the potatoes are tender, 4 to 8 minutes more.

3. Arrange the corn, mussels, clams and potatoes on serving platters. Remove lobster claws and tails by twisting them from the body. Cut the tails lengthwise (*see "How to Shell a Lobster"*). Discard the bodies. Add the split tails and claws to the platters. Serve immediately, with sauces (if using).

MAKES 4 SERVINGS.

PER SERVING: 274 calories; 3 g fat (0 g sat, 0 g mono); 56 mg cholesterol; 40 g carbohydrate; 24 g protein; 3 g fiber; 271 mg sodium; 564 mg potassium.

NUTRITION BONUS: Selenium (57% daily value), Vitamin C (50% dv), Iron (35% dv), Potassium (16% dv).

Eggs Italiano (page 176)

VEGETARIAN

DELICIOUS FEEDBACK

Fettuccine Alfredo

"This is a wonderful recipe! The sauce is wonderful...
even better than a normal high-fat alfredo sauce! It's a much
lighter taste, so you're not stuffed after you eat it. I highly
recommend it. Really easy to prepare as well."

—Sophie, Austin, TX

Tofu Parmigiana

"What a great way to work tofu into your diet!
You'd swear it was eggplant. Delicious—and
even better the next day."

—Mike, Los Angeles, CA

BAKED MAC & CHEESE

H↑F

ACTIVE TIME: 25 MINUTES | **TOTAL:** 55 MINUTES

TO MAKE AHEAD: Prepare through Step 4. Cover and refrigerate for up to 2 days or freeze for up to 3 months. Thaw in the refrigerator, if necessary, then bake for 35 to 45 minutes.

Elbow macaroni in a cheesy sauce can be a true comfort on a gloomy day, but you might not feel so great about all the fat and cholesterol most recipes dish up. In our healthy update we take advantage of the superior flavor of extra-sharp Cheddar, but combine it with creamy low-fat cottage cheese to balance things out. Spinach tucked into the middle of this casserole is great with the cheesy pasta and may help get picky eaters to down their vegetables. Whole-wheat pasta adds robust flavor and extra fiber.

- 3 tablespoons plain dry breadcrumbs (*see Tip, page 246*)
- 1 teaspoon extra-virgin olive oil
- ¼ teaspoon paprika
- 1 16-ounce *or* 10-ounce package frozen spinach, thawed
- 1¾ cups low-fat milk, divided
- 3 tablespoons all-purpose flour

- 2 cups shredded extra-sharp Cheddar cheese
- 1 cup low-fat cottage cheese
- ⅛ teaspoon ground nutmeg
- ¼ teaspoon salt
- Freshly ground pepper to taste
- 8 ounces (2 cups) whole-wheat elbow macaroni *or* penne

1. Put a large pot of water on to boil. Preheat oven to 450°F. Coat an 8-inch-square (2-quart) baking dish with cooking spray.

2. Mix breadcrumbs, oil and paprika in a small bowl. Place spinach in a fine-mesh strainer and press out excess moisture.

3. Heat 1½ cups milk in a large heavy saucepan over medium-high heat until steaming. Whisk remaining ¼ cup milk and flour in a small bowl until smooth; add to the hot milk and cook, whisking constantly, until the sauce simmers and thickens, 2 to 3 minutes. Remove from heat and stir in Cheddar until melted. Stir in cottage cheese, nutmeg, salt and pepper.

4. Cook pasta for 4 minutes, or until not quite tender. (It will continue to cook during baking.) Drain and add to the cheese sauce; mix well. Spread half the pasta mixture in the prepared baking dish. Spoon the spinach on top. Top with the remaining pasta; sprinkle with the breadcrumb mixture.

5. Bake the casserole until bubbly and golden, 25 to 30 minutes.

MAKES 4 SERVINGS.

PER SERVING: 576 calories; 22 g fat (11 g sat, 2 g mono); 69 mg cholesterol; 63 g carbohydrate; 37 g protein; 9 g fiber; 917 mg sodium; 403 mg potassium.

NUTRITION BONUS: Vitamin A (290% daily value), Calcium (70% dv), Folate (37% dv), Iron (15% dv).

> ## MAKEOVER TIP
>
> **ADD VEGETABLES TO BAKED PASTA DISHES OR CASSEROLES AS WE DO IN THIS SPINACH-STUDDED VERSION OF MACARONI & CHEESE.**

BEAN BOLOGNESE

H↑F H♥H

ACTIVE TIME: 40 MINUTES | **TOTAL:** 40 MINUTES

Fiber-rich beans stand in for the beef and pork in this surprisingly rich-tasting vegetarian take on pasta Bolognese. Without the meat, the dish has only a third of the fat and 80 percent less saturated fat. To make the perfect meal, serve with a peppery arugula salad and warm, crusty Italian bread. **SHOPPING TIP:** A can of salad beans, a mixture of chickpeas, kidney and pinto beans, adds depth and variety to this recipe. Look for it in the natural-foods section of larger supermarkets or natural-foods stores. If you can't find it, substitute a can of your favorite beans.

1	14-ounce can salad beans (*see Shopping Tip*) *or* other beans, rinsed, divided	4	cloves garlic, chopped
2	tablespoons extra-virgin olive oil	1	bay leaf
1	small onion, chopped	½	cup white wine
½	cup chopped carrot	1	14-ounce can diced tomatoes
¼	cup chopped celery	¼	cup chopped fresh parsley, divided
½	teaspoon salt	8	ounces whole-wheat fettuccine
		½	cup freshly grated Parmesan cheese

MAKEOVER TIP

RINSE CANNED BEANS BEFORE ADDING THEM TO RECIPES TO REDUCE SODIUM BY UP TO 35%.

1. Put a large pot of water on to boil. Mash ½ cup beans in a small bowl with a fork.

2. Heat oil in a medium saucepan over medium heat. Add onion, carrot, celery and salt; cover and cook, stirring occasionally, until softened, about 10 minutes. Add garlic and bay leaf; cook, stirring, until fragrant, about 15 seconds. Add wine; increase heat to high and boil until most of the liquid evaporates, 3 to 4 minutes. Add tomatoes and their juices, 2 tablespoons parsley and the mashed beans. Bring to a lively simmer and cook, stirring occasionally, until thickened, about 6 minutes. Add the remaining whole beans; cook, stirring occasionally, until heated through, 1 to 2 minutes more.

3. Meanwhile, cook pasta in the boiling water until just tender, about 9 minutes or according to package directions. Drain.

4. Divide the pasta among 4 bowls. Discard the bay leaf and top the pasta with the sauce; sprinkle with Parmesan and the remaining parsley.

MAKES 4 SERVINGS, ABOUT ¾ CUP SAUCE EACH.

PER SERVING: 443 calories; 11 g fat (3 g sat, 6 g mono); 9 mg cholesterol; 67 g carbohydrate; 19 g protein; 14 g fiber; 707 mg sodium; 281 mg potassium.

NUTRITION BONUS: Vitamin A (70% daily value), Vitamin C (25% dv), Magnesium (24% dv), Calcium (20% dv).

FETTUCCINE ALFREDO

H↑F H♥H

ACTIVE TIME: 35 MINUTES | **TOTAL:** 50 MINUTES

Most Alfredo sauces are made with copious amounts of butter and heavy cream—not at all what the doctor ordered. Here, a blend of garlic-infused low-fat milk, reduced-fat cream cheese and Parmesan cheese makes a flavorful sauce to coat the pasta. With plenty of fiber from whole-wheat pasta and only 6 grams of fat per serving, you can put Alfredo back into your pasta repertoire.

2 cups low-fat milk
8 large cloves garlic, peeled
½ teaspoon salt
Freshly ground pepper to taste
Pinch of ground nutmeg

1 pound whole-wheat fettuccine
2 tablespoons reduced-fat cream cheese (Neufchâtel)
¾ cup freshly grated Parmesan cheese, divided
3 tablespoons chopped fresh parsley

1. Put a large pot of water on to boil.

2. Combine milk and garlic in a heavy medium saucepan; bring to a simmer over low heat. Simmer gently until the garlic is tender and the milk has reduced to 1½ cups, 15 to 25 minutes. Let cool slightly.

3. Puree milk and garlic in a blender until smooth. (Use caution when blending hot liquids.) Return to the pan and season with salt, pepper and nutmeg. Keep the sauce warm.

4. Meanwhile, cook fettuccine until just tender, 8 to 10 minutes or according to package directions. Drain and transfer to a warmed large bowl.

5. Whisk cream cheese and ½ cup Parmesan into the sauce. Add to the fettuccine and toss well. Sprinkle with parsley. Serve immediately, passing the remaining ¼ cup Parmesan separately.

MAKES 6 SERVINGS.

PER SERVING: 361 calories; 6 g fat (3 g sat, 2 g mono); 17 mg cholesterol; 63 g carbohydrate; 19 g protein; 10 g fiber; 413 mg sodium; 210 mg potassium.

NUTRITION BONUS: Selenium (83% daily value), Magnesium (28% dv), Calcium (26% dv).

> ## MAKEOVER TIP
>
> **TRY REDUCED-FAT CREAM CHEESE IN PLACE OF HEAVY CREAM IN CREAM-BASED PASTA SAUCES LIKE ALFREDO TO REDUCE SATURATED FAT.**

SPINACH & CHEESE STUFFED SHELLS

H↑F

ACTIVE TIME: 1 ¼ HOURS | **TOTAL:** 2 HOURS

Our stuffed shells are based on a recipe that calls for frozen creamed spinach. By substituting plain fresh or frozen spinach, adding sautéed onions and using part-skim ricotta, we've reduced the fat by half without sacrificing flavor at all. The shells hold and reheat well, which makes them great for entertaining.

24	jumbo pasta shells (8 ounces)
1 ½	teaspoons extra-virgin olive oil
2	onions, finely chopped
2	pounds fresh spinach, trimmed and washed, *or* two 10-ounce packages frozen chopped spinach, thawed and squeezed dry
2	cups part-skim ricotta cheese
⅔	cup plain dry breadcrumbs

½	cup freshly grated Parmesan cheese, divided
¼	teaspoon ground nutmeg
⅛	teaspoon salt
	Freshly ground pepper to taste
1	large egg white, lightly beaten
3	cups prepared marinara sauce, preferably low-sodium

1. Preheat oven to 375°F. Cook shells in a large pot of boiling water, stirring often, until just tender, about 15 minutes or according to package directions. Drain and rinse under cold water. Set aside.

2. Heat oil in a large nonstick skillet over medium-high heat. Add onions and cook, stirring occasionally, until softened, about 3 minutes. If using fresh spinach, add it in batches and toss with tongs until wilted. Drain in a colander, pressing out excess moisture with the back of a spoon. Let cool. If using thawed frozen, add it to the onions and toss to mix well. Set aside.

3. Combine ricotta, breadcrumbs, ¼ cup Parmesan and nutmeg in a bowl; mix well. Add the reserved spinach and season with salt and pepper. Stir in egg white.

4. Stuff each of the reserved shells with a generous 2 tablespoons of the ricotta mixture. Spread 1 cup marinara sauce in the bottom of a 9-by-13-inch baking dish. Arrange the stuffed shells in a single layer. Top with the remaining 2 cups of the sauce and sprinkle with the remaining ¼ cup Parmesan cheese. Bake until the top is golden and the shells are heated through, about 30 minutes. (If the top browns too quickly, tent loosely with foil.) Let cool for 10 minutes before serving.

MAKES 6 SERVINGS.

PER SERVING: 438 calories; 12 g fat (6 g sat, 4 g mono); 32 mg cholesterol; 59 g carbohydrate; 25 g protein; 7 g fiber; 574 mg sodium; 1,121 mg potassium.

NUTRITION BONUS: Vitamin A (315% daily value), Vitamin C (104% dv), Folate (86% dv), Calcium (51% dv), Magnesium (47% dv), Potassium (45% dv), Iron (41% dv), Selenium (30% dv), Zinc (21% dv).

TOFU PARMIGIANA

H)(W   L ↓ C

ACTIVE TIME: 30 MINUTES | **TOTAL:** 30 MINUTES

Instead of having a greasy, battered coating, the tofu "steaks" in our revamped Parmigiana are breaded and lightly pan-fried in just a small amount of oil. Topped with part-skim mozzarella, fresh basil and your favorite marinara sauce, this Italian classic will please even those who are tofu-phobic.

¼ cup plain dry breadcrumbs	1 small onion, chopped
1 teaspoon Italian seasoning	8 ounces white mushrooms, thinly sliced
1 14-ounce package firm *or* extra-firm water-packed tofu, rinsed	¼ cup grated Parmesan cheese
¼ teaspoon garlic powder	¾ cup prepared marinara sauce, preferably low-sodium
¼ teaspoon salt	½ cup shredded part-skim mozzarella cheese
2 teaspoons plus 1 tablespoon extra-virgin olive oil, divided	2 tablespoons chopped fresh basil

1. Combine breadcrumbs and Italian seasoning in a shallow dish. Cut tofu lengthwise into 4 steaks and pat dry. Sprinkle both sides of the tofu with garlic powder and salt and then dredge in the breadcrumb mixture.

2. Heat 2 teaspoons oil in a large nonstick skillet over medium heat. Add onion and cook, stirring, until beginning to brown, about 3 minutes. Add mushrooms and cook until they release their juices and begin to brown, 4 minutes more. Transfer to a bowl.

3. Add the remaining 1 tablespoon oil to the pan. Add the tofu steaks and cook until browned on one side, about 3 minutes. Turn over and sprinkle with Parmesan. Spoon the mushroom mixture over the tofu, pour marinara over the mushrooms and scatter mozzarella on top. Cover and cook until the sauce is hot and the cheese is melted, about 3 minutes. Sprinkle with basil and serve.

MAKES 4 SERVINGS.

PER SERVING: 262 calories; 16 g fat (5 g sat, 7 g mono); 13 mg cholesterol; 15 g carbohydrate; 16 g protein; 3 g fiber; 597 mg sodium; 443 mg potassium.

NUTRITION BONUS: Calcium (40% daily value), Selenium (15% dv).

MAKEOVER TIP

READ MARINARA SAUCE LABELS TO PICK ONE WITH RELATIVELY LOW SODIUM.

EGGS ITALIANO

H✕W   H↑F

ACTIVE TIME: 40 MINUTES | **TOTAL:** 40 MINUTES

This sophisticated take on Eggs Benedict swaps a full-flavored, chunky vegetable medley for Canadian bacon and hollandaise sauce. Add whole-wheat English muffins and poached eggs and this combo makes a lovely brunch or an elegant light supper when served with a salad. (*Photograph: page 166.*)

¼ cup distilled white vinegar
2 teaspoons extra-virgin olive oil
1 shallot, minced
1 clove garlic, minced
1 pound zucchini (about 2 medium), diced
12 ounces plum tomatoes (3-4), diced
3 tablespoons thinly sliced fresh basil, divided

1 tablespoon balsamic vinegar
½ teaspoon salt
 Freshly ground pepper to taste
8 large eggs
4 whole-wheat English muffins, split and toasted
2 tablespoons freshly grated Parmesan cheese

MAKEOVER TIP

GET CREATIVE AND REPLACE HIGH-CALORIE SAUCES LIKE HOLLANDAISE WITH RICH VEGETABLE SAUCES AS WE DO IN THIS ENLIGHTENED TAKE ON EGGS BENEDICT.

1. Fill a large, straight-sided skillet or Dutch oven with 2 inches of water; bring to a boil. Add white vinegar.

2. Meanwhile, heat oil in a large nonstick skillet over medium-high heat. Add shallot and garlic and cook, stirring, until fragrant, about 1 minute. Stir in zucchini and tomatoes and cook, stirring occasionally, until the zucchini is tender, about 10 minutes. Remove from the heat; stir in 1 tablespoon basil, balsamic vinegar, salt and pepper.

3. Meanwhile, reduce the boiling water to a gentle simmer; the water should be steaming and small bubbles should come up from the bottom of the pan. Crack each egg into a small bowl and slip them one at a time into the simmering water, taking care not to break the yolks. Cook for 4 minutes for soft set, 5 minutes for medium set and 8 minutes for hard set. Using a slotted spoon, transfer the eggs to a clean kitchen towel to drain.

4. To serve, top each muffin half with some of the vegetable mixture, an egg, a sprinkling of cheese and the remaining basil.

MAKES 4 SERVINGS.

PER SERVING: 329 calories; 14 g fat (4 g sat, 6 g mono); 425 mg cholesterol; 31 g carbohydrate; 22 g protein; 5 g fiber; 675 mg sodium; 570 mg potassium.

NUTRITION BONUS: Vitamin C (43% daily value), Vitamin A (26% dv), Folate (22% dv), Potassium (16% dv).

CORN & BROCCOLI CALZONES

H)(W   H♥H

ACTIVE TIME: 30 MINUTES | **TOTAL:** 45 MINUTES

A calzone is the perfect vehicle to get your family to eat more veggies. Here we use a summery combination of corn and broccoli, but you can use whatever you have in your fridge. Part-skim ricotta and mozzarella make our pizza pockets lower in saturated fat. Plus a whole-wheat crust adds a nutty flavor and extra fiber. Serve with your favorite marinara sauce for dipping. **SHOPPING TIP:** Look for balls of whole-wheat pizza dough at your supermarket, fresh or frozen and without any hydrogenated oils.

1½ cups chopped broccoli florets
1½ cups fresh corn kernels (about 3 ears; *see Tip, page 246*)
1 cup shredded part-skim mozzarella cheese
⅔ cup part-skim ricotta cheese
4 scallions, thinly sliced
¼ cup chopped fresh basil

½ teaspoon garlic powder
¼ teaspoon salt
¼ teaspoon freshly ground pepper
All-purpose flour for dusting
20 ounces prepared whole-wheat pizza dough (*see Shopping Tip*), thawed if frozen
2 teaspoons canola oil

1. Position racks in upper and lower thirds of oven; preheat to 475°F. Coat 2 baking sheets with cooking spray.

2. Combine broccoli, corn, mozzarella, ricotta, scallions, basil, garlic powder, salt and pepper in a large bowl.

3. On a lightly floured surface, divide dough into 6 pieces. Roll each piece into an 8-inch circle. Place a generous ¾ cup filling on one half of each circle, leaving a 1-inch border of dough. Brush the border with water and fold the top half over the filling. Fold the edges over and crimp with a fork to seal. Make several small slits in the top to vent steam; brush each calzone with oil. Transfer the calzones to the prepared baking sheets.

4. Bake the calzones, switching the pans halfway through, until browned on top, about 15 minutes. Let cool slightly before serving.

MAKES 6 CALZONES.

PER CALZONE: 350 calories; 7 g fat (3 g sat, 3 g mono); 21 mg cholesterol; 50 g carbohydrate; 17 g protein; 4 g fiber; 509 mg sodium; 250 mg potassium.

NUTRITION BONUS: Vitamin C (35% daily value), Calcium (25% dv), Vitamin A (20% dv).

MAKEOVER TIP

SKIP FULL-FAT RICOTTA; USING REDUCED-FAT OR NONFAT RICOTTA IN RECIPES LIKE CALZONES OR LASAGNA—IT'S EVERY BIT AS RICH AND CREAMY— SAVES ABOUT 58 CALORIES AND 8 GRAMS OF FAT FOR EVERY ¼ CUP.

GRILLED EGGPLANT PARMESAN SANDWICH

H✂W H⬆F H❤H

ACTIVE TIME: 45 MINUTES | **TOTAL:** 45 MINUTES

Take battered and fried eggplant, lots of cheese and put it on some bread and you get one tasty sandwich…that has 60 grams of fat. This version uses tender, smoky grilled eggplant instead of fried, so it has a fraction of the fat and calories. To make these sandwiches a cinch to prepare, make sure to have all your ingredients ready before you head out to the grill.

1 large eggplant (1 ¼–1 ½ pounds), cut into 12 ¼-inch-thick rounds
Canola *or* olive oil cooking spray
¼ teaspoon salt
3 tablespoons finely shredded Parmesan *or* Asiago cheese
½ cup shredded part-skim mozzarella cheese

4 small pieces focaccia bread *or* rustic Italian bread
2 teaspoons extra-virgin olive oil
5 ounces baby spinach
1 cup crushed tomatoes, preferably fire-roasted
3 tablespoons chopped fresh basil, divided

1. Preheat grill to medium-high.

2. Place eggplant rounds on a baking sheet and sprinkle with salt. Coat both sides lightly with cooking spray. Combine Parmesan (or Asiago) and mozzarella in a small bowl. Brush both sides of focaccia (or bread) with oil.

3. Place spinach in a large microwave-safe bowl. Cover with plastic wrap and punch several holes in the wrap. Microwave on High until wilted, 2 to 3 minutes. Combine tomatoes and 2 tablespoons basil in a small microwave-safe bowl. Cover and microwave until bubbling, about 2 minutes.

4. Place all your ingredients on the baking sheet with the eggplant and take it to the grill. Grill the eggplant slices until brown and soft on both sides, 2 to 3 minutes per side. Grill the bread until toasted, about 1 minute per side. Return the eggplant and bread to the baking sheet. Reduce grill heat to medium.

5. Place 1 eggplant round on top of each slice of bread. Layer 1 tablespoon tomatoes, 1 tablespoon wilted spinach and 1 tablespoon cheese on each slice of eggplant. Repeat with the remaining eggplant, sauce, spinach and cheese. Sprinkle each stack with some of the remaining basil. Place the baking sheet on the grill, close the lid and grill until the eggplant stack is hot and the cheese is melted, 5 to 7 minutes.

MAKES 4 SERVINGS.

PER SERVING: 291 calories; 8 g fat (2 g sat, 3 g mono); 12 mg cholesterol; 48 g carbohydrate; 12 g protein; 9 g fiber; 756 mg sodium; 526 mg potassium.

NUTRITION BONUS: Vitamin A (38% daily value), Vitamin C (23% dv), Calcium (22% dv), Potassium (15% dv).

> ## MAKEOVER TIP
>
> **REDUCE CALORIES IN MAIN-COURSE SANDWICHES LIKE THIS EGGPLANT PARMESAN BY SERVING THEM OPEN-FACE WITH JUST ONE PIECE OF BREAD.**

PBT (PORTOBELLO, BASIL & TOMATO SANDWICH)

H⧖W H♥H

ACTIVE TIME: 25 MINUTES | **TOTAL:** 25 MINUTES

Don't get us wrong—we love bacon as much as the next person. But if you're itching for a BLT—but not all the fat—smoky grilled portobello mushrooms are a great substitute. Fresh basil takes the place of the lettuce, adding loads of summer flavor.

- 2 tablespoons low-fat mayonnaise
- 2 tablespoons nonfat sour cream *or* nonfat plain yogurt
- 1 teaspoon lemon juice
- 1 tablespoon extra-virgin olive oil
- 2 4-ounce portobello mushrooms, stems removed, caps sliced ½ inch thick
- ⅛ teaspoon salt
  Freshly ground pepper to taste
- 8 slices sourdough bread
- 1 clove garlic, halved
- 1 cup loosely packed basil leaves, torn into shreds (if large)
- 2 tomatoes, sliced

1. Preheat grill or broiler.

2. Stir mayonnaise, sour cream (or yogurt) and lemon juice in a small bowl.

3. Brush oil over cut sides of mushrooms. Grill or broil the mushroom slices until tender and golden, 2 to 3 minutes per side. Season with salt and pepper. Toast bread on the grill or under the broiler. Rub both sides of the bread with the cut sides of the garlic clove.

4. Spread half of the mayonnaise mixture over 4 toasted bread slices and arrange basil on top. Top with the grilled mushroom slices and tomato slices; season with pepper. Finish with a dollop of the remaining mayonnaise mixture and cover with the remaining pieces of toast. Cut sandwiches in half and serve immediately.

MAKES 4 SERVINGS.

PER SERVING: 335 calories; 5 g fat (1 g sat, 3 g mono); 1 mg cholesterol; 58 g carbohydrate; 13 g protein; 4 g fiber; 637 mg sodium; 456 mg potassium.

NUTRITION BONUS: Folate (40% daily value), Iron, Vitamin A & Vitamin C (20% dv).

SOUTHWESTERN CHEESE PANINI

H❨❩W   H⬆F

ACTIVE TIME: 25 MINUTES | **TOTAL:** 25 MINUTES

Lots of colorful vegetables and salsa make this cheesy panini prettier than any grilled cheese you've ever seen. The small amount of Cheddar cheese in this sandwich goes a long way because it is shredded and sharp. Serve with a mixed salad and you've got a delightful lunch or light supper. If you happen to have a panini maker, go ahead and skip Step 3 and grill the panini according to the manufacturer's directions.

4 ounces shredded sharp Cheddar cheese	1 tablespoon chopped pickled jalapeño pepper (optional)
1 cup shredded zucchini	8 slices whole-wheat bread
½ cup shredded carrot	2 teaspoons canola oil
¼ cup finely chopped red onion	
¼ cup prepared salsa	

1. Have four 15-ounce cans and a medium skillet (not nonstick) ready by the stove.

2. Combine Cheddar, zucchini, carrot, onion, salsa and jalapeño (if using) in a medium bowl. Divide among 4 slices of bread and top with the remaining bread.

3. Heat 1 teaspoon canola oil in a large nonstick skillet over medium heat. Place 2 panini in the pan. Place the medium skillet on top of the panini, then weigh it down with the cans. Cook the panini until golden on one side, about 2 minutes. Reduce the heat to medium-low, flip the panini, replace the top skillet and cans, and cook until the second side is golden, 1 to 3 minutes more. Repeat with another 1 teaspoon oil and the remaining panini.

MAKES 4 SERVINGS.

PER SERVING: 331 calories; 14 g fat (5 g sat, 2 g mono); 30 mg cholesterol; 37 g carbohydrate; 16 g protein; 5 g fiber; 523 mg sodium; 163 mg potassium.

NUTRITION BONUS: Vitamin A (50% daily value), Calcium (30% dv), Vitamin C (20% dv), Iron (15% dv).

MAKEOVER TIP

GET ABOUT 3 EXTRA GRAMS OF FIBER WHEN YOU USE WHOLE-WHEAT BREAD INSTEAD OF WHITE BREAD FOR PANINI OR OTHER SANDWICHES.

SLOW-COOKER BLACK BEAN-MUSHROOM CHILI

H✕W   H↑F

ACTIVE TIME: 25 MINUTES | **SLOW-COOKER TIME:** 5-8 HOURS
TO MAKE AHEAD: Cover and refrigerate for up to 2 days or freeze for up to 3 months.
EQUIPMENT: 5- to 6-quart slow cooker

Black beans, earthy mushrooms and tangy tomatillos combine with a variety of spices and smoky chipotles to create a fantastic full-flavored chili. It can simmer in the slow cooker all day, which makes it perfect for a healthy supper when the end of your day is rushed.

1	pound dried black beans (2½ cups), rinsed
1	tablespoon extra-virgin olive oil
¼	cup mustard seeds
2	tablespoons chili powder
1½	teaspoons cumin seeds *or* ground cumin
½	teaspoon cardamom seeds *or* ground cardamom
2	medium onions, coarsely chopped
1	pound mushrooms, sliced
8	ounces tomatillos (*see Ingredient Note, page 248*), husked, rinsed and coarsely chopped

¼	cup water
5½	cups mushroom broth *or* vegetable broth
1	6-ounce can tomato paste
1-2	tablespoons minced canned chipotle peppers in adobo sauce (*see Ingredient Note, page 247*)
1¼	cups grated Monterey Jack *or* pepper Jack cheese
½	cup reduced-fat sour cream
½	cup chopped fresh cilantro
2	limes, cut into wedges

STOVETOP VARIATION:
TOTAL: 4½ HOURS
In Step 2, increase broth to 8½ cups. Omit Step 3. Add the beans to the Dutch oven; cover and simmer the chili gently over low heat, stirring occasionally, until the beans are creamy to bite, about 3 hours.

MAKEOVER TIP

TOAST SPICES IN A SKILLET, AS WE DO IN THIS RECIPE, TO INTENSIFY FLAVOR WITHOUT ADDING CALORIES.

---

1. Soak beans overnight in 2 quarts water. (*Alternatively, place beans and 2 quarts water in a large pot. Bring to a boil. Boil for 2 minutes. Remove from heat and let stand for 1 hour.*) Drain the beans, discarding soaking liquid.

2. Combine oil, mustard seeds, chili powder, cumin and cardamom in a 5- to 6-quart Dutch oven. Place over high heat and stir until the spices sizzle, about 30 seconds. Add onions, mushrooms, tomatillos and water. Cover and cook, stirring occasionally, until the vegetables are juicy, 5 to 7 minutes. Uncover and stir often until the juices evaporate and the vegetables are lightly browned, 10 to 15 minutes. Add broth, tomato paste and chipotles; mix well.

3. Place the beans in a 5- to 6-quart slow cooker. Pour the hot vegetable mixture over the beans. Turn heat to high. Put the lid on and cook until the beans are creamy, 5 to 8 hours.

4. Garnish each serving with cheese, a dollop of sour cream and a sprinkling of cilantro. Serve with lime wedges.

MAKES 10 SERVINGS, GENEROUS 1 CUP EACH.

PER SERVING: 306 calories; 10 g fat (4 g sat, 2 g mono); 20 mg cholesterol; 40 g carbohydrate; 18 g protein; 13 g fiber; 415 mg sodium; 735 mg potassium.

NUTRITION BONUS: Fiber (52% daily value), Folate (47% dv), Iron (22% dv), Potassium (21% dv).

CHILAQUILES CASSEROLE

H)(W   H ↑ F

ACTIVE TIME: 20 MINUTES | **TOTAL:** 45 MINUTES
TO MAKE AHEAD: Prepare through Step 3 and refrigerate for up to 1 day.

A chilaquiles casserole is typically made with deep-fried tortillas and as much as a half-pound of cheese. Our version of this enchilada-style dish has only a third of the fat and is packed with nutritious beans and vegetables. Canned prepared enchilada sauce has great flavor and keeps the prep time quick. It can vary in heat level so find one that suits your taste. If you want to eliminate the heat altogether, try a green enchilada sauce (which is often milder than red) or substitute two 8-ounce cans of plain tomato sauce.

1	tablespoon canola oil
1	medium onion, diced
1	medium zucchini, grated
1	19-ounce can black beans, rinsed
1	14-ounce can diced tomatoes, drained
1½	cups corn, frozen (thawed) *or* fresh

1	teaspoon ground cumin
½	teaspoon salt
12	corn tortillas, quartered
1	19-ounce can mild red *or* green enchilada sauce
1¼	cups shredded reduced-fat Cheddar cheese

1. Preheat oven to 400°F. Lightly coat a 9-by-13-inch baking pan with cooking spray.

2. Heat oil in a large nonstick skillet over medium-high heat. Add onion and cook, stirring often, until starting to brown, about 5 minutes. Stir in zucchini, beans, tomatoes, corn, cumin and salt and cook, stirring occasionally, until the vegetables are heated through, about 3 minutes.

3. Scatter half the tortilla pieces in the pan. Top with half the vegetable mixture, half the enchilada sauce and half the cheese. Repeat with one more layer of tortillas, vegetables, sauce and cheese. Cover with foil.

4. Bake the casserole for 15 minutes. Remove the foil and continue baking until the casserole is bubbling around the edges and the cheese is melted, about 10 minutes more.

MAKES 10 SERVINGS.

PER SERVING: 243 calories; 10 g fat (5 g sat, 4 g mono); 23 mg cholesterol; 30 g carbohydrate; 9 g protein; 5 g fiber; 338 mg sodium; 267 mg potassium.

NUTRITION BONUS: Vitamin C (23% daily value), Fiber (22% dv).

MAKEOVER TIP

USE EXTRA VEGETABLES AND BEANS AND LESS CHEESE IN MEXICAN-STYLE CASSEROLES TO ADD FIBER AND KEEP PORTIONS GENEROUS WHILE REDUCING CALORIES AND FAT.

NASI GORENG

H)(W H♥H

ACTIVE TIME: 30 MINUTES | **TOTAL:** 30 MINUTES

Whole almonds add beneficial monounsaturated fats to EATINGWELL's spin on this Indonesian-style fried rice. To make it vegetarian we've substituted soy sauce for the fish sauce that's typically used as a seasoning. For added flavor, texture and nutritional oomph, our Nasi Goreng is brimming with fresh vegetables and accompanied with fresh slices of cool cucumber and tomato. Serve with Indonesian Tofu Satés (*page 186*).

3 large eggs, beaten
4 small shallots, peeled
3 cloves garlic, peeled
2 tablespoons whole almonds
2 small chile peppers, seeded and diced
2 tablespoons peanut *or* canola oil, divided
2 cups finely chopped or shredded vegetables, such as yellow bell pepper, cabbage and broccoli

2 tablespoons reduced-sodium soy sauce
2 tablespoons kecap manis (*see Ingredient Note*)
4 cups cooked and cooled brown rice
2 scallions, thinly sliced
1 medium tomato, sliced
1 small cucumber, sliced

INGREDIENT NOTE:

Kecap manis is a thick, palm sugar-sweetened soy sauce. It's used as a flavoring, marinade or condiment in Indonesian cooking. Find it in Asian food markets or online at *importfood.com*. To substitute for kecap manis, whisk 1 part molasses with 1 part reduced-sodium soy sauce.

1. Generously coat a wok or large skillet with cooking spray and heat over medium-high heat. Pour in eggs, reduce heat to medium-low and cook, lifting the edges so uncooked egg flows underneath, until mostly set, 1 to 2 minutes. Slide out of the pan onto a clean cutting board. When cool enough to handle, cut into thin strips.

2. Place shallots, garlic, almonds and chiles in a food processor. Process to a thick paste. Heat 1 tablespoon oil in the wok (or pan) over medium-high heat. Add the paste and cook until fragrant, about 2 minutes. Transfer to a small bowl.

3. Heat the remaining 1 tablespoon oil over medium-high heat. Add vegetables and cook, stirring, until crisp-tender, about 2 minutes. Add the shallot paste, soy sauce, kecap manis and rice and stir until combined and heated through, about 2 minutes more. Transfer the Nasi Goreng to a platter. Top with the strips of egg and scallions. Arrange tomato and cucumber slices around the edges.

MAKES 6 SERVINGS.

PER SERVING: 295 calories; 10 g fat (2 g sat, 4 g mono); 106 mg cholesterol; 40 g carbohydrate; 9 g protein; 4 g fiber; 380 mg sodium; 416 mg potassium.

NUTRITION BONUS: Vitamin C (60% daily value), Selenium (26% dv), Magnesium (19% dv), Vitamin A (15% dv).

SATISFYING A GLOBE-TROTTING FAMILY WITH SOPHISTICATED TASTES

Watching 14-year-old Taylor Carpenter skateboard fluidly around his family's large open kitchen, you might think he's one of the luckiest kids in the world. Sure, his parents, Jake and Donna Carpenter, own Burton Snowboards and Channel Islands Surfboards. Sure, the whole family took off on a 10-month, six-continent surf/snowboard odyssey a few years ago. But there's something even better. As Taylor sums it up: "My mom's a really, really great cook."

Donna has her own gourmet food shop, Harvest Market—complete with a brick oven where steaming loaves of sourdough are baked daily. And it's Donna who sees that Taylor, George (18) and Timmy (11)—all riders, skaters, surfers—are well fed and more or less healthy. "Finding something that they all like to eat is not always easy," she admits. "Jake tries to avoid meat and Timmy loves it."

After their worldwide adventure, Donna came back inspired by meals she had. When she's yearning for something ethnic, she makes Nasi Goreng, an Indonesian take on fried rice often served for breakfast. Typically made with leftover rice, spices, meats, shellfish, eggs and a cucumber/tomato garnish, this versatile dish can easily be made vegetarian.

Traditional Nasi Goreng can also be made healthier, as we discovered. We swapped out white rice for brown rice (which has nearly three times the fiber, magnesium, potassium and other nutrients) and loaded it up with fresh vegetables. Reduced-sodium soy sauce and a fiery paste made of shallots, garlic and chiles add flavor. Donna serves Indonesian Tofu Satés (*page 186*) alongside, using peanut butter as the basis for both a marinade and dipping sauce. And when the Carpenter family sits down at the table to gobble it down, there's little talk—a sure sign of enjoyment.

INDONESIAN TOFU SATÉS

H⟩⟨W   L↓C   H♥H

ACTIVE TIME: 40 MINUTES | **TOTAL:** 2½ HOURS
TO MAKE AHEAD: Prepare through Step 2 up to 1 day ahead.
EQUIPMENT: Six 12-inch skewers

Cubes of extra-firm tofu are threaded onto skewers and broiled for this vegetarian version of the popular Indonesian street food. The accompanying peanut sauce is filled with exquisite sweet, hot and salty flavors but omits the often-used coconut milk which is high in saturated fat. This flexible recipe works with tofu or chicken. If serving a group with some vegetarians and some meat eaters, prepare half chicken and half tofu and marinate them separately. These satés are great served with Nasi Goreng (*page 184*) or Peanut-Ginger Noodles (*opposite*).

¼ cup kecap manis (*see Ingredient Note, page 184*)
2 tablespoons reduced-sodium soy sauce
4 cloves garlic, minced
1 tablespoon peanut *or* canola oil
1 tablespoon rice vinegar
2 teaspoons ground cumin
1 teaspoon ground coriander

21 ounces (about 1½ packages) extra-firm water-packed tofu, patted dry and cut into 1-inch cubes
¼ cup smooth natural peanut butter
¼ cup water
2 tablespoons ketchup
1-2 teaspoons hot sauce

1. Combine kecap manis, soy sauce, garlic, oil, vinegar, cumin and coriander in a small bowl. Reserve 2 tablespoons of the marinade in a medium bowl. Place tofu in a large sealable plastic bag. Pour the remaining marinade into the bag. Marinate in the refrigerator for at least 2 hours or overnight.

2. Add peanut butter, water, ketchup and hot sauce to taste to the reserved marinade and whisk to combine. Refrigerate until ready to use.

3. Position rack in upper third of oven; preheat broiler. Line a broiler pan or baking sheet with foil and coat with cooking spray.

4. Remove the tofu from the marinade and thread equal amounts onto six 12-inch skewers. (If using wooden skewers, cover the exposed end of each skewer with foil to prevent burning.) Broil the skewers until the tofu is heated through, 6 to 8 minutes per side. Serve the satés with the reserved peanut sauce for dipping.

MAKES 6 SERVINGS.

PER SERVING: 232 calories; 14 g fat (2 g sat, 1 g mono); 0 mg cholesterol; 6 g carbohydrate; 14 g protein; 2 g fiber; 525 mg sodium; 37 mg potassium.

NUTRITION BONUS: Iron (15% daily value).

PEANUT-GINGER NOODLES

H✂W   H⬆F   H♥H

ACTIVE TIME: 30 MINUTES | **TOTAL:** 30 MINUTES

TO MAKE AHEAD: Cover and refrigerate for up to 2 days. To serve, stir in 2 tablespoons warm water per portion; serve cold or reheat in microwave.

Whole-wheat pasta adds nutty flavor plus extra nutrients and fiber to our version of this popular dish. If you like, add diced baked tofu to boost the protein and add calcium. **SHOPPING TIP:** If you can't find a bagged vegetable medley for this easy noodle bowl, choose 12 ounces of cut vegetables from your market's salad bar and create your own mix.

½ cup smooth natural peanut butter	1 teaspoon minced fresh ginger
2 tablespoons reduced-sodium soy sauce	8 ounces whole-wheat spaghetti
2 teaspoons minced garlic	1 12-ounce bag fresh vegetable medley,
1½ teaspoons chile-garlic sauce (*see Ingredient Note*), or to taste	such as carrots, broccoli, snow peas (*see Shopping Tip*)

1. Put a large pot of water on to boil.

2. Whisk peanut butter, soy sauce, garlic, chile-garlic sauce and ginger in a large bowl.

3. Cook pasta in the boiling water until not quite tender, about 1 minute less than specified in the package directions. Add vegetables and cook until the pasta and vegetables are just tender, 1 minute more. Drain, reserving 1 cup of the cooking liquid. Rinse the pasta and vegetables with cool water to refresh. Stir the reserved cooking liquid into the peanut sauce; add the pasta and vegetables; toss well to coat. Serve warm or chilled.

MAKES 6 SERVINGS, 1½ CUPS EACH.

PER SERVING: 280 calories; 11 g fat (1 g sat, 0 g mono); 0 mg cholesterol; 36 g carbohydrate; 11 g protein; 7 g fiber; 321 mg sodium; 95 mg potassium.

NUTRITION BONUS: Vitamin C (23% daily value), Vitamin A (20% dv).

INGREDIENT NOTE:

Chile-garlic sauce (or chili-garlic sauce, or paste) is a blend of ground chiles, garlic and vinegar and is commonly used to add heat and flavor to Asian soups, sauces and stir-fries. It can be found in the Asian section of large supermarkets and keeps up to 1 year in the refrigerator.

KUNG PAO TOFU

H✳W L↓C H↑F H♥H

ACTIVE TIME: 30 MINUTES | **TOTAL:** 30 MINUTES

In the Sichuan province of China where this dish originates, the tofu wouldn't be deep-fried like it is so often in America. Similarly, in our version of this takeout favorite we stir-fry the ingredients in only a little bit of oil. Our Kung Pao is loaded with fresh vegetables and has less than a third of the fat and calories, so next time think twice before grabbing that takeout menu.

- 1 14-ounce package extra-firm water-packed tofu, rinsed
- ½ teaspoon five-spice powder (*see Shopping Tip*), divided
- 1 tablespoon canola oil
- ½ cup water
- 3 tablespoons oyster-flavored *or* oyster sauce (*see Shopping Tip*)
- ½ teaspoon cornstarch

- 12 ounces broccoli crowns (*see Ingredient Note, page 247*), trimmed and cut into bite-size pieces (4 cups)
- 1 yellow bell pepper, cut into ½-inch dice
- 1 red bell pepper, cut into ½-inch dice
- 1 tablespoon minced fresh ginger
- 1 tablespoon minced garlic
- 2 tablespoons unsalted roasted peanuts
- 2 teaspoons hot sesame oil (optional)

1. Pat tofu dry and cut into ½-inch cubes. Combine with ¼ teaspoon five-spice powder in a medium bowl.

2. Heat canola oil in a large nonstick skillet over medium-high heat. Add tofu and cook, stirring every 1 to 2 minutes, until golden brown, 7 to 9 minutes total. Transfer to a plate.

3. Meanwhile, whisk water, oyster sauce, cornstarch and the remaining ¼ teaspoon five-spice powder in a small bowl.

4. Add broccoli, yellow and red bell pepper to the pan and cook, stirring occasionally, until beginning to soften, about 4 minutes. Add ginger and garlic and cook, stirring, until fragrant, about 30 seconds. Reduce heat to low, add the oyster sauce mixture and cook, stirring, until thickened, about 30 seconds. Return the tofu to the pan along with peanuts and stir to coat with sauce; stir in hot sesame oil (if using).

MAKES 4 SERVINGS, ABOUT 1 CUP EACH.

PER SERVING: 200 calories; 11 g fat (2 g sat, 5 g mono); 0 mg cholesterol; 16 g carbohydrate; 12 g protein; 5 g fiber; 622 mg sodium; 528 mg potassium.

NUTRITION BONUS: Vitamin C (230% daily value), Vitamin A (40% dv), Calcium & Folate (25% dv).

SHOPPING TIPS:

Five-spice powder is a blend of cinnamon, cloves, fennel seed, star anise and Szechuan peppercorns. Look for it in the spice section or with other Asian ingredients.

Be sure to use **"oyster-flavored" sauce** (it's oyster-free) to make this vegetarian; both it and oyster sauce are found in the Asian-food section or at Asian markets.

Easy Fiesta Beans (page 180)

SIDES & SAUCES

DELICIOUS FEEDBACK

Crispy Potato Latkes

"We adore potato latkes and really like that these are not fried. You don't lose any of the crispiness, and I think the flavor of the potatoes comes through even better."

—Sue, West Haven, CT

ONION RINGS

H✕W   H♥H

ACTIVE TIME: 20 MINUTES | **TOTAL:** 45 MINUTES

Crunchy, golden onion rings that aren't deep-fried—how can that be? We moisten the onions with tangy buttermilk and then dredge them in seasoned breadcrumbs and then here's the trick: we spray them lightly with olive oil before baking them to crispy perfection.

2 Vidalia onions	½ teaspoon salt
⅔ cup nonfat buttermilk (*see Tip, page 246*)	¼ teaspoon freshly ground pepper
¾ cup plain dry breadcrumbs	Canola *or* olive oil cooking spray

MAKEOVER TIP

INSTEAD OF DEEP-FRYING, COAT BREADED FOODS LIKE ONION RINGS WITH CANOLA OR OLIVE OIL SPRAY AND BAKE THEM IN THE OVEN—YOU'LL ENJOY ALL OF THE CRUNCH WITH A FRACTION OF THE FAT.

Preheat oven to 350°F. Coat a baking sheet with cooking spray. Cut onions into ½-inch rounds and separate into rings. Place in a bowl and toss with buttermilk. Combine breadcrumbs, salt and pepper in another bowl. Dredge the onion rings in the breadcrumbs and place on the prepared baking sheet. Coat with cooking spray. Bake until lightly browned, about 25 minutes.

MAKES 4 SERVINGS.

PER SERVING: 133 calories; 1 g fat (0 g sat, 0 g mono); 0 mg cholesterol; 27 g carbohydrate; 4 g protein; 2 g fiber; 452 mg sodium; 237 mg potassium.

NUTRITION BONUS: Folate (18% daily value).

OVEN FRIES

H❌W L⬇C H♥H

ACTIVE TIME: 5 MINUTES | **TOTAL:** 25 MINUTES

Coated with olive oil and baked in a hot oven, these fries are soft and buttery inside and crisp on the outside—the perfect combination.

2	large Yukon Gold potatoes, cut into wedges	½	teaspoon salt
4	teaspoons extra-virgin olive oil	½	teaspoon dried thyme (optional)

Preheat oven to 450°F. Toss potato wedges with oil, salt and thyme (if using). Spread the wedges out on a rimmed baking sheet. Bake until browned and tender, turning once, about 20 minutes total.

MAKES 4 SERVINGS.

PER SERVING: 102 calories; 5 g fat (1 g sat, 4 g mono); 0 mg cholesterol; 13 g carbohydrate; 2 g protein; 1 g fiber; 291 mg sodium; 405 mg potassium.

PARMESAN POTATO SKIN CHIPS

H❌W H♥H

ACTIVE TIME: 15 MINUTES | **TOTAL:** 40 MINUTES

The potato skins are the best part of the potato, nutrition-wise. Here, we toss the skins with olive oil, seasonings and Parmesan cheese and bake them to golden perfection.

5	large russet potatoes	¼	teaspoon salt
1	teaspoon extra-virgin olive oil	⅛	teaspoon cayenne pepper
½	teaspoon paprika	2	tablespoons freshly grated Parmesan cheese

Preheat oven to 400°F. Coat a baking sheet with cooking spray. With a paring knife, remove skin and about ⅛ inch of the flesh from potatoes in long 1- to 2-inch-wide strips. (Reserve peeled potatoes for another use.) Toss the potato skins with oil, paprika, salt and cayenne. Place in a single layer on the prepared baking sheet; sprinkle with Parmesan. Bake until tender and golden, 25 to 30 minutes.

MAKES 4 SERVINGS.

PER SERVING: 196 calories; 2 g fat (1 g sat, 1 g mono); 2 mg cholesterol; 40 g carbohydrate; 6 g protein; 4 g fiber; 202 mg sodium; 1,010 mg potassium.

NUTRITION BONUS: Vitamin C (30% daily value), Potassium (29% dv).

VERMONT CHEDDAR MASHED POTATOES

H ✙ W

ACTIVE TIME: 20 MINUTES | **TOTAL:** 45 MINUTES
TO MAKE AHEAD: Cover and refrigerate for up to 2 days. To serve, reheat in a double boiler and garnish with cheese and chives.

Extra-sharp Cheddar and buttermilk add a tangy punch to these potatoes. And, yes, we may be a bit biased, but we prefer Vermont Cheddar cheese.

3 pounds Yukon Gold potatoes, cut into 1 1/2-inch pieces	3/4 cup nonfat buttermilk (*see Tip, page 246*)
1 1/2 cups shredded extra-sharp Cheddar cheese, divided	1 teaspoon salt
	1/2 teaspoon freshly ground pepper
	1/4 cup sliced fresh chives, divided

Place potatoes in a large Dutch oven and add enough water to cover. Bring to a boil over high heat. Boil until very tender when pierced with a fork, 20 to 25 minutes. Remove from the heat. Drain and return the potatoes to the pot. Mash with a potato masher. Stir in 1 1/4 cups cheese until melted. Add buttermilk, salt and pepper and stir to combine. Gently fold in 3 tablespoons chives. Transfer to a serving dish and garnish with the remaining 1/4 cup cheese and 1 tablespoon chives.

MAKES 8 SERVINGS, ABOUT 1 CUP EACH.

PER SERVING: 223 calories; 6 g fat (4 g sat, 0 g mono); 19 mg cholesterol; 31 g carbohydrate; 8 g protein; 2 g fiber; 425 mg sodium; 935 mg potassium.

NUTRITION BONUS: Potassium (27% daily value), Calcium (15% dv).

AU GRATIN POTATOES

ACTIVE TIME: 45 MINUTES | **TOTAL:** 1 ½ HOURS
TO MAKE AHEAD: Prepare through Step 5; cover and refrigerate for up to 1 day.

We use flour-thickened low-fat milk combined with a modest amount of tangy sharp Cheddar to make a creamy cheese sauce for our healthy spin on au gratin potatoes. They're topped with additional cheese and some bread-crumbs, then baked until golden brown and bubbling; you'll find it hard to believe that these tasty potatoes have only a third of the fat of the original.

3	pounds red potatoes
1	small onion, halved
2	cloves garlic, peeled
¼	cup all-purpose flour
1 ½	teaspoons salt
1	teaspoon dry mustard
¼	teaspoon cayenne pepper

¼	teaspoon freshly ground pepper
3	cups low-fat milk, divided
1 ⅓	cups shredded sharp Cheddar cheese, divided
½	cup plain dry breadcrumbs
2	teaspoons extra-virgin olive oil

1. Preheat oven to 350°F. Coat a 9-by-13-inch baking pan with cooking spray.

2. Place potatoes in a large saucepan and cover with water. Bring to a boil, reduce heat to medium and cook, covered, until barely tender, 10 to 12 minutes. Drain, cool and slip off skins.

3. Coarsely shred the potatoes in a food processor or with the large-holed side of a box grater.

4. Place onion, garlic, flour, salt, dry mustard, cayenne and black pepper in a food processor; pulse until finely chopped. Add ½ cup milk and process until smooth. Scrape into a medium saucepan and add the remaining 2½ cups milk. Bring to a simmer over medium heat, stirring constantly. Simmer, stirring, until thickened, about 5 minutes. Remove from heat and stir in 1 cup Cheddar until melted.

5. Combine the potatoes and the cheese sauce. Transfer to the prepared pan. Combine the remaining ⅓ cup cheese, breadcrumbs and oil in a small bowl and mix with your fingers. Sprinkle the crumb mixture evenly over the potato mixture.

6. Cover the pan with foil and bake for 10 minutes. Uncover and bake until golden brown and bubbling, about 20 minutes more. Let stand for 10 minutes before serving.

MAKES 8 SERVINGS, 1 CUP EACH.

PER SERVING: 292 calories; 9 g fat (4 g sat, 1 g mono); 26 mg cholesterol; 42 g carbohydrate; 13 g protein; 4 g fiber; 665 mg sodium; 808 mg potassium.

NUTRITION BONUS: Calcium (28% daily value), Vitamin C (27% dv), Potassium (23% dv).

CRISPY POTATO LATKES

H⧓W   L⬇C   H♥H

ACTIVE TIME: 50 MINUTES | **TOTAL:** 1½ HOURS

It is a holiday tradition to fry latkes in hot oil, but there's no reason they can't be delicious with a little less oil. We give our shredded potato-and-onion pancakes a coating of matzo crumbs, pan-fry them in a small amount of oil and finish them in a hot oven for a few minutes. The golden-crisp results have only 4 grams of fat and 100 calories per serving—truly a miracle.

1½ pounds russet potatoes (about 2), shredded
1 medium white onion, shredded
2 medium shallots, minced (about ¼ cup)
1 teaspoon salt
1 large egg, lightly beaten

2 pieces whole-wheat matzo (6-by-6-inch), broken into pieces
½ teaspoon white pepper
3 tablespoons peanut oil *or* extra-virgin olive oil, divided

1. Toss shredded potato, onion, shallots and salt in a medium bowl. Transfer to a sieve set over a large bowl; let drain for about 15 minutes. Squeeze the potato mixture, a handful at a time, over the bowl to release excess moisture (don't oversqueeze—some moisture should remain). Transfer the squeezed potato mixture to another large bowl. Carefully pour off the liquid, leaving a pasty white sediment—potato starch—in the bottom of the bowl. Add the starch to the potato mixture. Stir in egg.

2. Put matzo pieces in a sealable plastic bag and crush with a rolling pin into coarse crumbs. Sprinkle the crumbs and pepper over the potato mixture and toss to combine. Cover and refrigerate until the matzo is softened, 20 to 30 minutes.

3. Preheat oven to 425°F. Coat a baking sheet with cooking spray.

4. Heat 1 tablespoon oil in a large skillet over medium-high heat. Stir the potato mixture. Cook 4 latkes per batch: place ¼ cup potato mixture in a little of the oil and press with the back of a spatula to flatten into a 3½-inch cake. Cook until crispy and golden, 1½ to 3 minutes per side. Transfer the latkes to the prepared baking sheet. Continue with 2 more batches, using 1 tablespoon oil per batch and reducing the heat as needed to prevent scorching. Transfer the baking sheet to the oven and bake until heated through, about 10 minutes.

MAKES 12 LATKES.

PER LATKE: 100 calories; 4 g fat (1 g sat, 2 g mono); 18 mg cholesterol; 15 g carbohydrate; 2 g protein; 2 g fiber; 204 mg sodium; 278 mg potassium.

NUTRITION BONUS: Vitamin C (20% daily value).

CORNBREAD & SAUSAGE STUFFING

H✖W   H♥H

ACTIVE TIME: 25 MINUTES | **TOTAL:** 50 MINUTES
TO MAKE AHEAD: Prepare through Step 3, cover and refrigerate for up to 1 day. Bake at 350°F until hot, about 30 minutes.

Cornbread stuffing, a Southern favorite, is a nice change from more traditional white-bread stuffing. Our delectable recipe uses Italian turkey sausage, rather than pork, and omits all the butter and cream to cut the fat by two-thirds. The stuffing is lower in sodium as well and so easy to make that it's sure to become a favorite side year-round.

1 pound sweet Italian turkey sausage (about 4 links), casings removed	2 pounds prepared cornbread, cut into ¾-inch cubes (about 12 cups)
2 cups finely chopped onion	¼ cup chopped fresh parsley
1½ cups finely chopped celery	1 tablespoon chopped fresh sage
¼ teaspoon salt	1½-3 cups reduced-sodium chicken broth
Freshly ground pepper to taste	

1. Preheat oven to 325°F. Coat a 9-by-13-inch baking pan with cooking spray.

2. Cook sausage in a large nonstick skillet over medium-high heat, stirring and breaking up with a wooden spoon, until browned, about 10 minutes. Add onion and celery; cover, reduce heat and cook, stirring occasionally, until tender, about 10 minutes. Transfer the mixture to a large bowl. Season with salt and pepper. Add cornbread, parsley and sage.

3. Bring broth to a simmer in a small saucepan. Pour 1 cup over the stuffing mixture and toss gently (the cornbread will break into smaller pieces). Add as much of the remaining broth as needed, ½ cup at a time, until the stuffing feels moist but not wet. Spoon the stuffing into the prepared pan and cover with foil.

4. Bake the stuffing until thoroughly heated, about 25 minutes. Serve warm.

MAKES 12 SERVINGS, SCANT 1 CUP EACH.

PER SERVING: 242 calories; 8 g fat (3 g sat, 0 g mono); 29 mg cholesterol; 34 g carbohydrate; 10 g protein; 2 g fiber; 692 mg sodium; 79 mg potassium.

WHOLE-GRAIN RICE PILAF

H✕W   L↓C   H♥H

ACTIVE TIME: 15 MINUTES | **TOTAL:** 30 MINUTES

Great-tasting whole-grain pilafs are available these days, and they are a step up (nutritionally speaking) from the original San Francisco treat, but unfortunately they are usually loaded with sodium. Our version combines whole-wheat pasta, onions and brown rice for delicious results with less sodium.

2 teaspoons extra-virgin olive oil *or* canola oil	1 cup instant brown rice
½ cup broken whole-wheat spaghetti pieces	¼ teaspoon salt
⅓ cup finely diced onion	1 bay leaf
1 14-ounce can reduced-sodium chicken broth	1 tablespoon chopped fresh parsley

MAKEOVER TIP

CHOOSING WHOLE-GRAINS—IN THIS CASE, BROWN RICE AND WHOLE-WHEAT PASTA—OVER REFINED GRAINS, SUCH AS WHITE RICE AND WHITE PASTA, ADDS FIBER.

Heat oil in a saucepan over medium-high heat. Add pasta and onion; cook, stirring, until starting to brown, about 3 minutes. Add broth, rice, salt and bay leaf; bring to a boil. Reduce heat to low, cover and cook until the liquid is absorbed and the rice is tender, 10 to 12 minutes. Let sit for 5 minutes. Discard the bay leaf. Fluff with a fork and stir in parsley.

MAKES 6 SERVINGS, ABOUT ⅔ CUP EACH.

PER SERVING: 98 calories; 2 g fat (0 g sat, 1 g mono); 1 mg cholesterol; 17 g carbohydrate; 3 g protein; 2 g fiber; 131 mg sodium; 32 mg potassium.

EASY FIESTA BEANS

H✕W   L↓C   H↑F   H♥H

ACTIVE TIME: 15 MINUTES | **TOTAL:** 15 MINUTES

This easy, tasty dish is a great way to jazz up canned beans. Opt for the fat-free refried beans and no-salt-added pinto beans to keep this dish as healthy as possible. (*Photograph: page 190.*)

1 16-ounce can nonfat refried beans, preferably spicy	½ cup prepared salsa
1 15-ounce can no-salt-added pinto beans, rinsed	⅔ cup shredded sharp Cheddar cheese, divided
	4 scallions, sliced

1. Position rack in upper third of oven; preheat broiler.

2. Combine refried beans, pinto beans, salsa and ⅓ cup cheese in a saucepan. Cook over medium heat, stirring, until the mixture is hot and the cheese is melted, 6 to 8 minutes. Spoon the bean mixture into a 2-quart baking dish and sprinkle with the remaining ⅓ cup cheese and scallions. Broil until the cheese is lightly browned, about 2 minutes.

MAKES 6 SERVINGS, GENEROUS ½ CUP EACH.

PER SERVING: 169 calories; 4 g fat (2 g sat, 0 g mono); 13 mg cholesterol; 21 g carbohydrate; 10 g protein; 7 g fiber; 519 mg sodium; 64 mg potassium.

NUTRITION BONUS: Calcium (15% daily value).

> **MAKEOVER TIP**
>
> **LOWER-SODIUM CANNED BEANS OR NO-SALT-ADDED BEANS ARE GREAT OPTION TO REDUCE THE OVERALL SODIUM IN A RECIPE.**

GARLIC-CHEESE GRITS

H ✂ W   L ↓ C

ACTIVE TIME: 20 MINUTES | **TOTAL:** 1-1 ½ HOURS
TO MAKE AHEAD: Prepare through Step 4, cover and refrigerate until ready to bake.

Garlic-cheese grits are a typically rich Southern dish, but the truth is you don't need a half a cup of butter and a pound of cheese to make them taste good. By using a pungent blend of super-sharp cheeses we've found you can use much less cheese and still get flavor-packed results.

4½ cups water	½ cup shredded extra-sharp Cheddar cheese
1 cup grits, quick *or* old-fashioned (*not* instant)	½ cup grated sharp Italian cheese, such as Pecorino Romano *or* Parmesan
¼ teaspoon salt	⅛-¼ teaspoon cayenne pepper *or* 1 teaspoon hot sauce, or to taste
2 teaspoons extra-virgin olive oil	
2 medium cloves garlic, minced	

1. Preheat oven to 350°F. Coat an 8-inch-square baking pan with cooking spray.

2. Bring water, grits and salt to a boil in a large saucepan, stirring occasionally. Reduce the heat and simmer until the grits are thick, 5 to 30 minutes, depending on the type of grits.

3. Meanwhile, combine oil and garlic in a small skillet and cook over medium heat, stirring often, until the garlic is fragrant but not browned, about 1 minute. Remove from heat.

4. Stir the oil and garlic into the grits along with the cheeses and cayenne (or hot sauce); transfer to the prepared pan.

5. Bake, uncovered, until bubbling and crusty on top, about 45 minutes.

MAKES 6 SERVINGS, ABOUT ⅔ CUP EACH.

PER SERVING: 168 calories; 6 g fat (3 g sat, 2 g mono); 16 mg cholesterol; 21 g carbohydrate; 7 g protein; 1 g fiber; 264 mg sodium; 35 mg potassium.

NUTRITION BONUS: Calcium (15% daily value).

OVEN-FRIED ZUCCHINI STICKS

H⊁W H♥H

ACTIVE TIME: 20 MINUTES | **TOTAL:** 30 MINUTES

When you get them in a restaurant, zucchini sticks have been cooked in a deep fryer, which means loads of fat and calories. Ours are oven-baked and taste every bit as good with only a fraction of the fat and calories. Serve with a side of your favorite marinara sauce for dipping.

Canola *or* olive oil cooking spray
½ cup whole-wheat flour
½ cup all-purpose flour
2 tablespoons cornmeal
1 teaspoon salt

½ teaspoon freshly ground pepper
1½ pounds zucchini (about 3 medium), cut into ½-by-3-inch sticks
2 large egg whites, lightly beaten

Preheat oven to 475°F. Coat a large baking sheet with cooking spray. Combine flours, cornmeal, salt and pepper in a large sealable plastic bag. Dip zucchini in egg white, shake in the bag to coat, and arrange, not touching, on the baking sheet. Coat all exposed sides with cooking spray. Bake on the center rack for 7 minutes. Turn the zucchini and coat any floury spots with cooking spray. Continue to bake until golden and just tender, about 5 minutes more. Serve hot.

MAKES 4 SERVINGS.

PER SERVING: 127 calories; 2 g fat (0 g sat, 0 g mono); 0 mg cholesterol; 23 g carbohydrate; 7 g protein; 4 g fiber; 427 mg sodium; 524 mg potassium.

NUTRITION BONUS: Potassium (15% daily value).

CREAMED SPINACH

H⊁W L↓C

ACTIVE TIME: 20 MINUTES | **TOTAL:** 20 MINUTES

There's nothing quite like a serving of creamed spinach served with a perfectly cooked steak. EATINGWELL's updated version has a low-in-fat cream sauce that's rich with Parmesan cheese and nutmeg.

2 teaspoons extra-virgin olive oil
¼ cup minced shallot *or* red onion
10 ounces fresh spinach, tough stems removed
1 tablespoon butter
1 tablespoon all-purpose flour
½ cup low-fat milk

⅛ teaspoon ground nutmeg
⅛ teaspoon salt
⅛ teaspoon freshly ground pepper
2 tablespoons grated Parmesan *or* Pecorino Romano cheese

1. Heat oil in a large nonstick skillet or Dutch oven over medium-high heat. Add shallot (or onion); cook, stirring, until fragrant, about 30 seconds. Add spinach and cook, stirring, until just wilted, about 2 minutes.

2. Heat butter in a small saucepan over medium-high heat. Add flour and cook, stirring, until smooth and bubbling, about 30 seconds. Add milk, nutmeg, salt and pepper; cook, whisking constantly, until thickened, about 1 minute. Stir the spinach into the sauce. Sprinkle with grated cheese and serve.

MAKES 2 SERVINGS.

PER SERVING: 203 calories; 13 g fat (6 g sat, 6 g mono); 23 mg cholesterol; 15 g carbohydrate; 9 g protein; 3 g fiber; 370 mg sodium; 870 mg potassium.

NUTRITION BONUS: Vitamin A (280% daily value), Folate (74% dv), Vitamin C (70% dv), Magnesium (30% dv), Calcium (28% dv), Potassium (25% dv).

ROASTED CARROTS WITH CARDAMOM BUTTER

H✕W L⬇C H⬆F

ACTIVE TIME: 15 MINUTES | **TOTAL:** 40 MINUTES

Roasting these carrots with only a bit of butter and some cardamom gives them a rich, nutty flavor that belies how healthy they are. A single serving gives you over 600 percent of the daily recommendation for vitamin A!

4 teaspoons butter, melted	½ teaspoon salt
2 teaspoons canola oil	2 pounds carrots, peeled and cut diagonally
1 teaspoon ground cardamom	into ¼-inch-thick slices

1. Position rack in lower third of oven; preheat to 450°F.

2. Combine butter, oil, cardamom and salt in a medium bowl. Add carrots and toss well to coat. Spread evenly on a rimmed baking sheet. Roast the carrots, stirring twice, until tender and golden, about 30 minutes. Serve immediately.

MAKES 4 SERVINGS, ABOUT ⅔ CUP EACH.

PER SERVING: 138 calories; 7 g fat (3 g sat, 2 g mono); 10 mg cholesterol; 20 g carbohydrate; 2 g protein; 6 g fiber; 430 mg sodium; 652 mg potassium.

NUTRITION BONUS: Vitamin A (680% daily value), Fiber (24% dv), Vitamin C (20% dv), Potassium (19% dv).

CREAMY MASHED CAULIFLOWER

H⊁W L↓C H♥H

ACTIVE TIME: 15 MINUTES | **TOTAL:** 30 MINUTES

Our savory cauliflower puree makes a perfect stand-in for mashed potatoes. It gets its fabulous flavor from garlic, buttermilk and a touch of butter and, best of all, it has about one-quarter of the calories of typical mashed potatoes. If you like, vary it by adding shredded low-fat cheese or chopped fresh herbs.

8 cups bite-size cauliflower florets (about 1 head)

4 cloves garlic, crushed and peeled

⅓ cup nonfat buttermilk (*see Tip, page 246*)

4 teaspoons extra-virgin olive oil, divided

1 teaspoon butter

½ teaspoon salt

Freshly ground pepper to taste

Snipped fresh chives for garnish

1. Place cauliflower florets and garlic in a steamer basket over boiling water, cover and steam until very tender, 12 to 15 minutes. (*Alternatively, place florets and garlic in a microwave-safe bowl with ¼ cup water, cover and microwave on High for 3 to 5 minutes.*)

2. Place the cooked cauliflower and garlic in a food processor. Add buttermilk, 2 teaspoons oil, butter, salt and pepper; pulse several times, then process until smooth and creamy. Transfer to a serving bowl. Drizzle with the remaining 2 teaspoons oil and garnish with chives, if desired. Serve hot.

MAKES 4 SERVINGS, ¾ CUP EACH.

PER SERVING: 107 calories; 7 g fat (1 g sat, 4 g mono); 3 mg cholesterol; 10 g carbohydrate; 5 g protein; 4 g fiber; 339 mg sodium; 288 mg potassium.

NUTRITION BONUS: Vitamin C (150% daily value), Folate (22% dv).

GREEN BEAN CASSEROLE

H⌘W H♥H

ACTIVE TIME: 30 MINUTES | **TOTAL:** 45 MINUTES

The original version of this holiday favorite, off the back of a box, was ripe for a makeover. This healthy revision skips the canned soup and all the fat and sodium that come with it. Our white sauce with sliced fresh mushrooms, sweet onions and low-fat milk makes a creamy, rich casserole.

3 tablespoons canola oil, divided
1 medium sweet onion (half diced, half thinly sliced), divided
8 ounces sliced mushrooms, chopped
1 tablespoon onion powder
1¼ teaspoons salt, divided
½ teaspoon dried thyme
½ teaspoon freshly ground pepper
⅔ cup all-purpose flour, divided
1 cup low-fat milk

3 tablespoons dry sherry (*see Ingredient Note, page 248*)
1 pound frozen French-cut green beans (about 4 cups)
⅓ cup reduced-fat sour cream
3 tablespoons buttermilk powder (*see Ingredient Note*)
1 teaspoon paprika
½ teaspoon garlic powder

INGREDIENT NOTE:

Buttermilk powder, such as Saco Buttermilk Blend, is found in the baking section or with the powdered milk in most supermarkets and can be used in place of fresh buttermilk. In this recipe, we just use the powder, without any added liquid. Store the unused portion in the refrigerator.

1. Preheat oven to 400°F. Coat a 2½-quart baking dish with cooking spray.

2. Heat 1 tablespoon oil in a large saucepan over medium heat. Add diced onion and cook, stirring often, until softened and slightly translucent, about 4 minutes. Stir in mushrooms, onion powder, 1 teaspoon salt, thyme and pepper. Cook, stirring often, until the mushroom juices are almost evaporated, 3 to 5 minutes. Sprinkle ⅓ cup flour over the vegetables; stir to coat. Add milk and sherry and bring to a simmer, stirring often. Stir in green beans and return to a simmer. Cook, stirring, until heated through, about 1 minute. Stir in sour cream and buttermilk powder. Transfer to the prepared baking dish.

3. Whisk the remaining ⅓ cup flour, paprika, garlic powder and the remaining ¼ teaspoon salt in a shallow dish. Add sliced onion; toss to coat. Heat the remaining 2 tablespoons oil in a large nonstick skillet over medium-high heat. Add the onion along with any remaining flour mixture and cook, turning once or twice, until golden and crispy, 4 to 5 minutes. Spread the onion topping over the casserole.

4. Bake the casserole until bubbling, about 15 minutes. Let cool for 5 minutes before serving.

MAKES 6 SERVINGS, ABOUT ¾ CUP EACH.

PER SERVING: 217 calories; 10 g fat (2 g sat, 5 g mono); 10 mg cholesterol; 24 g carbohydrate; 7 g protein; 3 g fiber; 625 mg sodium; 266 mg potassium.

NUTRITION BONUS: Calcium (16% daily value).

SWEET POTATO CASSEROLE

H✂W   H♥H

ACTIVE TIME: 30 MINUTES | **TOTAL:** 1 ¼ HOURS
TO MAKE AHEAD: Prepare through Step 4; cover and refrigerate for up to 2 days.

This scrumptious sweet potato casserole gets fabulous flavor from honey and freshly grated orange zest rather than the traditional stick of butter. To complete the healthy makeover we sprinkle a crunchy pecan streusel spiked with orange juice concentrate over the top. You can save the marshmallows for s'mores.

2½	pounds sweet potatoes (3 medium), peeled and cut into 2-inch chunks
2	large eggs
1	tablespoon canola oil
1	tablespoon honey
½	cup low-fat milk
2	teaspoons freshly grated orange zest
1	teaspoon vanilla extract
½	teaspoon salt

TOPPING

½	cup whole-wheat flour
⅓	cup packed brown sugar
4	teaspoons frozen orange juice concentrate
1	tablespoon canola oil
1	tablespoon butter, melted
½	cup chopped pecans

1. Place sweet potatoes in a large saucepan and cover with water. Bring to a boil. Cover and cook over medium heat until tender, 10 to 15 minutes. Drain well and return to the pan. Mash with a potato masher. Measure out 3 cups. (Reserve any extra for another use.)

2. Preheat oven to 350°F. Coat an 8-inch-square (or similar 2-quart) baking dish with cooking spray.

3. Whisk eggs, oil and honey in a medium bowl. Add mashed sweet potato and mix well. Stir in milk, orange zest, vanilla and salt. Spread the mixture in the prepared baking dish.

4. TO PREPARE TOPPING: Mix flour, brown sugar, orange juice concentrate, oil and butter in a small bowl. Blend with a fork or your fingertips until crumbly. Stir in pecans. Sprinkle over the casserole.

5. Bake the casserole until heated through and the top is lightly browned, 35 to 45 minutes.

MAKES 10 SERVINGS, ABOUT ½ CUP EACH.

PER SERVING: 242 calories; 10 g fat (2 g sat, 5 g mono); 46 mg cholesterol; 36 g carbohydrate; 5 g protein; 4 g fiber; 170 mg sodium; 351 mg potassium.

NUTRITION BONUS: Vitamin A (280% daily value), Vitamin C (25% dv).

CORN PUDDING

H✻W L↓C H♥H

ACTIVE TIME: 20 MINUTES | **TOTAL:** 1½ HOURS

We thought that lightening a corn pudding was as easy as leaving out a few of the egg yolks and using low-fat milk, but the resulting custard was disappointing. The Test Kitchen found that nonfat evaporated milk, rather than regular nonfat milk, produced a custard with a creamier consistency and less than half the fat. For additional creaminess, and to intensify the sweet corn flavor, we pureed half the corn.

2 cups fresh corn kernels (about 2 large ears), divided (*see Tip, page 246*)
2 tablespoons all-purpose flour
3 large eggs
3 large egg whites

1 cup nonfat evaporated milk
1 teaspoon salt
¼ teaspoon freshly ground pepper
1 teaspoon butter
2 tablespoons plain dry breadcrumbs

MAKEOVER TIP

BEURRE NOISETTE, "NUTTY BUTTER," IS THE FRENCH COOKING TERM FOR BUTTER THAT IS HEATED UNTIL IT TURNS LIGHT BROWN. IN DISHES WHERE THE TASTE OF BUTTER IS ESSENTIAL, YOU CAN GET AWAY WITH USING MUCH LESS IF YOU USE BEURRE NOISETTE AS WE DO IN THIS RECIPE.

1. Preheat oven to 325°F. Coat a 1½- or 2-quart soufflé or baking dish with cooking spray.

2. Combine 1 cup corn and flour in a food processor or blender; process until smooth. Whisk eggs and egg whites in a large bowl. Stir in the pureed corn, the remaining 1 cup kernels, evaporated milk, salt and pepper. Pour the mixture into the prepared dish. Bake for 30 minutes.

3. Meanwhile, melt butter in a small saucepan over low heat and cook until a light, nutty brown, 30 seconds to 4 minutes, depending on your stove. Add breadcrumbs and cook, stirring frequently, until the crumbs darken slightly, 1 to 1½ minutes.

4. When the pudding has baked for 30 minutes, sprinkle the breadcrumbs on top and continue to bake until a knife inserted near the center comes out clean, 25 to 35 minutes more. Serve immediately.

MAKES 6 SERVINGS.

PER SERVING: 145 calories; 4 g fat (1 g sat, 1 g mono); 109 mg cholesterol; 19 g carbohydrate; 10 g protein; 2 g fiber; 523 mg sodium; 348 mg potassium.

NUTRITION BONUS: Selenium (20% daily value).

Steamed vegetables make an easy, delicious side with any meal. If you need a little coaxing to enjoy your veggies, try them topped with one of the creamy sauces on the following pages.

TO STEAM VEGETABLES:

Bring 1 inch of water to a steady boil in a large saucepan over high heat. Place the vegetable of your choice in a steamer basket in the saucepan. Cover and steam until just tender. See chart below for timing.

	AMOUNT FOR 4 SERVINGS	COOKING TIME	ANALYSIS PER SERVING
ASPARAGUS	1 ½ pounds (1-2 bunches), trimmed	4 minutes	18 calories; 3 g carbohydrate; 2 g fiber.
BROCCOLI	1 pound (about 1 head), cut into 1-inch florets	6 minutes	30 calories; 6 g carbohydrate; 3 g fiber.
BRUSSELS SPROUTS	1 ½ pounds, stems trimmed	6 to 8 minutes	67 calories; 13 g carbohydrate; 5 g fiber.
CARROTS	1 ½ pounds, cut into ⅛-inch-thick rounds	4 minutes	55 calories; 13 g carbohydrate; 5 g fiber.
CAULIFLOWER	1 ½-2 pounds (1 head), cut into 1-inch florets	5 minutes	38 calories; 7 g carbohydrate; 4 g fiber.
GREEN BEANS	1 pound, trimmed	5 minutes	39 calories; 9 g carbohydrate; 4 g fiber.
POTATOES (BABY RED)	1 ½ pounds, scrubbed	10 to 15 minutes	119 calories; 27 g carbohydrate; 3 g fiber.
SNAP PEAS	1 pound, trimmed	4 to 5 minutes	55 calories; 10 g carbohydrate; 3 g fiber.
SUMMER SQUASH	1 ½ pounds, cut into ¼-inch-thick rings	4 to 5 minutes	29 calories; 6 g carbohydrate; 2 g fiber.

Creamy Tarragon Sauce

New Mornay Sauce

Sherry-Asiago Cream Sauce

Light Cheese Sauce

CREAMY TARRAGON SAUCE

ACTIVE TIME: 10 MINUTES | **TOTAL:** 10 MINUTES
TO MAKE AHEAD: Cover and refrigerate for up to 3 days.

This sauce is like a creamy béarnaise sauce except it skips the butter, egg yolks and fuss. It's spiked with lemon juice, zesty Dijon mustard and, of course, tarragon. Try it with poached eggs or even grilled steak.

- ½ cup low-fat plain yogurt
- 6 tablespoons low-fat mayonnaise
- 4 teaspoons chopped fresh tarragon *or* 1 teaspoon dried
- 1 tablespoon lemon juice
- 1 tablespoon water
- 2 teaspoons Dijon mustard
- ¼ teaspoon salt
  Freshly ground pepper to taste

Whisk yogurt, mayonnaise, tarragon, lemon juice, water, mustard, salt and pepper in a small bowl.

MAKES 1 CUP.

PER TABLESPOON: 11 calories; 1 g fat (0 g sat, 0 g mono); 0 mg cholesterol; 1 g carbohydrate; 0 g protein; 0 g fiber; 99 mg sodium; 21 mg potassium.

NEW MORNAY SAUCE

ACTIVE TIME: 10 MINUTES | **TOTAL:** 10 MINUTES

Our lightened Mornay is a great topping for almost any vegetable. Pureed low-fat cottage cheese contributes a rich dairy flavor and Gruyère and Parmesan add nuance to this classic sauce.

- 4 teaspoons all-purpose flour
- ⅔ cup nonfat milk, divided
- ¼ cup low-fat cottage cheese
- ¼ cup shredded Swiss cheese, preferably Gruyère
- ⅛ teaspoon salt
- ⅛ teaspoon white pepper
- 2 tablespoons freshly grated Parmesan cheese (optional)
- 1 tablespoon breadcrumbs (optional)

Stir flour and 2 tablespoons milk in a small bowl to make a smooth paste. Heat the remaining milk in a small heavy saucepan over medium heat until steaming. Whisk the flour paste into the hot milk and cook, whisking constantly, until thickened, about 1 minute. Remove from the heat and whisk in cottage cheese, Swiss cheese, salt and white pepper. Transfer the sauce to a food processor or blender and puree until smooth. Serve over steamed vegetables and top with Parmesan and breadcrumbs, if desired.

MAKES ¾ CUP.

PER TABLESPOON: 20 calories; 1 g fat (0 g sat, 0 g mono); 3 mg cholesterol; 2 g carbohydrate; 2 g protein; 0 g fiber; 55 mg sodium; 29 mg potassium.

SHERRY-ASIAGO CREAM SAUCE

ACTIVE TIME: 15 MINUTES | TOTAL: 15 MINUTES

A small amount of a full-flavored cheese like Asiago combines with low-fat milk and dry sherry for a sophisticated sauce that stands up to the assertive taste of vegetables like Brussels sprouts and broccoli.

> 1 tablespoon extra-virgin olive oil
> 2 tablespoons minced shallot
> 1 tablespoon all-purpose flour
> ⅔ cup low-fat milk
> 2 tablespoons dry sherry (*see Ingredient Note, page 248*)
> ⅓ cup finely shredded Asiago cheese
> ⅛ teaspoon salt
> Freshly ground pepper to taste

Heat oil in a small saucepan over medium heat. Add shallot and cook, stirring once or twice, until just starting to brown, 1 to 1½ minutes. Sprinkle in flour; stir until combined. Whisk in milk and sherry; bring to a simmer, whisking constantly. Reduce heat to medium-low and simmer, stirring often, until thickened and bubbly, about 3 minutes. Remove from heat; stir in cheese, salt and pepper.

MAKES ¾ CUP.

PER TABLESPOON: 40 calories; 3 g fat (1 g sat, 1 g mono); 4 mg cholesterol; 2 g carbohydrate; 1 g protein; 0 g fiber; 103 mg sodium; 9 mg potassium.

LIGHT CHEESE SAUCE

ACTIVE TIME: 10 MINUTES | TOTAL: 10 MINUTES
TO MAKE AHEAD: Cover and refrigerate for up to 2 days. Reheat before serving.

This cheese sauce, which can make almost anything taste better, is made with a combination of low-fat milk and flour to keep it light.

> 5 teaspoons all-purpose flour
> 1¼ cups nonfat milk, divided
> ⅔ cup grated sharp Cheddar cheese
> 1 teaspoon dry mustard
> ½ teaspoon sweet paprika
> Cayenne pepper to taste (optional)
> ¼ teaspoon salt

Whisk flour with ¼ cup milk in a small bowl until smooth. Heat the remaining milk in a small saucepan over medium-low heat until steaming. Add the flour mixture and cook, whisking constantly, until the sauce bubbles and thickens, about 4 minutes. Remove from the heat; stir in Cheddar, dry mustard, paprika, cayenne (if using) and salt.

MAKES 1¼ CUPS.

PER TABLESPOON: 23 calories; 1 g fat (1 g sat, 0 g mono); 4 mg cholesterol; 1 g carbohydrate; 2 g protein; 0 g fiber; 61 mg sodium; 26 mg potassium.

MAKEOVER TIP

DRY MUSTARD ENHANCES THE FLAVOR OF CHEESY SAUCES SO YOU CAN USE LESS CHEESE AND STILL HAVE PLENTY OF FLAVOR.

TARTAR SAUCE

ACTIVE TIME: 5 MINUTES | **TOTAL:** 5 MINUTES
TO MAKE AHEAD: Cover and refrigerate for up to 1 day.

Our sophisticated take on tartar sauce combines low-fat mayonnaise with chopped gherkins, pimientos and shallots.

¼ cup low-fat mayonnaise	2 tablespoons finely chopped jarred pimiento peppers
1 ½ teaspoons Dijon mustard	2 teaspoons minced shallot
2 sweet gherkin pickles, minced	

Combine mayonnaise, mustard, pickles, pimientos and shallot in a small bowl.

MAKES ⅔ CUP.

PER TABLESPOON: 10 calories; 0 g fat (0 g sat, 0 g mono); 0 mg cholesterol; 2 g carbohydrate; 0 g protein; 0 g fiber; 80 mg sodium; 6 mg potassium.

PESTO

ACTIVE TIME: 15 MINUTES | **TOTAL:** 15 MINUTES
TO MAKE AHEAD: Cover and refrigerate for up to 3 days or freeze for up to 2 months.

This pesto highlights the basil and pine nuts first and melds them together with just the right amount of freshly grated cheese and extra-virgin olive oil. Try it instead of red sauce on pizza or tossed with warm pasta.

1 cup loosely packed fresh basil leaves	1 tablespoon freshly grated Pecorino Romano *or* Parmesan cheese
3 tablespoons pine nuts	2 tablespoons extra-virgin olive oil
1 clove garlic, peeled	
½ teaspoon salt	

Place basil, pine nuts, garlic and salt in a food processor and pulse until a fairly smooth paste forms. Transfer to a small bowl. Stir in cheese, then stir in oil.

MAKES ⅓ CUP.

PER TABLESPOON: 86 calories; 9 g fat (1 g sat, 5 g mono); 1 mg cholesterol; 1 g carbohydrate; 1 g protein; 0 g fiber; 238 mg sodium; 54 mg potassium.

COCKTAIL SAUCE

ACTIVE TIME: 5 MINUTES | **TOTAL:** 5 MINUTES
TO MAKE AHEAD: Cover and refrigerate for up to 2 days.

Fresh dill and celery seed give this cocktail sauce a unique twist. It's great with New England Fried Shrimp (*page 160*).

1/3 cup bottled chili sauce, such as Heinz	1 tablespoon minced fresh dill
2 tablespoons ketchup	1 teaspoon Worcestershire sauce
1/2 teaspoon freshly grated lemon zest	1/4 teaspoon celery seed
2 tablespoons lemon juice	

Combine chili sauce, ketchup, lemon zest, lemon juice, dill, Worcestershire and celery seed in a small bowl.

MAKES 2/3 CUP.

PER TABLESPOON: 14 calories; 0 g fat (0 g sat, 0 g mono); 0 mg cholesterol; 4 g carbohydrate; 0 g protein; 0 g fiber; 277 mg sodium; 20 mg potassium.

CREAMY HORSERADISH SAUCE

ACTIVE TIME: 5 MINUTES | **TOTAL:** 5 MINUTES
TO MAKE AHEAD: Cover and refrigerate for up to 3 days.

Horseradish docs the talking in this creamy, pungent sauce. Serve with beef tenderloin, Cheddar mashed potatoes or as a sandwich spread.

1 1/4 cups reduced-fat sour cream	1 teaspoon kosher salt
1/3 cup prepared horseradish	1 teaspoon freshly ground pepper

Combine sour cream, horseradish, salt and pepper in a medium bowl. Chill until ready to serve.

MAKES 1 1/2 CUPS.

PER TABLESPOON: 19 calories; 2 g fat (1 g sat, 0 g mono); 5 mg cholesterol; 1 g carbohydrate; 0 g protein; 0 g fiber; 62 mg sodium; 24 mg potassium.

HOLLANDAISE SAUCE

ACTIVE TIME: 15 MINUTES | **TOTAL:** 15 MINUTES
TO MAKE AHEAD: Cover and refrigerate for up to 2 days. Reheat in a microwave on High for 1 to 1 ½ minutes, stirring once.

Fear not, you can still enjoy Eggs Benedict: buttermilk thickened with cornstarch, a touch of butter and fresh lemon creates a pleasant, tangy sauce that has only 1 gram of fat per tablespoon. It's also great drizzled over steamed vegetables.

1 tablespoon butter	½ teaspoon salt
¾ cup nonfat buttermilk (*see Tip, page 246*), divided	Pinch of cayenne pepper
	1 large egg, lightly beaten
1 tablespoon cornstarch	1 tablespoon lemon juice

1. Melt butter in a small saucepan over low heat. Cook, swirling the pan, until the butter turns golden, 30 to 60 seconds. Pour into a small bowl and set aside.

2. Whisk ¼ cup buttermilk, cornstarch, salt and cayenne in a heavy medium saucepan until smooth. Whisk in egg along with the remaining ½ cup buttermilk.

3. Set the pan over medium-low heat and cook the sauce, whisking constantly, until it comes to a simmer. Cook, whisking, for 15 seconds. Remove from heat and whisk in lemon juice and the reserved butter. Serve hot or warm.

MAKES ABOUT 1 CUP.

PER TABLESPOON: 17 calories; 1 g fat (1 g sat, 0 g mono); 15 mg cholesterol; 1 g carbohydrate; 1 g protein; 0 g fiber; 87 mg sodium; 6 mg potassium.

YOGURT-DILL RÉMOULADE

ACTIVE TIME: 10 MINUTES | **TOTAL:** 10 MINUTES

We replace mayonnaise with cool, tangy low-fat yogurt in this classic French sauce, which is an excellent accompaniment to shellfish or cold meats.

1 cup low-fat plain yogurt	1 ½ tablespoons chopped capers
1 teaspoon minced garlic	1 ½ tablespoons lemon juice
2 tablespoons minced red onion	1 tablespoon chopped fresh dill

Place yogurt in a small bowl and stir in garlic, onion, capers, lemon juice and dill.

MAKES 1 ½ CUPS.

PER TABLESPOON: 7 calories; 0 g fat (0 g sat, 0 g mono); 1 mg cholesterol; 1 g carbohydrate; 1 g protein; 0 g fiber; 27 mg sodium; 27 mg potassium.

BASIC BARBECUE SAUCE

ACTIVE TIME: 20 MINUTES | **TOTAL:** 30 MINUTES
TO MAKE AHEAD: Cover and refrigerate for up to 1 week.

Bottled barbecue sauces are often loaded with sodium and high-fructose corn syrup. In ours, strong coffee balances the sweetness of molasses and orange juice while the chiles and hot sauce provide subtle heat.

¾	cup strong brewed coffee		1	tablespoon Worcestershire sauce
1	cup ketchup		2	teaspoons Dijon mustard
¼	cup molasses		2	jalapeño *or* serrano chiles, pierced all over with a fork
2	tablespoons orange juice			Hot sauce to taste
2	tablespoons cider vinegar			

Combine coffee, ketchup, molasses, orange juice, vinegar, Worcestershire, mustard and chiles in a medium heavy saucepan; bring to a simmer, stirring. Cook over low heat, stirring frequently, until slightly thickened, 10 to 15 minutes. Let cool and discard the chiles. Add hot sauce to taste.

MAKES ABOUT 2 CUPS.

PER TABLESPOON: 16 calories; 0 g fat (0 g sat, 0 g mono); 0 mg cholesterol; 4 g carbohydrate; 0 g protein; 0 g fiber; 94 mg sodium; 75 mg potassium.

SPICY BLUE CHEESE DIP

ACTIVE TIME: 5 MINUTES | **TOTAL:** 5 MINUTES
TO MAKE AHEAD: Cover and refrigerate for up to 3 days.

Most blue cheese dips combine sour cream and mayo as well as cheese, a trifecta of fat and calories. Our lightened version still has plenty of intense blue cheese flavor to tame wings or complement crunchy vegetables.

⅔	cup reduced-fat sour cream		1	tablespoon distilled white vinegar
⅔	cup crumbled blue cheese		¼	teaspoon cayenne pepper

Whisk sour cream, blue cheese, vinegar and cayenne in a small bowl.

MAKES 1 CUP.

PER TABLESPOON: 33 calories; 3 g fat (2 g sat, 1 g mono); 8 mg cholesterol; 1 g carbohydrate; 2 g protein; 0 g fiber; 83 mg sodium; 28 mg potassium.

Strawberry Shortcake (page 218)

DESSERTS

DELICIOUS FEEDBACK

Oatmeal Chocolate Chip Cookies

"This is the very best oatmeal cookie recipe I've ever tried. These cookies
truly taste better than the more sinful traditional ones."

—Anonymous, Bellingham, WA

STRAWBERRY SHORTCAKE

ACTIVE TIME: 40 MINUTES | **TOTAL:** 1 HOUR

Besides succulent fresh, ripe strawberries, the key to a great strawberry shortcake lies in the quality of the biscuit. And this one is top-notch. These tender, sweet buttermilk biscuits are made with a blend of cake flour and whole-wheat flour and lightened by substituting reduced-fat cream cheese for some of the butter. As a delicately tangy alternative to whipped cream, we use a blend of cream and reduced-fat sour cream. (*Photograph: page 216.*)

SHORTCAKES
- 2 cups cake flour, plus more for dusting
- 1 cup white whole-wheat flour *or* whole-wheat pastry flour (*see Ingredient Note, page 248*)
- ¼ cup sugar
- 1 tablespoon baking powder
- 4 tablespoons cold unsalted butter, cut into small pieces
- 4 tablespoons (2 ounces) reduced-fat cream cheese (Neufchâtel)
- ¼ cup canola oil
- 1 large egg, lightly beaten
- 3 tablespoons nonfat buttermilk (*see Tip, page 246*)

FILLING
- 4 cups sliced hulled strawberries (about 1 ¼ pounds whole)
- 3 tablespoons sugar
- ½ cup whipping cream
- ½ cup reduced-fat sour cream

1. TO PREPARE SHORTCAKES: Preheat oven to 400°F.

2. Whisk cake flour, whole-wheat flour, sugar and baking powder in a large bowl. Cut in butter using two knives or a pastry cutter until the pieces are about the size of peas. Cut in cream cheese until it's the size of peas. Drizzle oil over the mixture; stir with a fork until just combined (the mixture will be crumbly). Make a well in the center and add egg and buttermilk. Gradually stir the wet ingredients into the dry ingredients with a fork until the mixture is evenly moist. Knead the mixture in the bowl two or three times until it holds together.

3. Turn the dough out onto a lightly floured surface. Dust with flour and roll into an 8-by-10-inch rectangle about ½ inch thick. Cut the edges square using a butter knife. Cut the dough into 12 equal shortcakes. Transfer to a baking sheet.

4. Bake the shortcakes until puffed and lightly golden, about 20 minutes. Let cool slightly.

5. TO PREPARE FILLING: Toss strawberries with sugar in a medium bowl. Whisk whipping cream in a medium bowl until it's thick and holds its shape, 1 to 2 minutes. Whisk in sour cream until combined.

6. To serve, split the shortcakes horizontally. Spoon the berries and juice onto the bottoms, top with the cream mixture and replace the shortcake tops.

MAKES 12 SERVINGS (1 shortcake & about ½ cup filling each).

PER SERVING: 303 calories; 14 g fat (6 g sat, 4 g mono); 48 mg cholesterol; 38 g carbohydrate; 5 g protein; 2 g fiber; 138 mg sodium; 157 mg potassium.

NUTRITION BONUS: Vitamin C (50% daily value), Folate & Iron (20% dv).

OLD-FASHIONED FRUIT CRUMBLE

H⬆F   H♥H

ACTIVE TIME: 10 MINUTES | **TOTAL:** 40 MINUTES

Typical crumble topping has as much as a half cup of butter—ours has just a tablespoon of canola oil and, for richness, chopped almonds, which are full of healthy monounsaturated fats.

2½	cups fresh *or* frozen fruit, such as blueberries, peaches, plums	½	cup rolled oats
1	tablespoon granulated sugar	¼	cup chopped almonds *or* pecans
3	tablespoons whole-wheat *or* all-purpose flour, divided	3	tablespoons brown sugar
1	tablespoon orange juice	¼	teaspoon cinnamon
		2	tablespoons canola oil

Preheat oven to 400°F. Combine fruit with granulated sugar, 1 tablespoon flour and orange juice. Divide among four 6-ounce ovenproof ramekins. Combine oats, nuts, brown sugar, the remaining 2 tablespoons flour and cinnamon. Drizzle with oil and stir to combine. Sprinkle over the fruit mixture. Place the ramekins on a baking sheet. Bake until the fruit is bubbling and the topping is golden, 20 to 25 minutes. Let stand for at least 10 minutes before serving.

MAKES 4 SERVINGS.

PER SERVING: 252 calories; 11 g fat (1 g sat, 7 g mono); 0 mg cholesterol; 38 g carbohydrate; 4 g protein; 5 g fiber; 1 mg sodium; 179 mg potassium.

EATINGWELL ALL-PURPOSE PIE CRUST

ACTIVE TIME: 10 MINUTES | **TOTAL:** 1 HOUR 10 MINUTES

TO MAKE AHEAD: Wrap tightly and refrigerate for up to 2 days or freeze for up to 6 months.

1¼	cups whole-wheat pastry flour (*see Ingredient Note, page 248*)	4	tablespoons cold unsalted butter
1¼	cups all-purpose flour	¼	cup reduced-fat sour cream
2	tablespoons sugar	3	tablespoons canola oil
½	teaspoon salt	4	tablespoons ice water

Whisk whole-wheat flour, all-purpose flour, sugar and salt in a large bowl. Cut butter into small pieces and, with your fingers, quickly rub them into the dry ingredients until the pieces are smaller but still visible. Add sour cream and oil; toss with a fork to combine with the dry ingredients. Sprinkle water over the mixture. Toss with a fork until evenly moist. Knead the dough with your hands in the bowl a few times—the mixture will still be a little crumbly. Turn out onto a clean surface and knead a few more times, until the dough just holds together. Divide the dough in half and shape into 5-inch-wide disks. Wrap each in plastic and refrigerate for at least 1 hour.

MAKES ENOUGH FOR TWO 9-INCH PIES *OR* ONE DOUBLE-CRUST PIE (10 SERVINGS).

PER SERVING: 207 calories; 10 g fat (4 g sat, 3 g mono); 14 mg cholesterol; 26 g carbohydrate; 3 g protein; 2 g fiber; 119 mg sodium; 25 mg potassium.

DEEP-DISH APPLE PIE

H ⬆ F

ACTIVE TIME: 1 ¼ HOURS | **TOTAL:** 4 HOURS (INCLUDING COOLING TIME)
TO MAKE AHEAD: Prepare the crust (STEP 1), wrap tightly and refrigerate for up to 2 days or freeze for up to 6 months.
EQUIPMENT: 9 ½-inch deep-dish pie pan

With all that delicious fruit an apple pie should be healthy, but the truth is a slice can have as much as 750 calories and 30 grams of fat. For the most part, the culprit is the crust. We use whole-wheat pastry flour to add fiber and lower the saturated fat by replacing some of the butter with canola oil. The brown sugar-sweetened filling in this pie is made with two kinds of apples for the perfect balance. A slice has half the calories of a typical version and only 10 grams of fat—sweet!

EatingWell All-Purpose Pie Crust (*page 219*)
6 cups thinly sliced peeled McIntosh apples (about 2 pounds)
6 cups thinly sliced peeled Granny Smith apples (about 2 pounds)
⅔ cup packed light brown sugar
1 tablespoon lemon juice

1 ¼ teaspoons ground cinnamon, divided
⅛ teaspoon ground nutmeg
Pinch of ground allspice
Pinch of salt
2 tablespoons all-purpose flour
1 teaspoon granulated sugar
1 large egg white, lightly beaten, for brushing

1. Prepare EatingWell All-Purpose Pie Crust. Wrap the dough in plastic and refrigerate for at least 1 hour.

2. Meanwhile, combine apples, brown sugar, lemon juice, 1 teaspoon cinnamon, nutmeg, allspice and salt in a large bowl. Reserving 4 cups, transfer the rest of the apple mixture to a Dutch oven. Cook over medium heat, stirring, until the apples are tender and beginning to break down, about 10 minutes. Remove from the heat, stir in the reserved apples and flour; let cool for about 30 minutes.

3. TO ASSEMBLE & BAKE PIE: Position a rack in lower third of oven; preheat to 425°F.

4. Remove the dough from the refrigerator; let stand for 5 minutes to warm slightly. Roll one portion between sheets of parchment or wax paper into a 13-inch circle. Peel off the top sheet and invert the dough into a 9½-inch deep-dish pie pan. Peel off the remaining paper. Scrape the filling into the crust. Roll the remaining portion of dough between sheets of parchment or wax paper into another 13-inch circle. Peel off the top sheet of paper and invert the dough onto the fruit. Peel off the remaining paper. Trim the crust so it overhangs evenly. Tuck the top crust under the bottom crust, sealing the two together and making a plump edge. Flute the edge with your fingers. Combine granulated sugar and the remaining ¼ teaspoon cinnamon in a small bowl. Brush the crust with egg white and sprinkle with the cinnamon-sugar. Cut 6 steam vents in the top crust.

5. Bake the pie on the bottom rack for 20 minutes. Reduce the oven temperature to 375° and continue baking until the crust is golden brown and the filling is bubbling, 25 to 35 minutes more. Let cool on a wire rack for about 1½ hours before serving.

MAKES 10 SERVINGS.

PER SERVING: 344 calories; 10 g fat (4 g sat, 3 g mono); 14 mg cholesterol; 62 g carbohydrate; 4 g protein; 5 g fiber; 143 mg sodium; 212 mg potassium.

PEACH-RASPBERRY PIE

ACTIVE TIME: 1 HOUR | **TOTAL:** 3 ½ HOURS (INCLUDING 1 ½ HOURS COOLING TIME)
TO MAKE AHEAD: Prepare the crust (STEP 1), wrap tightly and refrigerate for up to 2 days or freeze for up to 6 months.

A lightened pie crust plus the tart-sweet combination of peaches and raspberries is truly a winning recipe. Make this when peaches are at their most flavorful in midsummer.

	EatingWell All-Purpose Pie Crust (*page 219*)	⅔	cup sugar, plus 1 teaspoon for sprinkling
6	cups sliced peeled peaches (6-8 medium, ripe but firm; *see Tip*)	1	tablespoon lemon juice
		3	tablespoons cornstarch
1	cup fresh *or* frozen raspberries	1	large egg white, lightly beaten, for brushing

PEACH TIP:

Peaches that are ripe but still firm bake up perfectly tender while still holding their shape. To peel, dip peaches in boiling water for about 1 minute to loosen their skins. Let cool slightly, then remove the skins with a paring knife.

1. Prepare EatingWell All-Purpose Pie Crust. Wrap the dough in plastic and refrigerate for at least 1 hour.

2. Meanwhile, combine peaches, raspberries, ⅔ cup sugar and lemon juice in a large bowl; toss well to coat. Let stand for 5 minutes. Transfer the fruit mixture to a colander set over a medium bowl and let drain for 30 minutes. Pour the collected juice into a small saucepan. Return the fruit to the large bowl. Bring the juice to a boil over high heat and cook, gently swirling the pan, until reduced, syrupy and slightly darkened in color, 3 to 4 minutes. Add the syrup to the fruit along with cornstarch; gently toss until the cornstarch is completely dissolved.

3. TO ASSEMBLE & BAKE PIE: Position a rack in the center of the oven and place a foil-lined baking sheet on the rack below; preheat to 375°F.

4. Remove the dough from the refrigerator; let stand for 5 minutes to warm slightly. Roll one portion between sheets of parchment or wax paper into a 12-inch circle. Peel off the top sheet and invert the dough into a 9-inch pie pan. Peel off the remaining paper. Trim the crust with kitchen shears or a butter knife so it overhangs the edge of the pan by 1 inch. Scrape the filling into the crust. Roll the remaining portion of dough between sheets of parchment or wax paper into another 12-inch circle. Peel off the top sheet of paper and invert the dough onto the fruit. Trim the top crust so it overhangs evenly. Tuck the top crust under the bottom crust, sealing the two together and making a plump edge. Flute the edge with your fingers. Brush the top and edge with egg white and sprinkle with the remaining 1 teaspoon sugar. Cut 6 steam vents in the top crust.

5. Bake the pie on the center rack until the crust is golden brown and the fruit is bubbling, 50 to 60 minutes. Let cool on a wire rack for at least 1 ½ hours.

MAKES 10 SERVINGS.

PER SERVING: 313 calories; 10 g fat (4 g sat, 4 g mono); 14 mg cholesterol; 53 g carbohydrate; 5 g protein; 4 g fiber; 129 mg sodium; 220 mg potassium.
NUTRITION BONUS: Vitamin C (20% daily value).

FRENCH SILK PIE

H)(W   H♥H

ACTIVE TIME: 30 MINUTES | **TOTAL:** 4 ¼ HOURS (INCLUDING CHILLING TIME)
TO MAKE AHEAD: Cover and refrigerate for up to 2 days.

Bittersweet chocolate and Dutch-process cocoa meld with a shot of fresh brewed coffee to give an ultra-rich flavor to this creamy pie. A frothy meringue is the secret to lightening the brown sugar-sweetened filling.

CRUST
- 30 chocolate wafers
- 2 tablespoons chopped pitted dates
- 2 tablespoons water
- 1 tablespoon canola oil

FILLING
- 1 tablespoon brewed coffee
- 1 tablespoon water
- 1 ½ teaspoons unflavored gelatin
- 1 large egg
- ½ cup low-fat milk
- 8 tablespoons packed light brown sugar, divided
- ⅓ cup unsweetened cocoa powder, preferably Dutch-process
- 2 ounces bittersweet chocolate, chopped
- 1 ½ teaspoons vanilla extract
- 2 tablespoons dried egg whites (*see Ingredient Note, page 247*), reconstituted according to package directions
- ½ teaspoon cream of tartar

MAKEOVER TIP

MANY COMMERCIAL COOKIES AND WAFERS CONTAIN PARTIALLY HYDROGENATED OIL, A SOURCE OF TRANS-FATTY ACIDS. LOOK FOR BRANDS MADE WITHOUT THESE OILS, SUCH AS NEWMAN'S OWN ORGANICS AND MI-DEL, WHICH FORTUNATELY ARE EVERY BIT AS TASTY. FIND THEM IN THE NATURAL-FOODS SECTION OF LARGE SUPERMARKETS.

1. Preheat oven to 325°F. Coat a 9-inch pie pan with cooking spray.

2. TO PREPARE CRUST: Combine chocolate wafers and dates in a food processor; process until finely chopped. Add water and oil and process until moistened. Press into the bottom and sides of the prepared pan.

3. Bake until crisp, about 10 minutes. Cool completely on a wire rack.

4. TO PREPARE FILLING & GARNISH: Combine coffee and water in a small bowl. Sprinkle gelatin on top and set aside to soften.

5. Whisk egg, milk, 3 tablespoons brown sugar and cocoa in a small saucepan until smooth. Cook over low heat, whisking constantly, until thickened and an instant-read thermometer registers 160°F, 5 to 7 minutes. Do not let the mixture come to a simmer. Remove from the heat. Add the reserved gelatin mixture; stir until dissolved. Add chocolate and vanilla, stirring until melted. Set aside to cool to room temperature, about 30 minutes.

6. Beat reconstituted egg whites and cream of tartar in a large bowl with an electric mixer on low speed until frothy. Increase speed to high and beat until soft peaks form. Gradually add the remaining 5 tablespoons brown sugar, beating until the meringue is smooth and glossy.

7. Whisk one-fourth of the meringue into the cooled chocolate mixture until smooth. Scrape the chocolate mixture into the remaining meringue and fold in with a whisk. Spoon the filling into the crust and chill, uncovered, until set, about 3 hours.

MAKES 10 SERVINGS.

PER SERVING: 172 calories; 6 g fat (1 g sat, 1 g mono); 22 mg cholesterol; 29 g carbohydrate; 4 g protein; 2 g fiber; 88 mg sodium; 106 mg potassium.

PUMPKIN PIE WITH RUM

H ♥ H

ACTIVE TIME: 30 MINUTES | **TOTAL:** 1 HOUR 10 MINUTES
EQUIPMENT: 9-inch deep-dish pie pan

Dark molasses and dark rum put this pumpkin pie a cut above the rest. Nonfat evaporated milk, which stands in for heavy cream, does a fantastic job of cutting the fat in the filling. Add to that our blue ribbon butter-canola crust and you've dropped three-quarters of the fat and more than half the calories found in most similar pies. Don't use pumpkin-pie mix—buy canned pumpkin without added spices: the flavor will be superior.

CRUST
- ¾ cup all-purpose flour
- ¼ cup whole-wheat flour
- 1 tablespoon granulated sugar
- ⅛ teaspoon salt
- 1 tablespoon butter
- 3 tablespoons canola oil
- 1-2 tablespoons ice water

FILLING
- 2 large eggs
- 1 15- *or* 16-ounce can plain pumpkin puree
- 1 12-ounce can nonfat evaporated milk
- ¼ cup dark molasses
- 3 tablespoons dark rum *or* 1 tablespoon vanilla extract
- ½ cup packed dark brown sugar
- 1 tablespoon cornstarch
- 1 teaspoon ground cinnamon
- 1 teaspoon ground ginger
- ¼ teaspoon ground nutmeg
- ¼ teaspoon salt

1. TO PREPARE CRUST: Stir all-purpose flour, whole-wheat flour, sugar and salt in a medium bowl. Melt butter in a small saucepan over low heat. Cook, swirling the pan, until the butter turns a nutty brown, 30 seconds to 4 minutes, depending on your stove. Pour into a small bowl and let cool. Stir in oil. Slowly stir the butter-oil mixture into the flour mixture with a fork until the mixture is crumbly. Gradually stir in enough ice water so the dough holds together. Press the dough into a flattened disk.

2. Place two overlapping lengths of plastic wrap on a work surface. Set the dough in the center and cover with two more sheets of plastic wrap. Roll the dough into a 13-inch circle. Remove the top sheets and invert the dough into a 9-inch deep-dish pie pan. Remove the remaining wrap. Fold the edges under at the rim and crimp. Cover loosely with plastic wrap and refrigerate while you prepare the filling.

3. TO PREPARE FILLING & BAKE PIE: Position rack in lower third of oven; preheat to 350°F. Lightly whisk eggs in a medium bowl. Add pumpkin, evaporated milk, molasses and rum (or vanilla). Combine brown sugar, cornstarch, cinnamon, ginger, nutmeg and salt in a small bowl. Rub through a sieve into the pumpkin mixture and whisk until incorporated.

4. Pour the filling into the prepared crust. Bake the pie until the filling has set and a skewer inserted in the center comes out clean, 40 to 50 minutes; cover the edges with foil if they are browning too quickly. Cool on a wire rack.

MAKES 8 SERVINGS.

PER SERVING: 278 calories; 8 g fat (2 g sat, 4 g mono); 58 mg cholesterol; 43 g carbohydrate; 7 g protein; 3 g fiber; 187 mg sodium; 397 mg potassium.

NUTRITION BONUS: Vitamin A (137% daily value), Calcium (21% dv), Iron (15% dv).

KEY LIME PIE

ACTIVE TIME: 45 MINUTES | **TOTAL:** 5 HOURS (INCLUDES 4 HOURS CHILLING TIME)
TO MAKE AHEAD: Prepare through Step 3 up to 1 day in advance.

We tested this pie quite a few times and no one got tired of it. We lightened the filling with nonfat condensed milk blended with tangy low-fat plain yogurt and continued the makeover with a topping of lovely golden meringue rather than whipped heavy cream. Use Key limes if you can find them but common Persian limes work as well.

CRUST
- 1¼ cups graham cracker crumbs (about 10 crackers)
- 3 tablespoons butter, melted
- 3 tablespoons canola oil

FILLING
- 1 14-ounce can nonfat sweetened condensed milk
- ⅔ cup low-fat plain yogurt
- 2 teaspoons freshly grated lime zest, preferably Key lime
- ½ cup fresh lime juice (4-5 limes), preferably Key lime
- 2 tablespoons water
- 1½ teaspoons unflavored gelatin

MERINGUE
- 2 tablespoons dried egg whites (*see Ingredient Note, page 247*), reconstituted according to package directions
- ¼ teaspoon cream of tartar
- ½ cup sugar
- 1 teaspoon vanilla extract
  Lime slices for garnish

1. TO PREPARE CRUST: Preheat oven to 350°F. Coat a 9-inch pie pan with cooking spray.

2. Place graham cracker crumbs, butter and oil in a medium bowl. Blend with your fingertips until thoroughly combined. Press the mixture in an even layer on the bottom and sides of the pie plate. Bake until lightly browned, about 10 minutes. Cool on a wire rack.

3. TO PREPARE FILLING: Whisk condensed milk, yogurt, lime zest and juice in a medium bowl. Stir water and gelatin in a small heatproof cup or bowl. Microwave, uncovered, on High until the gelatin has completely dissolved but the liquid is not boiling, 20 to 30 seconds. (*Alternatively, bring ½ inch water to a gentle simmer in a small skillet. Set the bowl with the gelatin mixture in the simmering water until the gelatin has dissolved completely.*) Stir the gelatin mixture, then whisk into the lime mixture. Set that bowl over a larger bowl of ice water, stirring occasionally, until it begins to thicken, 15 to 20 minutes. Scrape the filling into the pie shell and refrigerate until chilled and set, at least 4 hours and up to 1 day.

4. TO PREPARE MERINGUE & FINISH PIE: Position oven rack about 6 inches below the broiler; preheat broiler.

5. Beat reconstituted egg whites and cream of tartar in a mixing bowl with an electric mixer on medium until soft peaks form. Gradually add sugar and continue mixing until the egg whites are glossy and hold stiff peaks. Blend in vanilla.

6. Spread the meringue over the top of the pie, sealing to the edge of the crust and decoratively swirling on top. Broil (leaving the oven door ajar and watching very carefully to prevent burning) until the meringue is lightly browned on top, 30 seconds to 1 minute. Serve garnished with lime slices.

MAKES 8 SERVINGS.

PER SERVING: 354 calories; 11 g fat (4 g sat, 4 g mono); 19 mg cholesterol; 56 g carbohydrate; 8 g protein; 0 g fiber; 167 mg sodium; 591 mg potassium.

NUTRITION BONUS: Calcium & Potassium (17% daily value).

BERRY-RICOTTA CHEESECAKE

ACTIVE TIME: 30 MINUTES | **TOTAL:** 3½ HOURS
TO MAKE AHEAD: Cover and refrigerate for up to 1 day.
EQUIPMENT: 9-inch springform pan

Much of the fat in a cheesecake comes from the cream cheese. Here, low-fat ricotta blended with reduced-fat Neufchâtel cheese gives this lighter, Italian-inspired cheesecake a great texture and all of the good cheese flavor you would want. We garnish the cake with mixed berries brushed with a red currant jelly glaze. With only 258 calories per slice, this dessert really is a worthwhile indulgence.

CRUST

- 4 hazelnut *or* almond biscotti (4 ounces)
- 1 tablespoon canola oil

FILLING

- 4 ounces reduced-fat cream cheese (Neufchâtel), softened
- 1 cup sugar
- 2 cups part-skim ricotta cheese
- ½ cup nonfat plain yogurt
- ⅓ cup cornstarch
- 2 large eggs
- 3 large egg whites
- 2 teaspoons freshly grated lemon zest
- 2 tablespoons lemon juice
- ¼ teaspoon salt

TOPPING & GLAZE

- 2 cups fresh berries, such as strawberries, blueberries, raspberries and/or blackberries
- ¼ cup red currant jelly

1. Preheat oven to 300°F. Coat a 9-inch springform pan with cooking spray.

2. TO PREPARE CRUST: Break biscotti into several pieces and pulse in a food processor until finely ground. Add oil and pulse until incorporated. Press the crumbs evenly into the bottom of the prepared pan.

3. TO PREPARE FILLING: Beat cream cheese in a large mixing bowl with an electric mixer until smooth. Add sugar and beat until smooth. Add ricotta, yogurt, cornstarch, eggs, egg whites, lemon zest, lemon juice and salt. Beat until well blended. (*Alternatively, mix ingredients in a food processor.*) Scrape the batter into the prepared pan and smooth the top.

4. Bake the cheesecake until the edges are puffed but the center still jiggles when the pan is tapped, 50 to 55 minutes. Turn off the oven and let the cheesecake stand, with the door ajar, for 1 hour. Transfer to a wire rack and let cool completely. (The top may crack.)

5. TO GLAZE & GARNISH CHEESECAKE: Place the cheesecake on a platter and remove pan sides. Arrange berries on top. Warm jelly in a small saucepan over low heat, stirring, until melted. With a pastry brush, coat the berries with the jelly glaze. Serve at room temperature or refrigerate until cold.

MAKES 12 SERVINGS

PER SERVING: 258 calories; 9 g fat (4 g sat, 2 g mono); 62 mg cholesterol; 37 g carbohydrate; 9 g protein; 1 g fiber; 176 mg sodium; 128 mg potassium.

NUTRITION BONUS: Vitamin C (16% daily value), Calcium (15% dv).

RUM-RAISIN BREAD PUDDING

H ❤ H

ACTIVE TIME: 20 MINUTES | **TOTAL:** 1 HOUR

Bread pudding is the king of comfort desserts. This version is inspired by the popular ice cream flavor and includes whole-wheat bread for added goodness. Nonfat evaporated milk subs for full-fat dairy and we use fewer eggs, all of which helps to lighten this warm dessert: it has only a tiny fraction of the fat and half the calories of a typical bread pudding. Enjoy it with a scoop of low-fat vanilla ice cream or frozen yogurt.

½ cup raisins
2 tablespoons rum *or* brandy
4 slices whole-wheat bread, torn into small pieces
2 large eggs

1 12-ounce can nonfat evaporated milk
¾ cup packed light brown sugar
1 tablespoon vanilla extract
½ teaspoon ground nutmeg

1. Preheat oven to 350°F. Coat an 8-inch-square baking pan with cooking spray.

2. Put raisins in a small bowl, sprinkle with rum (or brandy) and set aside to soak for 10 minutes. Spread bread in an even layer in the prepared pan.

3. Whisk eggs in a medium bowl. Add evaporated milk, brown sugar, vanilla and nutmeg; whisk until the sugar dissolves. Stir in the rum-soaked raisins. Pour the mixture over the bread. Mix in any unsoaked bread pieces with a fork. Let stand for 10 minutes.

4. Bake the pudding until puffed and set in the center, 35 to 40 minutes. Serve warm.

MAKES 6 SERVINGS.

PER SERVING: 278 calories; 3 g fat (1 g sat, 1 g mono); 73 mg cholesterol; 52 g carbohydrate; 10 g protein; 2 g fiber; 194 mg sodium; 411 mg potassium.

NUTRITION BONUS: Calcium (24% daily value).

HOMEMADE ICE CREAM

ACTIVE TIME: 15 MINUTES | **TOTAL:** 2¾ HOURS (INCLUDING 2 HOURS CHILLING TIME)
TO MAKE AHEAD: Store in an airtight container in the freezer for up to 1 week.
EQUIPMENT: Ice cream maker

Here's a simple "master recipe" for homemade low-fat ice cream that can be vanilla or chocolate—your choice. We've cut some of the egg yolks and we use low-fat milk along with fat-free sweetened condensed milk in place of heavy cream to cut the fat and calories while adding sweetness and a creamy texture.

1 ½ teaspoons unflavored gelatin
1 tablespoon water
3 cups low-fat milk, divided
3 large egg yolks
1 14-ounce can nonfat sweetened condensed milk

FOR VANILLA BEAN ICE CREAM:
1 vanilla bean
FOR CHOCOLATE ICE CREAM:
¼ cup unsweetened cocoa powder
2 ounces chopped unsweetened chocolate

1. Sprinkle gelatin over water in a small bowl; let stand, stirring once or twice, while you make the base for the ice cream.

2. Pour 1½ cups milk into a large saucepan.
   FOR VANILLA BEAN ICE CREAM: Cut vanilla bean in half lengthwise; scrape the seeds into the milk and add the pod.
   FOR CHOCOLATE ICE CREAM: Add cocoa and chocolate to the milk.

3. Heat the milk mixture over medium heat until steaming. Whisk egg yolks and condensed milk in a medium bowl. Gradually pour in the hot milk, whisking until blended. Return the mixture to the pan and cook over medium heat, stirring with a wooden spoon, until the back of the spoon is lightly coated, 3 to 5 minutes. Do not bring to a boil or the custard will curdle.

4. Strain the custard through a fine-mesh sieve into a clean large bowl. Add the softened gelatin and whisk until melted. Whisk in the remaining 1½ cups cold milk. Cover and refrigerate until chilled, at least 2 hours.

5. Whisk the ice cream mixture and pour into the canister of an ice cream maker. Freeze according to manufacturer's directions. If necessary, place the ice cream in the freezer to firm up before serving.

MAKES 8 SERVINGS, ½ CUP EACH (1 QUART).

PER SERVING (VANILLA BEAN):
H ⊁ W   H ♥ H

202 calories; 3 g fat (1 g sat, 1 g mono); 89 mg cholesterol; 36 g carbohydrate; 9 g protein; 0 g fiber; 104 mg sodium; 477 mg potassium.

NUTRITION BONUS: Calcium (25% daily value).

PER SERVING (CHOCOLATE):
245 calories; 7 g fat (4 g sat, 2 g mono); 89 mg cholesterol; 39 g carbohydrate; 10 g protein; 2 g fiber; 106 mg sodium; 576 mg potassium.

NUTRITION BONUS: Calcium (26% daily value), Magnesium (17% dv), Potassium (16% dv).

TIRAMISÙ

H ✣ W

ACTIVE TIME: 1 HOUR | **TOTAL:** 5 HOURS (INCLUDING CHILLING TIME)
TO MAKE AHEAD: Cover and refrigerate for up to 2 days.
EQUIPMENT: 3-quart trifle bowl or soufflé dish

Here's how we made our luscious Tiramisù with about a third of the fat and half the calories of most versions: we layer coffee-and-brandy-soaked ladyfingers with an ultra-light egg-white custard combined with rich mascarpone cheese and lower-fat Neufchâtel cheese. This healthier version of the triflelike dessert would pass muster in any Italian café.

8 ounces ladyfingers (60 ladyfingers)	¾ cup sugar
1 cup water	¼ teaspoon cream of tartar
4 tablespoons brandy, divided	4 ounces mascarpone cheese (½ cup)
1 tablespoon instant coffee (preferably espresso) granules	4 ounces reduced-fat cream cheese (Neufchâtel), softened
2 tablespoons dried egg whites (*see Ingredient Note, page 247*), reconstituted according to package directions	1 cup chocolate shavings (*see Tip*) Confectioners' sugar for dusting

1. If ladyfingers are soft, toast them in a 350°F oven for 6 to 8 minutes. Stir water, 3 tablespoons brandy and coffee granules in a small bowl until the granules are dissolved. Brush over the flat side of the ladyfingers.

2. Bring 1 inch of water to a simmer in a medium saucepan. Combine reconstituted egg whites, sugar and cream of tartar in a heatproof mixing bowl that will fit over the saucepan. Set the bowl over the simmering water and beat with an electric mixer at low speed for 4 to 5 minutes. Increase speed to high and continue beating over the heat for about 3 minutes more. (The mixture should form a ribbon trail.) Remove the bowl from the heat and beat until cool and fluffy, 3 to 4 minutes.

3. Beat mascarpone and cream cheese in a large bowl until creamy. Add about 1 cup of the beaten whites and the remaining 1 tablespoon brandy; beat until smooth, scraping down the sides. Fold in the remaining whites.

4. Line the bottom and sides of a 3-quart trifle bowl or soufflé dish with ladyfingers, flat sides toward the center. Spoon in one-fourth of the filling and top with a layer of ladyfingers. Repeat with two more layers of filling and ladyfingers, arranging the fourth layer of ladyfingers decoratively over the top, trimming to fit if necessary. Top with the remaining filling. Cover and chill for at least 4 hours or up to 2 days.

5. Before serving, sprinkle the tiramisù with chocolate shavings and dust with confectioners' sugar.

MAKES 12 SERVINGS, ⅔ CUP EACH.

PER SERVING: 216 calories; 7 g fat (4 g sat, 0 g mono); 29 mg cholesterol; 32 g carbohydrate; 4 g protein; 0 g fiber; 54 mg sodium; 47 mg potassium.

TIP:
To make chocolate shavings: Place a block of chocolate (2 ounces or larger) on wax paper and microwave on Defrost until slightly softened but not melted, 15 to 30 seconds. Use a swivel-bladed vegetable peeler to shave off curls. If the chocolate gets too hard to shave easily, warm it again.

CHOCOLATE CHIP CAKE

H ♥ H

ACTIVE TIME: 45 MINUTES | **TOTAL:** 2 HOURS
EQUIPMENT: 12-cup Bundt pan

Chocolate chip cake is always a hit at parties. This one has an amazing moist, dense texture and a healthy profile with egg whites, buttermilk, canola oil and whole-wheat pastry flour. We add plenty of chocolate chips for rich flavor.

CAKE

- 4 large egg whites
- ¼ teaspoon cream of tartar
- 1½ cups sugar, divided
- 1¼ cups whole-wheat pastry flour (*see Ingredient Note, page 248*)
- 1¼ cups all-purpose flour
- 2 teaspoons baking powder
- 1½ teaspoons baking soda
- ½ teaspoon salt
- 1½ cups nonfat buttermilk (*see Tip, page 246*)
- ¼ cup canola oil
- 1 tablespoon vanilla extract
- ½ cup mini chocolate chips

CHOCOLATE DRIZZLE

- ⅓ cup mini chocolate chips
- 2 tablespoons low-fat milk

1. TO PREPARE CAKE: Preheat oven to 350°F. Coat a 12-cup Bundt pan with cooking spray.

2. Beat egg whites in a large bowl with an electric mixer on low speed until foamy. Add cream of tartar, increase speed to medium-high and beat until soft peaks form. Gradually add ½ cup sugar, beating until stiff but not dry (this can take up to 5 minutes).

3. Combine the remaining 1 cup sugar, whole-wheat flour, all-purpose flour, baking powder, baking soda and salt in another large bowl. With the mixer on medium speed, beat in buttermilk, oil, vanilla and a heaping spoonful of whites. Fold in the remaining whites and ½ cup chocolate chips with a whisk. Scrape the batter into the prepared pan and smooth the top.

4. Bake the cake until a skewer inserted into it comes out clean, 40 to 50 minutes. Let cool in the pan on a wire rack for 10 minutes. Invert onto the rack and let cool completely.

5. TO PREPARE CHOCOLATE DRIZZLE: Combine ⅓ cup chocolate chips and milk in a small saucepan. Heat over low heat, stirring, until the chocolate is melted and the mixture is smooth. Drizzle over the cooled cake. Serve immediately or let stand until the chocolate is set, about 45 minutes.

MAKES 16 SERVINGS.

PER SERVING: 234 calories; 6 g fat (2 g sat, 3 g mono); 0 mg cholesterol; 41 g carbohydrate; 4 g protein; 2 g fiber; 296 mg sodium; 66 mg potassium.

MAKEOVER TIP

CONSIDER ENJOYING CAKE WITH A DRIZZLE OF MELTED CHOCOLATE ON TOP, AS WE DO IN THIS RECIPE, INSTEAD OF A THICK LAYER OF FROSTING.

ONE-BOWL CHOCOLATE CAKE

H⌘W   H♥H

ACTIVE TIME: 25 MINUTES | **TOTAL:** 1 HOUR 5 MINUTES

This cake is dark, moist, rich—and easy. Not quite as easy as boxed cake mixes, but those often contain trans fats. Our simple "from scratch" recipe dirties only one bowl and gives you a home-baked cake with healthful canola oil and whole-wheat flour.

¾ cup plus 2 tablespoons whole-wheat pastry flour (*see Ingredient Note, page 248*)

½ cup granulated sugar

⅓ cup unsweetened cocoa powder

1 teaspoon baking powder

1 teaspoon baking soda

¼ teaspoon salt

½ cup nonfat buttermilk (*see Tip, page 246*)

½ cup packed light brown sugar

1 large egg, lightly beaten

2 tablespoons canola oil

1 teaspoon vanilla extract

½ cup hot strong black coffee

Confectioners' sugar for dusting

1. Preheat oven to 350°F. Coat a 9-inch round cake pan with cooking spray. Line the pan with a circle of wax paper.

2. Whisk flour, granulated sugar, cocoa, baking powder, baking soda and salt in a large bowl. Add buttermilk, brown sugar, egg, oil and vanilla. Beat with an electric mixer on medium speed for 2 minutes. Add hot coffee and beat to blend. (The batter will be quite thin.) Pour the batter into the prepared pan.

3. Bake the cake until a skewer inserted in the center comes out clean, 30 to 35 minutes. Cool in the pan on a wire rack for 10 minutes; remove from the pan, peel off the wax paper and let cool completely. Dust the top with confectioners' sugar before slicing.

MAKES 12 SERVINGS.

PER SERVING: 139 calories; 3 g fat (1 g sat, 2 g mono); 18 mg cholesterol; 26 g carbohydrate; 2 g protein; 2 g fiber; 212 mg sodium; 60 mg potassium.

CREAM CHEESE POUND CAKE

ACTIVE TIME: 30 MINUTES | **TOTAL:** 3 HOURS (INCLUDING COOLING TIME)
TO MAKE AHEAD: Wrap and store at room temperature for up to 3 days or freeze for up to 1 month.
EQUIPMENT: 12-cup Bundt pan

This popular cake got its name from the original formulation: a pound each of sugar, flour, butter and eggs. Just the thought of it is enough to raise your cholesterol. Our version calls for half whole-wheat flour, less sugar, a modest amount of butter and loses quite a few egg yolks. To keep it rich we moisten the cake with reduced-fat cream cheese and buttermilk. It is every bit as delicious as the original, with only a third of the calories and fat.

1 ½ cups whole-wheat pastry flour (*see Ingredient Note, page 248*)
1 ½ cups all-purpose flour
1 ½ teaspoons baking powder
½ teaspoon salt
3 large eggs
½ cup nonfat buttermilk (*see Tip, page 246*)
⅓ cup canola oil

2 tablespoons light corn syrup
1 tablespoon vanilla extract
6 large egg whites
2 cups sugar, divided
½ cup (1 stick) unsalted butter, softened
8 ounces reduced-fat cream cheese (Neufchâtel)

1. Preheat oven to 325°F. Coat a 12-cup Bundt pan with cooking spray and dust with flour.

2. Whisk whole-wheat flour, all-purpose flour, baking powder and salt in a medium bowl. Whisk whole eggs, buttermilk, oil, corn syrup and vanilla in another medium bowl until well blended.

3. Beat egg whites in a large clean bowl with an electric mixer on high speed until light and foamy. Gradually beat in ½ cup sugar until stiff glossy peaks form.

4. Beat butter and cream cheese in a large bowl until creamy. Add the remaining 1½ cups sugar and beat, scraping down the sides of the bowl as needed, until pale and fluffy, about 4 minutes. Alternately add the flour and buttermilk mixtures, beating until just smooth. Fold in about one-third of the egg whites with a rubber spatula until just smooth and no white streaks remain. Fold in the remaining egg whites. Scrape the batter into the prepared pan, spreading evenly.

5. Bake the cake until a skewer inserted into it comes out clean and the top springs back when touched, 1 hour to 1 hour 10 minutes. Cool in the pan on a wire rack for 10 minutes. Loosen the edges with a knife and turn out onto the rack; let cool for at least 1 hour more before slicing.

MAKES 20 SERVINGS.

PER SERVING: 261 calories; 12 g fat (5 g sat, 3 g mono); 52 mg cholesterol; 35 g carbohydrate; 5 g protein; 1 g fiber; 167 mg sodium; 73 mg potassium.

MAKEOVER TIP

TRY SUBSTITUTING CANOLA OIL FOR UP TO HALF THE BUTTER IN CAKES OR OTHER BAKED GOODS. REPLACING ⅓ CUP OF THE BUTTER IN THIS RECIPE WITH CANOLA OIL CUT THE SATURATED FAT BY 2 GRAMS PER SERVING.

CARROT CAKE

ACTIVE TIME: 30 MINUTES | **TOTAL:** 1 HOUR 10 MINUTES (PLUS 1 HOUR COOLING TIME)

Carrots give carrot cake a health-halo effect—people think it's health food, but it's usually very high in fat and calories. But our version has about 40 percent less calories and 50 percent less fat than most. First, we use less oil in our batter. Then we skip the butter in the frosting (don't worry, it's still light and smooth). To ensure the cake is moist, we add nonfat buttermilk and crushed pineapple.

CAKE

- 1 20-ounce can crushed pineapple
- 2 cups whole-wheat pastry flour (*see Ingredient Note, page 248*)
- 2 teaspoons baking soda
- ½ teaspoon salt
- 2 teaspoons ground cinnamon
- 3 large eggs
- 1½ cups granulated sugar
- ¾ cup nonfat buttermilk (*see Tip, page 246*)
- ½ cup canola oil
- 1 teaspoon vanilla extract
- 2 cups grated carrots (4-6 medium)
- ¼ cup unsweetened flaked coconut
- ½ cup chopped walnuts, toasted (*see Tip, page 247*)

FROSTING

- 12 ounces reduced-fat cream cheese (Neufchâtel), softened
- ½ cup confectioners' sugar, sifted
- 1½ teaspoons vanilla extract
- 2 tablespoons coconut chips (*see Ingredient Note, page 247*) *or* flaked coconut, toasted

MAKEOVER TIP

NUTS ARE ESSENTIAL TO MANY RECIPES. THEY ADD FLAVOR TO BAKED GOODS, CRUNCHY TEXTURE TO TOPPINGS, AND, ALAS, FAT. TOASTING NUTS INTENSIFIES THEIR FLAVOR SO YOU CAN USE FEWER; TO LEARN HOW, SEE PAGE 247.

1. TO PREPARE CAKE: Preheat oven to 350°F. Coat a 9-by-13-inch baking pan with cooking spray.

2. Drain pineapple in a sieve set over a bowl, pressing on the solids. Reserve the drained pineapple and ¼ cup of the juice.

3. Whisk flour, baking soda, salt and cinnamon in a medium bowl. Whisk eggs, sugar, buttermilk, oil, vanilla and the ¼ cup pineapple juice in a large bowl until blended. Stir in pineapple, carrots and ¼ cup coconut. Add the dry ingredients and mix with a rubber spatula just until blended. Stir in the nuts. Scrape the batter into the prepared pan, spreading evenly.

4. Bake the cake until the top springs back when touched lightly and a skewer inserted in the center comes out clean, 40 to 45 minutes. Let cool completely on a wire rack.

5. TO PREPARE FROSTING & FINISH CAKE: Beat cream cheese, confectioners' sugar and vanilla in a mixing bowl with an electric mixer until smooth and creamy. Spread the frosting over the cooled cake. Sprinkle with toasted coconut.

MAKES 16 SERVINGS.

PER SERVING: 342 calories; 17 g fat (5 g sat, 7 g mono); 56 mg cholesterol; 43 g carbohydrate; 6 g protein; 3 g fiber; 349 mg sodium; 150 mg potassium.

NUTRITION BONUS: Vitamin A (40% daily value), Fiber (12% dv).

A SOUTHERN CAKE GETS A NEW LIFT

At White Oak Plantation, a hunting lodge in Tuskegee, Alabama, Hilda Pitman takes pride in serving truly Southern cooking. "But over the years," she wrote, "our hunters have become more conscious of the cholesterol and fat content of their food, since many have developed heart conditions. We are trying new recipes with more healthful approaches, but some of the dishes seem almost beyond help. I am enclosing one of our favorites, Fiesta Banana Cake. Is there anything you can do with it?"

When revising any recipe, the best policy is to preserve the nutritious ingredients while replacing or reducing those high in fat and calories. Butter and whipped cream are the two main sources of cholesterol-raising saturated fat in this cake and will not do the hunters—or anyone else—any good.

Luckily, however, the appealing cake already has healthful underpinnings. Bananas are one of the best dietary sources of potassium. By increasing the bananas, we were able to replace the butter with a smaller amount of canola oil.

To further bolster the cake's nutritional content, we used whole-wheat pastry flour in place of some of the white flour. Higher in trace minerals than white flour, it contains as much of the fiber-rich bran and germ as regular whole-wheat flour.

We reduced the amount of whipped cream—the second-highest contributor of saturated fat in the recipe—by stirring together a thick, stable base of nonfat milk, sugar and gelatin and then folding in half the whipped cream. The resulting cake was so delicious it was gone in a matter of minutes from our staff kitchen.

BANANA CREAM LAYER CAKE

ACTIVE TIME: 45 MINUTES | **TOTAL:** 2½ HOURS
TO MAKE AHEAD: Prepare through Step 3. Wrap the cooled layers in plastic and store at room temperature for up to 1 day.

This cake is for banana lovers. Delicate banana-buttermilk cake is layered with a fluffy Bavarian-style cream that's made low-fat by combining nonfat milk with a reasonable amount of whipping cream. The rich taste makes it hard to believe that this cake has only 300 calories and 3 grams of saturated fat per slice.

CAKE

2   large eggs
1   cup sugar
⅓   cup canola oil
1½ cups mashed very ripe bananas (about 3),
    plus 2 whole bananas, divided
½   cup nonfat buttermilk (*see Tip, page 246*)
1   teaspoon vanilla extract
1   cup whole-wheat pastry flour (*see Ingredient
    Note, page 248*)

1   cup all-purpose flour
1   teaspoon baking powder
½   teaspoon baking soda
½   teaspoon salt

BAVARIAN CREAM

¾   cup low-fat milk
1   teaspoon unflavored gelatin
2   tablespoons sugar
½   teaspoon vanilla extract
½   cup whipping cream

1. TO PREPARE CAKE: Preheat oven to 375°F. Coat two 9-inch round cake pans with cooking spray and line the bottoms with wax paper or parchment paper.

2. Whisk eggs, 1 cup sugar and oil in a large bowl. Stir in mashed bananas, buttermilk and 1 teaspoon vanilla. Stir whole-wheat flour, all-purpose flour, baking powder, baking soda and salt in a medium bowl. Add to the banana mixture and fold in just until blended. Divide the batter between the pans.

3. Bake the cake until the tops spring back when touched lightly, 20 to 25 minutes. Let cool for 5 minutes, then turn out onto a wire rack and let cool completely.

4. TO PREPARE BAVARIAN CREAM: Place milk in a small saucepan, sprinkle gelatin over the milk and let stand for 1 minute to soften. Stir in 2 tablespoons sugar and heat over medium heat, stirring to dissolve the gelatin. Stir in ½ teaspoon vanilla and transfer to a medium bowl. Refrigerate, stirring occasionally, until the mixture has thickened to the consistency of raw egg whites, 40 to 45 minutes.

5. Beat whipping cream until soft peaks form. Whisk one-third of the whipped cream into the milk mixture. Fold in the remaining whipped cream. Refrigerate until set and thickened to the consistency of whipped cream again, about 1 hour.

6. TO ASSEMBLE CAKE: Shortly before serving, place 1 cake layer on a serving plate and spread half the Bavarian cream over it. Peel and slice the remaining bananas; arrange half the slices evenly over the cream. Top with the second cake layer. Spread the remaining cream over the cake and arrange the remaining banana slices decoratively over the top.

MAKES 12 SERVINGS.

PER SERVING: 300 calories; 11 g fat (3 g sat, 5 g mono); 47 mg cholesterol; 47 g carbohydrate; 5 g protein; 3 g fiber; 229 mg sodium; 204 mg potassium.

LEMON SQUARES

H✝W L↓C H♥H

ACTIVE TIME: 15 MINUTES | **TOTAL:** 2¾ HOURS (INCLUDING 2 HOURS COOLING TIME)
TO MAKE AHEAD: Cover and refrigerate for up to 3 days.

These updated lemon squares are sure to be the hit of any picnic or potluck. We've improved the shortbread crust by using white whole-wheat flour and a butter-canola oil blend to cut saturated fat. The velvety filling has fewer eggs and gets a flavor boost from freshly grated lemon zest.

CRUST

- 1 cup white whole-wheat flour *or* all-purpose flour
- ½ cup granulated sugar
- ¼ teaspoon salt
- 2 tablespoons butter, softened
- 2 tablespoons canola oil
- 1 teaspoon freshly grated lemon zest

FILLING

- ¾ cup granulated sugar
- 2 teaspoons freshly grated lemon zest
- ⅓ cup lemon juice
- 1 large egg
- 1 large egg yolk
- 1 tablespoon white whole-wheat flour *or* all-purpose flour
  Confectioners' sugar for dusting

MAKEOVER TIP

TRY REPLACING ALL-PURPOSE FLOUR WITH WHITE WHOLE-WHEAT FLOUR, WHICH HAS THE HEALTH BENEFITS OF WHOLE-WHEAT WITH LESS OF THE "WHEATY" TASTE. IT'S ESPECIALLY GOOD IN COOKIES, BARS AND QUICK BREADS.

1. TO PREPARE CRUST: Preheat oven to 350°F. Coat an 8-inch-square or 7-by-11-inch baking pan with cooking spray.
2. Stir flour, sugar and salt in a medium bowl. Stir in butter, oil and lemon zest until blended and crumbly. Press the dough in an even layer in the prepared baking pan. Bake the crust until firm to the touch, about 20 minutes.
3. TO PREPARE FILLING: Whisk sugar, lemon zest and juice, egg, egg yolk and flour in a medium bowl until smooth. Pour evenly over the hot crust.
4. Bake until set, 15 to 20 minutes. Let cool completely in the pan on a wire rack, at least 2 hours. Cut into squares with a lightly oiled knife. Dust with confectioners' sugar just before serving.

MAKES 16 SQUARES.

PER SERVING: 126 calories; 4 g fat (1 g sat, 1 g mono); 30 mg cholesterol; 22 g carbohydrate; 2 g protein; 1 g fiber; 42 mg sodium; 23 mg potassium.

DOUBLE CHOCOLATE BROWNIES

H✴W L↓C

ACTIVE TIME: 20 MINUTES | **TOTAL:** 1 ½ HOURS (INCLUDING 45 MINUTES COOLING TIME)
TO MAKE AHEAD: Wrap in plastic wrap and store at room temperature for up to 2 days or freeze for up to 2 months.

Applesauce is the secret ingredient that keeps these yummy brownies dense and chewy even without all the butter you would expect to find. We've used whole-wheat pastry flour for added fiber and nutrients and loaded the brownies with plenty of chocolate chips to keep them rich and satisfying. You won't even miss the 20 grams of fat we've lost in the makeover.

4 ounces unsweetened chocolate	3 large eggs
2 tablespoons butter	1 ⅓ cups packed light brown sugar
1 cup whole-wheat pastry flour (*see Ingredient Note, page 248*)	¾ cup unsweetened applesauce
¼ cup unsweetened cocoa powder	2 tablespoons canola oil
¼ teaspoon salt	1 teaspoon vanilla extract
4 large egg whites	½ cup semisweet chocolate chips
	⅓ cup chopped walnuts *or* pecans (optional)

1. Preheat oven to 350°F. Coat a 9-by-13-inch baking pan with cooking spray.
2. Melt chocolate and butter in a double boiler over barely simmering water. (*Alternatively, place in a small microwave-safe bowl and microwave on Medium, stirring every 30 seconds, until melted and smooth.*)
3. Whisk flour, cocoa and salt in a medium bowl.
4. Beat egg whites, eggs and brown sugar in a large mixing bowl with an electric mixer. Add applesauce, oil and vanilla; beat until blended. (*See Variation.*) Add the chocolate-butter mixture; beat until blended. Add the flour mixture and mix just until moistened. Stir in chocolate chips. Scrape the batter into the prepared pan, spreading evenly. Sprinkle with nuts, if desired.
5. Bake the brownies until the top springs back when touched lightly, 20 to 25 minutes. Transfer to a wire rack and let cool completely. Cut into bars.

MAKES 24 BROWNIES.

PER BROWNIE: 142 calories; 6 g fat (3 g sat, 2 g mono); 29 mg cholesterol; 21 g carbohydrate; 3 g protein; 2 g fiber; 48 mg sodium; 106 mg potassium.

VARIATION:

For a mocha flavor, in Step 4 stir in 4 teaspoons instant coffee granules dissolved in 2 tablespoons hot water.

MAKEOVER TIP

USE APPLESAUCE IN PLACE OF ALL OR MOST OF THE FAT IN BARS LIKE THIS BROWNIE—THEY'RE EVERY BIT AS MOIST AND DELICIOUS AS THOSE MADE WITH TONS OF BUTTER.

HOLIDAY SUGAR COOKIES

ACTIVE TIME: 30 MINUTES | **TOTAL:** 50 MINUTES
TO MAKE AHEAD: Store in an airtight container for up to 3 days. Freeze for longer storage.

These festive cookies are proof that you can add whole-wheat flour to a baked good without anyone ever knowing it. We've replaced some of the butter with healthier canola oil, cutting the saturated fat by about 75%. They freeze well so you may want to consider making extras to have on hand for a sweet treat.

1/2 cup sugar	3/4 cup unsifted cake flour
2 tablespoons butter, softened	1 teaspoon baking powder
2 tablespoons canola oil	1/4 teaspoon salt
1 large egg	Cookie Icing (*recipe follows*)
1 1/2 teaspoons vanilla extract	Colored sprinkles (optional)
3/4 cup whole-wheat flour	

1. Preheat oven to 350°F. Coat 2 baking sheets with cooking spray.

2. Combine sugar, butter and oil in a medium bowl and beat with an electric mixer until light and fluffy. Mix in egg and vanilla; beat until smooth. Sift whole-wheat flour, cake flour, baking powder and salt together over the sugar mixture; mix on low speed until just combined. Divide the dough in half and press each piece into a disk. Roll out dough on a well-floured surface to an even 1/8-inch thickness.

3. Cut out cookies with a 3-inch shaped cutter, rerolling and cutting any scraps. Place cookies 1/2 inch apart on the prepared baking sheets.

4. Bake in upper third of oven, 1 sheet at a time, until slightly golden on the edges, 5 to 7 minutes. Do not overbake. Transfer the cookies to wire racks to cool.

5. To decorate cookies, use a pastry brush to paint with icing, then top with sprinkles, if using. Let stand until the icing hardens. (If storing iced cookies, layer between sheets of wax paper.)

MAKES ABOUT 2 1/2 DOZEN COOKIES.

PER ICED COOKIE: 84 calories; 2 g fat (1 g sat, 1 g mono); 9 mg cholesterol; 16 g carbohydrate; 1 g protein; 0 g fiber; 41 mg sodium; 19 mg potassium.

COOKIE ICING

ACTIVE TIME: 10 MINUTES | **TOTAL:** 10 MINUTES

1 3/4 cups confectioners' sugar	Food coloring (optional)
1 1/2 tablespoons light corn syrup	1 1/2 tablespoons hot water
1/2 teaspoon vanilla extract	

Sift sugar into a bowl. Stir in corn syrup, vanilla, a few drops food coloring (if using) and hot water; mix until smooth. If the icing is too thick, add a few more drops of water.

MAKES ABOUT 3/4 CUP.

PER TABLESPOON: 76 calories; 0 g fat (0 g sat, 0 g mono); 0 mg cholesterol; 20 g carbohydrate; 0 g protein; 0 g fiber; 2 mg sodium; 1 mg potassium.

OATMEAL CHOCOLATE CHIP COOKIES

ACTIVE TIME: 15 MINUTES | **TOTAL:** 1 HOUR
TO MAKE AHEAD: Store in an airtight container for up to 2 days or freeze for longer storage.

Kids will love these cookies—if the adults leave any for them to eat. They have the familiar flavors of brown sugar and chocolate, but get a sophisticated twist from tahini (sesame paste). Tahini helps to lower the saturated fat by more than 66 percent while adding a nutty flavor to an old classic.

2	cups rolled oats (*not* quick-cooking)
½	cup whole-wheat pastry flour (*see Ingredient Note, page 248*)
½	cup all-purpose flour
1	teaspoon ground cinnamon
½	teaspoon baking soda
½	teaspoon salt
½	cup tahini (*see Ingredient Note*)
4	tablespoons cold unsalted butter, cut into pieces
⅔	cup granulated sugar
⅔	cup packed light brown sugar
1	large egg
1	large egg white
1	tablespoon vanilla extract
1	cup semisweet *or* bittersweet chocolate chips
½	cup chopped walnuts

1. Position racks in upper and lower thirds of oven; preheat to 350°F. Line 2 baking sheets with parchment paper.

2. Whisk oats, whole-wheat flour, all-purpose flour, cinnamon, baking soda and salt in a medium bowl. Beat tahini and butter in a large bowl with an electric mixer until blended into a paste. Add granulated sugar and brown sugar; continue beating until well combined—the mixture will still be a little grainy. Beat in egg, then egg white, then vanilla. Stir in the oat mixture with a wooden spoon until just moistened. Stir in chocolate chips and walnuts.

3. With damp hands, roll 1 tablespoon of the batter into a ball, place it on a prepared baking sheet and flatten it until squat, but don't let the sides crack. Continue with the remaining batter, spacing the flattened balls 2 inches apart.

4. Bake the cookies until golden brown, about 16 minutes, switching the pans back to front and top to bottom halfway through. Cool on the pans for 2 minutes, then transfer the cookies to a wire rack to cool completely. Let the pans cool for a few minutes before baking another batch.

MAKES ABOUT 45 COOKIES.

PER COOKIE: 102 calories; 5 g fat (2 g sat, 1 g mono); 7 mg cholesterol; 14 g carbohydrate; 2 g protein; 1 g fiber; 45 mg sodium; 53 mg potassium.

INGREDIENT NOTE:

Tahini is a paste made from ground sesame seeds. Look for it in natural-foods stores and some supermarkets.

CHOCOLATE VELVET PUDDING

H ✳ W

ACTIVE TIME: 20 MINUTES | **TOTAL:** 20 MINUTES

Although instant mixes and premade puddings abound in every supermarket, they just can't compare with homemade. This reduced-fat version is almost as quick as a mix and delivers a rich chocolate flavor.

1	large egg	2	cups low-fat milk
1/3	cup nonfat sweetened condensed milk	1	ounce bittersweet or semisweet (*not* unsweetened) chocolate, chopped
1/4	cup unsweetened cocoa powder	2	teaspoons vanilla extract
2	tablespoons cornstarch		
1/8	teaspoon salt		

1. Whisk egg, condensed milk, cocoa, cornstarch and salt in a heavy saucepan until smooth. Gradually whisk in milk. Bring to a boil over medium-low heat, whisking constantly, until thickened, 7 to 9 minutes.

2. Remove from the heat; add chocolate and vanilla, whisking until the chocolate melts. Transfer to a bowl. Place plastic wrap directly on the surface to prevent a skin from forming. Serve warm or refrigerate until ready to serve.

MAKES 4 SERVINGS, GENEROUS ½ CUP EACH.

PER SERVING: 196 calories; 5 g fat (3 g sat, 1 g mono); 64 mg cholesterol; 30 g carbohydrate; 9 g protein; 2 g fiber; 183 mg sodium; 348 mg potassium.

NUTRITION BONUS: Calcium (23% daily value).

VANILLA CREAM

ACTIVE TIME: 15 MINUTES | **TOTAL:** 1 ¼ HOURS (INCLUDING 1 HOUR TO DRAIN YOGURT)

TO MAKE AHEAD: The cream will keep, covered, in the refrigerator for up to 2 days.

This versatile creamy topping blends the nutritional virtues and creamy texture of drained nonfat yogurt with the luxury of a little whipped cream. Use it in place of full-fat whipped cream or dessert topping. If you like, you can make variations by using different flavors of yogurt or even whisking in a bit of cocoa powder.

1	cup low-fat *or* nonfat vanilla yogurt	2½	teaspoons confectioners' sugar (optional)
1/4	cup whipping cream		

1. Line a sieve or colander with cheesecloth and set over a bowl, leaving at least ½-inch clearance from the bottom. (*Alternatively, use a coffee filter lined with filter paper.*) Spoon in yogurt, cover and let drain in the refrigerator for 1 hour. Discard whey.

2. Whip cream in a small bowl until soft peaks form. Add sugar, if using, and continue whipping until firm peaks form. Fold in the drained yogurt.

MAKES ABOUT 1 CUP.

PER TABLESPOON: 24 calories; 1 g fat (1 g sat, 0 g mono); 5 mg cholesterol; 2 g carbohydrate; 1 g protein; 0 g fiber; 11 mg sodium; 37 mg potassium.

SEE IT : MAKE IT

RHUBARB-VANILLA COMPOTE

Combine 4 cups diced rhubarb, ½ cup sugar and ¼ tea-spoon cinnamon in a saucepan. Simmer until the rhubarb begins to break down, about 5 minutes. Remove from heat and stir in ½ teaspoon vanilla.

MAKES 4 SERVINGS, ½ CUP EACH. | PER SERVING: 125 calories, 0 g fat (0 g sat), 5 mg sodium.

GINGERSNAP-BANANA FROZEN YOGURT

Layer equal portions of: 2 cups softened vanilla frozen yogurt, 6 chopped gingersnaps, 2 sliced bananas and ¼ cup chopped toasted pecans into 4 small dessert cups. Freeze until firm, at least 10 minutes.

MAKES 4 SERVINGS. | PER SERVING: 287 calories, 12 g fat (4 g sat), 81 mg sodium.

CITRUS-INFUSED STRAWBERRIES

Combine 1 pound sliced strawberries, 2 tablespoons sugar, 1 tablespoon Grand Marnier and 1 teaspoon lemon juice in a bowl. Let stand, stirring twice, until juicy, about 10 minutes. Serve with Vanilla Cream (*page 244*), if desired.

MAKES 4 SERVINGS, ¾ CUP EACH. | PER SERVING: 74 calories, 0 g fat (0 g sat), 1 mg sodium.

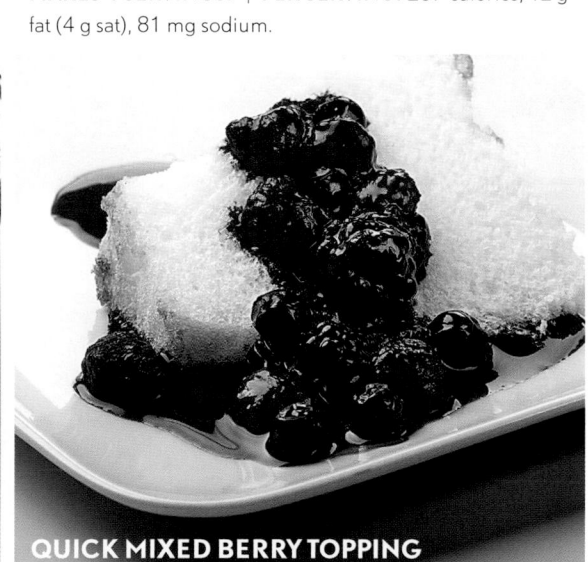

QUICK MIXED BERRY TOPPING

Toss 2 cups frozen mixed berries, 2 tablespoons sugar and 1½ teaspoons cornstarch in a large bowl. Microwave on High for 2 minutes. Stir; microwave until slightly thickened and steaming, about 2½ minutes more.

MAKES 8 SERVINGS, 2 TABLESPOONS EACH. | PER SERVING: 32 calories, 0 g fat (0 g sat), 0 mg sodium.

RESOURCES

KITCHEN TIPS:

To make **fresh breadcrumbs**, trim crusts from whole-wheat bread. Tear bread into pieces and process in a food processor until coarse crumbs form. One slice of bread makes about ½ cup fresh crumbs. For **dry breadcrumbs**, spread the fresh crumbs on a baking sheet and bake at 250°F until crispy, about 15 minutes. One slice of fresh bread makes about ⅓ cup dry crumbs. Or use prepared coarse dry breadcrumbs. We like Ian's brand labeled "Panko breadcrumbs." Find them in the natural-foods section of large supermarkets.

No **buttermilk**? You can use buttermilk powder prepared according to package directions. Or make "sour milk": mix 1 tablespoon lemon juice or vinegar to 1 cup milk.

To poach **chicken breasts**, place boneless, skinless chicken breasts in a medium skillet or saucepan and add lightly salted water to cover; bring to a boil. Cover, reduce heat to low and simmer gently until chicken is cooked through and no longer pink in the middle, 10 to 15 minutes. To shred the chicken, use two forks to pull it apart into long shreds.

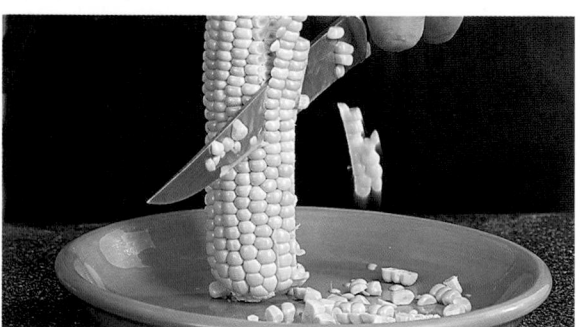

^
To remove **corn kernels** from the cob: Stand an uncooked ear of corn on its stem end in a shallow bowl and slice the kernels off with a sharp, thin-bladed knife. This technique produces whole kernels that are good for adding to salads and salsas. If you want to use the corn kernels for soups, fritters or puddings, you can add another step to the process. After cutting the kernels off, reverse the knife and, using the dull side, press it down the length of the ear to push out the rest of the corn and its milk.

To hard-boil **eggs**, place in a single layer in a saucepan; cover with water. Bring to a simmer over medium-high heat. Reduce heat to low and cook at the barest simmer for 10 minutes. Remove from heat, pour out hot water and fill the pan with a mixture of cold water and ice cubes; let stand until the eggs are completely cooled.

^
To oil the **grill rack**, oil a folded paper towel, hold it with tongs and rub it over the rack. (Do not use cooking spray on a hot grill.) When grilling delicate foods like tofu and fish, it is helpful to spray the food with cooking spray before placing it on the grill.

To clean **leeks**, trim and discard green tops and white roots. Split leeks lengthwise and place in plenty of water. Swish the leeks in the water to release any sand or soil. Drain. Repeat until no grit remains.

^
To clean **mussels**, scrub with a stiff brush under cold running water. Scrape off any barnacles using the shell of another mussel. Pull off the fuzzy "beard" from each one (some mussels may not have a beard).

To **toast nuts** (walnuts, pecans or hazelnuts), spread onto a baking sheet and bake at 350°F, stirring once, until fragrant, 7 to 9 minutes. To toast chopped (or small) **nuts**, **coconut** and **seeds**, cook in a small dry skillet over medium-low heat, stirring constantly, until fragrant and lightly browned, 2 to 5 minutes.

The dark gills found on the underside of a **portobello mushroom** cap are edible, but can turn a dish an unappealing gray/black color. Remove the gills with a spoon, if desired.

^
To skin a **salmon fillet**, place salmon on a clean cutting board, skin side down. Starting at the tail end, slip the blade of a long, sharp knife between the fish flesh and the skin, holding the skin down firmly with your other hand. Gently push the blade along at a 30° angle, separating the fillet from the skin without cutting through either.

^
To make **taco shells**, working with 6 tortillas at a time, wrap in a barely damp cloth or paper towel and microwave on High until steamed, about 30 seconds. Lay the tortillas on a clean work surface and coat both sides with cooking spray. Then carefully drape each tortilla over two bars of the oven rack. Bake at 375°F until crispy, 7 to 10 minutes.

INGREDIENT NOTES:

Andouille sausage is a smoky, mildly spicy pork sausage commonly used in Cajun cooking. Look for it with smoked sausages in large supermarkets or specialty-food stores.

Most supermarkets sell **broccoli crowns**, which are the tops of the bunches, with the stalks cut off. Although crowns are more expensive than entire bunches, they are convenient and there is considerably less waste.

Bulgur is made by parboiling, drying and coarsely grinding or cracking wheat berries. It simply needs a quick soak in hot water for most uses. Look for it in the natural-foods section of large supermarkets, near other grains, or online at *kalustyans.com*, *lebaneseproducts.com*.

Chicken tenders, virtually fat-free, are a strip of rib meat typically found attached to the underside of the chicken breast, but they can also be purchased separately. Four 1-ounce tenders will yield a 3-ounce cooked portion. Tenders are perfect for quick stir-fries, chicken satay or kid-friendly breaded "chicken fingers."

Chipotle peppers are dried, smoked jalapeño peppers. Ground chipotle chile pepper can be found in the specialty spice section of most supermarkets. **Chipotle chiles in adobo sauce** are smoked jalapeños packed in a flavorful sauce. Look for the small cans with the Mexican foods in large supermarkets. Once opened, they'll keep up to 2 weeks in the refrigerator or 6 months in the freezer.

Coconut chips—large thin flakes of dried coconut— make attractive garnishes. Find them in the bulk or baking section of large markets.

Dried egg whites are pasteurized—a wise choice when making meringue toppings that may not reach 160°F (the temperature at which eggs are considered "safe"). You'll find them in the baking or natural-foods section of most supermarkets. Reconstitute according to package directions.

Look for **precooked diced potatoes** in the refrigerated section of most supermarket produce departments—near other fresh, prepared vegetables. To make your own, peel 2¼ pounds Yukon Gold potatoes, cut into ½-inch pieces and boil until tender (about 15 minutes).

Be sure to buy "dry" sea **scallops** (scallops that have not been treated with sodium tripolyphosphate, or STP). Scallops that have been treated with STP ("wet" scallops) have been subjected to a chemical bath and are not only mushy and less flavorful, but will not brown properly.

Sherry is a type of fortified wine originally from southern Spain. Don't use the "cooking sherry" sold in many supermarkets—it can be surprisingly high in sodium. Instead, purchase dry sherry that's sold with other fortified wines in your wine or liquor store.

Shrimp is usually sold by the number needed to make one pound. For example, "21-25 count" means there will be 21 to 25 shrimp in a pound. Size names, such as "large" or "extra large," are not standardized, so to be sure you're getting the size you want, order by the count (or number) per pound. Both wild-caught and farm-raised shrimp can damage the surrounding ecosystems when not managed properly. Fortunately, it is possible to buy shrimp that have been raised or caught with sound environmental practices. Look for fresh or frozen shrimp certified by an independent agency, such as Wild American Shrimp or Marine Stewardship Council. If you can't find certified shrimp, choose wild-caught shrimp from North America—it's more likely to be sustainably caught.

Smoked paprika is available in three varieties: sweet, bittersweet and hot. Sweet is the most versatile, but choose hot if you like a bit of heat. It can be purchased in gourmet markets and online at *tienda.com*.

Tomatillos are tart, plum-size green fruits that look like small, husk-covered green tomatoes. Find them in the produce section near the tomatoes. Remove the outer husk and rinse them well before using.

Whole-wheat pastry flour, lower in protein than regular whole-wheat flour, has less gluten-forming potential, making it a better choice for tender baked goods. You can find it in the natural-foods section of large supermarkets and natural-foods stores. Store in the freezer.

MAKEOVER TIP INDEX

RECIPE INDEX

Our thanks to the fine food writers whose work has appeared in EATINGWELL Magazine.
(Page numbers in italics indicate photographs.)

OTHER EATINGWELL BOOKS

(available at *www.eatingwell.com/shop*):

The Essential EatingWell Cookbook

(The Countryman Press, 2004)

ISBN: 978-0-88150-630-3 (hardcover)

ISBN: 978-0-88150-701-0 (softcover, 2005)

The EatingWell Diabetes Cookbook

(The Countryman Press, 2005)

ISBN: 978-0-88150-633-4 (hardcover)

ISBN: 978-0-88150-778-2 (softcover, 2007)

The EatingWell Healthy in a Hurry Cookbook

(The Countryman Press, 2006)

ISBN: 978-0-88150-687-7 (hardcover)

EatingWell Serves Two

(The Countryman Press, 2006)

ISBN: 978-0-88150-723-2 (hardcover)

The EatingWell Diet

(The Countryman Press, 2007)

ISBN: 978-0-88150-722-5 (hardcover)

ISBN: 978-0-88150-822-2 (softcover, 2008)

EatingWell for a Healthy Heart Cookbook

(The Countryman Press, 2008)

ISBN: 978-0-88150-724-9 (hardcover)

TRUCS OF THE TRADE

101 Tricks, Tips, and Recipes from America's Greatest Chefs

Edited by Frank Ball and Arlene Feltman

Illustrations by Art Glazer

HarperPerennial
A Division of HarperCollinsPublishers

FIRST EDITION

Designed by Charles Kreloff

Library of Congress Cataloging-in-Publication Data
Trucs of the trade: 101 tricks, tips, and recipes from America's greatest chefs / edited by Frank Ball and Arlene Feltman.
    p.   cm.
Includes index.
ISBN 0-06-096595-9
1. Cookery. I. Ball, Frank. II. Feltman, Arlene.
TX652.T786 1992
641.5—dc20
                              92-52622

92 93 94 95 96 ❖ /RRD 10 9 8 7 6 5 4 3 2 1

CONTENTS

INTRODUCTION

What is a *truc*, anyway?

And how do you say it?

It's easy to say, but it's a little harder to say what it is.

Let's start with the easy part. *Truc* is a French word. When it's pronounced it sounds like *true* with a *k* at the end: *true* + *k* = *TRUC*.

Now for the hard part.

Truc is, basically, "trick." Not a magic trick, based on illusion, but a trick in a bigger, more universal sense—a trick that offers the inherent satisfaction of beating reality, of finding a better, cheaper, easier, faster way of getting something done. A trick that, the mere knowing of which, makes you feel smug.

Trucs have particular relevance in the kitchen. Take potatoes, for instance. Potatoes have a natural, built-in tendency to get mushy and fall apart when they are boiled. But there's a trick—a better way—revealed here by Giuliano Bugialli, to keep potatoes intact. Every single time. That trick is a *truc*.

Sometimes a *truc* is a shortcut, a way of doing something faster—like chilling champagne in 20 minutes flat (*Truc #101*). That shortcut is a *truc*.

At times a *truc* is a gimmick—like cooking fish in paper, for instance (*Truc #76*), or tenderizing meat with wine corks (*Truc #66*). These gimmicks are definitely *trucs*.

At other times a *truc* is a tip, a special little procedure that delivers better results. Like the *truc* André Soltner uses to ensure that the omelets at Lutèce don't stick (*Truc #42*). Or the *truc* Anne Rosenzweig developed for creating the perfect hamburger (*Truc #63*). Or the *truc* master baker Jim Dodge uses to coax the pesky skin off hazelnuts (*Truc #89*).

Finally, a *truc* is sometimes an out-and-out secret. Like the way to cook perfect rice (*Truc #45*), gleefully revealed by Chef Patrick Clark who advises, "Begin by ignoring the directions on the box …"

Trucs are not created in the scholarly vacuum of a laboratory. Rather, they are discovered and developed in the heat of real-world kitchens, through the daily interaction between cooks and ingredients, implements and processes. Once discovered, *trucs* are shared and passed around from one cook to another, constituting a legacy, a treasure trove of professional knowledge.

INTRODUCTION

No matter what their form or their source, though, all *trucs* share a single characteristic: a real *truc* is *genuinely helpful*. And that's the point.

We hope you enjoy learning these *trucs* and that you'll find them to be genuinely helpful. We are grateful to our many friends who shared their *trucs* with us, first for a videotape and now in this book. They were genuinely helpful. Their generosity reflects that of Kobrand Corporation, merchants of fine wines, who sponsored the production of the video.

In purchasing this book, you too have been genuinely helpful. A portion of the proceeds from this project—both video and book—goes to support the work of Share Our Strength (SOS), a network of food industry and other creative professionals united to fight hunger in the United States and overseas. Further information about the work of this organization and the video version of this book can be obtained by calling SOS at (800) 222-1767.

Thank you. And keep on *trucin'*.

F. B. & A. F.

THE TRUCS

VEGETABLES

#1

OPENING ARTICHOKES

When Mother Nature invented the packaging for artichokes, she created a doozie. Jimmy Schmidt features artichokes so frequently on his menu that he had to find a fast, workable way to get to the heart of the matter. He developed this three-stroke truc for delivering the heart in four neat pieces.

Quarter the cooked artichoke, lengthwise, cutting through the heart. Cut across each quarter, just at the point where the purple leaves peak. When the knife stops naturally, gently peel the heart and choke away from the tough leaves. Remove the fibrous choke from the heart by making a cut about ½ inch deep at the base of the choke fibers. Flick the blade of the knife up and the choke will pull right out, leaving the heart.

#2
PICTURE-PERFECT AVOCADOS

Picture-perfect avocado halves, deftly peeled to reveal their smooth green flesh, are lovely to behold. Their violin-like shape and their velvet texture coalesce to become a thing of beauty. Occasionally. More frequently the shape disappears and the texture is totally mutilated as we wrestle the peel off. Robert Del Grande says the truc is in thinking small.

Don't try to remove the peel in one piece. With the tip of a sharp paring knife, make two lengthwise slits, equally spaced, just through the skin of the avocado. Avoid cutting the flesh beneath. With the edge of the blade, lift the corner of the outside strip of skin and roll it off. Repeat with the other two strips.

#3
PITTING AVOCADOS

When most of us North-of-the-border types try to open and pit an avocado, we end up with a handful of guacamole. Chef Robert Del Grande has an ingenious two-step truc that he gratefully learned from a Mexican colleague.

Start by trimming off the stem end of an unpeeled avocado. Then, hold the avocado on its side and work a knife around the seed, cutting it full circle. Remove the knife and give both sides of the avocado a gentle twist. The avocado will pull right apart into two halves. To remove the seed: hit the top of the seed with the heel of a heavy knife. Give the knife a slight turn and lift; the seed will emerge stuck to the blade.

To remove the seed from the knife, reach over the top of the blade with forefinger and thumb and push down, with a squeezing action, until the seed pops off.

#4

CONTROLLING THE TEXTURE OF DRIED BEANS

One of life's abiding mysteries: why do cooked dried beans sometimes come out mushy and creamy and, at other times, firm and whole. Is it due to the age of the beans, the preparation (soaking versus parboiling), the cooking liquid (broth versus water), the heat source (gas versus electric), the kind of pot (metal versus clay), or the size of the pot? Chef Judy Rogers made a breakthrough discovery when she realized that the beans, the preparation, the liquid, the heat, and the pot are irrelevant factors; the truc to reliable bean cookery is in the lid.

For soft and creamy beans, cook with the lid on.
For firmer beans, cook with the lid off.

Soft Beans

Firm Beans

#5

SNAPPING FAVA BEANS

Those strange, lumpy-looking oversized pods that show up in the market during the spring and summer are called fava beans. And they're good for you. They sport a rich, smooth taste that makes them a welcome accompaniment to meat, fish, and fowl. But many of us pass on favas for a simple reason: we don't know how to peel them. Daniel Boulud to the rescue, with a truc that makes peeling favas a snap.

Working down the pod, snap to release each fava bean and push it out with thumb and forefinger. Blanch the beans for 30 seconds in boiling water, then plunge them into iced water to cool. Break the seam of each bean with a fingernail, pushing the fava bean out of its sleeve.

#6
REMOVING BEET STAINS

Daniel Boulud has developed a defensive strategy against beet stains. When working with fresh beets, he covers himself and his work surface with a thin membrane of protection that ensures the stains end up in the trash and not on the cook or the kitchen.

Cover the work surface with wax paper and wear disposable rubber gloves when preparing fresh beets. At cleanup time, toss the gloves and the paper—and the stains.

#7
CARROTS THAT TASTE LIKE CARROTS

Carrots are a lot like tomatoes—they can be intensely flavorful or they can be intensely tasteless. Giuliano Bugialli, observing that a great deal of the carrot's flavor resides in the carrot's skin, uses that skin to intensify the sweet, "carroty" flavor of boiled carrots. His truc:

Don't peel the carrots. Wash them and cook with the peels on, in salted boiling water. Once they are soft enough to pierce with a fork, plunge them into cool water. The peels will rub right off, leaving behind their distinctive flavor.

#8
ODORLESS CAULIFLOWER COOKING

Among the special pleasures of home-cooked food is the delightful smell that emanates from the kitchen. Unless it's cauliflower. Then everyone wants to eat out. For as good as cauliflower can taste on the plate, it can really smell up a house while it's cooking. Antoine Bouterin's truc, which also works with broccoli and cabbage, is like a breath of fresh air.

Tear a slice of bread into small pieces and add it to the pot with the cauliflower and its cooking liquid. The bread will absorb and contain the cooking odor.

#9
CUTTING CUCUMBER FANS WITH CHOPSTICKS

One of Barbara Tropp's most popular dishes is Ma-La Szechwan Cucumber Fans—marinated pieces of cucumber cleverly cut and splayed to resemble fans. Chef Tropp reveals her chopstick trick for making these fanciful fans (and points out that the same approach will work with zucchini, carrots, potatoes, and so forth).

Place two chopsticks flat on the counter and bring the thicker ends together to form a *V*. Put a 2- to 3-inch piece of peeled cucumber on the counter, in between the chopsticks. Cut the cucumber into thin slices. (The chopsticks will automatically stop the knife from cutting through the cucumber.) Apply light pressure on the vegetable to spread open the slices and reveal the fan shape.

#10
EGGPLANT GENDER

Male or female, which is sweeter? If we're talking people, the jury's still out. But if we're talking eggplant, the males win hands down—they've got fewer bitter seeds. So to end up with better eggplant dishes, start out with male eggplants. Granted, a good male is hard to find, but Lidia Bastianich knows how ... and she's telling.

To determine the gender of eggplants, look at the bottom of the vegetable where the flower

Male

Female

was once attached. The male eggplant has a well-rounded bottom with a smooth, even stem area. The female has a narrow bottom with an elliptical, deeply indented stem area.

#11
A SMASHING WAY TO PEEL GARLIC

Removing the peel from garlic is sufficiently frustrating to make even a patient cook want to smash it. And that, according to our friend the late Leslee Reis, is exactly what should be done.

Place the head of garlic on the counter and press on the root end to loosen the cloves. Separate a clove from the head and set it on a cutting board. Lay the flat side of a chef's knife on the clove and press down firmly until the clove snaps. Pick up the clove and the peel will come right off.

#12
MELLOWING GARLIC

The lusty, robust taste of garlic is just right for most people. But for those who want their garlic slightly less lusty and a little less robust, Michel Richard discloses this Gallic truc for mellowing the taste of garlic.

Peel the skin from a clove of garlic. Using a sharp paring knife, make a vertical incision halfway into the clove, removing the bitter green shoot, if present, from the center. Put the clove in a pot of water and boil for 5 minutes.

#13
MINCING GARLIC WITH A FORK

When making a vinaigrette or other salad dressing that calls for minced garlic, using a garlic press or a cutting board to mince the garlic just creates more things to wash. Alain Sailhac shares an ingenious little truc he learned from his father—a way to mince the garlic using just the bowl and fork used to make the dressing.

Place a fork, tines pointing up, on the bottom of the salad bowl. Gently rub a peeled garlic clove across the ends of the tines, mincing the garlic. When garlic is minced, add remaining ingredients and proceed with the recipe.

#14

NO-FUSS GARLIC PURÉE

Puréeing garlic in a garlic press couldn't be easier. Cleaning a garlic press couldn't be harder. So Susan Feniger uses her garlic press as seldom as possible. Instead, when she needs to purée garlic, she resorts to this truc.

Cut a garlic clove in half lengthwise and place it flat-side down on a work surface. Make several vertical cuts, then several horizontal cuts on each

Salt

Minced Garlic

half of the clove. Finish by cutting straight down across the clove, mincing the garlic. Sprinkle the garlic with a little salt and, using the flat side of a chef's knife, mash the garlic and salt together. The abrasiveness of the salt helps turn the garlic into a smooth purée.

#15
GETTING THE GARLIC ON THE BREAD

In Italy, garlic bread is called bruschetta. *The concept is simple: slices of hearty peasant bread are toasted, rubbed with garlic, and topped simply with tomatoes, mushrooms, and/or olive oil. There's one special trick involved in this process: how do you get the garlic rubbed on the bread without mangling and tearing the bread's crisp, toasted surface? Native Tuscan* Pino Luongo *imparts this native Tuscan truc.*

Rub a clove of garlic liberally *on just the crusty edges* around the perimeter of the toasted bread. The rough texture of the crust grates the garlic and flavors the whole slice.

#16
TEARLESS ONION DICING

Susan Feniger has been working on a truc to make all existing onions practically no-tear. She's discovered that by dicing an onion in a way that minimizes the loss of its juices, the onion has better flavor, caramelizes evenly when cooking—and, most important, doesn't cause tears. Here's how it's done.

Minimize the release of the onion's tear-causing juice by cutting the onion cleanly, precisely, and as few times as possible. Set the onion on its root end and cut it in half, right through the core. Place a half, flat-side down on the cutting board and make several lengthwise cuts, then several crosswise. Dice finely by cutting straight down through the onion.

1. Vertical Cuts

3. Cut
Straight
Down

2. Horizontal Cuts

#17

KEEPING THE SWEETNESS
IN RAW ONION

Ever notice how raw onion gets stronger as it sits? How a bowl of potato salad with onion becomes, after a few hours, a bowl of onion salad? How a sprightly fresh tomato/onion salsa turns on you to become salsa from hell? Well, there's a reason: chemicals within onions are released when an onion is cut. These chemicals oxidize as they sit, becoming increasingly strong, bitter, and unpleasant. The solution? A simple chemical truc from Mr. Wizard, Rick Bayless.

Place diced or chopped onion in a strainer. Dip the strainer several times into a bowl filled with water and and a little bit of vinegar. Drain the onion, shaking off excess liquid. The acid in the water prevents the onion from turning bitter.

#18
BETTER SCALLION CHOPPING

Finely chopping scallions isn't as easy as it might seem. Cutting across the white part reveals a series of concentric rings which, if they separate, is great; if they don't; scallion chunks result. And cutting across the green part frequently produces something akin to grade school paper dolls—a string of semi-detached scallion rings which appear to be holding hands. Barbara Tropp contributes a most helpful truc to achieve perfectly chopped scallions.

Before cutting a scallion crosswise, make one vertical slice all the way from the root to the tip. This one extra cut will allow the rings to separate easily and will double the number of scallion pieces produced.

#19

PEELING PEPPERS QUICKLY

One of the few vegetables that a vegetable peeler won't peel is a fresh pepper. The peel is so thin and so tightly bound to the flesh that it takes heat to get it off. The usual method is to blacken the skin over an open flame (impossible with an electric range) or under the broiler. The pepper has to be repeatedly turned to expose different areas to the flames, and even then, there are nooks and crannies that escape. This inefficient process takes several minutes and it is incredibly boring. Zarela Martinez has a truc that takes the pepper from the fire into the frying pan—and polishes off the job in less than 30 seconds.

Pour vegetable oil into a skillet to a depth of approximately ½ inch; heat until almost smoking. Make a small slit in the side of the pepper to prevent it from popping. Put the pepper into the skillet of hot oil and cook for a few seconds until the pepper turns beige in color and the skin becomes transparent. Turn and repeat on the other side. Remove the pepper, cool on a paper towel, and slip off the peel under running water.

#20
CUTTING PEPPERS FROM THE INSIDE OUT

The slick, waxy skin on bell peppers makes them a potential hazard on the cutting board—it's all too easy for a knife blade to slip when confronting this kind of surface. So Chef Michael Foley turns things around with an inside-out truc for safely cutting bell peppers.

After the pepper is seeded and deveined, place it on a cutting board *shiny side down.* Proceed to cut through the moist underside. The knife cuts easily through this surface and is less likely to slip.

#21
INSTANT GLOVES

Everybody knows that the skin and seeds of chili peppers contain hot resins that will burn a cook's hands. And everybody's been told endlessly to wear rubber gloves when working with chilies. And everybody usually ignores this advice because it's too much trouble to find the rubber gloves and put them on, particularly when working with just a few chilies. And everybody's been burned. And, therefore, everybody will love Stephan Pyles's truc for instant gloves.

To don instant gloves, rub the hands liberally with vegetable oil. This coating will protect the skin from the fiery resins in chili peppers.

#22
CLEANING DRIED CHILIES

Dean Fearing, *one of the guiding lights in Southwestern cuisine, illuminates for us a three-step truc for cleaning dried chilies quickly.*

To clean a dried chili, start by removing its stem. Then pull the chili apart, lengthwise, splitting it in half. Brush the seeds from both halves and the chili is ready to cook.

#23
QUICK PEPPER SEEDING

Most recipes which use fresh peppers specify that they be seeded. (In the case of sweet bell peppers and other mild varieties, the seeds have no taste and are extraneous; in the case of chili peppers, the seeds contain heat that overpowers the taste of the pepper.) Cutting the pepper in half and trying to dig out the seeds makes one feel like a strip miner or a dentist. The pros go about it a whole different way, a secret shared by Robert Del Grande.

Cut both ends off the pepper. Stand the pepper on the counter and slice straight down with a sharp knife, removing the flesh in four or five pieces from around the core. Discard the seeds and the core.

#24
KEEPING BOILED POTATOES FIRM

Sliced or cubed, potatoes boiled for salad need to be cooked until they're tender, but still retain their shape. Giuliano Bugialli shares a secret-ingredient truc he uses to keep the boiled potatoes from becoming mushy and falling apart.

Fill a pot with 2 parts water and 1 part vinegar. Add a dash of kosher salt and bring to a boil. Add the potatoes, which are already trimmed or peeled, and gently boil them until cooked.

#25
BAKING POTATOES ON COPPER PIPES

David Burke is known to be highly inventive in his novel combination of ingredients. And in the case of one of his signature garnishes, a crispy arched potato wafer, his inventiveness led him to devise a new kind of copper cookware—pipes.

Place a 2-inch-wide copper pipe (available at plumbing and building supply stores) on a baking sheet, using crumpled aluminum foil under the ends to keep the pipe from rolling. Preheat the pipe for 10 minutes in a 325° oven.

Thinly slice a peeled potato on a mandolin. Soak the slices in either flavored oil or clarified butter. Lay the slices across the pipe and bake in a 325° oven for 5 to 7 minutes. Once baked, the crispy wafers will easily slide off the pipe and retain their arched shape.

#26
EASY TOMATO PEELING

Peeling tomatoes with a knife is not only tedious and wasteful, but it yields a tomato that looks slightly brutalized. There's a better way. Andy D'Amico's truc makes peeling fast and easy, and delivers tomatoes with smooth, unnicked flesh. (This same approach, by the way, works well with peaches.)

Cut the core from the center of the tomato. Turn it over and score the bottom with a shallow X Drop the tomato into boiling water, letting it simmer for about 10 seconds. With a slotted spoon, scoop up the tomato and plunge

it into iced water. After cooling 30 seconds, the skin will slip right off.

#27
CUBING TOMATOES

Recipes frequently ask for tomatoes that are "peeled, seeded, and chopped." Peeling is easy (see Truc #26). But seeded and chopped is a little more daunting. If we cut the tomato in half and squeeze it to get the seeds out, we've effectively crushed it and cut it into a shape that's difficult to chop. If we section it and chop it first, we end up with several dozen nicely chopped pieces—all containing seeds. Paula Wolfert has come up with a new approach that solves these problems and delivers neat square shapes from round tomatoes. Paula calls this "cubing."

To cube a peeled tomato, begin by cutting across the tomato, about 1 inch down from the top, until the blade reaches the far side. Turning the knife blade, continue the cut down the side of the tomato. This creates a long strip of tomato; set that strip aside. Continue cutting around and down the tomato removing the flesh in a series of petals, using the natural contour of the tomato as a guide while cutting down its sides. With the tip of a finger, flick out any seeds that

are attached to the petals and any remaining in the central core. The tomato is now peeled and seeded, ready to chop into neat squares, large or small as the recipe requires.

#28
A QUICK WAY TO CRUSH TOMATOES

Professional chefs use their hands in a variety of clever ways that don't normally occur to amateurs. Pino Luongo shares his truc for a "handy" tomato crusher.

Open a can of whole tomatoes, drain if desired, and pour the tomatoes into a large bowl. With one hand squeeze and crush them into either a rough or smooth consistency as required by the recipe.

#29
ROASTING TOMATOES

Modern tomatoes need all the help they can get. Rick Bayless reports that roasting is a kind of culinary shock treatment that makes ordinary tomatoes good, and good tomatoes extraordinary. "High heat so concentrates and enhances the flavor," says Rick, "that the tomatoes acquire an entirely new taste dimension, perfect for soups and sauces." Roasting tomatoes couldn't be easier:

Place a single layer of tomatoes on a foil-lined baking sheet, making sure the tomatoes don't touch. Place under a preheated broiler, several inches below the element, and roast for 10 to 15 minutes, turning them once. When the tomatoes blister and blacken on all sides, remove them from the oven. When cool enough to handle, slip off the peels.

#30
SAVING LEFTOVER TOMATO PASTE

Many recipes calls for tomato paste. More accurately, many recipes call for 1 tablespoon of tomato paste. What, then, does one do with the rest of the can? The late Leslee Reis shared with us her resourceful truc for saving tomato paste.

Measure leftover tomato paste by the tablespoon into individual compartments of an ice cube tray. Freeze, then pop the frozen spoonfuls of tomato paste into a zipper-seal bag and hold in the freezer for future use.

FRUITS

#31
"EFFICIENT" JUICING

Getting more for less is the height of efficiency. Stephan Pyles squeezes out a particularly efficient truc that helps him get the most juice out of a citrus fruit with the least amount of effort.

Pressing down on the fruit, roll it several times back and forth over a hard surface before cutting it in half. Squeezing the juice out will be effortless.

#32
PEELING AND SEGMENTING CITRUS FRUITS

Individual peeled segments of lemon, lime, orange, or grapefruit are a wonderful garnish. Patrick Clark has a truc for preparing whole, membrane- and pith-free segments.

The secret is in the approach: first cut off both ends of the fruit with a sharp paring knife and set the fruit flat on a work surface. Work the knife down along the natural rounded shape of the fruit, cutting off both the bitter pith and peel. Then hold the peeled fruit and slice down between the membranes to free each segment.

#33
BROAD-STROKE ZESTING

Many recipes call for the grated zest of citrus, the colored part of the peel that contains the fragrant oil. Most often a hand grater is used, a choice that yields tiny gratings. But Robert Del Grande goes about it differently. He removes the zest in large pieces, expanding the options for how it can be shaped and used—minced, chopped, or julienned.

Use a vegetable peeler to scrape a ribbon of peel off the fruit. Remove only the colored peel,

Minced

Julienned

leaving the bitter white pith attached to the fruit. Finish the peel by mincing, chopping, or julienning as desired.

#34
GRATING CITRUS PEEL A BETTER WAY

Removing the tiny bits of grated peel from a grater can be the toughest part of adding citrus zest, or peel, to a recipe. Giuliano Bugialli has a special truc for removing these stubborn bits from the grater with a paper-thin layer of . . . paper!

Cover the side of a grater with a piece of parchment paper. Rub the citrus fruit back and forth, turning the fruit as the peel is scraped off. Lift the parchment paper off the grater. The grated peel remains on the paper and can be easily scraped into a bowl. The bitter white pith is left behind on the grater and can be simply washed away.

#35
DRY-POACHING PEARS IN SALT

Pears are well suited to poaching in either sugar, syrup, or wine. But there's one drawback—the poaching liquid dilutes somewhat the delicate taste of the pear. So Jimmy Schmidt dry-poaches his pears with a truc that sears in the pear's juices, trapping them beneath the peel. The key to successful dry-poaching is baking the salt until it is extremely hot, otherwise a salty taste will permeate through the peel. Cooked properly, the fruit will have no taste of salt and will be delicious served with a wine sauce or ice cream—or both.

Preheat a deep baking pan filled with kosher salt to 450° for 60 minutes. Insert a wooden skewer into the top of the fruit. Bury the fruit in the hot salt, leaving only a portion of the wooden skewer exposed. Bake for 15 minutes or until the fruit softens. Remove the fruit and brush off any clinging salt. Cool before serving.

#36
PORCUPINE-CUT MANGO

Craig Claiborne visited Bali and came home with a neat truc that seems to be the right way to cut and serve a mango. In Bali, this presentation is dressed with a lime wedge.

Hold the mango on end and slice the fruit in half, cutting down alongside the flat side of the broad seed. Take a mango half and score the flesh diagonally, making diagonal cuts every ¾ inch. Be careful not to cut through the rind. Give the fruit a quarter turn and continue scoring the flesh, cutting it into a diamond-

shaped pattern. Pick up the fruit and, using thumbs, push the skin up, pressing the fruit outward, as if turning a tennis ball inside out. The flesh opens to reveal little porcupine-like spikes of mango, which can easily be lifted from the peel with the edge of a spoon.

#37
SEEDING A POMEGRANATE NEATLY

Paula Wolfert makes great use of pomegranates. She sprinkles the seeds on salads, adds them to stuffings, and squeezes them and uses the juice for tenderizing marinades. This versatile fruit has only one drawback—the seeds stain like crazy. The trick is knowing how to open a pomegranate and remove the seeds so they don't stain everything in sight. Here's how Paula liberates those seeds—her "stainless steal" truc.

Make a slit in the center of the fruit, large enough to insert both your thumbs. Submerge the fruit in a bowl of water. Insert your thumbs in the slit and pull the fruit apart into two pieces. Loosen the seeds with your fingers; they will float to the surface, rinsed and ready to be scooped out and used.

#38
TELLING A BOILED EGG FROM A RAW ONE

Raw eggs and hard-boiled eggs are radically different on the inside, but from the outside they look alike. How does one, from the outside, manage to tell what's going on inside? Chef Hubert Keller's truc reveals the egg's status with a simple twist of the wrist.

To determine whether an egg is raw or hard-boiled, give it a spin. A hard-boiled egg will spin easily; a raw egg won't spin at all.

Cooked

Raw

#39
COOKING THE "PERFECT" HARD-BOILED EGG

Many people have a litany of troubles concerning their hard-boiled eggs: the eggs crack while cooking, they're undercooked, they have a sinister gray rim around the yolk, or they stick to the shell and won't peel. André Soltner imparts a three-step truc that solves all the problems.

Start with eggs that are at least one day old and are at room temperature. In a pot large enough to hold the eggs in a single layer, bring cold water to a boil. When the water is boiling, not

before, place the eggs in the pot. Boil 8 minutes for small eggs; 10 minutes for large ones. Remove eggs from heat and cool immediately in several changes of cold water.

Boil 8 to 10 Minutes.

#40
HARD-BOILED EGG GARNISH

The hard-cooked egg is a universal plate decoration, usually presented in familiar slices or wedges. Daniel Boulud has a truc that elevates the ordinary hard-boiled egg into a delicate, elegant garnish, classically known as mimosa.

Separate the white from the yolk. Rub the egg white through one side of a fine-mesh sieve, set aside. Then rub the yolk through other side of the sieve. Sprinkle the white and yolk in alternating circles to create an attractive garnish.

#41

OPENING QUAIL EGGS

Quail eggs are turning up on lots of menus, usually presented poached or fried where their diminutive size is shown to best advantage. The problem is that quail eggs are really tiny (about the size of a thumbnail) and fragile—and are, therefore, tricky to open. How do those in the know manage to crack and open the shell without smashing the egg inside? Jean-Louis Palladin reveals the best, and probably the only, way to open a quail egg.

Notice that a quail egg has both a pointed end and flat end. Working at the flat end, take a small paring knife and gently press the tip of the blade into the shell, cracking the shell while turning the egg. Make a continuous circle around the egg, lift off the top, and carefully pour out the egg.

KEY TO A PERFECT OMELET

#42

"In France, when a young chef shows up at a restaurant looking for work, they ask him to make an omelet," remembers André Soltner. "And properly so. There's so much technique involved that if a chef makes a perfect omelet—you know, you just know, that chef's been well trained." Is there a truc? Definitely. "If your pan isn't clean, you'll never have a good omelet because your eggs will stick," says André. Here's his truc for getting the pan spotlessly clean.

Pour some kosher salt into the skillet and rub vigorously with a kitchen towel over the side and bottom of the pan. The abrasiveness of the salt will put a fine polish on the skillet. Discard the salt and proceed with the recipe.

GRAINS

#43
QUICK BRICK OVEN TRICK

The disappointing results which most home bakers face when they try to create hearty thick-crusted peasant bread or thin-crisp pizza crust has very little to do with ingredients and proportions; it has a lot to do with having the wrong kind of oven. A brick oven contributes uniquely and unmistakably to the texture and taste of these breads. Giuliano Bugialli has a quick brick trick for obtaining these results from any oven.

Place a single layer of large unglazed terra cotta tiles (available from a brickyard, masonry supply, or tile store) on an oven rack. Preheat the oven. Then place the bread or pizza directly on the tiles and bake.

#44
MAKING LUMP-FREE POLENTA

"I've been eating polenta ever since I was a kid—and cooking it since I was big enough to reach the pot," says Lidia Bastianich. *"About the only way it should not be served is with lumps." She accomplishes lump-free polenta with this truc she learned from her grandmother.*

Cold Water

The secret of lump-free polenta is starting with cold water. Mix the cornmeal thoroughly with the cold water, then season with salt and a bay leaf, and cook. Many recipes specify warm or hot water, but lump-free polenta starts with cold water.

#45
MAKING PERFECT RICE EVERY TIME

"The secret to turning out perfectly cooked rice," according to Patrick Clark, "lies in completely ignoring the directions on the back of the box." Patrick's truc for preparing perfectly cooked rice couldn't be easier.

Rice   Oil   Water

In a saucepan over medium heat, sauté the rice in a little oil until the kernels are well coated.

Add an amount of water equal to the amount of rice (1 cup to 1 cup, for example). Bring the water to a boil, stir, and then reduce the heat to a simmer. Cover and cook the rice for 10 minutes. Remove the pan from the heat and, with the lid still on, let it sit for 15 minutes. Fluff the rice with a fork.

#46

SALVAGING BURNED RICE

That ancient Chinese New Year's greeting, "May your rice never burn," tells us that this is not a new problem. The late Felipe Rojas-Lombardi had a new truc for solving this old problem, a way of actually salvaging scorched rice with ... onion skins.

To remove the smoky, unpleasant taste from scorched rice, scoop the rice into a clean pot, being careful *not* to scrape in any of the crusty bottom at the same time. Place a single layer of onion skins on top of the rice. Cover the pot and let it sit for 10 to 15 minutes. The onion skins will remove the acrid taste from the rice. Discard the onion skins and serve.

#47
MEASURING RICE FOR RISOTTO

To make risotto, that creamy, rich Italian specialty made with short-grain Arborio rice, an unspecified quantity of liquid is added to an unspecified quantity of rice and cooked for an unspecified period of time—"until the rice is soft and will absorb no more liquid." So how much rice to start with? Pino Luongo's truc offers a good rule of thumb for figuring this out.

For risotto, use one handful of raw Arborio rice for each person being served.

#48
ARTICHOKE-FLAVORED RICE

Rice is often served as an edible sponge for gravy or sauce. With some plain, unsauced entrées, plain boiled rice would be the perfect accompaniment—if only it had some flavor. The late Felipe Rojas-Lombardi unveiled a secret that gives boiled rice a haunting, elusive, intriguing flavor—and makes it good enough to stand unclothed.

Cut a whole raw artichoke into quarters. Place one or more quarters of the artichoke in the pot along with the rice and water and cook as usual. Remove the artichoke before serving.

#49
SOFTENING TORTILLAS IN A MICROWAVE OVEN

Rolling up ingredients inside a corn tortilla is fundamental in Mexican cooking. Such popular dishes as enchiladas, taquitos, and flautas capitalize on the appeal of this edible envelope. But rolling commercially made tortillas is not easy because they tend to be dry and brittle and, therefore, tend to crack and split as they're rolled. Zarela Martinez developed a speedy truc for making corn tortillas soft, pliable, and easy to roll.

Place several tortillas into a plastic bag and loosely close the bag. Microwave on high for 30 seconds. The tortillas will emerge soft and pliable enough to roll easily, without breaking.

HERBS AND SPICES

#50

PRESERVING FRESH HERBS

When herbs are fresh and abundant, Lidia Bastianich preserves her favorites in an elegantly simple manner—she freezes them. Then for the rest of year, Lidia has a plentiful supply of fragrant herbs.

To preserve fresh herbs, pick the unbruised leaves from their stems and splash them with cold water. Pack several tablespoonfuls into small paper cups, fill the cup with water, and freeze. To use, defrost under running water and proceed as with fresh herbs.

#51
KEEPING FRESH CILANTRO FRESH

Fresh cilantro is an essential ingredient in much Mexican and Asian cooking. Since there's no substitute for it, it's the kind of ingredient that's good to have on hand. But keeping cilantro fresh for more than a day is a real challenge. The leaves begin to bruise and turn black very quickly. Andy D'Amico has discovered a truc for keeping cilantro fresh, green, and usable for several days.

Pick the leaves off the stem and place them in a single layer on a moist paper towel. Roll up the towel, and wrap it tightly in plastic wrap or seal it in a zipper-seal plastic bag, squeezing out the excess air. Refrigerate; the cilantro will stay green and fresh for several days.

#52
REFRESHING WHOLE SPICES

Peppercorns, juniper berries, and other whole spices lose some of their pungency after being packaged for a long time. Andrew D'Amico has a truc for refreshing tired spices and restoring their punch.

Roast dried whole spices in a preheated 350° oven for a few minutes. When the spices become aromatic, remove them from the oven and grind or use whole as the recipe requires.

#53

PRESERVING FRESH BASIL IN OIL

"Oh, I love the smell of sweet basil!" enthuses Michel Richard. To use that flavor all year long, Michel has a wonderful truc for keeping the basil fragrant and fresh. But wait, there's more. This truc yields a bonus—basil-flavored oil that's perfect to use in risottos, pastas, vinaigrettes, and bruschetta.

Pick off the unbruised basil leaves from the stem. Pack the leaves in a jar and then cover completely with olive oil. Close the lid tightly and refrigerate.

#54
USING FRESH HERB STEMS

The late Felipe Rojas-Lombardi used fresh herbs extensively in his cooking. He used the leaves, of course, for finishing dishes and for garnish—but he also used the stems. He reminded us that "the flavor of the herb is in the stem as well as the leaves," and then disclosed an economical truc for using the stems.

Use the stems of fresh herbs in preparing soups, stocks, and long-simmered sauces. The stems will deliver flavor just like the leaves, and because they have less chlorophyll, they will not tint the product green.

#55
CUTTING FRESH HERBS

Most of us have trouble turning out precise, fine cuts of the larger herb leaves, such as basil and sorrel; we usually end up with a pile of hacked, bruised leaves of wildly different shapes and sizes. There is a better way. Larry Forgione lets us in on the secret.

Remove fresh herb leaves from the stems and stack them. Roll the leaves lengthwise tightly. With a small knife, cut across the rolled bundle of leaves in thin strips. This creates long, thin julienned slices of herb. For finely minced herbs, turn the julienned slices (still rolled) 45° and cut crosswise into very thin strips.

Unroll For
Julienne

Cut Crosswise
To Mince

#56
HEALTHY HERBS

Chef David Bouley has discovered yet another benefit of vitamin C—it keeps fresh herbal oils from turning brown. Here's his prescription.

For each 6 ounces of oil, use one 500-milligram tablet of vitamin C. Crush the vitamin tablet and combine it with the oil in a blender; blend until dissolved. Add fresh green herb leaves and blend until they are completely puréed. Refrigerated, this oil will keep its green color indefinitely.

SAUCES, BROTHS, AND DRESSINGS

#57
INTENSE FISH STOCK

Fish stock is the foundation on which memorable fish chowders, soups, stews, and countless other fish dishes are built. The most important requirement of fish stock is that it be intensely fishy. Most cooks know that cooking down a meat stock intensifies its flavor; the same technique does not work for fish stock. Jasper White shares the surprisingly obvious truc behind intense fish stock.

Intense fish stock depends on fish, not cooking time. Fish stock cooked more than 20 minutes will begin to turn bitter. The only way to intensify fish stock is to start with a larger quantity of fish parts.

Only 20 Minutes!

#58
MAKING A LIGHTER VINAIGRETTE

Sometimes traditional vinaigrette formulations seem too heavy in weight and overpowering in taste for dressing tender, delicate salad green suchs as Boston lettuce or mâche. Jean-Georges Vongerichten divulges a truc that'll lighten even the heaviest vinaigrette.

When making vinaigrette, either by hand or in a food processor, add a couple of teaspoons of boiling water after the dressing emulsifies.

Boiling Water

#59
MAKING PERFECT WINE SAUCE

A *well-made wine sauce is smooth tasting, redolent with the flavor of the wine, but bearing no harsh acidic edge. There's a truc to pulling that off. The trick is in preparing the wine before it's incorporated into the sauce. Georges Perrier, renowned for his classic technique, shares the secret.*

Bring the wine to a boil, then ignite it with a match. The flame will burn off the wine's alcohol and acidity at the same time. Then bring back the wine's sweetness by adding just a touch of sugar. This mixture is now ready to incorporate into the sauce.

#60
HOW NOT TO SPOIL THE BROTH

Contrary to popular wisdom, it's not too many cooks that spoil the broth, it's bacteria. During the cooling-down period—after the stock is cooked and before it's refrigerated—bacteria can begin to form, multiply, and sour the stock. Marcel Desaulniers shares his truc for quickly getting stock cooled down and ready for the refrigerator.

To cool a soup or stock as quickly as possible, place the pot into an ice bath, one that reaches midway up the stock's container. Stir the stock often, and it will cool quickly. Once the stock is cool to the touch, refrigerate immediately.

#61
REPAIRING A TOO-SALTY SAUCE

Adding salt to a sauce is easy. Removing salt from a sauce is a little tricky. Fortunately, Antoine Bouterin has a little truc.

Dip a sugar cube into the too-salty sauce and pass it back and forth in a zigzag motion across the surface of the sauce. Repeat three or four times. Taste and repeat if necessary.

#62
FIXING "BROKEN" MAYONNAISE

Homemade mayonnaise, that delightful blend of egg yolks, oil, and seasonings, is a special pleasure, better by far than store-bought. But homemade mayo has an undeserved reputation for being "difficult." Many a cook's had a nice batch of mayonnaise suddenly "break" and lose its texture, turning thin and soupy. André Soltner has a wonderfully simple truc for rebinding broken mayonnaise, whatever the cause.

When mayonnaise breaks, take a clean bowl and add a couple of spoons of warm (not boiling) water. Very slowly pour the broken mayonnaise into the second bowl, whisking to incorporate the water. The mayonnaise will re-emulsify, thicken up ... and be "fixed."

Broken Mayonnaise

Warm Water

Fixed Mayonnaise

MEATS AND POULTRY

#63

MAKING THE PERFECT HAMBURGER

Grilling a hamburger patty presents a culinary challenge: how to cook it fast enough and hot enough so it'll be seared and browned on the outside, yet remain rare and juicy on the inside. Anne Rosenzweig engineered the solution: pack something cold and flavorable in the middle of the patty. This is the truc behind (inside?) her famous burger.

Before grilling, tuck a tablespoon-size nugget of frozen herb butter (parsley and shallots is a good combination) into the center of a freshly ground hamburger patty. This nugget keeps the hamburger rare in the center, while giving it an extra burst of flavor.

#64
UNNATURAL SAUSAGE CASING

The toughest part to making homemade link sausages is locating a source for the natural casings. In many parts of the country they're almost impossible to find. But Michel Richard has discovered an easy substitute for natural casing, universally available in every supermarket in the land.

Prepare the filling for your favorite sausage. Lay a piece of plastic wrap flat on a counter and place the sausage filling along the near edge. Fold the plastic wrap over the filling and press the wrap tightly against it, making it as tight as possible. Roll the sausage into a log shape, keeping the roll tight. Twist the endstogether and tie them off with a knot. Simmer this sausage in broth or water until it is cooked.

Once cooked, rewrap the sausages and refrigerate. To brown the sausages, remove wrapping and sauté before serving.

#65
SELF-BASTING BIRDS

Everyone knows that frequent basting helps ensure a beautifully browned, succulent roasted chicken. Michael Roberts has a truc for achieving that same result without the need for frequent basting. A real time-saver, Michael's truc also works with capons, turkeys, and other birds, either stuffed or unstuffed.

Season and prepare the chicken for roasting. Before placing the bird in the oven, lay a piece of cheesecloth saturated with olive oil or melted chicken fat over the bird so that the bird's completely covered. Roast as usual. Then, once cooked, remove the cheesecloth to reveal a golden brown, moist bird.

Olive Oil Or Chicken Fat

Cheesecloth

#66
TENDERIZING MEAT WITH WINE CORKS

Long-cooked, slow-simmered stews may be the ultimate comfort food. The only problem is that, by definition, the cooking process is long and slow. The late Felipe Rojas-Lombardi uncorked a truc that delivers that long-cooked, slow-simmered taste faster.

When making a stew, add at least three wine corks to the pot. These corks release enzymes that help tenderize the meat quickly and reduce the cooking time by as much as half. Remember to remove the corks before serving.

#67
SEVEN-MINUTE "ROASTED" CHICKEN

Preparing oven-roasted chicken with its characteristic crispy skin and moist, juicy flesh takes well over an hour. But Anne Rosenzweig has developed an ingenious truc for putting this culinary staple on the table in about 7 minutes!

Bone a 3½-pound chicken, keeping the breast and thigh meat in one piece. (Reserve remainder of chicken for another use.) Season with salt and pepper. Heat 1 tablespoon of oil medium-high in a skillet. When hot, add the chicken, skin side down, and cook until the skin gets very crispy, about 2 minutes. Place the pan in a preheated 400° oven for approximately 5 minutes until the chicken is done.

FISH AND SEAFOOD

#68

A COOL WAY TO OPEN CLAMS

Intimidated about opening clams? Lidia Bastianich has some advice. "Relax. Both you and the clams." It's easy to relax when you know Lidia's truc for getting the clams to relax.

Before opening clams, arrange them in a single layer in a pan and place in the freezer for 15 minutes. The intense cold relaxes the clams' muscles and makes opening them a snap.

#69
KEEPING LOBSTER TAILS UNCURLED

Lobster tails will curl when cooking. And that's fine, unless you have in mind an elaborate presentation requiring flat, uncurled lobster tails. Jean-Louis Palladin frequently has that need, so he devised this truc for "lobster on a stick."

To keep a lobster tail straight when cooking, insert a bamboo skewer through the back of the lobster tail and out the front. Remove the skewer when the lobster is cooked and the tail will stay straight.

#70
CRACKING A LOBSTER CLAW

A whole lobster claw, neatly extracted from its shell in one perfect piece, is the height of elegant presentation. But shelling the claw in one neat piece requires one neat truc. And Hubert Keller's got one.

Break off the lobster claw from the body. Twist the small pincher and pull it off the claw. Using the heel of a chef's knife, crack the claw across its broad middle area. Twist the knife back and forth until the shell cracks and begins to break. Open the shell, and the claw meat will pull out easily in one piece.

#71
KEEPING A LOBSTER ALIVE FOR A WEEK

Lobsters are sold live, and they should stay that way until cooked. Keeping them alive at home, though, requires a truc. "It's easy if you've got a lobster tank," says Chef André Soltner. "But if you don't, just give the lobster a newspaper and keep it cool. It'll stay alive for at least a week."

Soak several pieces of newspaper in a pan filled with cool water. Place the paper on a flat work surface and set the lobster on top. Roll the

lobster up in the paper, enclosing it completely, and refrigerate. It will keep at least a week.

#72
CLEANING SOFT-SHELL CRABS

When soft-shell crabs are served in a restaurant, they're completely edible. But that's because the kitchen staff removed the three inedible parts—eyes, lungs, and apron before serving. "It's easy," says Emeril Lagasse. "Three steps, two fingers, and you're done."

First, use thumb and forefinger to pinch off the crab's eyes. Second, lift the pointed ends of the shell and pinch out the lungs—the saclike, spongy organs on either side. And third, turning the crab onto its back, pry up and pull off the flap, or apron. The crab is now fully cleaned, completely edible, and ready to cook.

#73
ROUNDING OUT A SALMON CARPACCIO

Want a show-stopping presentation for smoked salmon? Present a perfectly round circle of salmon, perfectly centered on an elegant serving plate. How? Yannick Cam reveals the truc.

Place thinly sliced smoked salmon in the center of a serving plate. Place a piece of plastic wrap over the plate and brush it lightly with oil. Use the back of a spoon to press against the wrapped salmon, stretching the fish toward the rim of the plate. Place a second serving plate, identical to the first, on top of the fish, serving side up. Press down firmly and give the plate a twist. Remove the top plate, the plastic wrap and any scraps of fish from the edge of the plate. Garnish and serve.

#74
FORMING THE PERFECT CARPACCIO OF TUNA

Diners at Charles Palmer's restaurant marvel at the wide, thin, flat carpaccio of yellowfin tuna that emerges from his kitchen. How does he get the tuna that wide, that flat, that thin? "The truc involves ounces and pounds," says Charlie. "Three ounces of tuna, and many, many pounds."

Put a piece of plastic wrap on a work surface and brush it lightly with olive oil. Place a 3-ounce piece of raw tuna on the plastic wrap, loosely folding the wrap over the fish. Using the flat side of a cleaver, slap the wrapped fish firmly, stretching the fish as it's pounded. After two or three pounds, turn the fish and pound again. Repeat this process until the tuna is completely flattened and very thin. Remove the plastic wrap and turn the *carpaccio* onto a plate. Serve chilled.

#75
BONING FISH

Chef Jacky Pluton has an inspired truc for removing those pesky bones from raw fish fillets. It just takes a flick of the wrist and, of all things ... a vegetable peeler!

Run the peeler over the fillet, catching the bones in the center slit of the peeler. Twist the peeler slightly in the opposite direction and pull the bones right out.

#76

COOKING FISH IN PAPER

Cooking fish in a paper wrapper is a classic New Orleans technique that's ideal for such delicate fish as pompano, sole, and catfish. The concept is simple: fish, spices, and vegetables are sealed in a paper package and baked in a hot oven. The fish and vegetable juices, trapped within the package, provide flavorful steam that gently cooks the fish. The trick, of course, is in the bag—creating a package that holds in the steam. Emeril Lagasse shares a native truc for sealing the paper so that the fish steams and cooks perfectly.

Cut a circle from a heavy piece of cooking paper such as parchment or, preferably, butcher's wrap. (If neither is available, use aluminum foil.) Brush with melted butter or olive oil. Place the ingredients on one half of the circle, folding the other half over to cover. Seal the edges together with a series of small overlapping folds, working all the way around the paper. Twist the last fold several times, ensuring that the paper package, or *papillote*, is sealed

tightly. Turn the *papillote* over and set it on a baking sheet. The fish is now ready to bake in its perfectly sealed package.

#77
FILLETING FRESH SALMON

Chef Hubert Keller fillets a lot of salmon. He's developed a lightning-quick method that, according to conventional wisdom, is completely backward—he starts at the head of the fish. "It's faster and easier," says Hubert. Vive la différence!

Start at the head end of the fish, not the tail. Cut around the gills until the knife hits the backbone. Then, holding the knife flat against

the backbone, cut toward the tail using the backbone as a guide. With just one stroke, the entire side of salmon is filleted.

#78
SMOKING SEAFOOD IN A SKILLET

Cold-smoking is an exotic technique for subtly flavoring food before cooking. It's an approach that works especially well with shrimp, scallops, and other mild seafood. The usual method is to fire up the grill and then make yourself crazy trying to regulate the heat so that it's hot enough to create smoke but not hot enough to cook the food. Jean-Michel Diot has a low-tech, stove-top truc that's a lot less trouble.

Place dried thyme sprigs in the bottom of a cold skillet. Top with fresh green thyme sprigs, then light the dried sprigs with a match. Place the seafood on a heavy china or Pyrex plate and set it on top of the burning herbs. Cover the skillet and let the seafood smoke for 30 minutes. Proceed to cook as usual.

BAKING AND DESSERTS

#79
ROLLING COLD DOUGH

"Most pastry recipes require that the dough be chilled thoroughly before rolling and baking. But rolling a cold dough is not easy," says Jacques Pépin. He reveals a truc for making chilled dough so pliable that it can be rolled right after it's taken out of the refrigerator.

Place the dough on the counter. With a rolling pin, pound the surface of the dough several times, making ridges. Place the rolling pin in the ridges and press down, spreading the dough slightly. Then turn the dough 90° and repeat the process until the dough is pliable and easy to roll.

#80
BAKING PIE SHELLS UPSIDE DOWN

It's one thing to put a perfectly shaped pie shell into the oven to bake; it's another to have it retain that perfect shape while baking. High heat causes the dough to contract and shrink as it bakes, and gravity causes it to slide down inside the pan. Jim Dodge put gravity on his side, and developed this upside-down truc for baking a perfectly shaped pie shell.

Start with two identical metal pie plates. Line one with pie dough that's been rolled into a sheet. Chill until the dough becomes firm to the touch. Set a second pie plate inside the dough-lined plate. Invert the plates onto a baking sheet, then bake. When the edge of the pie shell has turned a golden brown, the shell is baked. Take the baking sheet from the oven and turn the pie plates right side up, removing the inside plate.

Bake Until Edge
Is Golden Brown

#81 _1/29/96_

REMOVING STUCK PARCHMENT PAPER FROM CAKES

As cakes cool after baking, they sometimes stick to their paper pan liners. Trying to remove the paper usually results in a tug-of-war that causes the cake to crumble. When Jacques Torres encounters that kind of resistance, he brushes it aside with this clever truc.

When parchment paper sticks to the bottom of a cake, brush the paper with a little warm water. After 10 to 20 seconds, the paper can easily be peeled right off the cake.

#82
CUTTING PAN LINERS

Perla Meyers has been teaching baking classes in New York City for years. Her truc for cutting paper linings for cake pans, origami-style, has saved many of her students' cakes from sticking to the bottom of the pans.

Take a piece of parchment paper large enough to cover the bottom of a cake pan. Fold the paper in half lengthwise, then crosswise. Fold diagonally to create a triangle. Fold the triangle in half lengthwise, forming a cone shape. Continue folding the cone shape lengthwise until it becomes quite narrow. Turn the cake pan over and place the tip of the paper cone at the center of the pan. With scissors, snip the paper where it meets the edge of the pan.

Unfold the paper cone to reveal a circle that will perfectly fit the bottom of the cake pan.

#83
ULTIMATE DISPOSABLE PASTRY BAG

Even a passionate baker like Rose Levy Beranbaum doesn't like to wash pastry bags. So she set about to concoct a whole new disposable pastry bag system that makes cleanup unnecessary. Here's how:

Take a heavy-duty zipper-seal plastic bag and snip off one corner, making a slightly curved cut. Using a standard two-piece plastic coupler (available wherever cake decorating supplies are sold), insert the larger piece into the hole.

Choose a tip and secure it with the coupler's ring. Fill the bag and zip the top closed. Decorate away, then remove the coupler/tip assembly and toss the bag. No messy cleanup!

#84
SWIRLING TWO COLORS FROM ONE PASTRY BAG

Swirling two different colors and flavors of mousse together makes for a dramatic visual and gustatory effect. Jacques Torres has a simple truc that employs two pastry bags to achieve one magical look.

To swirl two mousses together decoratively, scoop each mousse into its own pastry bag. Then slide both pastry bags, side by side, into one larger bag. Gather the larger pastry bag around the two smaller ones and squeeze. As the mousse emerges from the bag, it will appear swirled.

#85

BAKING REAL "CUP" CAKES

One of Mary Sue Milliken's most popular desserts is a "gourmet" version of an American snack favorite: the Hostess cupcake. In developing the recipe, Mary Sue sought to duplicate the rich, moist texture of the commercial version. The solution was in her cupboard. She discovered that to bake a rich, moist "cup" cake takes more than a good recipe—it also takes the right cup.

Butter and flour heavy, ovenproof porcelain coffee cups. Spoon cake batter into the cups, filling each two-thirds full. Bake in a preheated

325° oven for 20 to 25 minutes. Once baked, let the cakes cool slightly; then invert and pop them out of their cups.

#86

CRISPLY GLAZING CRÈME BRÛLÉE AT HOME

In restaurants, crème brûlée arrives at the table covered with a crisp, thin layer of caramelized sugar. But homemade versions of this classic usually lack this distinctive feature, having been made without the high-heat broilers found in restaurant kitchens. Hubert Keller has solved the problem; he has a truc for creating a restaurant-style crème brûlée crust at home.

First, go to a hardware store and buy a propane torch. Then, sprinkle a thin dusting of granulated sugar over the top of the crème brûlée. Apply the lighted torch, keeping it several inches above the dish, moving the flame quickly back and forth. The sugar will melt, forming a thin, crisp crust.

#87
INSTANT CHOCOLATE DECORATOR

In The Cake Bible, Rose Levy Beranbaum shares her secrets for making and decorating perfect cakes. None is more ingenious than what she calls her "instant chocolate decorator," an easily wrought pastry bag filled with piping chocolate.

Put 1 cup of mini chocolate chips into a heavy duty zipper-seal plastic bag. Set the bag into a bowl of hot water for about 5 minutes, or until the chips melt. Pat the zipper-seal bag dry with a towel. Press the melted chocolate into one corner and zip the top closed. With scissors, clip off a small corner from the bottom of the bag. (Start small—you can always enlarge it.) Pipe away.

#88
MAKING CHOCOLATE RIBBONS

New York's Le Cirque is known for its impeccable service, its stellar food, and the stunning desserts created by its pastry chef, Jacques Torres. Jacques's chocolate cake is topped with a deliciously delicate chocolate bow and festooned with chocolate ribbons. Jacques unwraps his truc for making this spectacular decoration.

Cut a strip of cellophane (not plastic wrap) about 1½ inches wide. Place the cellophane strip on a cool table and brush it with melted chocolate, covering it. To make the bow, cut the strip into smaller lengths, 5 to 7 inches long. Working quickly, lift these strips and bring the two ends together to form a loop. When the

chocolate hardens (this happens very quickly), peel off the cellophane and arrange several of these loops together on top of the cake to form a bow. Use the same technique to create the ribbons, forming them into flat or rippled shapes as desired.

#89

A BETTER WAY TO HUSK HAZELNUTS

Even a famous pastry chef like Jim Dodge had about as much trouble as the rest of us in getting the skins off hazelnuts. Until, that is, he discovered the benefits of steam heat and developed this truc for removing those stubborn skins without endless rubbing.

Place hazelnuts in a single layer on a cookie sheet and mist them with water. Bake in a preheated oven at 400° for 5 minutes. This small amount of water creates enough steam to loosen the skins so they slip right off the nuts.

#90
STRING-CUTTING CHEESECAKE

Rose Levy Beranbaum's mother is a dentist, which may explain why Rose uses dental floss instead of a knife to cut cheesecake. But it may just be that she uses dental floss because it does a superior job—quicker, neater, and better than a knife.

Cut a piece of dental floss several inches longer than the diameter of the cheesecake. Holding it taut, set the floss on the top surface of the cake. Press the floss right down through the cake until it reaches the bottom. Let go one end of the floss and pull it out through the other side of the cheesecake. Repeat this process to cut the desired number of slices.

#91

KEEPING IT IN THE BAG

"Nothing is more frustrating than loading up a pastry bag only to have the filling leak out through the tip," says Jim Dodge. Jim's discovered a truc that keeps the filling in the bag "and out of your shoes."

Twist the pastry bag just above the tip, making a knot. Press this knot into the tip and then fill the pastry bag. When the bag is filled, untwist the knot and squeeze the filling into the tip area.

#92
RESTORING CURDLED CRÈME ANGLAISE

With its briefly cooked blend of egg yolks, cream, and sugar, crème anglaise may be the world's most popular dessert sauce. But if it's overcooked (and that's easy to do), the yolks curdle to create very sweet, very creamy scrambled eggs. Patrick Clark has a truc for repairing the curdled crème.

Pour the curdled crème into a blender and give it a 2-second jolt on high. The crème will regain its velvety smooth texture.

#93
FOOD PROCESSOR GRATING

Lots of dessert recipes call for grated lemon zest. This onerous task cannot be done in the food processor because the air currents from the blade causes the lightweight peel to fly around the bowl. Rose Levy Beranbaum found that adding an abrasive ingredient to the workbowl solves the problem. Fortunately, most desserts call for this ingredient anyway.

To grate zest in a food processor, add a small quantity of sugar. The sugar traps the peel and whirls it into the blades, resulting in a fine, powdery amalgamation of peel and sugar—perfect for desserts.

MISCELLANEOUS

#94

SHAVING PARMESAN CHEESE

Judy Rogers adorns many of her soups, salads, and main dishes with wide, luxurious shavings of Parmesan instead of measly little gratings. Her razor? An ordinary vegetable peeler.

Push a swivel-blade vegetable peeler across a large, flat piece of Parmesan cheese, letting the shavings fall directly on the food to be garnished. Vary the pressure, speed, and depth to achieve different-size shavings.

#95
SLICING DELICATE TERRINES

Nothing is more disheartening than watching a perfectly baked terrine crumble into pieces when it's sliced. Gerard Pangaud knows how to keep delicate terrines from breaking under the pressure of a knife. Here's his truc for guaranteeing a perfect slice.

Unmold the terrine and completely wrap it in a piece of aluminum foil. Place the wrapped terrine on a counter, steady it with one hand, and slice through the foil with a very sharp knife. Set the slice on a serving plate and remove the foil.

#96
PAN FRYING WITHOUT HOT OIL SPLASHES

Maneuvering ingredients in a pan of sizzling oil can be a harrowing experience. All too often, the oil splashes on the cook and spills on the stove, inviting a fire. Larry Forgione has a two-step truc to prevent this mayhem when pan frying.

Place food in the skillet starting at the side nearest you, unfolding it away from you toward the back of the pan. That way, if any grease splashes, it will splash away from the cook. When it's time to turn the food, tilt the pan to one side, letting the hot oil slide in that direction. Turn the item over into the *drier* area of the pan. Then lay the pan flat, letting the oil once again cover the bottom, and continue cooking.

#97

THREE-HANDED COOKING USING ONLY TWO

When Patrick Clark needs to pour with one hand, whisk with one hand, and steady a bowl with one hand—he keeps this truc close at hand … just in case no one else is.

Twist a wet kitchen towel into a tight ring and wrap it around the base of the bowl. This will

steady the bowl on the counter, leaving your hands free to pour and whisk simultaneously.

#98

PREVENTING BOIL-OVERS

Watched pots never boil. But unwatched pots do. And in a busy restaurant kitchen, they sometimes boil over. Mary Sue Milliken doesn't worry about pots boiling over, because she knows this whisk truc.

Keep a whisk next to the stove at all times.
When a boil-over is imminent, plunge the whisk into the pot and beat rapidly. The bubbles will recede immediately, allowing enough time to remove the pot from the heat before its contents spill over.

#99
PAINTING WITH SAUCE

When it comes to getting sauce on a plate, most of us reach for a spoon, a ladle, or a sauceboat and simply pour it on. Jean-Jacques Rachou has a different approach. He "paints" the plate with sauces to create a variety of decorative effects. His signature look is a plate painted with intricate designs in sauces of contrasting colors, which serve as edible background for the food. It takes a special "paintbrush" to achieve this look—a dime-store squeeze bottle.

Fill a squeeze bottle with smooth, lump-free sauce and pipe designs directly onto the plate. Endless designs are possible by varying the color of the sauces, the size of the opening in the nozzle, and blending techniques (dragging the tip of a paring knife blade creates fanciful swirls). Experiment!

#100

SQUEEZING OUT THE OIL

"Coat lightly with olive oil" is a direction frequently employed in preparing such contemporary favorites as foccacia or bruschetta, meat, fish, or vegetables headed for the grill, or a bowl of greens needing a light dressing. But the truth is that coating lightly with olive oil is almost impossible using a pastry brush or even fingertips, the usual techniques. Hubert Keller has a better way—he squeezes it on.

Fill a plastic squeeze-trigger bottle with olive oil. Holding the bottle 12 to 18 inches from the ingredients, give a couple of quick squeezes to provide a light, even coating of oil.

#101
QUICK-CHILLING CHAMPAGNE

Champagne, the celebration beverage, is at its best served very cold, around 43°. In the average refrigerator, this takes well over an hour to achieve. But for those celebrations that just won't wait, Eileen Crane shares an ingenious professional truc that does the job in 20 minutes flat. (For more modest celebrations, this truc works equally well with beer and white wines.)

Fill an ice bucket half full of ice cubes. Pour in several cups of cold water and add 4 tablespoons of salt. Plunge the champagne into the ice bucket, adding additional water and ice to almost fill the bucket. Let sit for 20 minutes.

Water

Salt

THE RECIPES

STARTERS

Avocado Dip . . . . *Robert Del Grande*

Potato-Herb Wafers . . . . *David Burke*

Tuna *Carpaccio* with Citrus Vinaigrette . *Charles Palmer*

Thinly Sliced Norwegian Salmon in a Corn Pancake
with Golden Caviar . . . . *Hubert Keller*

Paillard of Salmon with Oyster Tartar . . . . *Jacky Pluton*

Carrot Soup with Dill. . . . . *Mary Sue Milliken*

Shoepeg Corn and Peanut Soup . . . . *Marcel Desaulniers*

Ancho and Navy Bean Soup . . . . *Dean Fearing*

New England Fish Chowder. . . . . *Jasper White*

Bruschetta . . . . *Pino Luongo*

Quail Eggs in Brioche with Caviar
and Smelt Roe. . . . . *Jean-Louis Palladin*

Lobster with Snail Butter . . . . *André Soltner*

DRESSINGS AND SAUCES

Mayonnaise . . . . *André Soltner*

Roasted Tomatillo Salsa with Cilantro,
Mint, and Avocado . . . . *Rick Bayless*

My Father's Vinaigrette . . . . *Alain Sailhac*

Green Herb Oil . . . . *David Bouley*

RICE AND POLENTA

Perfect Rice. . . . . *Patrick Clark*

Artichoke-Flavored Rice . . . . *Felipe Rojas-Lombardi*

Basic Polenta . . . . *Lidia Bastianich*

ENTRÉES

Meat Dishes

The Arcadia Burger . . . . *Anne Rosenzweig*

Salad of Short Ribs and Beets
with Tarragon. . . . . *Daniel Boulud*

Lamb Loin Chops with Mint Pesto
and Artichokes. *Jimmy Schmidt*

Lamb Curry with Fried Onions . . . . *Susan Feniger*

DESSERTS

Poultry Dishes

Seafood Dishes

Vegetarian Dishes

STARTERS

AVOCADO DIP

• ROBERT DEL GRANDE •

2 servings

¼ cup chopped yellow onion

4 cloves garlic, peeled (see Truc #11)

2 jalapeño peppers, stems removed

1½ cups water

2 tablespoons white wine vinegar

2 poblano chilies, peeled and seeded (see Truc #19)

⅓ cup toasted, shelled pumpkin seeds

2 avocados, peeled and pitted (see Trucs #2 and #3)

½ cup roughly chopped fresh cilantro (or to taste)

1 teaspoon salt (or to taste)

1 teaspoon coarsely ground black pepper

1. In a small saucepan, combine onion, garlic, and jalapeño peppers with the water and vinegar. Bring the liquid to a boil and simmer for 15 minutes. Allow to cool.

2. Transfer the cooked ingredients and the liquid to a blender. Add the poblano chilies, pumpkin seeds, avocados, and cilantro, and purée for approximately 15 seconds. Do not overblend. Add the salt and pepper.

3. Let cool and serve with *crudités* and chips as a festive hors d'oeuvres.

POTATO-HERB WAFERS

• DAVID BURKE •

35 to 40 wafers

Two 2-inch copper pipes, the length of a cookie sheet (see Truc #25)

8 tablespoons (1 stick) unsalted butter

Two 6- to 7-ounce large baking potatoes, peeled

2 tablespoons finely chopped fresh herbs such as tarragon, cilantro, chives, sage, or basil (see Truc #55)

Coarse salt

1. Secure the copper pipes on a cookie sheet using crumpled aluminum foil to cradle the ends.

2. Melt the butter over low heat in a small saucepan. Remove from the heat and let sit until milky solids settle to bottom of the pan. Pour off the clarified butter and reserve.

3. Preheat oven to 325°.

4. Slice the potatoes on a mandolin so thinly that each slice is translucent. Soak the slices in the clarified butter.

5. Lay a potato slice over a pipe and sprinkle with approximately ½ teaspoon of chopped herbs. Then press another potato slice firmly against it, sealing the potato slices together and sandwiching the herb mixture in between.

6. Bake for 10 to 15 minutes, just until the potatoes are lightly brown and crisp. Season with salt and serve as a garnish or hors d'oeuvres.

TUNA CARPACCIO WITH CITRUS VINAIGRETTE

• CHARLES PALMER •

6 servings

Citrus Vinaigrette

½ cup extra-virgin olive oil
2 tablespoons freshly squeezed lemon juice (see Truc #31)
1 tablespoon freshly squeezed orange juice (see Truc #31)
1 tablespoon finely grated lemon zest (see Truc #34)
1 tablespoon white wine vinegar
1 tablespoon coarse salt
1 teaspoon freshly cracked white pepper
1 teaspoon chopped fresh chives
1 teaspoon chopped fresh parsley (see Truc #55)

Tuna
Six 3-ounce pieces center-cut yelloufin or bluefin tuna, ¼ to ½ inch thick
Olive oil for pounding
½ cup mixed salad greens

1. Prepare the vinaigrette by combining all the ingredients, except the chives and parsley. Whisk and refrigerate until ready to use. Just before serving, add the chives and parsley.

2. Place the tuna on a sheet of oiled plastic wrap and pound until thin—see *Truc #74*. Place the *carpaccio* on a serving plate with a bouquet of fresh salad greens. Spoon the vinaigrette over the tuna and greens and serve immediately.

THINLY SLICED NORWEGIAN SALMON IN A CORN PANCAKE WITH GOLDEN CAVIAR

• HUBERT KELLER •

6 appetizer servings

3 to 4 ears of corn, husked
3 eggs
2 tablespoons flour
Salt
Freshly ground pepper
1 cup watercress leaves
1½ teaspoons butter
1 tablespoon chopped shallots
1 tablespoon white wine
⅔ cup heavy cream
6 ounces filleted Norwegian salmon
(see Trucs #75 and #77)
12 teaspoons (3 ounces) golden caviar
2 tablespoons vegetable oil
2 tablespoons sour cream
1 tablespoon chopped chives
18 cooked asparagus tips

1. *To make the pancake batter:* Bring 4 quarts of salted water to a boil. Add the corn and cook for 5 minutes, then immediately plunge into a bowl of cold water. Scrape the kernels off the cobs and set aside.

2. In a food processor, combine the corn, eggs, flour, a pinch of salt, and a few grindings of pepper. Process into a chunky purée. Check the seasonings, adding more salt and pepper if necessary. Set aside.

3. *To make the watercress sauce:* Wash the watercress leaves under cool water. Simmer the leaves in boiling salted water for 3 minutes; plunge into cold water to stop the cooking and then squeeze out the moisture with your hands.

4. Melt the butter in a small saucepan over medium heat. Add the shallots and sauté until golden. Stir in the white wine and simmer until the moisture evaporates. Add the cream. Bring to a boil, then lower the heat and simmer for 5 minutes. Add the watercress leaves and cook for 1 minute. Season with salt and pepper. Keep warm.

5. *Prepare the salmon:* Slice the fillet into 6 thin slices. Put them flat on a plate and top each with a teaspoon of caviar. Fold the salmon over the caviar so that the caviar is sealed inside. Season the salmon with salt and pepper.

6. Heat the oil in a skillet over medium heat. Drop about 1½ tablespoons of pancake batter into the pan. Top with a scallop of salmon, then spoon another 1½ tablespoons of pancake mixture over the salmon, just to cover. Cook 4 to 6 pancakes at a time, turning them once.

7. *To assemble:* Spoon the warm watercress sauce into the center of a plate. Place a pancake in the center of the sauce and top with 1 teaspoon of sour cream, 1 teaspoon of caviar, and a sprinkling of chopped chives. Decoratively place 3 asparagus tips around the plate. Repeat for the remaining pancakes. Serve warm.

PAILLARD OF SALMON WITH OYSTER TARTAR

· JACKY PLUTON ·

4 servings

Olive oil

1½-pound salmon fillet, cut into four 6-ounce pieces (see Truc #75*)*

8 oysters

3 tablespoons finely chopped shallots

2 teaspoons finely chopped capers

1 teaspoon Tabasco sauce

1 teaspoon Worcestershire sauce

1 heaping tablespoon finely chopped chervil or parsley leaves (see Truc #55*)*

1 hard-boiled egg

Salt

Freshly ground pepper

¼ cup lemon juice

Warm toast

1. Brush a 12-inch-square piece of plastic wrap with olive oil. Place 1 piece of salmon on the wrap and fold it over the salmon. Using the flat side of a meat cleaver, pound the salmon, pressing it out until it is about ¼ inch thick and forms a rectangle approximately 6 × 4 inches.

2. Heat a large skillet and cook the salmon paillard for 20 seconds over medium-high heat; turn it over and cook it for another 10 seconds. Cook all the salmon, then set aside.

3. *For the tartar,* open the oysters and set their juice aside. Finely chop the muscle. Combine the chopped oysters with the shallots, capers, Tabasco sauce, Worcestershire sauce, chervil, and reserved oyster juice.

4. Separate the egg white from the egg yolk. First press the egg white and the yolk through a fine sieve (see *Truc #40*). Set aside in separate piles.

5. Sprinkle a plate decoratively with salt and pepper. Lay a salmon paillard on the plate and brush with olive oil and lemon juice. Place a spoonful of oyster tartar in the center of the salmon paillard. Fold the salmon over, pocketing the tartar in the middle. Sprinkle the edge of the fish with egg white and egg yolk. Repeat with remaining salmon. Serve paillard cold with warm toast.

CARROT SOUP WITH DILL

· MARY SUE MILLIKEN ·

4 to 6 servings

2 tablespoons unsalted butter
¾ cup sliced onions
2 teaspoons salt
½ teaspoon white pepper
1 bunch fresh dill
4 cups chicken stock or canned broth (see Truc #60)
1 pound carrots, peeled and finely chopped (3½ to 4 cups)
1 cup heavy cream
1 cup half-and-half

1. Melt butter over medium-low heat in a large stockpot or Dutch oven. Cook onions with salt and pepper until soft, about 5 minutes.

2. Chop dill in half, crosswise, separating the leaves from the stems. Reserve the leaves for garnish. You should have about 1 cup. Tie the stems with string and place in the pot (see Truc #54). Add the chicken stock and cook over medium heat, uncovered, about 15 minutes.

3. Remove and discard the dill stems and add the carrots. Bring to a boil, lower heat to a simmer, and cook, uncovered, until the carrots are soft, about 10 minutes.

4. Purée the soup in a blender or food processor until smooth. Strain back into the pot, pressing with the back of a ladle to extract all juices. Add the cream and half-and-half. Bring to a boil and remove from the heat. Serve immediately, garnished with dill leaves.

SHOEPEG CORN AND PEANUT SOUP

· MARCEL DESAULNIERS ·

8 servings

6 cups Vegetable Stock (recipe follows)
1 cup (about 5 ounces) shelled, unsalted Virginia peanuts, skinned
7 tablespoons safflower oil
1 tablespoon water
1½ cups diced celery
½ cup diced onions (see Truc #16)
Salt
Freshly ground pepper
2 cups (about 2 ears) white shoepeg corn (or other variety) kernels
½ cup all-purpose flour
4 tablespoons creamy peanut butter

VEGETABLE STOCK

8 cups

3 quarts water
2 medium onions, chopped (1 cup) (see Truc #16)
4 stalks celery, chopped (1½ cups)
1 medium potato (about 4 ounces), peeled and cut into 1-inch pieces
2 leeks, white part only, chopped (½ cup)
1 medium carrot, washed and chopped (¾ cup)
1 medium tomato, cored and chopped (½ cup) (see Truc #26)
1 teaspoon salt
2 medium garlic cloves, peeled (see Truc #11)
1 teaspoon chopped fresh parsley
½ teaspoon whole black peppercorns

1. Heat ½ cup of the water in a 5-quart saucepan over medium-high heat. Add the onions, celery, potatoes, leeks, carrots, tomato, and salt. Cover and steam for 5 minutes.

2. Add remaining water, garlic, parsley, and peppercorns. Bring liquid to a boil, reduce heat, and simmer for 2 hours.

3. Strain the stock and cool (see Truc #60). Stock can be refrigerated for 2 days or frozen for up to 1 month.

1. Prepare Vegetable Stock. Cool.

2. Preheat the oven to 300°.

3. Spread the peanuts on a cookie sheet and roast them in the oven for 25 to 30 minutes, until golden brown. Set aside.

4. Heat 1 tablespoon of the oil and the water in a 5-quart sauce pan over medium heat. Add the celery and onions, cook for 5 minutes. Season with salt and pepper. Add the corn kernels and sauté for 5 minutes. Add the Vegetable Stock and bring to a boil. Reduce heat and simmer for 15 minutes.

5. In a small saucepan, heat the remaining oil over low heat, add the flour and stir. Add the peanut butter and blend. Cook for 6 minutes, stirring constantly so that the peanut butter won't scorch.

6. Add 4 cups of the soup's broth to the peanut butter mixture, whisking vigorously until smooth. Whisk this mixture into the soup and blend. Simmer for 10 minutes. Season with salt and pepper to taste.

7. To serve, sprinkle the roasted peanuts over the soup.

ANCHO AND NAVY BEAN SOUP

· DEAN FEARING ·

4 servings

2 cups dried white navy beans, picked over and rinsed
4 thick slices smoked bacon
1 large onion, peeled and chopped (see Truc #16)
1 stalk celery, trimmed and chopped
2 large shallots, peeled and chopped
2 cloves garlic, peeled and chopped (see Truc #11)
2 serrano chilies, chopped
4 cups Ham Stock (recipe follows)
4 cups chicken stock
1 cup Ancho Chili Paste (recipe follows)
Salt
Freshly squeezed lime juice (see Truc #31)
1 red onion, peeled and cut into ¼-inch dice (see Truc #16)
8 fresh cilantro leaves (see Truc #51)

1. Cover navy beans with at least 8 cups of cold water. Allow to soak at least 8 hours. Drain well.

2. Render fat from bacon in a large stockpot over medium heat. Add onion, celery, shallots, garlic, and serrano chilies and sauté for 3 minutes. Add beans, Ham Stock, and chicken stock. Bring to a boil, reduce heat, and simmer for 40 minutes.

3. When done, combine soup and Ancho Chili Paste in a blender and purée until smooth. Stir in salt and lime juice to taste. Strain and recheck seasoning. Pour soup into 4 warm soup bowls and garnish with red onion and cilantro leaves just before serving.

HAM STOCK

4 cups

2 tablespoons bacon fat
1 large onion, peeled and chopped (see Truc #16)
2 stalks celery, trimmed and chopped
1 carrot, chopped
1 bunch fresh cilantro, chopped (about ¾ cup)
2 jalapeño peppers seeded and chopped (see Truc #23)
1 pound ham bones
1 pig's foot
1 bay leaf
1 tablespoon chopped fresh or 1½ teaspoons dried thyme leaves
1 teaspoon whole black peppercorns
4 quarts cold water

NEW ENGLAND FISH CHOWDER

- JASPER WHITE -

8 to 10 servings

3½ pounds fresh cod fillets, skinned
¼ pound meaty salt pork, cut in ¼- to ½-inch dice
12 tablespoons unsalted butter
3 cups diced onions, cut into ¾-inch dice (see Truc #16)
3 bay leaves
1 tablespoon chopped fresh thyme leaves
3 or 4 large Maine or other boiling potatoes, peeled and cut lengthwise in half, then into ¼-inch slices
3 cups strong Fish Stock (recipe follows) (see Truc #57)
2 cups heavy cream
Salt
Freshly ground black pepper
2 tablespoons chopped fresh parsley and/or chervil (see Truc #55)

1. Prepare the fish by removing any excess skin and picking out any bones with a pair of tweezers. If you use a knife to cut out bones, be sure to leave the fillets in as large pieces as possible.

2. Render the fat from the salt pork, medium-high, in a large soup pot until it begins to crisp. Add 4 tablespoons

1. Heat bacon fat in a large saucepan over medium-high heat. Add onion, celery, carrot, cilantro, and jalapeño peppers and sauté for 4 minutes or until transparent. Do not brown the vegetables.

2. Add ham bones, pig's foot, bay leaf, thyme, and peppercorns. Cover with the water and bring to a boil. Lower heat and simmer for 4 hours.

3. Strain stock through a fine sieve, discarding solids, and cool quickly (see *Truc #60*). Refrigerate for up to 2 days or freeze for up to 1 month.

ANCHO CHILI PASTE

1 cup

1 cup chicken stock
4 ancho chilies, seeded (see Truc #22)
1 small onion, peeled and chopped (see Truc #16)
1 clove garlic, peeled and chopped (see Truc #11)
1 small bunch fresh cilantro (about 10 sprigs)

1. Place all the ingredients in a small saucepan over medium heat. Simmer for 10 minutes.

2. Pour into a blender and purée until smooth. Cool quickly (see *Truc #60*). Set aside until ready to use, or refrigerate for up to 2 days or freeze for up to 1 month.

of the butter, the onions, bay leaves, and thyme. Cook for 5 minutes until the onions become soft. Add the potatoes and Fish Stock and simmer for 20 minutes, until the potatoes are tender.

3. Remove the bay leaves and add the cod fillets and heavy cream. Simmer slowly until the fish is cooked through and begins to flake (about 8 to 10 minutes). Season to taste with salt and pepper. Stir in the chopped parsley. Remove from heat.

4. Using a slotted spoon, transfer the chunks of fish, the onions and potatoes to soup plates, then ladle over the piping hot broth. Put a dollop of butter into each plate of soup and serve with crackers or biscuits.

FISH STOCK

8 cups

2½ to 3 pounds fish bones
2 tablespoons unsalted butter
1½ cups finely chopped leeks
1 cup finely chopped onions (see Truc #16)
1½ cups finely chopped celery
1½ cups thinly sliced carrots, peeled
3 bay leaves
2 sprigs thyme
4 or 5 parsley stems (see Truc #54)
½ teaspoon whole black peppercorns
1 cup dry white wine
Salt (optional)

1. Cut the fish bones into pieces 2 to 3 inches across. Trim the bones of any excess skin or viscera that may still be attached. Rinse or soak if necessary in cold water to remove completely any traces of blood.

2. Melt the butter in a stockpot over low heat and add the leeks, onions, celery, carrots, bay leaves, thyme, parsley stems, and peppercorns. Cook for about 5 minutes, stirring a few times.

3. Add the wine and place the fish bones on top of the vegetables. Cover the pot and allow the bones to sweat in the aromatic steam. After 20 minutes, remove the lid and pour in 4 cups of water, enough to cover the fish bones.

4. Raise the heat and bring the stock to a boil. Skim the top, then reduce the heat to a slow simmer. Simmer for 10 minutes and remove from the heat. Allow the stock to sit for another 10 minutes. If you like, you can lightly salt the stock.

5. Gently strain the stock through a fine strainer and chill as quickly as possible (see *Truc #60*). Freeze any leftover stock for up to 1 month.

BRUSCHETTA

- PINO LUONGO -

2 servings

3 ripe plum tomatoes, cored and diced small (about ¾ cup) (see Truc #27)

Salt

Freshly ground pepper

2 basil leaves, cut into fine ribbons (see Truc #55)

3 tablespoons olive oil

Two ¾-inch-thick slices crusty peasant bread

1 medium clove garlic, peeled (see Truc #11)

1. In a bowl, combine the tomatoes, salt and pepper to taste, basil, and 1½ tablespoons of oil. Set aside.

2. Toast the bread lightly on both sides.

3. Slightly bruise the garlic clove and rub it over the perimeter of the bread, using the crusty edge to grate the garlic (see Truc #15).

4. Drizzle the bread using 1½ tablespoons of olive oil. Sprinkle with salt.

5. Toss the tomato mixture to blend and spoon onto the warm bread. Serve immediately.

QUAIL EGGS IN BRIOCHE WITH CAVIAR AND SMELT ROE

- JEAN-LOUIS PALLADIN -

4 servings

8 to 10 quail eggs

8¼-inch-thick slices brioche

Vegetable oil

Freshly ground black pepper

2 ounces mixed caviar (about 2 teaspoons each of beluga, ossetra, American golden caviar, and smelt roe) or 1¼ ounces (about 8 teaspoons) smelt roe

½ teaspoon minced fresh chives (optional)

SPECIAL UTENSILS:

Two or more cookie cutters of assorted geometric shapes, each about equal in area to a 3-inch-round cookie cutter, for cutting brioche into shapes

One 1-inch round cookie cutter

Cookie sheet or baking pan large enough to hold 8 brioche shapes and also fit under broiler

1. Heat oven to 400° and preheat broiler, if you have a separate broiler unit.

(continued)

138

2. Open the quail eggs (see *Truc #41*), setting the opened eggs in an "egg carton" fashioned from crumpled aluminum foil. Set aside.

3. Use the larger cookie cutters to cut out 8 geometric shapes of brioche, then use the smaller round cutter to cut out a hole in the center of each.

4. Oil the cookie sheet and heat it in the oven, about 1 minute. Remove cookie sheet from oven (leave oven on) and arrange the brioche shapes on it in a single layer. Gently pour the quail eggs into the center holes of the shapes. Return cookie sheet, uncovered, to the oven and bake for 2 minutes; then immediately broil for just a few seconds, about 4 inches from the heat source, until brioche is lightly toasted and egg whites are opaque (the yolks should still be very runny). Remove from broiler. Season tops with pepper.

5. *To assemble:* Transfer 2 brioche shapes to each of 4 heated serving plates. With 2 teaspoons, mold the caviar or smelt roe into 8 quenelles (oval shapes) allowing about 1 level teaspoon of caviar and/or smelt roe for each. As each is formed, place on top of one of the brioche shapes, next to the egg. Sprinkle with chives, if desired. Serve immediately.

Note: You will need 8 eggs for this recipe, but it's a good idea to have extras in case any break.

LOBSTER WITH SNAIL BUTTER

· ANDRÉ SOLTNER ·

2 appetizer servings

2 tablespoons unsalted butter, softened
1 tablespoon chopped parsley (see Truc #55)
2 tablespoons chopped shallots
1 clove garlic, peeled and chopped (see Truc #11)
¼ teaspoon salt
Freshly ground pepper
1 tablespoon Pernod or Ricard
1¼-pound live lobster (see Truc #71)

1. *To make the snail butter:* In a food processor, combine the butter, parsley, shallots, garlic, salt, pepper, and liqueur. Set aside.

2. Preheat the oven to 450°.

3. With a sharp knife, split the lobster in half, lengthwise. Discard the stomach (the small sac behind the eyes) and the intestinal vein.

4. Place the lobster in a round shallow gratin dish and cover with snail butter. Roast in a very hot oven for 10 minutes and serve immediately.

Note: There are no snails in the snail butter; André calls it *snail/butter* because it is the same butter that he uses to cook snails at Lutèce.

DRESSINGS AND SAUCES

MAYONNAISE

▪ ANDRÉ SOLTNER ▪

1 quart

4 large egg yolks (room temperature)
1½ teaspoons Dijon mustard
1 teaspoon white vinegar
Pinch of salt
White pepper to taste
4 cups vegetable oil (room temperature)

1. Whisk egg yolks together with mustard, vinegar, salt, and pepper.

2. Begin to add oil slowly, a few drops at a time, while continuing to whisk vigorously. After the mayonnaise emulsifies and begins to thicken, the oil can be added a little more quickly.

3. Continue whisking until all the oil is incorporated and the mayonnaise is thick and smooth. Adjust seasoning, if necessary.

Note: If at any point the mayonnaise breaks—loses its texture and becomes runny—see *Truc #62.*

ROASTED TOMATILLO SALSA WITH CILANTRO, MINT, AND AVOCADO

▪ RICK BAYLESS ▪

1¾ cups

½ pound (about 5 or 6) fresh tomatillos (Mexican green tomatoes), husked and washed
1 jalapeño pepper or 2 serrano chilies, stemmed, halved, and deveined, seeds reserved (see Truc #23)
½ small onion, finely chopped (¼ cup) (see Truc #16)
3 tablespoons vinegar
6 sprigs fresh cilantro, finely chopped (2 tablespoons)
2 small sprigs mint, finely chopped
1 avocado, pitted, peeled, and diced (see Trucs #2 and #3)
½ teaspoon salt

1. Preheat broiler.

2. Place the tomatillos on a cookie sheet and roast them 6 inches below the broiler, turning them gently as they blister and brown on all sides. Set aside to cool.

3. In a food processor, roughly chop the jalapeño pepper. Add the tomatillos and process into a smooth purée. Transfer to a small mixing bowl.

4. Put the onion in a small strainer and dip several times into a bowl of water mixed with about 3 tablespoons of vinegar. This rinses away the souring juices (see *Truc* #17). Shake off excess water and add to the bowl of tomatillos along with the cilantro, mint, and avocado. If the salsa is too thick, add ¼ cup water. Season with salt. Let the salsa sit for 30 minutes before serving.

Note: In Southwestern cooking, tomatoes, tomatillos, garlic, and green peppers are frequently roasted to blacken their peels and intensify their flavor. This roasting is accomplished either under a broiler, as in this recipe, or in an iron skillet over high heat, as in Zarela Martinez's recipe for Roasted Tomato Sauce (page 153).

MY FATHER'S VINAIGRETTE

· ALAIN SAILHAC ·

2 servings

1 medium garlic clove, peeled (see Truc #11)
1 teaspoon Dijon mustard
1 tablespoon red wine vinegar
Dash of salt
13 twists of the pepper mill
3 tablespoons olive oil

1. Grate the garlic with the tines of a fork (see *Truc* #13). Add the mustard, vinegar, salt, and pepper. Blend together, using the fork. Very slowly add the olive oil, whisking all the while.

2. Toss with salad greens just before serving.

GREEN HERB OIL

· DAVID BOULEY ·

1 cup

⅓ cup extra virgin olive oil
⅓ cup vegetable oil
One 500-milligram vitamin C tablet
½ cup chopped fresh leafy green herbs—basil, parsley, tarragon, or cilantro (see Truc #55)

1. Combine the oils in a blender and place in freezer until very cold, about ½ hour.

2. Crush the vitamin C tablet into a fine powder. Combine with the oil and blend until the tablet is dissolved (see *Truc* #56).

3. Add the herbs and blend until the leaves are fully puréed and emulsified in the oil.

4. Store in the refrigerator.

RICE AND POLENTA

PERFECT RICE

• Patrick Clark •

4 servings

1 cup rice
2 teaspoons vegetable oil
1 cup water or stock

1. In a saucepan, over medium heat, sauté the rice in the oil until the individual grains are coated and just beginning to turn opaque, about 1 minute.

2. Add water or stock and bring to a boil. Stir rice, cover, and reduce heat to a simmer.

3. Cook for 10 minutes, then remove from heat. Do not uncover. Let sit for 15 minutes, then remove lid. Fluff the rice with a fork and serve (see *Truc #45*).

ARTICHOKE-FLAVORED RICE

• Felipe Rojas-Lombardi •

6 servings

1 tablespoon olive oil
1 or 2 cloves garlic, peeled and crushed (see Truc #11)
2 cups long-grain rice
4 cups water or stock
1 large artichoke, quartered
Coarse salt to taste

1. In a saucepan, heat the oil over low heat. Add the garlic and sauté until lightly browned on all sides, about 4 minutes. Do not burn the garlic.

2. Remove the garlic, add the rice, and sauté for about 5 minutes.

3. Add 4 cups water and the artichoke quarters; bring to a boil over high heat (see *Truc #48*). Cover the pan tightly, reduce heat to low, and simmer for 10 to 12 minutes, or until rice has absorbed all the liquid.

4. Remove the artichoke quarters, and fluff the rice with a fork. Season with salt and serve.

BASIC POLENTA

• LIDIA BASTIANICH •

4 servings

4 cups cold water (2 cups milk plus 2 cups water can be
used for a richer taste)
1 tablespoon unsalted butter
1 bay leaf
2 tablespoons coarse salt
1½ cups coarse yellow cornmeal

1. Place the water in a medium-size cast-iron saucepan
or other heavy pot. Add the butter, bay leaf, and salt.

2. Very slowly, begin to sift the cornmeal into the pan
through the fingers of one hand, stirring constantly with
a wooden spoon or whisk. (This operation will be greatly
facilitated if the meal is scooped by the handful from a
wide bowl.) Gradually sift all the meal into the pan (see
Truc #44).

3. Place the pan over high heat and stir until the mixture begins to simmer. Then reduce heat to medium-low
and cook, stirring constantly, until the polenta is smooth,
thick, and pulls away from the sides of the pan as it is
stirred, about 30 minutes. Discard the bay leaf. Pour the
polenta into a serving bowl or onto a wooden board, and
allow it to rest for 10 minutes.

4. To serve from the bowl, dip a large spoon into hot
water and scoop the polenta onto individual dishes, dipping the spoon into the water between scoops. To serve
from the board, cut the polenta into segments with a thin,
taut string or a knife and transfer to plates with a spatula
or cake server. The polenta can also be fried or grilled.
Serve as a side dish with stews, poultry, and seafood.

ENTRÉES

MEAT DISHES

THE ARCADIA BURGER

• ANNE ROSENZWEIG •

8 servings

Herb Butter
8 tablespoons butter
1 tablespoon finely chopped fresh thyme leaves
2 tablespoons finely chopped fresh basil leaves (see Truc #55)
1 tablespoon chopped fresh parsley leaves (see Truc #55)

Hamburgers
6 pounds freshly ground chuck (20 to 22% fat)
Herb Butter
Salt
Freshly ground pepper
16 ½-inch-thick slices Italian peasant bread
1½ cups olive oil
16 to 24 slices ripe tomato
16 thin slices red onion
1 cup freshly squeezed lemon juice (see Truc #31)

1. Make the Herb Butter by softening the butter and combining with the chopped herbs. Shape into a log, wrap in plastic wrap, and freeze. To use, slice into 8 pieces.

2. Divide the meat into 8 balls, touching it only lightly as you work. Make an indentation in each ball and press a nugget of herb butter into the meat (see *Truc #63*). Close the indentation and shape the meat into patties about 1 inch thick. Season with salt and pepper. Grill over medium flame, about 4 minutes on each side.

3. Brush the bread slices on one side, using ½ cup of the olive oil. Place the slices, oiled side down, on the grill and lightly toast. Turn over and toast the other side.

4. Combine the tomato and onion slices in a bowl with the remaining olive oil, the lemon juice, and salt and pepper to taste.

5. Serve the burgers on the grilled bread, with the tomato-onion salad offered as a topping.

SALAD OF SHORT RIBS AND BEETS WITH TARRAGON

▪ DANIEL BOULUD ▪

4 to 6 servings

4 pounds thick beef short ribs
4 leeks, rinsed well (separate greens from whites)
1 carrot, peeled and split in half
1 teaspoon celery salt
¼ teaspoon crushed black peppercorns
1½ teaspoon salt
1 pound beets, cleaned (see Truc #6)
½ pound small redskin potatoes, scrubbed, but not peeled
1 teaspoon finely chopped shallots
1 clove garlic, peeled and chopped (see Truc #11)
3 tablespoons chopped parsley leaves (see Truc #55)
1 tablespoon chopped fresh tarragon leaves
5 tablespoons of red wine vinegar
8 to 10 tablespoons olive oil
Salt
Freshly ground pepper
1 head Boston lettuce
⅓ cup fresh chives, cut into 1-inch pieces

1. Place the short ribs in a Dutch oven and cover with 4 quarts of water.

2. Add the leek greens, carrot, celery salt, crushed black pepper, and 1½ teaspoons of salt. Boil gently for 1 hour.

3. In a separate pot, boil the beets in water until done (60 minutes minimum).

4. Remove the short ribs from their pot, strain the bouillon, discard the vegetables (or keep them for soup), and return the ribs and bouillon to the Dutch oven.

5. Add the potatoes and the leek whites and bring to a boil. Cook for another 30 to 45 minutes, then drain. (Quickly cool and refrigerate the cooking bouillon to use in sauces or as a soup. See Truc #60.)

6. Cut the meat in ½-inch slices. Discard the bones and the fat.

7. Slice the potatoes into ¼-inch dice and quarter the leek whites. In a bowl, toss the meat and vegetables together while still warm.

8. Add the shallots, garlic, 2 tablespoons of the parsley, and 1 teaspoon of the tarragon. Sprinkle with 3½ tablespoons of the vinegar, 5 to 7 tablespoons of the olive oil, and salt and freshly ground pepper to taste. Toss carefully to avoid mashing the vegetables.

9. Drain the beets, cool, peel and cut into thin wedges. Season with the remaining parsley and tarragon, 1 tablespoon of the vinegar, 2 tablespoons of the olive oil, and salt and freshly ground pepper to taste.

(continued)

10. Toss the lettuce with the remaining vinegar and olive oil. Place the lettuce leaves on the bottom and around the sides of a large salad bowl. Place the short rib mixture in the center of the lettuce and surround with the beet mixture. Sprinkle the salad with chives.

LAMB LOIN CHOPS WITH MINT PESTO AND ARTICHOKES

- JIMMY SCHMIDT -

4 servings

Salt

4 medium artichokes

¾ cup olive oil

6 cloves garlic, roasted and minced

Eight 4-ounce lamb loin chops

1 cup chopped fresh mint leaves

½ cup chopped fresh parsley leaves

¼ teaspoon freshly ground black pepper

1 tablespoon Balsamic vinegar

¼ cup fresh whole mint leaves

1. Bring 4 quarts of water to a boil in a large saucepan. Add 2 tablespoons salt and the artichokes. Cook until tender, about 45 minutes. Test for doneness by inserting a skewer through the base of the artichoke. When tender, drain the water and set the artichokes aside to cool.

2. Once the artichokes are cool enough to handle, quarter them, remove the hearts, and set aside (see *Truc* #1).

3. In a small mixing bowl, blend one third of the garlic with 2 tablespoons of the olive oil. Rub the mixture over the surface of the lamb chops.

4. Preheat the broiler or grill.

5. In a food processor or blender, combine the remaining garlic and olive oil with the chopped mint and parsley and pepper. Process until finely chopped, then add the vinegar. Season with salt to taste. Set aside at room temperature.

6. Broil the chops for 5 minutes, turn them and continue broiling for another 4 minutes—they will be medium-rare.

7. *To serve:* spoon mint pesto over each chop. Garnish with whole mint leaves and the quarered artichoke hearts.

LAMB CURRY WITH FRIED ONIONS

• SUSAN FENIGER •

6 servings

4 pounds boneless, trimmed lamb shoulder
Salt
Freshly ground pepper
1 cup vegetable oil
1½ cups diced onions (see Truc #16)
2 tablespoons puréed garlic (see Truc #14)
2 tablespoons black mustard seeds
2 tablespoons garam marsala
2 teaspoons turmeric
2 teaspoons ground cardamom
2 teaspoons ground cumin
1 teaspoon dried red pepper flakes
2 quarts brown lamb stock or canned chicken broth
4 cups cooked white rice (basmati preferred)
1 cup plain yogurt
Fried Onions (recipe follows)

1. Cut meat, as uniformly as possible, into 2 × 3-inch cubes. Generously sprinkle with salt and pepper.

2. Heat oil in a large Dutch oven over high heat. Cook meat until golden on all sides; reserve on a platter.

3. In the same pot, cook the diced onions, stirring occasionally, until golden. Reduce heat to medium, add garlic and all dry spices, and cook 3 minutes, stirring constantly.

4. Return the meat to pan and pour in stock. Bring to a boil, reduce heat to a simmer, and cook, uncovered, 1 hour and 15 minutes. Occasionally skim and discard the fat that rises to top.

5. Ladle warm stew over a bed of white rice. Garnish with yogurt and Fried Onions. Serve immediately.

FRIED ONIONS

6 servings

1 large onion
¼ cup vegetable oil

1. Peel the onion and slice it as thinly as possible—more like a shave than a cut—across the width. (You may need to use a meat slicer or food processor fitted with a 1-millimeter blade to slice it this fine.)

2. Heat the oil over moderate heat in a small skillet. Working in small batches, fry the onion, constantly shaking the pan, until crispy and golden, about 3 minutes.

3. Remove the slices with tongs or a slotted spoon and drain on paper towels.

POULTRY DISHES

ROAST CHICKEN À LA TRUC

• MICHAEL ROBERTS •

4 servings

One 4- to 5-pound roasting chicken, seasoned with salt and
    pepper
⅓ cup olive oil, melted butter, margarine, or chicken fat
4 tablespoons all-purpose flour
¼ cup dry white wine
1½ cups chicken stock or canned low-sodium chicken broth

1. Preheat the oven to 425°. Place the bird, breast side
down, in a roasting pan and place in the oven. Reduce the
heat to 350° and roast for 10 minutes.

2. Soak a double layer of cheesecloth (large enough to
cover the chicken) with the olive oil. Set aside (see *Truc*
#65).

3. Turn the bird breast side up and cover with the
cheesecloth. Return to oven and roast 60 minutes, basting
with pan juices every 15 minutes. (When well cooked, the
thigh will move freely in its joints.)

4. Remove the bird from the pan and place on a serving platter.

5. Set the roasting pan on the stove over medium heat.
With a wooden spoon, stir in the flour. Add wine and
broth and bring to a simmer, scraping up concentrated
juices that cling to the bottom of the pan. Reduce the
broth by one-third. Check seasoning. Pour the gravy into
a sauce boat.

6. Untruss the bird and serve immediately, with gravy.

CHICKEN BOUDIN BLANC

- MICHEL RICHARD -

6 servings

¾ cup finely chopped onion (see Truc #16)
2 cups heavy cream
1 pound boneless skinned chicken breast, cut into chunks
¼ teaspoon freshly grated nutmeg
½ teaspoon salt
3 drops Tabasco sauce
4 large eggs
Plastic wrap (see Truc #64)

1. Simmer the onions in the heavy cream over low heat for 30 minutes. Stir occasionally to prevent scorching. Strain cream into a small bowl, discarding the onions. Set bowl in an ice bath to cool cream.

2. In a food processor, purée the chicken with the cooled cream, nutmeg, salt, and Tabasco sauce. Once the mixture is smooth, add the eggs and continue to process.

3. Lay 3 feet of plastic wrap on the counter. Fit a pastry bag with a ½-inch tube. Fill the bag with the chicken mixture (see Truc #91). Pipe chicken mixture on the plastic wrap, beginning 3 inches up from the long edge. Pipe so the sausage is 1 inch in diameter.

4. Roll the sausage tightly, tying each end with a piece of string. Pinch the sausage roll at 6-inch intervals, tying each pinch with a piece of string.

5. Drop the sausage roll into a pot of barely simmering water. Poach for 30 minutes, until the sausage firms up. Once cooked, plunge immediately into a bowl of iced water to cool.

6. Refrigerate until ready to serve. Before serving, unwrap the sausages and pan fry in a lightly oiled nonstick pan until the sausages turn a golden brown. Serve hot.

CHICKEN FLAUTAS

- ZARELA MARTINEZ -

4 to 6 servings

2 tablespoons lard or oil
½ cup finely chopped onion (see Truc #16)
1 teaspoon minced garlic (see Truc #11)
3 cups shredded poached chicken meat
Salt
Freshly ground pepper
16 corn tortillas (see Truc #49)
Vegetable oil for frying

1. Heat the lard in a skillet over medium heat. Add the onions and garlic and cook until translucent, about 3 minutes. Add the chicken, stir well, season with salt and pepper to taste, and cook for 5 minutes.

2. *To prepare the flautas:* Soften tortillas in the microwave, four at a time. Lay them flat on the counter and place 2 tablespoons of chicken mixture in the center of each. Roll each into a tight cylinder, securing it with a toothpick. Place the rolled tortillas in a plastic bag until you are ready to cook.

3. *To cook:* Pour 3 inches of oil into a deep saucepan. Heat to 350°. Fry 2 or 3 flautas at a time until golden, about 5 minutes. Drain on a plate lined with paper towels. Serve hot with salsa or guacamole.

POBLANOS RELLENOS
· ZARELA MARTINEZ ·

6 servings

½ cup pimiento-stuffed green olives
½ cup each pitted prunes, dried apricots, and dried peaches
6 large poblano chilies
Vegetable oil for frying
8 tablespoons (1 stick) unsalted butter
¾ cup chopped onion (see Truc #16)
2 garlic cloves, peeled and minced (see Truc #11)
1½ teaspoons ground cumin
½ teaspoon Cassia cinnamon (or 1½ teaspoons Ceylon cinnamon, more popular in Mexico)
¼ teaspoon ground cloves
2 cups shredded cooked chicken
Salt
Roasted Tomato Sauce (recipe follows)

1. Preheat the oven to 425°.

2. Slice the olives and coarsely dice the dried fruit. Set aside.

3. Make a slit in each of the poblano chilies (do not cut through) and fry in hot oil to remove the peel (see *Trucs* #19 and #96). Seed the chilies and set them aside.

4. Melt the butter in a large skillet over medium heat. Add the onions and garlic and sauté for 3 minutes. Stir in the olives and dried fruit and sauté for another 3 minutes. Add the spices and chicken and cook for 2 minutes, stirring. Season with salt to taste.

5. Spoon the chicken mixture into the peppers through the slit. Place the stuffed chilies on an oiled baking pan and bake for 7 minutes. Spoon the Roasted Tomato Sauce onto a serving plate and arrange the poblanos *rellenos* on top.

ROASTED TOMATO SAUCE
(SALSA DE TOMATE ASADO)

1½ cups heavy cream
8 cloves of garlic, unpeeled
1 medium onion, unpeeled and cut crosswise
2¾ pounds (about 3 to 4 large) tomatoes
Salt

1. In a small saucepan, simmer the cream until reduced to 1 cup.

2. Heat a heavy cast-iron skillet over high heat until it is hot to the touch. Roast the garlic and onion in the pan. Turn them several times until the garlic is dark on all sides and has softened, and the onion is partly blackened. Set aside.

3. Roast the tomatoes the same way until they blister on all sides. Let cool.

4. Peel the garlic, onion, and tomatoes and put in a blender. Purée on medium until smooth. Add the cream and blend until mixed. Season with salt. Return to the saucepan and simmer gently over low heat. Serve warm.

PHEASANT IN CHOCOLATE SAUCE

▪ FELIPE ROJAS-LOMBARDI ▪

6 to 8 servings

Two 2½-pound pheasants, each cut into 8 serving pieces
1 cup olive oil
2 cloves garlic, peeled and minced (see Truc #11)
1 or 2 fresh jalapeño peppers, seeded and minced (see Truc #23)
2 cups chopped onions (see Truc #16)
2 tablespoons chopped unsweetened chocolate
4 stalks celery, deveined and cut on the diagonal into ¼-inch slices (about 2 cups)
4 carrots, peeled and cut into ¼ inch slices (about 2 cups)
¼ cup all-purpose flour
1 tablespoon coarse salt
2 quarts chicken stock
4 links Morcilla sausages (or other blood sausages), skinned and chopped
3 wine corks (see Truc #66)

1. Pat the pheasant pieces dry and set aside.

2. Heat the oil in a sauté pan over medium-high heat. Brown the pheasant pieces evenly on all sides. Remove the pheasant from the pan and set aside. Discard all but ¼ cup of the oil.

3. Reduce the heat to medium-low and add the garlic, jalepeño peppers, and onions. Cook until the onion turns golden, about 10 minutes.

4. Add the chocolate and cook 2 minutes, then add the celery and carrots. Raise the heat to medium and cook for another 3 minutes.

5. Sprinkle the flour over the vegetables and stir until

they are coated. Season with salt and add 2 cups of stock. Bring the stock to a boil, stirring constantly. Reduce the heat, and simmer for 5 minutes.

6. Add the pheasant, sausages, remaining stock, and the wine corks. Return to a boil, then reduce the heat and simmer for 30 to 45 minutes, until the pheasant is tender.

7. Once cooked, remove the corks and season with salt if necessary. Serve over white rice.

SEAFOOD DISHES

FRIED SOFT-SHELL CRABS WITH CRAB SALAD

• EMERIL LAGASSE •

4 servings

2 cups all-purpose flour
2 eggs
1 cup milk
1½ cups dry bread crumbs
2 tablespoons Creole Seasoning *(recipe follows)*
Four 5- to 6-ounce jumbo soft-shell crabs, cleaned *(see Truc #72)*
Vegetable oil
Creole Tomato Sauce *(recipe follows)*
Crab Salad *(recipe follows)*

1. Put the flour into a shallow pan, set aside. Combine the eggs with the milk in a shallow pan, set aside. In a third shallow pan, toss the bread crumbs and Creole Seasoning together.

2. Dredge the crabs in the flour, shaking off any excess. Dip crabs into the milk mixture and, finally, dredge them in the seasoned bread crumbs.

3. Deep fry the crabs in 375° oil for 2 minutes, just until the crabs turn golden. Remove and drain on paper towels.

4. *To serve:* Pool the Creole Tomato Sauce on the bottom of each plate. Put one soft-shell crab on top of the sauce, along with ½ cup Crab Salad.

CREOLE SEASONING

7 tablespoons

2½ tablespoons salt
2 tablespoons sugar
2 tablespoons freshly ground pepper
1 tablespoon cayenne

1. Combine all ingredients and mix thoroughly. Pour into a glass jar and seal tightly.

2. Creole Seasoning keeps indefinitely. Use the remainder to season grilled chicken, fish, and meat.

CREOLE TOMATO SAUCE

4 servings

6 medium tomatoes
2 tablespoons unsalted butter
¼ cup dry white wine
½ cup finely chopped onion
½ cup chopped fresh cilantro leaves (see Truc #55)
3 tablespoons Creole Seasoning (recipe precedes)
Freshly ground pepper to taste
Salt to taste

1. Preheat broiler.
2. Place tomatoes on a foil-lined baking sheet and roast, turning frequently, until skin has blistered and turned black (see *Truc #29*). Cool, remove skin, and chop tomatoes.
3. Melt the butter in a skillet over medium-high heat. Add wine and cook for 30 seconds.
4. Add tomatoes and remaining ingredients and simmer for 4 to 5 minutes, until the sauce thickens slightly. Keep warm until ready to serve.

CRAB SALAD

4 servings

2 cups water
½ cup packaged crab boil
1 tablespoon salt
½ teaspoon whole black peppercorns
1 clove garlic, peeled (see Truc #11)
2 ears corn
2 scallions, sliced (see Truc #18)
2 teaspoons Creole Seasoning (recipe precedes)
1 cup diced red bell pepper (see Truc #20)
2 tablespoons olive oil
2 tablespoons freshly squeezed lemon juice (see Truc #31)
1 pound jumbo lump crabmeat

1. In a saucepan combine the water, crab boil, salt, peppercorns, and garlic. Bring to a boil. Add the corn and simmer for 2 minutes. Remove the corn and cool.
2. Scrape the corn kernels from the ears and reserve.
3. In a bowl combine the corn kernels, scallions, Creole Seasoning, and red bell pepper. Using a fork, toss together. Add the olive oil and lemon juice and mix thoroughly. Refrigerate until ready to serve.
4. Gently fold the crabmeat into the salad. Refrigerate until ready to serve. (No longer than 1 day in advance.)

4. Cook the pasta in boiling, salted water. Prepare the sauce by combining ¼ cup of the poaching liquid with the caviar butter in a saucepan. Do not overheat or the sauce will separate.

5. *To serve:* Pile the pasta high in the center of each plate. Arrange slices of lobsters around the mound of pasta and ladle on some of the caviar butter sauce. Top each with a sprig of chervil and serve.

LOBSTER TAILS WITH SQUID INK PASTA AND CAVIAR BUTTER

• JEAN-LOUIS PALLADIN •

4 servings

½ cup unsalted butter
½ cup pressed caviar
2 lobster tails, in shell
2 cups lobster consommé or fish broth (see Truc #57)
½ pound fresh squid ink pasta (black pasta)
4 sprigs chervil

1. To prepare the caviar butter, combine the butter and caviar in a food processor and process until well mixed. Refrigerate until firm, about 2 hours.

2. Insert a wooden skewer at the back of each lobster tail, pressing it out the front (*see Truc #69*). Poach the tails in the consommé until the meat is cooked, approximately 6 minutes. Reserve poaching liquid.

3. Remove both the shell and skewer from each lobster tail and cut each crosswise into 8 slices. Cover with a kitchen towel and reserve.

ROASTED LOBSTER PACKETS ON A CORIANDER AND TOMATO COULIS

· HUBERT KELLER ·

4 servings

Bouquet garni (made with bay leaf, thyme, and parsley)

Salt to taste

Freshly ground pepper to taste

Two 1¼-pound live lobsters (see Truc #71)

⅔ cup heavy cream

2 medium leeks, chopped

1 tablespoon chopped chives

12 large spinach leaves

2 tablespoons olive oil

1 tablespoon chopped shallots

1 small garlic clove, peeled and finely chopped (¼ teaspoon) (see Truc #11)

3 large tomatoes, peeled, seeded, and diced (2 cups) (see Truc #27)

¼ teaspoon sugar or to taste

1 tablespoon finely chopped fresh cilantro leaves (see Truc #55)

4 quail eggs (see Truc #41)

Chopped fresh chervil leaves, for garnish (see Truc #55)

1. Line a 1½-quart casserole, 9 × 13 inches, with parchment paper.

2. *To cook the lobsters:* Bring 6 quarts of water to a boil in a large stockpot. Add bouquet garni, salt, pepper, and lobsters. Poach for 8 minutes. Remove the lobsters and cool. Break each lobster's tail off where the tail meets the body. With scissors, cut off the soft underpart of the tail, then remove the meat in one piece. Remove the claw meat, also in one piece (see *Truc #70*). Set the meat aside.

3. Bring the cream to a boil in a medium saucepan. Add the leeks and season with salt and pepper. Reduce heat, cover and simmer for 6 to 8 minutes or until the leeks become tender. Add the chives and set aside to cool.

4. Quickly blanch the spinach leaves in lightly salted boiling water, set aside.

5. Dice the lobster meat and add to the cream mixture. Toss to blend.

6. Preheat the oven to 350°.

7. Lay the spinach leaves flat on the counter. Spoon the lobster mixture into the center of each spinach leaf. Fold each leaf around the lobster mixture, creating an envelope. Arrange the stuffed leaves, seam side down, in the prepared casserole. Sprinkle the leaves with 1 tablespoon of the olive oil and roast for 6 minutes.

8. *To make the tomato* coulis: Heat the remaining olive oil in a small saucepan. Add the shallots and cook until golden. Add the garlic and tomatoes, then season with salt, pepper, and sugar to taste. Reduce heat and simmer for 5 minutes, until the tomato *coulis* thickens. Add the cilantro and adjust seasonings.

9. *To serve:* Spoon 1 tablespoon of tomato *coulis* into the center of each plate. Arrange 3 lobster packets around the sauce. Cook the quail eggs, sunny-side up, and place one in the center of each plate. Sprinkle with chervil.

POMPANO COOKED IN PAPER

• EMERIL LAGASSE •

4 servings

¼ *cup olive oil*
4 *tablespoons unsalted butter*
½ *cup thinly sliced fresh basil leaves (see* Truc #55)
Four 12-ounce pompano fillets
¼ *cup Creole Seasoning (page 155)*
8 *medium plum tomatoes, cut into ½-inch slices*
1 *onion, cut into ¼-inch slices*

1. Preheat the oven to 450°.

2. Cut 4 pieces of parchment paper into large heart shapes. Lay the hearts flat on the counter. Brush half of each heart with olive oil and then dot with a tablespoon of butter.

3. Sprinkle half the basil evenly over the oiled paper. Place a fish fillet on top of the basil, then season with Creole Seasoning. Top the fish fillets with remaining basil.

4. Make a single layer of tomatoes on top of each fish fillet and then top with a single layer of onions.

5. Fold the paper over the fish. Seal the fish inside by making a series of overlapping folds around the perimeter (see *Truc #76*). Twist the last fold several times to ensure that the paper packages are completely sealed.

6. Place the paper-wrapped fish on a baking sheet and bake for 10 to 15 minutes. When the paper package balloons and browns, the fish has steamed inside.

7. Bring the fish to the table in their paper packages, letting guests open their own. A wonderful aroma will waft from the fish as the packages are opened.

SALMON FILLET COOKED ON ONE SIDE ONLY

• PAULA WOLFERT •

2 servings

¾ pound center-cut fresh Atlantic salmon fillet, skin on
1 tablespoon olive oil
½ teaspoon sea salt
2 teaspoons unsalted butter
8 small capers, rinsed, drained, and chopped
3 tablespoons sliced scallions, white part only (see Truc #18)
1 ripe tomato, peeled, seeded, and cut into ¼-inch cubes (about ⅔ cup) (see Truc #27)
3 tablespoons cubed lemon flesh, with rind, pith, and seeds removed (see Truc #32)

Salt

Freshly ground pepper
2 tablespoons shredded fresh sorrel leaves (see Truc #55)
2 tablespoons snipped chives

1. Cut the salmon crosswise into 2-inch-wide strips. Lightly brush with olive oil and sprinkle with sea salt. Place the salmon, skin side down, on a heated, well-seasoned iron skillet or griddle and cook over low heat for 20 minutes *without turning*. Use a dome lid or foil to cover the salmon for the last 5 minutes to finish the cooking. (Note that the color of the salmon will not turn dull and the texture will be very juicy.) Scrape off any globules of fat and reserve.

2. Meanwhile, melt the butter in a small skillet, add the capers and scallions and cook, stirring, 1 minute. Add the tomato and lemon and cook 30 seconds. Season to taste with salt and pepper. Swirl in the reserved salmon fat.

3. Raise the heat under the large skillet to crisp the skin of the fish at the last minute. Serve the salmon, skin side down, with the warm tomato garnish, sorrel, and chives.

VEGETARIAN DISHES

LUTÈCE'S FAMED OMELET

• ANDRÉ SOLTNER •

1 serving

1 tablespoon kosher salt (approximately)
3 eggs
Table salt
1 tablespoon butter
Freshly ground pepper

1. Sprinkle kosher salt into omelet pan and rub vigorously with a paper towel. Discard salt (see *Truc #42*).

2. Crack the eggs into a bowl and beat vigorously with a fork until the whites and yolks are thoroughly blended. Once the eggs are pale yellow in color and well beaten, add a sprinkling of table salt.

3. Add the butter to the pan and let it melt over high heat. Roll the butter around the pan, coating the bottom. Give the eggs one last quick beating with a fork and then pour them into the pan. Using a fork, stir and fold the eggs while they cook. Be careful not to overcook them, otherwise they become rubbery.

4. Once the eggs have cooked, tilt the pan over a serving plate and slide the eggs toward the edge of the pan. Fold the top of the eggs into the middle, and continue rolling toward the bottom of the pan. Flip the eggs onto the plate. Straighten the omelet, so that it is cigar-shaped. Season with a few grindings of pepper.

EGGPLANTS STUFFED WITH WALNUTS AND POMEGRANATE SEEDS

· PAULA WOLFERT ·

4 to 6 servings

1 ¾ teaspoons salt
8 to 10 baby eggplants, halved lengthwise (see Truc #10)
2 cups coarsely chopped walnuts
1 garlic clove, peeled and minced (see Truc #11)
½ teaspoon hot Hungarian paprika
¼ teaspoon ground turmeric
⅓ cup chopped celery leaves
¼ cup shredded fresh basil leaves (see Truc #55)
⅓ cup chopped fresh cilantro leaves (see Truc #55)
¼ cup minced red onion
2 tablespoons rice wine vinegar
¼ cup pomegranate seeds (see Truc #37)
1½ tablespoons olive oil
Italian parsley for garnish

1. Sprinkle 1 teaspoon of the salt over the cut side of the eggplants. Place them, flat side down, on paper towels. Set a plate on top of the eggplants, weighing them down for 20 minutes. Rinse the eggplants under cool water and gently squeeze out the moisture. Pat dry with paper towels. Set aside.

2. Place the remaining salt, the walnuts, garlic, paprika, and turmeric in a food processor. Process until mixture becomes an oily paste. Add ⅓ cup of water and process to blend. Transfer the paste to a mixing bowl and stir in the celery leaves, basil, cilantro, onion, and vinegar. Fold in the pomegranate seeds. Cover with plastic wrap and set aside.

3. In a 9-inch skillet, heat the olive oil over medium-low heat. Add the eggplant, flat side down. Cover tightly and cook until the flesh is golden and the eggplant is tender, about 15 minutes. Transfer the eggplant to paper towels to drain and cool slightly.

4. With your fingers, split open the flesh of the cut side of the eggplant. Mound the walnut filling into the slit and serve warm or at room temperature. Garnish with parsley and extra pomegranate seeds.

EGGPLANTS FILLED WITH PASTA AND CHEESE
(TUBETTINI ALLA SICILIANA)

▪ LIDIA BASTIANICH ▪

4 servings

Four 6- to 8-ounce round male eggplants (see TRUC #10)
3 tablespoons olive oil
½ cup cooked pasta, such as ditalini or tubettini
8 ounces mozzarella cheese, diced
2 tablespoons grated Parmesan cheese
Salt
Freshly ground pepper
½ cup tomato sauce

1. Preheat oven to 375°.

2. Wash the eggplants and cut off the tops. Scoop out the pulp and mince it, reserving the shells.

3. Heat 2 tablespoons of the olive oil in a skillet over medium heat. Add the eggplant pulp and cook, covered, for 5 minutes. Stir the pulp occasionally.

4. Combine eggplant pulp with pasta, mozzarella cheese, a sprinkle of Parmesan cheese, salt and pepper to taste, and the remaining olive oil.

5. Add enough tomato sauce to moisten the pulp mixture. Blend well. Mound the filling in the eggplant shells. Top with remaining tomato sauce and Parmesan cheese.

6. Bake for 30 minutes, or until golden.

DESSERTS

FLEUR-DE-LYS'S CRÈME BRÛLÉE WITH CARAMELIZED APPLES AND ORANGE ZEST

▪ HUBERT KELLER ▪

6 servings

3 cups heavy cream
The grated zest of 1 lemon (see Truc #34)
The grated zest of 1 orange (see Truc #34)
9 large egg yolks
¼ cup granulated sugar
3 tablespoons butter
2 large Granny Smith apples, peeled and sliced into 15
   slices each
¼ cup packed light brown sugar

SPECIAL UTENSIL:
Propane torch

1. Preheat the oven to 275°. Butter the sides and bottoms of 6 shallow 4-ounce crème brûlée molds. Set aside.

2. In a saucepan, bring the cream and lemon and orange zests to a boil.

3. Meanwhile, whisk together the egg yolks and granulated sugar. Once the cream comes to a boil, remove from heat and gradually add it to the egg yolk mixture, whisking constantly.

4. Fill the prepared molds with the crème brûlée mixture and set them in a roasting pan. Place the pan in the oven and add enough boiling water to reach halfway up the sides of the molds. Bake for 40 minutes.

5. Melt the butter in a sauté pan over high heat. Add the apple slices and sauté until brown and slightly softened. Set aside.

6. When the crème brûlée is firm, remove from the oven and water bath. Fan five apple slices over the top of each mold. Sprinkle with brown sugar.

7. With a propane torch, melt the brown sugar (see Truc #86). When the crème brûlée cools slightly, it will have a thin, crispy crust. Serve warm or at room temperature.

CORDON ROSE CHEESECAKE

· ROSE LEVY BERANBAUM ·

8 to 12 servings

Two 8-ounce packages cream cheese, at room temperature

1 cup sugar

1 tablespoon cornstarch

3 large eggs

3 tablespoons freshly squeezed lemon juice (see Truc #31)

1½ teaspoons vanilla extract

¼ teaspoon salt

3 cups sour cream

SPECIAL UTENSIL:
Dental Floss

1. Preheat the oven to 350°. Butter an 8 × 2½-inch springform pan and line the bottom with greased parchment or wax paper.

2. In a large mixing bowl beat the cream cheese and sugar until very smooth (about 3 minutes), preferably with a whisk beater.

3. Beat in the cornstarch if desired. Add the eggs, one at a time, beating after each addition until smooth; scrape down the sides of the bowl. Add the lemon juice, vanilla, and salt and beat until incorporated. Beat in the sour cream, just until blended.

4. Pour the batter into the prepared pan. Set the pan in a larger pan and surround it with 1 inch of very hot water. Bake 45 minutes. Turn off the oven. Without opening the door, let the cake cool for 60 minutes. Remove to a rack and cool to room temperature (about 60 minutes). Cover with plastic wrap and refrigerate overnight.

5. *To unmold:* Have ready a serving plate and one flat plate at least 8 inches in diameter, covered with plastic wrap. Place pan on heated burner and move it around for 15 seconds. Wipe the side of the pan with a hot, damp towel.

6. Run a thin metal spatula around the side of the cake and release the side of the springform pan. Place the plastic-wrapped plate on top and invert. Remove the bottom of the pan and the parchment paper. Reinvert the cake onto the serving plate and use a small metal spatula to smooth the side. Refrigerate until shortly before serving.

7. *To cut:* Use the dental floss method (see *Truc #90*).

Note: For a richer, denser cheesecake that completely holds its moisture without cornstarch, replace the 3 whole eggs with 6 egg yolks.

An 8 × 3-inch solid cake pan can be used instead of a springform. To unmold the cake, run a thin spatula around the side, place the pan on heated burner for 10 to 20 seconds, moving the pan back and forth, and then invert. If the cake does not release, return to the hot burner for a few more seconds.

CUPCAKES HOSTESS-STYLE

• MARY SUE MILLIKEN •

18 cupcakes

5 ounces unsweetened chocolate, chopped
1 cup packed brown sugar
1 cup milk
4 large egg yolks
8 tablespoons butter
1 cup granulated sugar
2 cups all-purpose flour
1 teaspoon salt
1 teaspoon baking soda
¼ cup heavy cream
1 teaspoon vanilla extract
3 large egg whites
2½ cups Pastry Cream (recipe follows)
¾ cup Ganache (recipe follows)
½ cup Pure White Frosting (recipe follows)

1. Preheat oven to 325°. Butter and flour a 12-cup and a 6-cup muffin tin, or prepare 18 ovenproof porcelain cups (see *Truc #85*).

2. Melt the chocolate in the top of a double boiler or in a bowl over simmering water. In another bowl, combine brown sugar, ½ cup of the milk and 2 of the egg yolks. Whisk until combined. Add to melted chocolate and cook over simmering water, stirring constantly, until mixture is shiny and thick, about 3 minutes. Set aside to cool.

3. In a clean bowl, cream the butter and granulated sugar until light. Add the remaining 2 egg yolks, one at a time, beating well after each addition.

4. In another bowl, mix together flour, salt, and baking soda.

5. Combine cream, vanilla, and remaining ½ cup milk in a small bowl and reserve.

6. Pour the cooked chocolate mixture into the butter and sugar mixture. Whisk until smooth. Add the cream mixture and dry ingredients in three stages, alternating liquid and dry ingredients, and ending with liquid.

7. Beat the egg whites until soft peaks form. Gently fold, all at once, into the batter. Spoon the batter into the muffin cups, about two-thirds full.

8. Bake 20 to 25 minutes, until a toothpick inserted in center comes out clean. Set aside to cool, in the pan, on rack, about 10 minutes. Invert and set aside on a lined sheet pan to cool, about 60 minutes. Prepary Pastry Cream, Ganache, and Pure White Frosting.

9. Using the tip of a small paring knife, cut a small cone from the bottom of each cupcake. Reserve cones. Scoop out about 1 teaspoon of cake from the center of each cupcake. Fill a pastry bag fitted with a plain tip with Pastry

Cream (see *Truc #91*). Pipe the cream into cupcakes, then replace the reserved cones. Place the cupcakes bottom-side down on a lined sheet pan and chill.

10. When the Ganache has cooled, dip the cupcakes in to coat the tops. Fill a plain-tipped pastry bag with Pure White Frosting (see *Truc #91*) and decorate each cupcake with a squiggle across the top, Hostess-style. Store in the refrigerator until serving time (up to 1 day).

PASTRY CREAM

2½ cups

½ cup sugar
¼ cup cornstarch
4 large egg yolks
2 cups milk
½ teaspoon vanilla extract

1. Mix ¼ cup of the sugar and the cornstarch in a bowl until smooth. Add the egg yolks and mix until a paste is formed. Stir in ½ cup of the milk.

2. Combine the remaining milk and sugar in a saucepan and bring to a boil. Pour the hot mixture into the bowl with the egg yolks, whisking constantly. Pour back into the saucepan.

3. Cook over moderate heat, stirring constantly, until smooth and thick. Remove from heat and stir an additional minute. Stir in the vanilla and transfer to a bowl. Cover with buttered parchment paper that touches top of the cream and chill a minimum of 2 hours (up to 2 days).

GANACHE

¾ cup

3 ounces semisweet chocolate, chopped
⅓ cup plus 1 tablespoon heavy cream

1. Place chocolate in a medium bowl.

2. Bring cream to a boil and pour into the chocolate. Stir until chocolate is completely melted.

3. Let cool until mixture is less than body temperature.

PURE WHITE FROSTING

½ cup

⅔ cup confectioners' sugar
1 tablespoon milk

1. Mix in a small bowl until smooth.

TINY FRUITCAKE GEMS

• ROSE LEVY BERANBAUM •

3½ dozen

8 tablespoons unsalted butter
½ cup small mixed candied fruit
2 tablespoons candied citron
¼ cup dried currants
¼ cup pecan halves
½ cup Myer's dark rum
½ cup unsifted cake flour, without leavening
¼ teaspoon cinnamon
¼ teaspoon salt
⅛ teaspoon baking soda
¼ cup packed dark brown sugar
1 large egg
¼ liquid cup unsulfured molasses (preferably Grandma's)
2 tablespoons milk
1 teaspoon vanilla extract
¼ cup minced candied cherries, optional

1. Place the oven rack in the center of the oven and preheat the oven to 325°. Set the tartlet tins on a baking sheet so that the edges don't touch.

2. Soften the butter with the beater of an electric mixer, set aside.

3. Finely chop the candied fruit, citron, currants, and pecans. Put them in a small mixing bowl and combine with ¼ cup of the rum. Set aside.

4. In another small mixing bowl, combine the flour, cinnamon, salt, and baking soda. Set aside.

5. In a large mixing bowl, cream the butter and brown sugar together until light and fluffy. Beat in the egg and gradually add the flour mixture in 3 batches, alternating with the molasses and milk. Add the candied fruits (with the soaking rum) and the vanilla, then beat until blended.

6. Scrape the batter into a 1-gallon zipper-seal plastic freezer bag. Cut a small piece from one of the corners of the bag. Pipe the batter into the tartlet molds, filling them three-quarters full (see *Truc #83*).

7. Bake 15 to 17 minutes, or just until the batter begins shrinking away from the sides of the molds and the top springs back when lightly touched.

8. Unmold the gems on a buttered piece of wax paper. Brush the tops with the remaining rum. As an option, place ¼ teaspoon of minced candied cherries in the center of each gem. Once cooled, wrap each in a small piece of plastic wrap.

ESPRESSO CHOCOLATE AND HAZELNUT CAKE WITH BRANDY-SOAKED CANDIED FRUIT

• PERLA MEYERS •

10 servings

Cake

¼ cup finely minced excellent-quality candied fruit

¼ cup brandy

8 ounces bittersweet chocolate (preferably Lindt)

5 tablespoons strong prepared coffee mixed with 1 teaspoon instant espresso

8 tablespoons unsalted butter, cut into pieces and chilled

3 extra-large eggs, separated

⅔ cup granulated sugar

4½ tablespoons cake flour

⅔ cup ground hazelnuts (see Truc #89)

Whipped cream

Glaze

3 ounces bittersweet chocolate (preferably Lindt)

2 tablespoons strong prepared coffee

1 tablespoon confectioners' sugar

3 tablespoons unsalted butter, cut into pieces and chilled

1. Preheat the oven to 375°.

2. Butter the inside of an 8-inch round cake pan, preferably one with a high, straight side or a springform. Cut a piece of parchment paper to fit bottom of pan (see *Truc #82*). Butter the parchment paper. Sprinkle the pan lightly with flour, shaking out the excess, and set aside.

3. *To make the cake:* In a small bowl, combine the candied fruit with the brandy and let macerate for at least 60 minutes.

4. In the top of a double boiler, combine the chocolate and 5 tablespoons of coffee, set over warm water, and stir until smooth. Remove from heat, let cool slightly, and whisk in 8 tablespoons of butter, 1 tablespoon at a time, until completely incorporated. Reserve.

5. Combine the egg yolks with ½ cup of the granulated sugar in a large mixing bowl and beat until fluffy and pale yellow. Add the chocolate mixture and whisk until just blended. Add the flour, hazelnuts, and candied fruit and brandy mixture and fold gently but thoroughly.

6. In a large bowl, combine the egg whites with the remaining granulated sugar and beat until they hold firm peaks. Fold the beaten whites gently but thoroughly into the chocolate and hazelnuts, being careful not to deflate the mixture. Pour the batter into the prepared cake pan.

7. Place the pan in the center of the oven and bake for 20 minutes. Remove the cake from the oven and let it sit on a wire cake rack for 15 minutes. Run a knife around the inside of the cake pan, if necessary, and invert the cake onto a serving platter. Carefully peel off and discard the parchment paper (see *Truc #81*). Let the cake cool for 6 hours or refrigerate overnight.

8. *To make the glaze:* Combine the chocolate, 2 tablespoons of coffee, and the confectioners' sugar in the top of a double boiler set over warm water and stir until smooth. Remove from heat, cool slightly, and stir in 3 tablespoons of butter, 1 tablespoon at a time, until thoroughly incorporated. Pour the glaze over the cake and smooth evenly with a spatula. Let the cake sit 30 minutes before serving.

9. *To serve:* Cut into wedges and top each with a dollop of whipped cream.

BALINESE MANGO ICE CREAM WITH RUM

• CRAIG CLAIBORNE •

8 to 10 servings

2 fresh, ripe, unblemished mangoes
1 cup sugar
1 cup heavy cream
2 cups milk
5 large egg yolks
Salt
1 teaspoon vanilla extract
¼ cup dark rum

1. Cut the mango in half, discarding the seed. "Porcupine cut" each half, following *Truc #35*. Cut the flesh away from the outer peel.

2. Roughly chop the flesh and combine it in a mixing bowl with ½ cup of the sugar. Toss and then let it sit until the sugar dissolves, about 3 minutes.

3. In the top of a double boiler combine the cream, milk, egg yolks, remaining sugar, salt, and vanilla. Cook the custard, stirring continually so it does not stick to the pan.

4. Continue stirring until the custard is as thick as heavy cream and a candy thermometer reads 180°. Remove the custard from heat immediately, continuing to stir the mixture for 1 to 2 minutes more. Let the custard cool.

5. Add the mango mixture to the custard and blend. Stir in the rum.

6. Pour the mixture into the container of an ice-cream maker and freeze according to the manufacturer's instructions.

UPSIDE-DOWN PIE SHELL

• JIM DODGE •

One 9-inch crust

1 cup all-purpose flour
1½ teaspoons sugar
1 pinch salt
8 tablespoons (1 stick) unsalted butter
3 tablespoons heavy cream

SPECIAL UTENSILS:
2 metal 9-inch pie plates (see Truc #80)

1. Preheat the oven to 350°.

2. Combine the flour, sugar, and salt. Cut the butter into small pieces and blend with the flour until a coarse meal is formed.

3. Add the cream and carefully blend until the dough is smooth.

4. On a floured table, roll the dough into a 10-inch circle. Fold into quarters and unfold over one of the 9-inch pie plates. Trim the edges and place the other pie plate on top. Turn both plates upside down and bake on a sheet pan for 20 minutes. Turn over and remove the top pie plate. Continue baking until the bottom, center, and edge of the shell are golden. Set aside to cool.

DRY-POACHED PEARS WITH RED WINE SAUCE

• JIMMY SCHMIDT •

4 servings

Wine Sauce
1¼ cups red wine (preferably Pinot Noir)
1 cup sugar
3 tablespoons balsamic vinegar

Poached Pears
One 3-pound box kosher salt
4 large Comice pears
2 tablespoons unsalted butter
2 cups cinnamon ice cream
4 sprigs mint for garnish

1. *To make the wine sauce:* Bring the wine and sugar to a boil, reduce heat, and simmer until the wine reduces to 1 cup, about 20 minutes. Cool to room temperature and stir in vinegar. Set aside.

2. Preheat the oven to 450°.

3. Select a medium-size ovenproof pot, deep and wide enough to later accommodate all 4 pears. Fill the pot with the salt and heat in the oven for 60 minutes (see *Truc*

BARTLETT PEARS IN PUFF PASTRY

▪ JACQUES PÉPIN ▪

6 servings

1 cup flour—measured by dipping the cup directly into the flour and leveling it off with the hand
⅛ teaspoon salt
8 tablespoons unsalted butter, very cold (almost frozen), cut into 8 pieces
⅓ cup iced water
6 tablespoons sugar
¾ teaspoon ground cinnamon
Three 9-ounce ripe Bartlett pears
2 tablespoons freshly squeezed lemon juice (see Truc #31)
2 tablespoons unsalted butter at room temperature
⅓ cup water at room temperature
Heavy cream or sour cream, for garnish (optional)

1. Place the flour, salt and cold butter in a food processor and process for approximately 5 seconds. The butter should be lumpy and visible throughout the flour. Add the iced water and process another 4 to 5 seconds, just long enough for the mixture to become moist, even if it does not hold together completely and form a ball.

2. Transfer the contents to a lightly floured board, press

#36). Remove the pot and carefully pour out two-thirds of the salt and reserve. (Remember the salt is 450°!)

4. Insert a wooden skewer into each pear. Position the pears on top of the salt remaining in the pan. Don't let the pears touch each other. Pour the reserved hot salt back into the pan, burying the pears completely. Put the pan back into the oven and bake for 15 minutes, until tender.

5. Remove the pan from the oven and carefully pour out the salt. Brush away any clinging salt from the pears and set them on a platter to cool.

6. *To serve:* Spoon a puddle of wine sauce on the bottom of each plate. Put a pear in the middle of the sauce, add a scoop of ice cream on the side, and garnish with a mint sprig.

together to form a compact ball, and roll into a rectangle about ¼ inch thick. Fold the ends of the rectangle until they meet in the center, then fold again to create a 4-layer dough. (This is called a *double turn*.) Immediately roll the dough again into a rectangle and fold it again into a double turn. Wrap in plastic wrap and refrigerate. The dough is now ready to use and can be prepared up to this point up to 1 day ahead.

3. Mix the sugar and cinnamon together and set aside. Peel the pears and cut in half lengthwise. Remove the core and seeds from each and arrange, cut side down, in one layer in a gratin dish. Sprinkle with the lemon juice and half the cinnamon-sugar mixture.

4. Preheat the oven to 375°.

5. Roll out the puff pastry (see *Truc* #79) and cut into 6 pieces, each about 5 × 3 inches. Lay a pastry piece on top of each pear and, as the pastry warms and relaxes slightly, press each piece gently around the pear so it takes on the shape of the pear half. Sprinkle with the remaining cinnamon-sugar mixture and dot with the butter.

6. Place the gratin dish on a cookie sheet and bake for about 25 minutes. The pastry should be browning nicely and the mixture around the pears should be bubbly and caramelized. Pour the water around the pears and return to the oven for 5 minutes. The water will melt the caramel and create a sauce. Eat lukewarm, with heavy cream or sour cream, if desired.

THE TRUCSTERS

We are grateful to these fine chefs—our trucsters—who welcomed us into their kitchens and showed us their trucs:

Lidia Bastianich, executive chef and co-owner of Felidia in New York City; author of *La Cucina di Lidia.*

Rick Bayless, executive chef and owner of Frontera Grill in Chicago, author of *Authentic Mexican.*

Rose Levy Beranbaum, author of *The Cake Bible* and *Rose's Christmas Cookies.*

David Bouley, executive chef and owner of Bouley, New York City.

Daniel Boulud, executive chef of Le Cirque in New York City.

Antoine Bouterin, executive chef of Le Perigord in New York City, author of *Cooking with Antoine at Le Perigord.*

Giuliano Bugialli, author of *Bugialli on Pasta,* and *The Fine Art of Italian Cooking, Foods of Italy,* and *Classic Techniques of Italian Cooking.*

David Burke, executive chef of the Park Avenue Café in New York City.

Yannick Cam, formerly of Le Pavillon in Washington, D.C., now executive chef of Yannick Cam at the Raddison Hotel in Alexandria, Virginia.

Craig Claiborne, former food editor for *The New York Times* and author of *The New York Times Cookbook, Craig Claiborne's Favorites,* and *A Feast Made for Laughter.*

Patrick Clark, formerly of Metro in New York City, now executive chef of Bice in Beverly Hills, California.

Eileen Crane, managing director and chief operating officer, Domaine Carneros by Taittinger, Carneros, California.

Andrew D'Amico, executive chef of Sign of the Dove in New York City.

Robert Del Grande, executive chef and co-owner of Cafe Annie in Houston.

Marcel Desaulniers, executive chef and owner of The Trellis in Williamsburg, Virginia, and author of *The Trellis Cookbook.*

Jean-Michel Diot, executive chef and co-owner of Park Bistro and Les Halles, New York City.

Jim Dodge, owner of American Baker in San Francisco and author of *Baking with Jim Dodge.*

Dean Fearing, executive chef of The Mansion on Turtle

Creek in Dallas and author of *Dean Fearing's Southwest Cuisine*.

Susan Feniger, chef and co-owner of City in Los Angeles and co-author of *City Cuisine*.

Michael Foley, executive chef and owner of Printer's Row in Chicago.

Larry Forgione, executive chef and owner of An American Place in New York City.

Hubert Keller, executive chef and co-owner of Fleur de Lys in San Francisco.

Emeril Lagasse, formerly of Commander's Palace, now executive chef and co-owner of Emeril's in New Orleans.

Pino Luongo, executive chef and co-owner of Le Madri in New York City and author of *A Tuscan in the Kitchen*.

Zarela Martinez, executive chef and owner of Zarela's in New York City.

Perla Meyers, author of *Perla Meyers' Art of Seasonal Cooking*.

Mary Sue Milliken, executive chef and co-owner of City in Los Angeles and co-author of *City Cuisine*.

Jean-Louis Palladin, executive chef and co-owner of Jean-Louis at the Watergate, Washington, D.C., and

author of *Jean-Louis' Cooking with the Seasons*.

Charles Palmer, executive chef and co-owner of Aureole in New York City.

Gerard Pangaud, formerly of Aurora, now executive chef of The Ritz Carlton Hotel in Arlington, Virginia.

Jacques Pépin, chef and author of *The Short-Cut Cook, The Art of Cooking* (Vols. 1 and 2), *La Technique, La Methode,* and *Everyday Cooking with Jacques Pépin*.

Georges Perrier, executive chef and owner, Le Bec-Fin, Philadelphia.

Jacky Pluton, formerly of Le Truffe, Philadelphia, now executive chef at La Vieille Maison, Boca Raton, Florida.

Stephan Pyles, executive chef and co-owner of Routh Street Cafe in Dallas.

Jean-Jacques Rachou, executive chef and owner of La Côte Basque in New York City.

Leslee Reis, the late executive chef and owner of Café Provençal in Evanston, Illinois.

Michel Richard, executive chef and owner of Citrus in Los Angeles.

Michael Roberts, executive chef and co-owner of Trumps, Los Angeles, author of *Secret Ingredients*.

Judy Rogers, executive chef of Zuni Cafe in San Francisco.

Felipe Rojas-Lombardi, the late executive chef and co-owner of The Ballroom in New York City and author of *The Art of South American Cooking.*

Anne Rosenzweig, executive chef and co-owner of Arcadia in New York City and author of *The Arcadia Seasonal Mural and Cookbook.*

Alain Sailhac, dean of culinary studies, French Culinary Institute, New York City.

Jimmy Schmidt, executive chef and co-owner of The Rattlesnake Club in Detroit and author of *Cooking for All Seasons.*

André Soltner, executive chef and owner of Lutèce in New York City.

Jacques Torres, executive pastry chef of Le Cirque in New York City.

Barbara Tropp, executive chef and owner of China Moon Cafe in San Francisco and author of *The Modern Art of Chinese Cooking.*

Jean-Georges Vongerichten, executive chef and co-owner of JoJo in New York City and author of *Simple Cuisine.*

Jasper White, executive chef and co-owner of Jasper's in Boston and author of *Jasper White's Cooking from New England.*

Paula Wolfert, author of *Paula Wolfert's World of Food, Couscous and Other Good Food from Morocco,* and *The Cooking of Southwest France.*

INDEX

D

E

cubing, *37*
peeling, *36*
roasting, *39*
  in salsa, *140–41*
Tomato paste, saving leftover, *40*
Tomato sauce, roasted, *152, 153*
Torres, Jacques, *99, 102, 106*
Tortillas, softening, *62*
Tropp, Barbara, *19, 28*
Trucs, characteristics of, *7–8*
Tuna, carpaccio of, *91, 129*
Turkeys, self-basting, *81*

V

Vegetables
  entree recipes for, *161–63*
  trucs about, *11–40*
Vegetable stock, *133*
Vegetarian dishes, *161–63*
Vinaigrette
  citrus, *129*

  making a lighter, *73*
  my father's, *141*
Vitamin, C, *70*
Vongerichten, Jean-Georges, *73*

W

Wafers, potato-herb, *128–29*
Walnuts, as filling/stuffing, *162*
Watercress sauce, *130–31*
White, Jasper, *72, 135–36*
Wine sauce, *74, 172–73*
Wolfert, Paula, *37, 48, 160, 162*

Z

Zucchini, cutting, *19*

